B.C.		
1200		
	About 1200 Exodus from Egypt.	PROPHETIC TEACHINGS
	1150-1100 Settlement of Canaan.	
1100		C H R
		E U E
	1030 Establishment of Saul's Kingdom.	R M L
	1010 David's Coronation at Hebron.	E A I
1000		M N G
	975 Solomon's Coronation.	DECALOGUE O E I
	965 Completion of the Temple.	OF THE N O
	937 Division of the Hebrew Empire.	I A U
		TWO TABLETS A L E S
		L DECALOGUES
900		(Ex.20 23-26, 22 21- 23 19)
	875-850 Work of Elijah.	
	854 839 Campaigns of Shalmaneser II.	JUDEAN
850		
	850-795 Work of Elisha.	VERSION
	842 Jehu's Tribute to Shalmaneser II.	(Ex. 34)
	810 Joash's Tribute to Hazael.	
		EPHRAIMITE BOOK
800		(Ex.20 23
	781-740 Reign of Jeroboam II.	
	750-740 Preaching of Amos.	**PRIMITIVE CODES**
750		
	745-736 Work of Hosea.	
	737-690 Work of Isaiah.	
	722-721 Capture of Samaria.	DECISIONS
700		OF
	686-641 Reactionary Reign of Manasseh.	LATER PROPHETIC
	663 Ashurbanipal's Capture of Thebes.	JUDGES DECALOGUE
650		(Ex.20 2-17)
	626 Earlier Sermons of Zephaniah and Jeremiah.	
	621 Great Reformation of Josiah.	LAW BOOK OF JOSIAH
600		(Dt. 12-19, 26) Dt. 5-11
	597 The First Captivity. Work of Ezekiel.	**DEUTERONOMIC CODES**
	586 The Final Captivity.	(Book of Dt.)
	560 Expulsion of Foreigners from Egypt.	
550		
	538 Capture of Babylon by Cyrus.	
	520-516 Rebuilding of the Temple.	
	520-516 Reorganization of Persian Empire.	
500		
	490 Battle of Marathon.	
	480 Battles of Thermopylæ and Salamis.	
	470 Expulsion of Persians from Europe.	
450		
	445 Rebuilding the Walls of Jerusalem.	
	432 Nehemiah's Second Visit.	
400		
	400 Adoption of the Priestly Law by the Judean Community.	
350		

PROBABLY CURRENT ONLY IN ORAL FORM

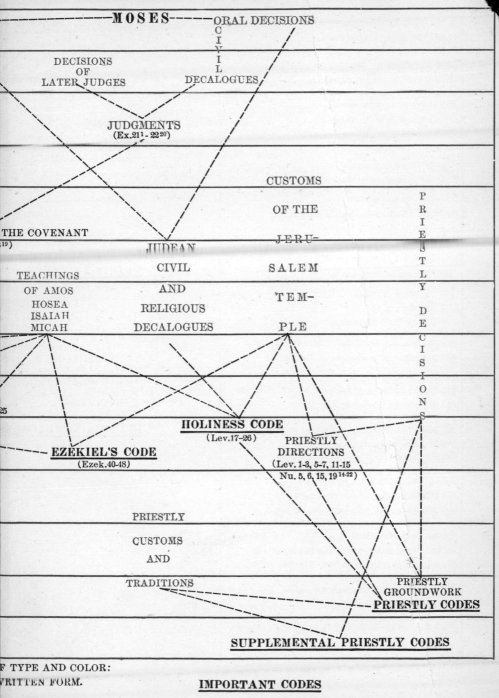

MOSES———ORAL DECISIONS

CIVIL

DECISIONS
OF
LATER JUDGES

DECALOGUES

JUDGMENTS
(Ex.21¹ - 22²⁰)

CUSTOMS

OF THE

THE COVENANT

JUDEAN

JERU—

CIVIL

SALEM

TEACHINGS
OF AMOS
HOSEA
ISAIAH
MICAH

AND

RELIGIOUS

TEM—

DECALOGUES

PLE

PRIESTLY DECISIONS

HOLINESS CODE
(Lev.17–26)

PRIESTLY
DIRECTIONS
(Lev. 1-3, 5-7, 11-15
Nu. 5, 6, 15, 19¹⁴⁻²²)

EZEKIEL'S CODE
(Ezek.40-48)

PRIESTLY

CUSTOMS

AND

TRADITIONS

PRIESTLY
GROUNDWORK
PRIESTLY CODES

SUPPLEMENTAL PRIESTLY CODES

F TYPE AND COLOR:
RITTEN FORM.

IMPORTANT CODES

The Student's Old Testament

ISRAEL'S
LAWS AND LEGAL PRECEDENTS

THE STUDENT'S OLD TESTAMENT

LOGICALLY AND CHRONOLOGICALLY
ARRANGED AND TRANSLATED

BY

CHARLES FOSTER KENT, Ph.D.

WOOLSEY PROFESSOR OF BIBLICAL LITERATURE IN YALE UNIVERSITY

ARRANGEMENT OF VOLUMES

The Student's Old Testament

ISRAEL'S
LAWS AND LEGAL PRECEDENTS

FROM THE DAYS OF MOSES TO THE CLOSING OF
THE LEGAL CANON

BY

CHARLES FOSTER KENT, Ph.D.

Woolsey Professor of Biblical Literature in Yale University

WITH PLANS AND DIAGRAMS

NEW YORK
CHARLES SCRIBNER'S SONS
1907

PREFACE

THE *Torah* represents the first edition of the Old Testament, and in the life and thought of Judaism it has always retained that first place. In the reaction from this extreme emphasis upon the law, Christianity has perhaps underestimated the permanent value of the Old Testament legal literature. In rejecting that which is only national and temporal, it has also overlooked much that is vital and eternal. Law and prophecy are not antithetic, as is sometimes imagined, but rather different expressions of the same divine revelation, the one through the life and institutions of the nation, the other through the experience and minds of certain divinely enlightened men. The prophets proclaimed the principles which the lawgivers applied practically and concretely to the needs of their day and race. Both labored in their characteristic way to realize the will of God in the life of the nation and individual; but the lawgivers were in closest touch with that life and therefore in their writings picture it most concretely and vividly.

That inner history, however, is almost completely obscured by the confused order in which the laws at present are found. Civil and ceremonial, criminal and humane, secular and religious, ancient and late laws and legal precedents are all mingled together, with little trace of systematic classification. The one who seeks to read or study them is constantly distracted, as in the book of Proverbs, by the sudden transitions; if he desires to determine the teaching of the Old Testament on a given theme, it is only after the most laborious research that he is able to bring similar laws together. Even when this preliminary work has been done, the result is often perplexing, for many of the laws contradict each other.

The present confused order is the inevitable result of the complex process of collecting, editing and supplementing through which each of the legal books has passed. The laws of many ancient and modern nations present close analogies. Since law through gradual growth is adapted to the varying needs of succeeding generations, there is an inevitable lack of order unless the whole body of enactments is frequently and thoroughly codified.

The first requisite, therefore, if the Old Testament legal literature is to be studied intelligently and profitably, is that similar laws be grouped together, and then that those in each resulting group be arranged in their chronological order. For practical purposes it is important that all the regulations relating to a given subject be reproduced, even at the cost of occasional repetitions. It is also desirable to follow, as far as it can be discovered, the original Hebrew order of classification. In Exodus 21^1–23^{19}, which contains the oldest collection of laws in the Old Testament,

v

there is evidence of careful arrangement (cf. p. 27 and Appendix II). It is in general: (1) personal and family laws; (2) criminal laws, comprising injuries to persons, property, and society; (3) humane laws, emphasizing the duty of kindness to animals and men; (4) religious laws, defining obligations to God; and (5) ceremonial laws, containing minute directions regarding worship and the ritual. Inasmuch as this order is both logical and in general accord with the relative historical development of these different groups of laws, it has been followed in the system of classification adopted in the present volume. The minor sub-divisions are determined by the nature of the laws themselves and the modern principles of legal codification. The laws within each section are also arranged in their chronological order, so that the history and development of each Israelitish law and institution can be readily followed from their earliest to their latest stages. Nowhere in all legal literature can the genesis and growth of primitive law be traced so clearly as in Israel's codes thus restored. They also represent the most important corner-stones of our modern English laws and institutions and therefore challenge and richly reward the study of all legal and historical students.

The Old Testament laws, arranged in their chronological order, reveal the deeper currents and forces in the life of ancient Israel of which the external events in that remarkable history were but the effect. In each successive code the presence and power of God can be clearly recognized. Through that divine influence, customs, originally very rude and barbarous, are gradually transformed and ennobled, until they worthily express and effectively enforce the eternal standards of justice and love and mercy. It is also because these laws reveal Israel's and therefore humanity's faith and ethics in the making that they possess a great and permanent value. Each succeeding lawgiver, as did the great Teacher of Nazareth (cf. Mt. $5^{17,\ 21\text{-}48}$), felt under obligation to revise and bring to more perfect expression the divine ideals constantly revealed in fuller measure to each succeeding generation.

My great debt to the scholars who have contributed richly to our knowledge on the many subjects considered in this volume is suggested in the list of detailed references in Appendix I. The translations of the laws of Hammurabi are from Johns' *Babylonian and Assyrian Laws, Contracts and Letters*—a work with which all students of Israel's laws should be acquainted. Again I am under great obligation to the members of my Biblical and Hebrew seminars for many valuable suggestions, and especially to the Reverend Roy Mac Houghton in connection with the work of codification, to Mr. Darwin Ashley Leavitt for collaboration in the translation of the priestly laws, and to the Reverend Morgan Millar for aid in revising the copy.

C. F. K.

YALE UNIVERSITY,
May, 1907.

CONTENTS AND CLASSIFICATION

INTRODUCTION

THE HISTORY OF ISRAEL'S LAWS AND LEGAL PRECEDENTS

PERSONAL AND FAMILY LAWS

A. PERSONAL RELATION AND CONDITION.	Classification of the Codes					
	Primitive	Deuteronomic	Holiness	Priestly	Supplemental Priestly	
I. Parents and Children.						
§ 1. Honor and Obedience Due Parents	Ex. $21^{15, 17}$	Dt. $5^{16, 21}$ 18-21, 27^{16} [Ex. 20 12]*	Lev. $19^{3a,}$ 20^9	....	....	PAGE 51
§ 2. Authority of Father over Unmarried Daughter.	....	....	....	....	Nu. 30^{3-5}	52
II. The Marriage Relation.						
§ 3. Relatives between Whom Marriage is Illegitimate	....	Dt. 22^{30}, $27^{20,22,23}$	Lev. 18^{6-18}, 23, 24	....	....	53
§ 4. Marriage with a Captive	....	Dt. 21^{10-14}	....	....	....	54

* References in brackets represent duplicate passages not reproduced in text; those in parentheses are to later additions to earlier codes.

CONTENTS AND CLASSIFICATION

CONTENTS AND CLASSIFICATION

ix

CONSTITUTIONAL LAWS

CONTENTS AND CLASSIFICATION

CONTENTS AND CLASSIFICATION

CONTENTS AND CLASSIFICATION

xiv

CONTENTS AND CLASSIFICATION

CONTENTS AND CLASSIFICATION

CONTENTS AND CLASSIFICATION

CONTENTS AND CLASSIFICATION

LAWS DEFINING OBLIGATIONS TO JEHOVAH

CONTENTS AND CLASSIFICATION

CEREMONIAL LAWS

CONTENTS AND CLASSIFICATION

CONTENTS AND CLASSIFICATION

CONTENTS AND CLASSIFICATION

CONTENTS AND CLASSIFICATION

CONTENTS AND CLASSIFICATION

CONTENTS AND CLASSIFICATION

APPENDIX

CONTENTS AND CLASSIFICATION

INDEX OF BIBLICAL PASSAGES

CHART AND DIAGRAMS

INDEX OF BIBLICAL PASSAGES

INDEX OF BIBLICAL PASSAGES

INDEX OF BIBLICAL PASSAGES

INDEX OF BIBLICAL PASSAGES

EXPLANATION OF TYPOGRAPHICAL SYMBOLS AND ABBREVIATIONS

Text in roman type.

Supplemental and editorial additions to an older section in smaller type.

Superscriptions IN SMALL CAPITALS.

Poetical passages are distinguished by smaller type and broken lines.

Explanatory clauses, found in the original, in ( ).

English equivalents of the more significant Hebrew proper names in [ ].

Words implied by the context or supplied to restore the original narratives, where these have been abridged in the process of editorial fusion, *in italics.*

Foot-notes, presenting the reasons for the analysis and classification of the material, significant alternate readings, and explanatory material, in small roman type.

Interpretative side-headings, giving a condensed summary of the accompanying text, on the margins in small roman type.

Chapter numbers in arabic figures. **Verse numbers** in small figures placed above the line. **Successive portions of a verse** indicated by ^{a}, ^{b} or ^{c}, placed after the verse number. Thus, Genesis II. 4 (second part of the verse) to IV. 6 (first half) inclusive is written 2^{4b}–4^{6a}.

Complete stories or literary units (with their parallels, if any) are numbered with arabic numerals successively throughout the entire volume and are referred to as sections. Thus, § 2 refers to § 2, **The Primitive Story of Man's Creation and Fall,** pp. 53–56.

General Abbreviations

AmRV = American Revised Version (1901).
AV = Authorized Version (1611).
Apocr. = Apocrypha or apocryphal.
Aram. = Aramaic.
Assyr. = Assyrian.
Bab. = Babylonian.
cf. = compare.
e. g. = for example.
f. = and following.
Gk. = Greek B (Vatican) text of the O.T.

Gk.A = Alexandrian Gk. text of the O.T.
Gk. ℵ = Sinaitic Gk. text of the O.T.
Heb. = Hebrew.
i. e. = that is.
Jos. = Josephus.
Lat. = Latin (Vulgate) text of Jerome.
Lit. = literally.
Luc. = Lucian's Recension of the Greek O.T.
N.T. = New Testament.

Old Lat. = Old Latin Version of the O.T.
Origen = Reading found in Origen's *Hexapla.*
O.T. = Old Testament.
Pent. = Pentateuch.
RV = Revised Version (1885).
Sam. = Samaritan Version of the Pent.
Sem. = Semitic.
Syr. = Syriac Version of the O.T.
Targ. = Targum.
Vs. = verse.

Abbreviations for the Old Testament and Apocryphal Books

Gen. = Genesis.
Ex. = Exodus.
Lev. = Leviticus.
Num. or, Nu. = Numbers.
Dt. = Deuteronomy.
Josh. = Joshua.
Judg. = Judges.
Sam. = Samuel.
Kgs. = Kings.
Chr. = Chronicles.
Neh. = Nehemiah.
Esth. = Esther.
Ps. = Psalms.
Pr. = Proverbs.
Ecc. = Ecclesiastes.
Sg. of Sgs. = Song of Songs.

Is. = Isaiah.
Jer. = Jeremiah.
Lam. = Lamentations.
Ezek. = Ezekiel.
Dan. = Daniel.
Hos. = Hosea.
Am. = Amos.
Ob. = Obadiah.
Jon. = Jonah.
Mic. = Micah.
Nah. = Nahum.
Hab. = Habakkuk.
Zeph. = Zephaniah.
Hag. = Haggai.
Zech. = Zechariah.
Mal. = Malachi.

Esdr. = Esdras.
Wisd. Sol. = Wisdom of Solomon.
B. Sir. = Ben Sira or Ecclesiasticus.
Bar. = Baruch.
Sg. of Three = Song of the Three Children.
Sus. = Susanna.
Pryr. of Man. = Prayer of Manasses.
Mac. = Maccabees.
Enoch = Book of Enoch.
Ps. of Sol. = Psalms of Solomon.

THE HISTORY OF ISRAEL'S LAWS AND LEGAL PRECEDENTS

INTRODUCTION

I

THE BABYLONIAN BACKGROUND OF ISRAEL'S LAWS

IN the light of recent discoveries, the study of ancient law begins to- The day, not with the legal system of Israel, of Greece, or of Rome, but with dawn of civil- that of early Babylonia. Long centuries before the days of Moses or ization in an- Minos or Romulus, the peoples living between the lower waters of the cient Tigris and the Euphrates developed legal codes that deeply influenced all Baby-lonia subsequent legislation. This early rise of law in ancient Babylonia is primarily traceable to the physical contour and position of the land itself. For countless generations beyond the dawn of history, the rich alluvial territory lying between the two great rivers attracted the nomadic peoples of every quarter of southwestern Asia. The soil of this coveted region could be reclaimed from the annual floods, and permanently held against the strong foes ever pressing in from the east and west, only by the most arduous toil of hand and head. While Nature early spurred the mixed, virile population of ancient Babylonia to develop a high type of civilization, she generously rewarded its persistent labor. In return for skilful cultivation the land furnished lavish harvests; for the development of the arts it also provided abundant facilities, not the least of which was the soft clay of the riverbanks, a material early utilized for buildings, for military defences, and for literary records.

Natural gate-ways opened in every direction for commerce. The Tigris Why it and Euphrates with their tributaries penetrated far into the populous high- was a com- lands to the east and north of Babylonia. On the west, the Arameans and mercial Arabs, the great land traders, carried Babylonian wares to the Phœnicians, civili-zation Egyptians, and southern Arabians, and in turn brought back the products of those other centres of ancient civilization. To the south, the Persian Gulf opened into the Indian Ocean and commanded the trade of Arabia and India. It is not strange, therefore, that Babylonia early developed a rich, dominantly commercial civilization, the influence of which radiated throughout the known world.

This intense commercial activity explains why the art of writing and the Early making of law attained in Babylonia so high a stage of development; com- devel-opment merce demands for its development exact written records and the protection of law and the of just and well-defined laws. Hence, for more than a thousand years before art of the days of Moses, the Babylonians had so far perfected their system of writing writing that it was in as general use as writing was among the Greeks or

3

Romans, or as it is to-day among most oriental peoples. The scribes constituted a large and important class in the community. Every important transaction was recorded in written contracts, usually duplicated to guard against injury to individual copies. All important judicial decisions were likewise recorded. Hundreds of thousands of these legal documents have already been discovered in the ruins of Babylonia and Assyria. Obviously, this remarkable command of the art of writing was of great service in the development of definite laws and legal codes. Among a primitive nomadic or agricultural people a few simple customs, at first transmitted orally from generation to generation, sufficed to meet the popular needs; but in a complex commercial civilization, a great variety of legal questions arose and were decided. It was the Babylonian custom to commit to writing all legal decisions; and these became the basis of an ever-growing body of written laws.

The Sumerian family laws

The few popular traditions attributing to a certain god the origin of Babylonian law, throw no light upon its earliest beginnings. Its origin is far older than the most primitive history and literature of the human race. In the legal phrase-books of the later scribes chance has preserved to us seven so-called Sumerian laws; they are written in the archaic language of the very early, though highly civilized, people that occupied the southern part of the Tigris-Euphrates valley before it came under the sway of the Semites. These laws were probably in existence in the fourth millennium B.C.; the origin of some of them doubtless goes thousands of years farther back. The fragments which have been preserved treat of family relations; as, for example, *If a son has said to his father, "You are not my father," he may brand him, lay fetters upon him, and sell him* (cf. for the others, Appendix II). The literary form and themes are the same as those of the later Babylonian and the early Old Testament laws.

The recently discovered Code of Hammurabi

By far the most important code yet discovered comes from about 2250 B.C. It bears the name of the real founder of the Babylonian empire, already well known to scholars through his letters and historical inscriptions, the great Hammurabi. The laws are clearly inscribed in forty-four columns on an almost square block of black diorite. It was found by French excavators at Susa in December, 1901, and January, 1902. Five columns of the original inscription have been erased by the Elamite king who carried it off as spoil, probably from the temple of Shamash at Sippara where it was first set up. Three thousand six hundred lines, however, still remain. These were arbitrarily divided into sections and numbered by the first translator, Professor V. Scheil of Paris, and this division into sections has been generally adopted for reference.

Purpose of this code

In the remarkable epilogue which he appended, Hammurabi plainly states the motives that guided him as a ruler, and led him to prepare and set up this body of laws. He describes himself as the shepherd chosen by the gods to care for his people, to lead them into safe pastures, and to make them dwell in peace and security. *That the great should not oppress the weak, to counsel the widow and orphan, to render judgment and to decide the decisions of the land, and to succor the injured,* he wrote these noble words on his stele

4

and placed them before his likeness. *By the command of Shamash, the judge supreme of heaven and earth, that justice might shine in the land,* he set up a bas-relief to preserve his likeness. At the head of the laws is an exceedingly suggestive picture representing Hammurabi receiving them from the seated sun-god Shamash. The epilogue also adds: *The oppressed who has a suit to prosecute may come to my image, that of a righteous king, and read my inscription and understand my precious words, and may my stele elucidate his case. Let him see the law he seeks, and may he draw his breath and say, "This Hammurabi was a ruler who was to his people like the father who begot them. He obeyed the order of Marduk his lord, he followed the commands of Marduk above and below. He delighted the heart of Marduk his lord, and granted happy life to his people forever." Let him recite the document.* These words betray a benign, God-fearing, paternal ruler, actuated by the principles that underlie all just legislation.

The contents of the code confirm the implications of its epilogue. The code consists entirely of civil laws dealing with specific legal questions that were constantly arising in the empire over which Hammurabi ruled. Briefly and clearly the given offence or case of dispute is stated; then the penalty or course of legal action is definitely outlined; as, for example, *If a man has borne false witness in a trial, or has not established the statement that he has made, if that case be a capital trial, the man shall be put to death.* The code was evidently prepared for the guidance of judges no less than for those seeking justice. The aim, apparently, was not to present every possible case, but, leaving the more unusual to be decided by the judge, to register the common and typical. Unlike most oriental literary products, the laws have been systematically classified. They are included under three great heads with subdivisions: I. Introduction on evidence and decisions; II. Property, (1) personal, (2) real, and (3) in trade; III. Persons, (1) the family, (2) injuries, (3) laborers and labor. Within the smaller groups of laws, those defining the rights and obligations of the patrician classes precede those relating to the plebeians and slaves. *[Contents and general character]*

This entire collection of laws is properly called the *Code of Hammurabi*. Under his personal direction it undoubtedly assumed its present form, and by him it was publicly promulgated and made the law of the empire. He states distinctly that he received it from the god Shamash. The meaning of this statement, however, must be interpreted in the light of the code itself. Some of the laws, doubtless, were first formulated by Hammurabi; to this class may well belong those which attempt to fix a uniform price for hire and labor; but it is certain that the code as a whole rests on far older foundations. Many of its laws are assumed to be already in existence, and not a few of its legal phrases are found in contracts dating long before the time of Hammurabi. Like the Indian *Laws of Manu*, or the Greek *Gortyan Code*, or the Roman *Twelve Tables*, the code is evidently a compilation incorporating many very early laws and customs. So comprehensive and so well adapted to the needs of Babylonia was the wonderful Code of Hammurabi that for more than fifteen hundred years it continued to be the fundamental law of the Babylonian and Assyrian empires. *[Origin and history]*

Its influence upon Israel's laws

How far did this highly developed Semitic code influence the laws of the Hebrews? The fact that it was in force through a large part of southwestern Asia for over a thousand years before the advent of the Hebrews, and that it bears striking analogy in theme, content, and form to many Old Testament laws, naturally prompts this query. The question is one that concerns not the reality but the method of divine revelation; for that revelation is as broad as human life and history. The vital consideration is whether the Infinite Judge made known the eternal principles of justice through the minds and life of the Babylonians as well as of the Hebrews? If so, the history of the origin and growth of Israelitish law begins in ancient Babylonia long before the days of Hammurabi; and the code of that truly noble ruler marks, like the Book of the Covenant (Ex. 21–23) and Deuteronomy, one of the great receptive epochs of divine revelation through human laws and institutions.

Early Babylonian influence in Canaan

The final answer to this important question must, of course, be based on a detailed and careful comparison of the codes as a whole, and of the individual laws; to approach the study a glance at some historical points of contact between Babylonian and Israelitish civilization must here suffice. It is probable that out of the same peculiar nomadic life of north Arabia came the ancestors of the Hebrews and those of the Babylonian line of rulers to which Hammurabi belonged. A common Arabian origin may go far to explain the many points of analogy between the two legal systems. In the oldest Babylonian inscriptions, far antedating the days of Hammurabi, the more ambitious rulers of the lower Tigris-Euphrates valley tell of conquests of theirs which extended to the eastern shore of the Mediterranean. Even during the periods when military prowess did not prepare the way, traders, bearing the civilization and thought and institutions of the East, carried on the peaceful but no less effectual conquest of Palestine. For three millenniums at least their conquests continued, until, as we know from contemporary chronology and the testimony of archæology, the pre-Hebraic civilization of Canaan reflected predominantly that of Babylonia.

Later contact between Babylon and Israel

There can be no doubt that the Babylonian culture influenced the Israelites through their own Semitic ancestors, and still more strongly through the Canaanites; but there are two periods in their history when that influence was overwhelming. The first period was when the Assyrians, the heirs and conquerors of Babylon, held Palestine for nearly two centuries in their iron grasp; the second, when the new Babylonian empire under Nebuchadrezzar conquered Judah and carried away to an exile under the shadow of the mistress of the East, the political, intellectual, and religious leaders of the Israelitish race.

Nature of the Babylonian influence

The intricate manner in which the history of these two peoples is constantly interwoven is one of the most remarkable and significant facts of antiquity. That the younger and weaker was deeply influenced by the older and stronger is patent; in the case of the specific laws, however, that influence, though marked, appears to have been indirect rather than direct. Gradually, probably unconsciously, assimilating that which they inherited

6

from the Semitic past, the early Israelites, wrought upon by the Divine, developed their own peculiar institutions and laws; for, striking as are the external analogies with the laws of other ancient people, especially in ceremonial regulation, the majority of the Old Testament laws are informed by a spirit and purpose which have no ancient parallel.

II

THE ORIGIN AND GROWTH OF ISRAELITISH LAW

Mean-
ing of
the
Hebrew
word
for law In derivation and variety of meanings there is a wealth of suggestion in
the term *torah*, the Hebrew word for law. It comes from a verb which means
to point out, to direct, and this in turn is probably to be traced back to an
earlier root signifying *to cast* or *throw* the sacred lot or arrows employed in
early times to determine the divine will. The verb is thus used in Joshua
18⁶ to describe the casting of lots. Hence *torah* meant originally the decision
obtained by the lot, and then it stood for the authoritative direction or decision
that came from Jehovah and was made known to the people by his official
representatives.

Differ-
ent
kinds
of
torah Since Jehovah was represented in ancient Israel by several different classes
of teachers, there were various kinds of *torahs*. One of the oldest and most
significant was the *torah* or decision of a judge like Moses, which soon came
to be recognized as a precedent to be followed when cases similar to that
which called it forth arose (Ex. 18¹⁵, ¹⁶, ²⁰). The *torah* was sometimes the
designation also of social and moral teachings (Is. 5²⁴), of political counsels
(Is. 8¹⁶, ²⁰), and of religious doctrines (Is. 1¹⁰) of prophets like Isaiah. In the
prophetic books it frequently denotes the teachings of the prophets as a whole
(*e. g.*, Jer. 6¹⁹, 9¹³, 16¹¹, 26⁴). And constantly the wise men or sages throughout their writing refer to their own characteristic teachings that were usually
cast in the form of proverbs (*e. g.*, Pr. 1⁸, 3¹, 4², Job 22²²) as the *torah* or
instruction. In Psalm 78¹ a psalmist uses the same broad term to describe the
didactic poem that follows. In all these passages the common idea is that
the *torah* consists of a body of definite and authoritative directions or teachings coming ultimately from Jehovah himself.

The
torah
of the
priests From statements like that in Jeremiah 18¹⁸, however, it is clear that the
torah was early regarded as the especial contribution of the priest. The
enemies of Jeremiah justify their attack upon him by asserting that *the torah*
(or *law*) *shall not perish from the priest, nor counsel from the wise, nor the
word from the prophet* (cf. also Ezek. 7²⁶). In its earliest and limited sense
the *torah* was the specific decision or direction given by the priest, and ascer-
tained by him, usually in response to some definite question, by means of
the oracle or lot or other accepted method of ascertaining the will of the Deity.
Thus according to Malachi 2⁶, *the torah of truth was in the mouth of the priest
. . . and the people should seek the torah at his mouth.* In Haggai 2¹¹ the
people are commanded to ask a *torah* from the priests in regard to a certain
ceremonial question. In the prophetic books charges are not infrequently
brought against the priests because they have misused their authority as
guardians of the *torah* (Mi. 3¹¹, Zeph. 3⁴, Ezek. 22²⁶, Mal. 2⁸, ⁹). From

the earliest times the priests, since they were the guardians of the oracles and constituted an established religious class that could readily be found at the different local sanctuaries, were resorted to as arbiters and judges in cases civil as well as ceremonial. According to the later Deuteronomic codes the supreme court of appeal included both priests and laymen; and its decision on a specific question was still called the *torah* or direction (Dt. 17[11]).

As in the case of the teachings of the prophets and sages, *torah* in like manner became in time the regular designation of a group of technical directions regarding some specific subject, as, for example, the *torah* of the burnt-offering, of the cereal-offering, or of the Nazirite (Lev. 6[9, 14, 25], 7[1, 11, 37], 11[46], 12[7], 13[59], Nu. 5[29, 30]). Primarily these rules appear to have been intended for the guidance of the laity rather than the priests. Soon, however, the *torah* or law was the name applied to a code of laws (as, for example, that found in Dt. 1[5], 4[8, 44], 17[18, 19], etc.), or appeared in the familiar phrase *the torah* or *law of Moses*, which described the collection of codes ascribed by later generations to the first great leader of the Hebrew race (Josh. 1[7, 8], 8[31, 32], I Kgs. 2[3], II Kgs. 10[31], 17[13, 34], 21[8]). In the later Old Testament books and in the New Testament, *The Torah* has become the prevailing designation of the combination of narrative, poetry, and law found in the first five books of the Hebrew Bible (I Chr. 16[40], II Chr. 31[3], Ezra 3[2], Neh. 8[1]). The legal *torah* in its broad application, therefore, included all the directions—civil, judicial, moral, ceremonial, or religious—that came from the lips or pens of priests or priestly scribes. *Later literary content of the term Torah*

As has been pointed out, when the early priest by the use of the oracle or sacred lot, or on his own authority as God's representative, rendered the decision, it was Jehovah's *torah*. When this and kindred decisions became the precedents by which later judges were guided in deciding similar cases, they felt that they were simply applying Jehovah's law. Priestly editors who recorded the customary laws that grew up on the basis of these precedents, or else expanded or modified the primitive customs in order to adapt them to new conditions, felt, as did Ezekiel (cf. Ezek. 40–48), that they were simply the agents of Jehovah. *Origin of the belief in the divine origin of law*

To be sure, the concrete, naïve form in which they often expressed this fundamental belief cannot be interpreted with a blind literalness. The declaration that Jehovah talked face to face with Moses or wrote with his finger on tablets of stone reflects the primitive, anthropomorphic conceptions of God which are so prominent in the story of the Garden of Eden and the earliest patriarchal narratives. But this is only the early graphic manner of stating the eternal fact that God communicated his truths directly to his prophets and people, and inscribed a knowledge of his law, not with his finger on perishable stone but by means of individual and national experiences, upon the imperishable consciousness of the Israelitish race. The process of revelation was indeed more natural and sublimely accordant with God's methods of accomplishing his purpose than Israelitish tradition pictured it; and yet these concrete pictures impressed upon the minds of the early Hebrews the divine origin of the law much more clearly and vividly than a more exact and therefore more abstract statement of the fact would have done.

9

Pro-
gressive
nature
of
divine
revela-
tion
through
the law

For the child now, as for the human race in its childhood, these concrete pictures have a practical value, for they emphasize the essential truth that the ancient laws embody the will and possess the authority of God himself. To some mature minds, however, that picture language obscures the almost equally important fact that the revelation of God's will through the Old Testament laws was progressive and adapted to the developing consciousness of the race. A *torah* was given only when demanded by human needs, and originally it gave in each case specific directions to anticipate those immediate needs. That the different laws and codes reflect the developing moral and religious consciousness of many different ages, the character of the laws and codes themselves is conclusive evidence. The testimony of Israelitish history also confirms the conclusion that the ethical standards and laws varied greatly from generation to generation. Acts like the torture of enemies (II Sam. 8$^{2, 13}$) or the sacrifice of human beings to appease Jehovah (II Sam. 21$^{1-6}$), which were regarded as entirely legitimate by David and his contemporaries, were unsparingly condemned by an Amos (1$^{3, 13}$) or a Micah (6$^{7, 8}$). Jesus himself proclaimed the fundamental principle of religious evolution to be, *First the blade, then the ear, and then the full corn in the ear.* His statement, that he came to *fulfil the law*, that is, to bring it to full and perfect expression, is equivalent to affirming that it represented a progressive unfolding not yet complete. Repeatedly he declared, *Ye have heard that it was said to them of olden time, but I say to you*, and then proceeded to substitute for the ancient law a nobler command.

Origin
of the
tradi-
tional
concep-
tion of
the law

It was only very late Judaism that attributed all the Old Testament laws to one man and age. There was a twofold reason for this; it was partly due to a mistaken worship of the authority of the past, a worship which failed to realize that God's revelation was progressive, leading upward rather than downward; and it was due partly to the tendency of later rabbis to recognize as authoritative only those books which were associated with the name of some early prophet or hero of the faith, such as Samuel or David or Solomon or Isaiah. The Old Testament itself, as is well known, does not directly attribute to Moses the literary authorship of even a majority of its laws; the passages that place them in his mouth belong to the later editorial framework of the legal books.

Moses'
real re-
lation
to the
Old
Testa-
ment
legisla-
tion

The oldest records of Moses' work, and the history of the *torah*, suggest the great leader's real relation to Israelitish legislation as a whole and justify the title, *The Law of Moses*, so often applied to that legal lore. As a prophet and leader he called the Israelitish race into being; and he it was who inspired it with ideals, moral and religious, of which its later history and institutions were but the realization. There are good grounds for believing that the simple religious principles which he impressed upon his people were but the germinal ideas which, in the school of trying national experience, gradually unfolded into the *torahs* of the subsequent prophets and priests. His own age had no need of elaborate written codes. To his followers in the desert the detailed laws which grew up about the later monarchy and temple would have been meaningless. Exodus 18$^{13-27}$ tells us that he gave the Israelites of his day what they needed; and the need was definite, detailed

10

directions and decisions on questions of doubt or dispute as these questions arose. From morning until evening the people crowded about him to inquire the will of God; and like a Bedouin sheik or a priestly judge of later Israelitish history, he investigated each case and rendered a decision. As he thus decided which of two litigants was in the right, he also *made known the statutes of God and his decisions*, and thereby laid the foundation of later Israelitish law. As customary law gradually grew up on this concrete foundation, tradition naturally attributed its origin to Moses. When later scribes codified and committed to writing the constantly expanding body of oral laws, they also preserved the traditions of Mosaic origin. Even though they modified or supplemented the older laws in order to adapt them to new conditions and to embody the higher principles set forth by later prophets, they felt neither desire nor justification for altering the traditional title. The tendency, rather, of exilic and post-exilic Judaism was so to magnify and give graphic expression to the ancient title that practically all of the Old Testament laws were made to come directly from the mouth of Moses.

In the same dramatic manner are set forth the two great truths that underlie the authority of Israel's laws. The first truth is: back of the laws lie the work and teachings of the great prophets of Israel who proclaimed the exalted principles which the laws embody. The second truth is: back of the prophets, and speaking through them and the conscience of the Israelitish race, was Israel's God. The various processes and stages whereby the different laws attained their final form may be traced in detail; but they are of minor importance compared with the supreme fact that Israel's laws contain God's directions, adapted at each point to the intelligence and needs of the race. *The divine authority underlying Israel's law*

The fact that many of Israel's laws and institutions were inherited from an older Semitic past does not affect the divineness of their origin; to receptive souls, however limited their spiritual perspective, the infinite God has in all ages and to all races revealed truth as fast as they have been able to receive it. Hammurabi and most ancient lawgivers not only acknowledged but openly proclaimed their debt to the Divine. Israel received much from the past; but more than this, she developed unceasingly her own gift; her laws take on a wide human significance because they constantly incorporate the ampler principles enunciated by the nation's inspired prophets. It is this new element, reflecting as it does a nobler conception of God, of duty to him and to fellow-men, that makes the Old Testament laws unique. *The uniqueness of Israel's laws*

We have referred to the part played by *torah*; there are still other Old Testament legal terms equally suggestive of the processes by which Israel's laws gradually grew. *Mishpat*, derived from the same root as the Hebrew word for judge, meant originally a *judgment* or a *decision* given in connection with a specific case. Like *torah*, however, it was soon used to designate the enactment or law which grew up on the basis of the original decision, and embodied its underlying principle. In this sense it is used in Exodus 21^1 and 24^3, as a title to the body of specific laws found in 21^1–22^{27} (introduced in each case by *when* or *if*) which anticipate certain crimes and prescribe definite penalties. At first it appears to have included only civil laws, as in Exodus and Numbers 27^{11} and 35^{24}, but in time it was applied to ceremonial laws *Meaning of a mishpat or decision*

11

as well (*e. g.*, Lev. 18[4, 5, 26], 19[37]). In the historical books it is sometimes used in the sense of *custom*, suggesting the intermediate stage between a verbal decision and a fixed law.

Other Hebrew synonyms for law
 The other synonyms for law are comparatively late. *Commandment* is a characteristic term in the Deuteronomic legislation. It emphasizes the divine authority back of the given law (*e. g.*, Dt. 4[2, 40], 5[29, 31]). *Testimonies* (*êdwôth, êdôth*) is another Deuteronomic term (Dt. 4[45], 6[17, 20]), especially applied to moral and religious enactments solemnly proclaimed and attested by Jehovah. *Precepts* (*pekkudîm*) is found only in the Psalms (note especially Ps. 119). *Statute*, from a root meaning to *inscribe* or *engrave*, suggests a period when writing on stone was well known. This term recalls the divine command to Isaiah (Is. 8[1]) to write the essence of his prophecy on a tablet and set it up before the eyes of the people. The practice of inscribing the more important laws on tablets and putting them up before the people was common in antiquity, as witness the Code of Hammurabi, the Gortyan Laws of Crete, and the Twelve Tables of the Romans. The word *statutes* also occurs frequently in the Deuteronomic and priestly codes and suggests that the custom was not unknown among the Hebrews (cf. Dt. 27[2-4]). In general it emphasizes the importance and established authority of the laws thus designated.

Authorities that rendered the original decisions which shaped later laws
 In the light of these studies, and of analogies among other kindred peoples, it is thus possible to trace definitely the processes by which Israel's individual laws came into being. The original decisions that constituted the precedents upon which oral and customary law grew up, were rendered, (1) by regularly appointed judges, usually leaders of the nation like Moses or heads of families (*e. g.*, Ex. 18[13-26], Dt. 1[9-18]); (2) by military chieftains or kings like David. In I Samuel 30[24, 25], for instance, there is a most instructive example showing that the law regarding the distribution of booty, which Numbers 31[27] attributes to Moses, first arose as the result of a decision given by David after an expedition against the Amalekites. In addition to the authorities instanced under (1) and (2), we have to add (3) that the great majority of the Old Testament laws doubtless grew out of the decisions of the priests (Mal. 2[6, 7]), or (4) later, out of the renderings of the supreme court of appeal at Jerusalem (Dt. 17[8-12]).

Editorial work of the priests
 There is no evidence, however, that a special legal commission or legislative body was ever intrusted with the task of formulating laws or of collecting or codifying existing customs. This was contrary to the theory of ancient Israelitish law, the origin of which was early traced back directly through Moses, or the *torahs* of the priests, to Jehovah himself. To the priests, as proclaimers, interpreters, and guardians of the *torah*, fell the responsibility of collecting and codifying and also of developing the law. This is distinctly implied in Zephaniah 3[4] and Ezekiel 22[26], where they are charged with having done violence to the *torah*. Thus the theory and practice underlying Israelitish law explain how it was possible readily to absorb foreign elements and at the same time to develop in accord with the higher moral standards and needs of each age.

 In the history of Israel's legal system five distinct periods may be distinguished. The first is the nomadic, the period which preceded the settlement in Canaan. At this stage the customary Semitic law of the desert, supplemented by the specific rulings of their leaders and priests, sufficed for the people's simple needs. The second may be designated as the early agricultural or Canaanite period. It began with the settlement in Canaan and extended down to the revolution of Jehu in 842 B.C. It was then that the nomadic Hebrews gradually absorbed the Canaanites by conquest and intermarriage and adopted largely their civilization, laws, institutions, sanctuaries, and, as the prophets frequently complain, not a few of their religious ideas and customs. The third may be denominated the prophetic period; that during which the great heralds of ethical and social righteousness impressed their new and revolutionary principles upon the conscience of the race. This period, extending from 842 to 586 B.C., was one of intense political and religious activity. It was in the interval between these two dates that the great moral and humane laws probably took form. The fourth period embraces the exilic and post-exilic times; it extends from 586 to about 300 B.C. The nation rested under the shadow of the exile, and its religious leaders under the spell of the Babylonian and Persian religions. With the hierarchy in the ascendancy, the whole tendency of the age was toward ceremonialism. The end of this period marks the probable date at which the canon of the law was closed. The fifth period is that of the oral law, and extends on beyond New Testament times. In theory the legal canon was forever closed, but in practice the expansion of the law still went on in the schools of the scribes. Until after the fall of Jerusalem (70 A.D.), however, the results of these scribal labors were preserved simply in the form of oral tradition.

The five great epochs in the development of Israel's laws

Until the exile wrought a radical transformation in their habits, the Israelites were not, as were the ancient Babylonians and Egyptians, a literary people. Abhorring commerce as they did, their life was comparatively simple; their own individual and national problems commanded most of their attention. Oral communication being easy, it was not until real needs arose that laws were likely to be committed to writing, or, at least, to gain wide currency in written form. Even the *Book of the Covenant*, though solemnly accepted as law in the days of Josiah, was simply read to the people (II Kgs. 23²). There is no evidence that more than one copy of it was made at the outset. In the numerous introductions to the laws in the Pentateuch, introductions written comparatively late, the references are chiefly to the oral reception and presentation of those laws. Only in connection with the early decalogues is it distinctly stated that they were written down (*e. g.*, Ex. 24⁴, 31¹⁸, 32¹⁶, 34²⁷, ²⁸, Dt. 9¹⁰); and then the aim of the statement is to emphasize their divine origin. During the nomadic period there was no need for written laws.

The long period of oral transmission

The ultimate conquest of the Canaanites and the absorption of their civilization, gave the Hebrews their system of writing; in all probability, also, it introduced them directly or indirectly to the legal codes inherited from Babylonia. It is possible that certain rules for the guidance of judges were placed on record as early as the days of David. The reference in Hosea 8¹² may seem to imply the existence in Northern Israel of written *torahs* or direc-

The earliest traces of written laws

13

tions; but the context indicates that they were simply the moral teachings of the prophets, applied, possibly, in the form of laws to the life of the people. For the nation as a whole, oral law and custom undoubtedly sufficed far into the prophetic period, even until the reformation of Josiah, an event which we know was based on a definite written code. And the account we have of that reform movement makes it clear that the *Book of the Covenant* had its genesis in the desire to correct prevailing usages and to regulate the life of the nation in accordance with the new doctrines of the prophets.

Influences of the exile that made the Israelites a literary race
The influences most potent in promoting the growth and study and use of the written law date from the beginning of the Babylonian exile. It was then that writing became the principal means of communication between the scattered remnants of the Israelitish race. The example of the Babylonians and Egyptians, among whom the leaders of Israel found themselves, could hardly fail to influence them. With the future of their race and religion depending largely upon the preservation of the rich heritage from the past, with the temple and sacred city in ruins and the ceremonial institutions in abeyance, the demand became imperative for written records of the customs and rules hitherto transmitted from priest to priest by usage and oral teachings. Torn from the temple and without occupation, the priests had, like Ezekiel, both leisure and incentive to become scribes and cast their inherited customs and laws into permanent form—a literary form which at once conserved Israel's heritage and adapted it to the changed conditions and beliefs that the exile brought in its train. Hence during the period beginning a little before 621 and ending about 300 B.C. with the closing of the canon of the law, the great majority of the Old Testament laws were, it is safe to say, not only first committed to writing, but also edited, codified, and given their final form.

Testimony of the laws themselves to their gradual growth
The character and present literary structure of the Old Testament laws confirm, at every point, the plain implications of Israelitish history and contemporaneous reference. Among the many indications of their gradual unfolding into successive codes is the fact that the same law is often repeated twice and, in some cases, four or five times; a fact obviously inconsistent with the late Jewish theory of their derivation from the one age and lawgiver. Then again, laws dealing with the same subjects as, for example, those defining the rights of slaves, inheritance, and temple dues, are found to stand in a progressive relation to each other; for in Deuteronomy these laws are given with much detail and often fundamentally modify the similar enactments in Exodus 21–23; and in Leviticus the corresponding laws introduce various other elements not logically consistent with the preceding, if all are assigned to the same age. Furthermore, certain laws supplant each other; as, for example, that in Deuteronomy 12, decreeing that all sacrifice must be offered in Jerusalem, is in obvious contradiction to the law of Exodus 20$^{24, 26}$; since this law in Exodus provides for the rearing of a sacrificial altar at any suitable place and is in perfect keeping with the prevailing usage until the days of Josiah (cf. *e. g.,* I Sam. 9$^{12, 22-25}$, I Kgs. 18$^{30-37}$).

There is further evidence, of the most convincing character, that the various

early ritual. At least three of the commands assume that the Hebrews are agriculturists, and therefore already settled in Canaan. Others, as for example the command not to seethe a kid in its mother's milk, are clearly inherited from the nomadic period, and may well go back to the days of Moses. As a whole, however, these ten words in their present form cannot be definitely dated earlier than the days of the united kingdom.

This decalogue appears to have had a place from the first in the early Judean narratives. Important evidence has already been presented (Vol. I, notes §§ 75, 76) to the effect that the familiar prophetic decalogue of Exodus 20[1-17] was substituted by a late prophetic editor for the older decalogue of Exodus 34. The importance of the former amply justified the transfer, although it assigned to the beginning of Israel's history certain principles (as, for example, the rejection of all images) which were only gradually revealed to the more mature consciousness of the race. This substitution, however, was in perfect keeping with the tendency that finds illustration in every department of Old Testament literature. In the light of the higher teachings and ideals of the prophets, the primitive definition of the obligations of the people to Jehovah had been supplanted by one much nobler. Exodus 19[25] states that Moses had gone down from the mount of revelation, although its present sequel (Ex. 20[1-17]) implies that he was still on the mountain in the presence of God. The natural and immediate continuation of the early Judean prophetic narrative of 19[20-25] is found not in 20 but in 34; for the latter opens with the command to Moses to go up again on the mountain with tablets to receive the words of the covenant (cf. for the restored order, Vol. I, §§ 183, 184). The reference to the second tablets of stone in [1b, 4b] are evidently from the editor who substituted the prophetic decalogue of Exodus 20[1-17]. Fortunately he preserved the older version by resorting to the harmonistic method often employed by the editors of the Pentateuch when confronted by two conflicting parallel versions, and assigned it to a later setting. The Ephraimite or Northern Israelitish account of the sin of the people and of the destruction of the two tablets (32[15-19]) suggested a method of reconciling the presence of two distinct decalogues. Accordingly the editor introduced the older immediately after this account. The great inconsistency of his theory, however, is left unreconciled; for he offers no hint or explanation why one decalogue was inscribed on the first tablets and a totally different one on the duplicate tablets, notwithstanding the fact that the context clearly implies identical contents in both cases.

Deuteronomy confirms (5[22, 31], 6[1]) the testimony of the earliest source, that only ten words or commands were publicly given to Moses at the mount of revelation. This evidence is important, for it clearly implies that when the original book of Deuteronomy was written the additional laws now associated with Sinai must have stood in a different connection. The suggestion of the learned Dutch scholar, Kuenen, is at least plausible. It is that the editor who assigned the Deuteronomic code to its present position in Israel's history, just before the crossing of the Jordan, did so because this was already the setting of the main collection of primitive laws. The only considerable body of early Hebrew laws of which there is any record is that now found in

Evidence that it was found originally immediately after Exodus 19

Original position of the laws now found in Exodus 20[23]–23[19]

17

Exodus 20^{23}–23^{19}. A position at the close of Moses' career and just before the people passed over the Jordan to enter upon that agricultural life of Canaan, which these laws contemplate, was most appropriate. But in following this ancient precedent for the assignment of the body of the laws of Deuteronomy to this setting, it was impossible for the editor to leave the older enactments there, for the Deuteronomic legislation modifies and in some cases absolutely annuls certain of their commands. Nothing remained, therefore, but to transfer them to the earlier setting and to join them, as now found, with the ten words. This, be it noted, was in perfect harmony with the tendency, traceable from the exile, to associate more and more of Israel's laws with the initial revelation at Sinai. It was, moreover, exactly parallel with the corresponding tendency to attribute all to Moses.

Original unity and independence of the *Judgments* in Exodus 21–22^{20}

The theory that the code in Exodus 20^{23}–23^{19} was transferred from a later setting to its present position by a late prophetic editor, certainly has the advantage of explaining, in a simple and reasonable manner, a great number of most puzzling facts. It may be questioned, however, whether the whole of this composite group of laws or only the major collection of case laws found in 21^1–22^{10} was thus transferred. The unity of this group is clearly marked. They all deal with civil and criminal questions. They all employ practically the same formula and are expressed in the third person rather than the second person singular. They are also introduced by the independent superscription: *Now these are the Judgments that thou shalt set before them* (21^1). If these *Judgments* were not originally found among Moses' farewell words, they may appropriately have followed the account in Exodus 18^{13-26} of his work as judge, but this hypothesis suggests no sufficient cause for their transfer. Hence, Kuenen's conjecture is still the most probable. Their remarkable unity in form and content, and the presence also of a distinct superscription, leaves little doubt that they once constituted an independent group by themselves, and that they did not originally stand in the midst of the collection of ceremonial and humane laws which they divide into two unequal parts.

Date and origin of the remaining ceremonial and humane laws

The first question to be answered, therefore, is, What were the origin and primary position of the small groups of ceremonial and humane laws which remain (20^{23-26}, 22^{18}–23^{19}) after the *Judgments* have been removed? Some later explanatory and hortatory glosses can be readily recognized (*e. g.*, 22^{21b}, 24, $23^{9b, 13, 15b}$); but the majority evidently came from an early period in Israel's history. The permission to build altars and offer sacrifices at many different places (Ex. 20^{24-25}) suggests either greater antiquity than even Exodus 34^{26}, or else the less restricted usage of Northern Israel. Furthermore, this permission is one of the primitive regulations abrogated by Deuteronomy 12. There is nothing in these groups of laws distinctly pointing to a date later than that of the united Hebrew kingdom. Their vocabulary connects them with the early Ephraimite rather than the Judean narratives. The early prominence of the prophets, the broader and more complex life of the northern kingdom, lead us to expect that there, rather than in little Judah, legal institutions first expanded and found record in detailed written laws.

The ceremonial enactments are but the repetition or expansion of the laws Their
in Exodus 34; laws which are the prototypes of the later and more detailed real
priestly laws of Leviticus. The humane commands reflect the spirit of the char-
early Ephraimite narratives and embody certain fundamental ethical prin- acter
ciples, like those of kindness to the poor and justice toward dependents, which
are constantly assumed by Amos and Hosea in their addresses to the Northern
Israelites as universally accepted. They represent the early Hebrew formulation of the noble humanitarian ideals that had already been partly incorporated in Hammurabi's code and that were destined later in Israelitish
and Christian law to find their fullest and most exalted expression.

It is a most significant fact that within this rather heterogeneous collection The
there are found in three groups, which stand by themselves (20^{23}, 22^{29-31}, and variant
23^{12-19}), practically all of the ten words of the primitive Judean decalogue in of the
Exodus 34. The many and striking variations in order and form furnish Judean
conclusive proof that the two decalogues represent distinct versions and not logue
mere scribal transcription from one original. Of course, the exact form and
content of the ten words or commands alluded to in Exodus 34^{28b}, and found
in the preceding verses of the same chapter, cannot be absolutely determined,
since they have been expanded and supplemented by later explanatory notes.
Likewise, the initial commands in Exodus 20^{23} have evidently been changed by
a later editor; for, under the influence of the obviously later introductory
phrase (^{22b}), the prevailing form of address in the second person singular
(*thou*) has been changed to the second person plural (*ye*). The frequency of
this particular change is illustrated by a comparison of the variations of
identical passages in the Greek and Hebrew versions—even where there is no
apparent cause (*e. g.*, Ex. $22^{18, \ 20, \ 23}$). Conversely, in Exodus 21^2 the regular
formula of the judgments has been changed from the third to the second person
singular, because this form is found in the immediately preceding passage.
The following table will facilitate the comparison of the two versions of the
primitive decalogue; in it the order of the Judean has been followed and the
fuller form given. The original *thou* of Exodus 20^{23} has also been restored.
The first command has evidently suffered in transmission, for in its present
form it reads, *Ye shall not make with me*, and the Greek version represents
a futile attempt to correct it. It is exceedingly probable that this command was
originally identical with the Judean version.

Early Judean Prophetic Version	*Early Ephraimite Parallel*	
I. **Exodus 34** ^{14}Thou shalt worship no other God, for Jehovah, whose name is Jealous, is a jealous God.	**Exodus 20** ^{23a}Thou shalt make no [other gods] with me (?).	The two variant versions of the primitive decalogue
II. ^{17}Thou shalt make thee no molten gods.	**20** ^{23b}Thou shalt make thee no gods of silver or gold.	
III. ^{18a}The feast of unleavened bread shalt thou observe: seven days shalt thou eat unleavened bread.	**23** ^{15a}The feast of unleavened bread shalt thou observe: seven days shalt thou eat unleavened bread.	

Early Judean Prophetic Version	*Early Ephraimite Parallel*
IV. [19, 20a, b]Every first-born is mine: even all the male cattle, the first-born of ox and sheep. And the first-born of an ass shalt thou redeem with a lamb; and if thou wilt not redeem it, then thou shalt break its neck. All the first-born of thy sons shalt thou redeem.	22 [29b, 30]The first-born of thy sons shalt thou give to me. Likewise shalt thou do with thy ox and thy sheep; seven days shall it remain with its mother; on the eighth day thou shalt give it to me.
V. [21]Six days shalt thou toil, but on the seventh thou shalt rest; in plowing time and harvest thou shalt rest.	23 [12]Six days thou shalt do thy work, but on the seventh thou shalt rest, that thine ox and thine ass may have rest and that the son of thy handmaid and the resident alien may be refreshed.
VI. [22]Thou shalt observe the feast of weeks, even of the first-fruits of wheat harvest, and of the ingathering at the end of the year.	[16][Thou shalt observe] the feast of harvest, the first-fruits of thy labors, which thou sowest in the field, and the feast of ingathering at the end of the year, when thou gatherest in thy labors from the field.
VII. [25a]Thou shalt not offer the blood of my sacrifice with leaven.	23 [18a]Thou shalt not offer the blood of my sacrifice with leaven.
VIII. [25b]The fat of the feast of the passover shall not be left all night until the morning.	[18b]The fat of my feast shall not be left all night until the morning.
IX. [26a]The best of the first-fruits of thy land shalt thou bring to the house of Jehovah thy God.	22 [29a]Thou shalt not delay to bring offerings from the abundance of thy harvests and the outflow of thy presses.
X. [26b]Thou shalt not seethe a kid in its mother's milk.	23 [19b]Thou shalt not seethe a kid in its mother's milk.

It is possible that the command in Exodus 34[20c], *none shall appear before me empty*, is original. It departs, however, from the prevailing formula; in Exodus 23[15c] it breaks the connection and is probably a scribal insertion from 34. Its content also strongly suggests that it is a later addition; but, if not such an addition, the eighth command could reasonably be counted as one. Even if this change be adopted, the close correspondence between the two versions is not affected. In four cases (III, VII, VIII, X) this correspondence is absolutely identical; in purport it is complete throughout the ten words. Both the variations and the remarkable points of agreement can be explained only on the hypothesis that they go back to a common original.

It is sometimes claimed that the Ephraimite prophetic narratives had no decalogue; yet such statements as those in Exodus $24^{3, 12a}$, 31^{18b}, 32^{16} Evidence that the (which belong to the northern history), plainly declare that it, like the early Ephraimite Judean prophetic narratives, at first contained only the laws of the decalogue narratives inscribed on two tablets. Exodus $20^{21, 22a}$ is probably the original Ephraimite contained introduction to the ten words or brief commands that once immediately a decalogue followed it, an introduction giving the account of the covenant at Horeb as that account originally stood in the Ephraimite narrative before the additional religious and humane laws were combined with it.

While it is impossible to determine with absolute certainty the exact form Date of the of the original ten words or commands underlying the two early prophetic original decalogue decalogues, the probabilities all go to show that they antedate the division of the two kingdoms in 937 B.C. In the light of all the evidence obtainable there is good ground for concluding that this original decalogue was promulgated at least as early as the days of the united monarchy. The character of its commands, and their prominence in all later codes, strongly support this comparatively early date.

On the basis of the two variant versions it may be conjecturally restored Its conjectural restoration as follows:

I. Thou shalt worship no other God.

II. Thou shalt make thee no molten gods.

III. The feast of unleavened bread shalt thou observe.

IV. Every first-born is mine.

V. Six days shalt thou toil, but on the seventh thou shalt rest.

VI. Thou shalt observe the feast of weeks and ingathering at the end of the year.

VII. Thou shalt not offer the blood of my sacrifice with leaven.

VIII. The fat of my feast shall not be left until morning.

IX. The best of the first-fruits of thy land shalt thou bring to the house of Jehovah.

X. Thou shalt not seethe a kid in its mother's milk.

Two significant facts should here be noted: first, the persistence of the Persistence of tradition that this simple primitive decalogue was early inscribed on two tablets the tradition of of stone; second, the emphasis that is laid upon it in all the different groups the two of narratives, except the late priestly, which substitutes for it the large body tablets of legislation found in Exodus 26–31, 35–40, and Leviticus. The different prophetic versions only reveal variations that are inevitable when a very early tradition is transmitted through different channels. The early Judean prophetic narratives represent the words as having been written on the tablets by Moses (Ex. $34^{27, 28}$). The early Ephraimite narratives state that the words were inscribed on the two tablets by the finger of God (Ex. 24^{12}, 31^{18b}). The Deuteronomic narrative as usual follows the Ephraimite tradition (Dt. 5^{22}, $9^{9, 10}$). A later Deuteronomic editor, possibly the one who transferred the early Judean decalogue to its present position in Exodus 34, reproduces the contents of that chapter; but at one point he abandons it in favor of the later tradition representing Jehovah himself as writing the words (Dt. 10^4). He also adds (possibly following a lost Judean original, or the temple records quoted in I Kgs. 8^9) that at Jehovah's command Moses, before going up on the mount to receive the tablets of the law, prepared an ark of acacia wood, and that when he returned he put them in the ark that he had made (Dt. 10$^{2, 3, 5}$).

Elements common to all the earliest narratives

In the light of these facts it seems clear that the original tradition, namely, that the earliest decalogue was written on two tablets of stone, also goes back at least to the early days of the united monarchy, a time when both the North and the South shared it in common. Furthermore, a tradition so persistent must have had an historical basis. The variations can easily be traced to the different narratives in which they appear; but the permanent elements, shared by all versions, are: (1) that the ten words were presented to the people by Moses as Jehovah's prophet; (2) that they were promulgated at the mount of revelation; (3) that they contained the terms of the solemn covenant which bound Israel as a nation to Jehovah; and (4) that they were inscribed on two tablets of stone.

Evidence of an original Mosaic oral decalogue

Of the elements just named the first is exceedingly important, for it represents the genesis of that tendency, which later became so prominent, to attribute the giving of the law to Moses. The second reflects the beginning of that parallel tendency to trace the origin of legal institutions to the beginning of Israel's history, which ultimately led the later editors of the law to associate the great body of the Old Testament legislation with Mount Sinai. As has already been noted, the contents of these commands support the conclusion that at least the majority of them may well come from the time of Moses. In early Hebrew thought Sinai-Horeb long continued to be regarded as the place where Jehovah dwelt and where he could be consulted. The account of Elijah's flight to Horeb is a familiar illustration of this belief (I Kgs. 19$^{8-14}$). Back of the decalogue in its present versions, anticipating as they do settled agricultural conditions in Canaan, there was probably a more primitive oral decalogue, which came, as the tradition asserts, directly from Moses and the mount of God.

Evidence that there was an early decalogue inscribed on two tablets

The third element, the belief that the ten words embodied the terms of the original covenant which bound Israel as a nation to Jehovah, indicates that when the early variant traditions first took form these ten words or commands were regarded as possessing an absolute and unique authority. It is not too much to say that they represent the first stage in that process of canonization which ultimately gave us the Old Testament. Out of a larger body of traditional laws and institutions these ten commands stood forth invested with overshadowing authority. By following their injunctions the continued protection and favor of Israel's national God was assured. What gave these ten words their commanding position? The fourth permanent element in the tradition suggests the simplest answer. It was because they were actually inscribed on two tablets of stone, and in characters which in time became archaic. It is impossible satisfactorily to explain this early and constantly recurring *motif* in the tradition on any other basis.

Excellent Semitic parallels are found in the Code of Hammurabi and the Marseilles tablet. The second example, although comparatively late, is especially to the point because it reflects a Phœnician, and, therefore, a Canaanite custom. The tablet was set up in a temple and was intended to guide the people in the discharge of their religious duty in connection with the ritual (cf. Appendix VIII). The command in Exodus 34^{26a} to bring the best of the first-fruits of the land *to the house of Jehovah thy God* would also seem to indicate that the oldest decalogue was closely connected with a specific sanctuary; a sanctuary which, in the Judean narrative where it is found, could have been none other than Solomon's temple. The testimony of the extract from the temple records found in I Kings 8^9 also connects the original ten words with the ark and Solomon's temple. Tradition, resting probably on an ultimate basis of fact, assigns their origin to Moses and the mount of revelation; but the varied historical data, as well as the needs of the situation and the spirit of the age, suggest that the primitive ten words were not put in written form until the reign of Solomon and in connection with the royal sanctuary reared by him. The decalogue form indicates that they were at first simply inscribed on the popular memory. Date and histori- cal set- ting of the first written deca- logue

A careful study of Exodus 20^{23}–23^{19} demonstrates, after two or three obvious scribal errors have been corrected (*e. g.*, 20^{23}, 21^2 and 22^{18}, where the Hebrew should be translated, *a sorceress shall not live*), that the religious and humane laws are practically always cast in the form of a direct address in the second person singular (*thou*), and that the civil and criminal laws, where a definite penalty is imposed, are always, as in the corresponding Code of Hammurabi, cast in the form of case law and employ the third person, never the second person singular (*If a man do so and so, such shall be the penalty*). The same distinction reappears in the older laws preserved in Deuteronomy, although that code, assuming as a whole the prophetic point of view, uses *thou* prevailingly. The care with which this distinction is maintained is illustrated by Exodus 21^{14}, *And if a man attack another maliciously, to slay him by treachery; thou shalt take him from mine altar, that he may be put to death.* The mention of the altar introduces the religious *motif* with the result that the corresponding *thou* is employed. Dis- tinct forms of the civil and cere- monial laws

The fundamental reason is probably because the appeal in the one case is directly to the individual conscience, and a penalty is rarely imposed; while in the other, the fear of punishment is the *motif*, and the specific laws are intended for the guidance of judges as well as the people. The civil and criminal laws also go back to earlier decisions and precedents as the ultimate basis of their authority, and aim simply to formulate and fix customs already largely in force. Here too, the indirect influence of Hammurabi's epoch-making code may perhaps be recognized in determining the form of the early Hebrew civil laws. It is in this connection significant that the superscription to the oldest Hebrew group (21^1–22^{20}) is but a variant of the title *Judgments of Righteousness* which Hammurabi gave to his collection of case laws. On the other hand, the direct address (*thou*) is alone employed in the religious and humane laws, probably because each command in the earliest decalogue was first given by a priest or prophet as divine *torah*, and in response to a specific question presented by an individual; or else, as the traditions imply, because the first group of commands was addressed by Moses, speaking in the name of Jehovah, directly to the nation collectively. Origin of these distinct forms

The distinct form and classification of the civil and the religious laws in

Origin and classification of the case laws or judgments — the earliest collection indicate that, as among the Babylonians, these two great departments of Israel's laws originally grew up independently. Side by side with the ceremonial decalogues, which were in time supplemented and expanded, the judgments or case laws were taking form. The early Ephraimite prophetic tradition in Exodus 18^{12-26} associates their beginning with Moses. The *Judgments* in Exodus $21^1–22^{20}$ are the earliest written evidences of the growth of criminal and civil laws. By their use of the word *Elohim* instead of Jehovah ($21^{6, \ 13}$, $22^{8, \ 11}$), and by other linguistic marks, the *Judgments* reveal their relationship with the Ephraimite group of narratives. With this strand they are also connected in their present setting.

Evidences of their date and history — Their setting, however, gives little aid in determining their date, for, as has been noted, they have been placed in their present position by some later editor of the book of Exodus. The laws themselves furnish the only real answer to the question of their date. Many of them may come from Moses, others assume the settled agricultural conditions to which the Hebrews did not attain until after they entered Canaan (*e. g.*, $22^{5, \ 6}$). But Hebrew society is still primitive; there are no central courts of appeal; a decision can be secured at any one of the shrines or sanctuaries which the Israelites inherited from the Canaanites (Ex. $22^{8, \ 9}$); wealth consists of produce and cattle; the *lex talionis* is still prominent, though the more civilized principle of compensation is being introduced. There is, indeed, no reason for doubting that the majority, if not all, of these laws were in force in Israel as early as the days of David and Solomon. Their early date is also confirmed by the central place that is assigned to them in all later civil legislation. These facts, however, do not necessarily imply that they were committed to writing at this early time. If Kuenen's conjecture be correct, they were introduced into the Ephraimite narratives (about 750 B.C.) in connection with Moses' farewell. Their remarkable unity (cf. p. 18) also suggests that they were possibly once current as an independent law book. This conclusion would explain, further, why they have retained their unity, though introduced into the midst of distinctly different laws. Possibly they were not associated with the Pentateuch until assigned to their present position by a late editor. The indications, both of form and content, strongly indicate they must have been formulated long before 750 B.C.

Comparison of the Hebrew code with that of Hammurabi — The remarkable correspondence between many of these individual laws and those of Hammurabi, favors the conclusion that the principles underlying them, if not the detailed contents and form, were in part derived from the older code through the Canaanites. They deal with similar questions and assume very much the same social conditions. Out of the forty-five or fifty judgments at least thirty-five have points of contact with the laws of Hammurabi, and fully half are in part parallel. The variations are in most cases traceable to the different spirit and circumstances of the two peoples from whom they come. Thus, for example, there are great differences in the penalties imposed. As a rule the older code, which comes from a populous commercial nation, is much more severe in punishing any infringement of the rights of property; while the Hebrew laws, coming from a people whose

24

numbers were comparatively small, are more strenuous in protecting human life. The penalty for stealing an ox in the Hebrew code is five oxen (Ex. 22^1), but in Hammurabi's code thirty, or if the owner was a poor man, tenfold its value (§ 8). In general the same just and humane spirit is reflected in both systems, and the variations are those of degree rather than kind. The old law of *an eye for an eye and a tooth for a tooth*, however, still figures prominently in both. In the older code slaves for debt were to be set free at the end of three years instead of six (Ex. 21^2); under the Babylonian laws daughters had the right of inheritance, a right which was not granted to them in Israel until a much later period; the rights of widows also are more carefully guarded in the older code. On the whole, the Babylonian laws appear to reflect a much more highly developed stage of civilization; and this conclusion also favors the early dating of the Hebrew code.

The points of close agreement are many. Especially is this true of the laws of deposit (cf. Ex. 22^{7-12} and Hammurabi's code §§ 9–11, 120, 124–26), the punishment of kidnapping (cf. Ex. 21^{16} and H. C. § 14), of injury to a pregnant woman (cf. Ex. 21^{22-25} and H. C. §§ 209–14), of sorcery (cf. Ex. 22^{18} and H. C. §§ 1, 2), and the responsibility of shepherds (cf. Ex. 22^{10-13} and H. C. § 266). That the later Hebrew code owes much to the older system seems probable, for the atmosphere in which the former developed was surcharged with Babylonian legal ideas; yet the points of variation are so many and so significant that the originality and individuality of the Old Testament code do not need demonstration. *(margin: Significance of the points of agreement and variation)*

Both codes seek only to guard against crimes and to anticipate the more common cases of dispute, and thus to establish principles and precedents to guide judges in deciding similar questions. Where a customary usage is fixed, it is often assumed and not restated. Much was necessarily left to the discretion of judges. A study of the Hebrew code in the light of the needs of early Hebrew society, leads to the conclusion that it is not a fragment of a large code, but that the early code, with the probable exception of five laws, is preserved in its original and complete form. *(margin: Comparative completeness of the Hebrew code)*

Furthermore, the civil code, unlike the corresponding ceremonial and humane laws in Leviticus, Numbers, and Deuteronomy, has received only a few later supplemental additions. These can readily be recognized. The penalty to be visited upon a son who reviles his father (21^{17}) was probably added by a scribe who was reminded of this law in Leviticus 20^9 by the very similar enactment in [15]. This, first written in the margin, has later been awkwardly introduced into the text in the midst of a group of laws dealing simply with assault. Similarly, Exodus 21^{26} contemplates the same crime and is clearly the immediate sequel of [20, 21]. The primitive laws in [22-25], which introduce a new subject, may well have been added by an early editor familiar with the corresponding Babylonian and Assyrian usage. The Greek translators recognized the difficulty, but failed to eliminate it. Exodus $22^{2, 3}$ is evidently also an early gloss, for it separates verse [1] from its complement [4] and contains a different, although kindred, law. Furthermore [2, 3] assume that the thief is killed, while [4] provides for his punishment in case the thing stolen is still in his possession. *(margin: The few later additions to it)*

25

Earlier attempts to recover the original decalogues and pentads

During the first part of the last century the German scholar Bertheau* detected the presence of decads in this primitive code, although he failed to recognize the unity of each. Professors Ewald, Dillmann, and especially Professor Briggs,† traced these groups of ten still further; Briggs also recognized the recurrence of the minor unit five. Professor Paton,‡ by pointing out the secondary passages which had led preceding scholars astray, and by vigorously insisting on the principle that each decad contains only laws bearing on closely related topics, succeeded in restoring four complete decalogues in this code and pointed out several more in the ceremonial and humane sections of Exodus 20²³–23¹⁹. Professor Paton also called attention to the fact that the law in Deuteronomy 22²⁸, ²⁹ is identical with that in Exodus 22¹⁶, and that it is preceded (Dt. 22¹⁰⁻¹⁹, ²⁰⁻²¹, ²², ²³⁻²⁴, ²⁵⁻²⁷) by a pentad of what appear to be primitive laws, all of which relate to social purity and join naturally with the corresponding pentad in Exodus 22¹⁶, ¹⁷, ¹⁸, ¹⁹, ²⁰, thus restoring a fifth decalogue. That Deuteronomy is based on the primitive codes, and that it contains certain early laws not found in the older collections, are facts now generally recognized. The assumption, therefore, that Deuteronomy has here preserved a pentad of laws, originally found in the primitive code, but removed by some editor or scribe to whose moral sense they were repugnant, is exceedingly probable.

Evidence that Exodus 22¹⁶⁻²⁰ belongs with the original judgments

Although the pentad regarding social purity (Ex. 22¹⁶⁻²⁰) has, hitherto, been in part assigned by scholars to the group of religious laws, it is clear that it all belongs to the collection of judgments. The form is the same; the *thou* of the current translations of ¹⁸ is evidently due to a mistake. Hammurabi in his civil code (§§ 1, 2) provides for the punishment of sorcerers. Even the law against sacrificing to an alien god was classified by the Hebrew lawgivers among the enactments relating to social purity (Lev. 17⁷, Dt. 31¹⁶). In Leviticus 18²¹ the prohibition of sacrifice to Moloch or Milk is found between the laws against adultery and sodomy.

In the light of these facts it is now possible to distinguish the pentad of decalogues which probably constituted the original collection of judgments. The following analyses will indicate their contents as well as the nature of the code as a whole: §

JUDGMENTS

Analysis of the civil and criminal laws

First Decalogue : The Rights of Slaves

First Pentad: Males, Exodus 21², ³ᵃ, ³ᵇ, ⁴, ⁵⁻⁶.
Second Pentad: Females, 21⁷, ⁸, ⁹, ¹⁰, ¹¹.

Second Decalogue : Assaults

First Pentad: Capital Offences, 21¹², ¹³, ¹⁴, ¹⁵, ¹⁶.
Second Pentad: Minor Offences, 21¹⁸⁻¹⁹, ²⁰, ²¹, ²⁶, ²⁷.

---

* *Die sieben Gruppen mosäischer Gesetze in den mittleren Büchern des Pentateuchs*, 1840.
† *Higher Criticism of the Hexateuch*, pp. 211 ff.
‡ *Journal of the Society of Biblical Literature and Exegesis*, 1893, pp. 79–93.
§ For these laws arranged in their grouping, cf. Appendix II.

Third Decalogue : Laws Regarding Domestic Animals

First Pentad: Injuries by Animals, $21^{28, 29, 30, 31, 32}$.

Second Pentad: Injuries to Animals, $21^{33-34, 35, 36}$, $22^{1, 4}$.

Fourth Decalogue : Responsibility for Property

First Pentad: In General, $22^{5, 6, 7, 8, 9}$.

Second Pentad: In Cattle, $22^{10-11, 13, 14, 15a, 15b}$.

Fifth Decalogue : Social Purity

First Pentad: Adultery, Deuteronomy $22^{13-19, 20-21, 22, 23-24, 25-27}$.

Second Pentad: Fornication and Apostasy, Exodus $22^{16, 17, 18, 19, 20}$.

As in the Code of Hammurabi, a serious attempt at systematic classification is here apparent. The general order is: the rights of persons, the rights of property, and the rights of society. Within each decalogue there is evidence also of careful grouping. Each pentad is a unit by itself. Whence this surprising order which is lacking in so many other parts of the Old Testament? It may be due to the powerful influence of the older Babylonian code, or it may simply reflect the tendency of the legal mind. *(Principle of classification)*

The ceremonial and humane laws found in 20^{23-26} and 22^{21}–23^{19}, although evidently somewhat disarranged, still reveal unmistakable traces of a similar grouping in decalogues and pentads. The disarrangement, as a rule, does not affect the unity of the pentads. It should be expected, however, that the powerful example of the early decalogue (cf. Ex. 34) would affect the form of the kindred group of the religious even more than the civil laws where its influence has already been traced. The indications favor the conclusion that the primitive decalogue of Exodus 34 gradually developed in Northern Israel into four corresponding decalogues. At present Exodus 20^{23-26}, 22^{21}–23^{19} contain only seven complete pentads, and $23^{4, 5}$, which separate the kindred laws of 23^{1-3} and $6-9$, two commands of an eighth. The remaining three of the pentads are to be found in Deuteronomy 22^{1-7}, which in verses 1, 3 reproduce Exodus $23^{4, 5}$ word for word, only substituting *brother* for *enemy*. The two commands in Deuteronomy $22^{2, 3}$ are the immediate sequel of 1; and the remaining command, 6, 7, which enjoins kindness to birds, is evidently primitive and belongs with this cycle of laws. *(The four ceremonial and humane decalogues)*

Exodus 23^9 is a scribal duplicate of 22^{21}. Rejecting the minor editorial additions, which are readily recognized, the following decalogues appear:

CEREMONIAL AND HUMANE LAWS

First Decalogue : Kindness

First Pentad: Toward Men, Exodus $22^{21a, 22-23, 25a, 25b, 26-27}$.

Second Pentad: Toward Animals, Exodus 23^4 [Deuteronomy 22^1], $22^{2, 3}$, Exodus 23^5 [Deuteronomy 22^4], 22^{6-7}. *(Analysis of the ceremonial and humane laws)*

Second Decalogue : Justice

First Pentad: Among Equals, Exodus $23^{1a, 1b, 2a, 2b, 3}$.

Second Pentad: On the Part of Those in Authority, $23^{6, 7a, 7b, 7c, 8}$.

ISRAEL'S LAWS AND TRADITIONAL PRECEDENTS

Third Decalogue : Duties to God
First Pentad: Worship, Exodus $20^{23a,\ 23b,\ 24,\ 25,\ 26}$.
Second Pentad: Loyalty, Exodus $22^{28,\ 29a,\ 29b,\ 30,\ 31}$.

Fourth Decalogue : Sacred Seasons
First Pentad: Command to Observe them, Exodus $23^{10-11,\ 12,\ 15a,\ 16a,\ 16b}$.
Second Pentad: Method of Observing them, Exodus $23^{17,\ 18a,\ 18b,\ 19a,\ 19b}$.

Original order and extent of these decalogues
These decalogues have been so disarranged that it is impossible to determine with assurance their original order. If they followed the *Judgments*, they probably began with duties to men and led up to duties to God. If the prophetic decalogue of Exodus 20 (Dt. 5) is an index, the original order was the reverse. Possibly the influence of this prophetic decalogue, which was esteemed so highly, explains the transfer of the decalogue regarding duties to God; so that one pentad precedes the *Judgments* and the other pentad precedes the decalogue concerning justice to one's fellow-men. The remarkable symmetry discernible in the grouping of these laws, leads us to expect another decalogue; such a decalogue as would make complete the pentad of decalogues in the group of religious and humane laws corresponding to that of the *Judgments*. The later grouping of the law in the five books of the Pentateuch, the five divisions of the Psalter, and the apparently five-fold grouping in the original Matthew's collection of the Sayings of Jesus are but a few of the many analogies that might be cited. A fifth ceremonial or humane decalogue might be found in Deuteronomy, but the attempt to define it without any guides would be precarious.

The decalogue of Exodus 20^{1-17}
It is an interesting fact that a fifth religious decalogue is now found in the same context, and is none other than the familiar prophetic decalogue of Exodus 20^{1-17}. In its present arrangement the so-called *Greater Book of the Covenant* (Ex. 20–24), with the additions from Deuteronomy, consists of exactly ten decalogues. In the initial decalogue of Exodus 20 the same division into pentads is also apparent; the first laws concerning duties to God and parents, the second concerning duties to one's fellow-men.

Parallels to this decalogue
In addition to those already noted (p. 17) there are, however, serious difficulties involved in regarding this decalogue as originally associated with the primitive codes. Its first and second commands seem to be a briefer and more advanced version of the two laws in 20^{23}. The prototype of the third is perhaps to be found in 22^{28}, *Thou shalt not revile God.* The fourth is a duplicate of 23^{12}, *Six days thou shalt do thy work, but on the seventh thou shalt rest.* The fifth, sixth, seventh, and eighth are briefer, more emphatic, statements of the principles underlying the criminal laws of Exodus 22^{15-27}, $22^{13,\ 16}$; the ninth is but a restatement of the law in 23^{1}.

The original version and its date
The history of this noblest of decalogues must forever remain shrouded in mystery. Without any close connection with its context, it stands, as we have seen, alone. It is, indeed, a practical duplicate of the decalogue in Deuteronomy 5; the variations in the form of the original words of the fourth and tenth commandments, and the fact that a distinct and variant group of explanatory and hortatory glosses has grown up about many of the original

28

words (as for example, *Thou shalt not make unto thee a graven image*) indicate that each decalogue has had an independent history. At the same time it is clear that both versions go back to a common original. In the fourth command the Deuteronomic version employs the more primitive word *observe* (cf. Ex. 34^{22}), and the tenth command, that which forbids coveting a neighbor's *wife* (Dt. $5^{21\,a}$), suggests an earlier stage of society than the corresponding *house* of Exodus 20^{17}, which implies that the Hebrews are settled in Canaan; so that, on the whole, Deuteronomy 5 seems to represent the older original. The prominent position of this decalogue in Deuteronomy indicates, however, that it is older than its setting; how much older can never be determined. Internal evidence does not assign it as a whole to a period earlier than the latter part of the eighth century, a time when the influence of the prophets of ethical righteousness was beginning to be felt in Israel, and all use of images in worship was viewed with disfavor by the most enlightened leaders. Possibly it represents the briefer Judean version of the fuller and yet parallel Northern Israelitish decalogues in Exodus 20^{23}–23^{19}. Its present form may simply be due to prophetic revision; its basis is perhaps a very brief popular decalogue, intended for the guidance of the people in their daily relations; while the decalogue in Exodus 34 defined their duties in connection with the ritual and the sanctuary. It is important to note that, with the exception of the second, and possibly the tenth command, there is nothing in the decalogue of Deuteronomy 5 (Ex. 20) fundamentally inconsistent with the conclusion that it came, in its original and simplest form, from Moses himself.

In view of all these facts, and aided by means of analogy and imagination, it is possible to construct an approximate history of the growth of Israel's primitive codes. Why the decalogue, from the first and far down into Hebrew history, was the prevailing form into which all laws and precepts were cast, finds its simplest and perhaps most satisfactory explanation in the obvious fact that every normal man from earliest childhood has two hands with five fingers on each. These ten fingers are ever present and suggestive aids to the memory not only of children, but of men as well. If this be the true explanation, a system so simple and yet so effective, is worthy of a genius like that of Moses. There is no reason for doubting that through Israel's first great prophet there was transmitted a primitive decalogue—and possibly several—which defined in ten brief sentences the nation's obligations to its God. It is probable that these ten words were not originally inscribed on two tablets of stone by the finger of Jehovah, but upon the memory of each individual Israelite by association with the fingers of his two hands. In time the ceremonial decalogue, adapted to the new agricultural civilization and to the changed conditions and customs which the Israelites found in Canaan, was inscribed on two tablets of stone, and perhaps at first set up in the temple of Solomon. Naturally, after the division of the Hebrew kingdom, the Judean historians preserved the more exact version of it.

As new ideals dawned upon the consciousness of the race, this primitive decalogue was supplemented, and became, especially in the North, the nucleus about which grew up a much larger body of ceremonial and humane enact-

Origin of the deca- logue form

Growth of new laws and decalogues ments. All these laws were modelled after the older original, and hence were expressed in the form of a direct personal command (*thou*). Side by side with the memory that Moses was the author of the original ten words, was treasured the tradition that Jehovah's commands were cast in the form of decalogues and pentads. Possibly the priests in this effective way originally impressed the new enactments upon the minds of the people. As new needs arose and new standards were adopted, the priests could easily supplement the older laws by additional decalogues and pentads.

Development of corresponding civil and criminal decalogues Meantime the demands of the settled agricultural life had made necessary a corresponding group of civil and criminal laws. The customs of the agricultural Canaanites, the inheritors of the older Babylonian laws, were adapted to these new needs and were doubtless, in modified form, largely adopted by the Hebrews. When originally promulgated as a brief code, they were probably grouped in decalogues and pentads. If our explanation be correct, this form was intended primarily to aid the memory, and may be regarded as clear proof, therefore, that these laws, like the corresponding ceremonial group, were probably at first transmitted orally. This fact, then, would explain why all these primitive codes are cast in what at first glance seems to be a very artificial mould. The necessity of conforming to this mould would also explain why some subjects, which are passed over briefly in the Code of Hammurabi—as, for example, injuries by animals (cf. H. C. §§ 250–52 and Ex. 21^{28-32})—are expanded into five laws, while others, as for example the laws regarding property (Ex. 22^{5-15}), though deserving more detailed treatment, are accorded only the same space.

Approximate dates of the primitive codes It is also probable that the Northern Israelitish school of prophetic historians first committed these civil decalogues to writing. Possibly, as Kuenen has urged, they associated them with Moses' farewell words. Just when they were introduced into the midst of the ceremonial decalogues is not clear; possibly it was the work of the late prophetic editor who substituted the decalogue of Exodus 20^{1-17} and transferred the original Judean decalogue to its present position. At least it is probable that the majority of the laws found in Exodus 20^{23}–23^{19} and 34, were in force as early as the days of the united Hebrew kingdom; and that the five civil and criminal decalogues, and the four surviving ceremonial and humane decalogues, were to be found in written form by the eighth century B.C. These represent, therefore, the growth of Israel's laws and institutions from that early period, about 1150 to about 750 B.C., when Amos and Hosea and Isaiah appeared as the heralds of a new era in the political and religious life of the Hebrew race. To distinguish them from the legal systems of later periods, these oldest collections of laws may as a whole be appropriately designated as the *Primitive Codes;* for they record, in concrete form, the earliest revelation of the Divine will through the life and institutions of the ancient Israelites.

IV

THE DEUTERONOMIC CODES

THE appearance of Assyrian armies in Palestine about the middle of the Influ- eighth century and the resulting conquest of both Northern and Southern ences that Israel, not only destroyed the simplicity of early Hebrew life, but also intro- pro-duced duced new conditions and problems. Assyrian ideas and religious institutions the threatened to supplant completely the more austere worship of Jehovah. It new codes was the series of grave crises arising from this changed state of affairs that called forth the first, and in many ways the noblest, group of Israel's prophets, Amos, Hosea, Isaiah and Micah. Their teachings established new ethical and religious standards in Israel. New needs, new conditions and new ideals, therefore, made a recasting of the old primitive codes a necessity. Fortunately the theory and character of Israelitish law made the needed revision possible.

The prophet Isaiah, discouraged by faithlessness and apathy, turned Fruit- from the nobles and people to a little group of devoted disciples in whom he age of saw the earnest of an ultimate acceptance of his teachings by the nation. work of the *I will preserve the revelation and seal up the instruction among my disciples,* earlier were the words that he uttered, words full of promise for the future (Is. 8[16]). proph- The reactionary reign of Manasseh silenced the lips of the prophets. For ets forty or fifty years after the death of Isaiah, the old Canaanitish cults and especially the newly introduced Assyrian religion, commanded the devotion of the people of Judah and led them to forget almost entirely the exalted ethical teachings of the group of prophets who had followed Amos. The reaction, however, disclosed the crying needs of the situation; and these needs led the disciples of the true prophets to devote themselves to the formulation of the vital principles of their masters in laws so definite that the most obtuse could understand and apply them to the details of every-day thought and life. The noble results of the activity of these disciples are recorded in.the book of Deuteronomy.

The spirit of this wonderful book is prophetic rather than priestly. The Their emphasis is placed on deeds and spirit rather than ceremonial. Worship spirit pro- is important only as it is an expression of an attitude of loyalty to Jehovah. phetic Little is said about the ritual; and the prophet figures more prominently than the and popu- priest (cf. 18). Love to God, love to man, kindness to the needy and oppressed, lar and even to animals, are the dominant notes in the book. The appeal is not so much to fear of punishment as to the conscience of the individual. The exact penalty for a given crime is often left to the judge. The omission of all technical data and the popular form of the enactments indicate that this book was intended for the guidance of the people rather than of judges or priests. The whole is presented in the form of a farewell address in the mouth of

31

Moses. In him, as their first great representative, the prophets are made to rise above the temporal and local conditions that called them forth, and to proclaim, with divine authority and in specific terms, the principles, humane, political, social, ethical and religious that underlay all their teachings.

Their relation to earlier codes   Yet the codes of Deuteronomy do not represent a break with Israel's earlier legal traditions; they are, rather, a natural evolution. Three-fourths of the laws found in the previous codes are represented in Deuteronomy. Those which were omitted (found in Ex. 21^{18}–$22^{25, 28, 29b}$) were of interest only to judges when imposing penalties for specific crimes; and they did not, therefore, conserve the popular aim of the book of Deuteronomy. Although most of the earlier laws are reproduced in spirit, very few are quoted verbatim (cf. Ex. 34^{26b}, 23^{19b} and Dt. 14^{21c}). The days of a slavish worship of the letter of the law are, evidently, still in the future. Usually the purport of the primitive laws is reproduced in the peculiar language of the Deuteronomic writers, fully supplemented by explanations and exhortations (cf. e. g., Ex. 21^{2-7} and Dt. 19^{1-13}). Often the usage represented by the earlier codes is modified or entirely abrogated. Thus the law of Exodus 20^{24-26}, a law recognizing as perfectly legitimate the many altars scattered throughout ancient Israel, is annulled by the commands of Deuteronomy 12^{1-28}, $16^{5, 6}$ that declare illegal every sacrifice performed outside of Jerusalem.

Sources of the principles underlying Deuteronomy   In most instances the reasons for the new rulings can be traced either to the changed political and social conditions or to the teachings of some earlier prophet. Hence an endeavor to guard against a heathen reaction like that in the days of Manasseh, made it possible, after the fall of Samaria, to centralize all worship in Jerusalem. Amos and Hosea regarded the local shrines of Palestine with little favor (Am. 5^5, 7^9, Hos. 4^{13}). The lofty ideals of justice and social righteousness that permeate the book of Deuteronomy, are clearly traceable to the sermons of Amos and Isaiah; and its distinctive spirit, that of love to God and man, is the clear reflection of the central doctrine of Hosea. It was this epoch-making prophet, Hosea, who declared that the worship of heathen gods and the practising of heathen rites was whoredom, treason to Jehovah, and the cause of the nation's undoing. He demanded nothing less than that his people *love Jehovah with all their heart and with all their soul, and with all their might.*

Moses' relation to the Deuteronomic codes   The assignment by the later editors of Deuteronomy of all the laws of this noble prophetic law-book to Moses, is singularly appropriate. The public address was the characteristic prophetic method of presenting truth. This is illustrated not only by the so-called oral prophecies but also by the prophetic histories, wherein long speeches containing the doctrines of their late prophetic editors, are put in the mouths of Moses, Joshua, Samuel and David. Indeed this literary form is common in all literature, especially in ancient writings (cf. Vol. II, p. 4). Israelitish history and tradition also united in attributing all primitive laws to the master-mind that first moulded the race. These laws furnished the foundation of the new codes. Not to have acknowledged the supreme debt to Moses would have been unwarranted. It is but fair to say that they represent what the great prophet would have taught had he been confronted by the later needs and stood in the light of later revelation.   Through all the laws, early and late alike, the same God was making known his will to men.   It mattered little who was his spokesman; the laws themselves bore on their face the credentials of their divine origin.

The evidence that the mass of the laws in Deuteronomy are a century or two later than those of the primitive codes, is cumulative and conclusive. Kingship, as well as prophecy, has become an important element in the state (17[14-20]).   The crimes of such rulers as Solomon and Ahab are evidently in the mind of the prophet lawgivers ([16, 17]).   A supreme court at Jerusalem has been established (17[8-13]).   Not only the many shrines but also the sacred pillars and asherahs (consecrated tree-poles), which were countenanced in the early prophetic narratives and tolerated without protest from the prophets far down into the Assyrian period, are placed under the ban (12[3], 16[22]). Many other heathen institutions that flourished during the reigns of Ahaz and Manasseh, are also strictly forbidden (17[3-5]).   The Babylonian exile, be it said, casts its dark shadow across certain pages of Deuteronomy (*e. g.*, 4[25-29]). The marks of that period are distinctive; the peculiar language and ideas of Deuteronomy are closely related to those of Jeremiah and the disciples who edited his book of prophecies. *(margin: Evidence that Deuteronomy is later than the primitive codes)*

The evidence regarding the date of the Deuteronomic laws all points to the latter part of the seventh century.   The evils of the reign of Manasseh have become patent; and the prophetic lawgivers take up the task of guarding Israel against them for all future time.   The spirit of the books as a whole is decidedly hopeful.   Its authors seem to contemplate not the distant but the immediate possibility of reform.   The rigorous enactments regarding the punishment of the devotees of the ancient heathen cults, strongly suggest the spirit of the early reformers under Josiah, rather than the dark, reactionary reign of Manasseh.   From beginning to end it is essentially a reform book. It seems probable, though the question can never be absolutely decided, that the original edition of Deuteronomy was completed somewhere between the beginning of Josiah's reign in 639 and the great reform in 621 B.C., rather than in the days of Manasseh or earlier, as has been sometimes urged. *(margin: Date of the original edition)*

That this was the *Book of the Covenant*, found, according to II Kings 22, by Hilkiah the priest while conducting repairs in the temple, has been recognized by scholars since the days of Jerome.   The reforms, instituted by the king after the newly discovered law-book had been verified by the prophetic order, and publicly read and promulgated by him, are in perfect accord with the demands of Deuteronomy.   All the symbols of the heathen cults were first cast out of the temple and destroyed (cf. Dt. 12[3], 17[3]).   All the high places, their altars, and the sacred pillars, were broken down; the asherahs were hewn in pieces (Dt. 12).   Necromancy and witchcraft were suppressed (Dt. 18[11]).   Practically every recorded act in that great reformation is in accord with a specific command of Deuteronomy.   Henceforth until the days of Nehemiah and Ezra the life of the Jews of Palestine was regulated by this wonderful law-book. *(margin: Evidence that it was the basis of Josiah's reforms)*

Aside from the later introductions in 1–4, and the farewell speeches, exhortations, and blessings (cf. Vol. I, p. 42), the book of Deuteronomy consists

Analysis of the laws of Deuteronomy

of seven rather loosely defined groups of laws. These are found in the distinctively legal sections, 5–26. The first includes the prophetic decalogue, 5^{6-21}, and is followed by a series of exhortations based on the first command. The second group, 12^1–17^7, consists of ceremonial and religious laws. The third, 17^8–18^{22}, describes the appointment and duties of the officials —the judges, the king, the priests and the prophets—in the theocracy. In the fourth, 19, is found a collection of criminal laws. With this group is associated, by community of subject, the law in 21^{1-9} regarding the expiation of an untraced murder. The fifth group, 20, 21^{10-14}, consists of military laws to be observed in case of war. The sixth, 21^{15}–25^{19}, includes a miscellaneous collection of civil, criminal, humane, and religious laws. No systematic principle of classification is here apparent. Many of these laws are closely related to those found in the other groups. They seem to represent the result of compilation, and to be a series of supplements added to the preceding collections. The seventh group, 26, relates to the presentation of the first-fruits and the triennial tithe.

Lack of logical arrangement

The laws of Deuteronomy are in general characterized by lack of logical order and arrangement, though, compared with the primitive codes, there is evidence of an attempt at classification. Except in the commands of 5^{6-21}, and in a few citations from earlier collections (e. g., $22^{1-4,\ 13-30}$), the system of grouping in decalogues and pentads has been abandoned; a fact probably due to the authors' expectation that their laws would be promulgated not in oral but in written form.

Evidences that the laws come from a school of writers

It is obvious, also, that the book of Deuteronomy does not consist of one code coming from the same hand; for it bears all the marks of a collection of minor codes which have been gradually brought together into their present relations. The same subjects are treated in widely separated sections; and, conversely, entirely disconnected themes are brought into close connection. In addition to the primitive enactments of Exodus 20–23, many other earlier laws have evidently been utilized as the basis of these revised codes. These, as a rule, can readily be recognized by their more primitive form and content (cf. 22). Yet so homogeneous are the phraseology, spirit, and purpose which characterize all the different codes that they establish the underlying unity of the book as a whole. This is more marked and significant than the evidence for different groups of laws from widely different dates. That the different collections or codes are the work of the same school of writers, who from time to time expanded and supplemented the original nucleus of laws, seems to be the true explanation of the repetitions and minor variations in language and point of view.

The original Book of the Covenant

Both the peculiar structure of the book of Deuteronomy and the report of Josiah's reformation in II Kings 22, favor the conclusion that the original Book of the Covenant, the basis alike of Deuteronomy and of the initial reforms, is represented by chapters 12–19 and 26. With this nucleus was probably associated from the first the original form of the blessings and curses in 28. These sections contain all the regulations which are reported to have been enforced by the reformers.

To make the new code the comprehensive law-book of the realm, the mis-

cellaneous groups of laws in 20–25 were doubtless early added. Then, with Com-
the same aim, and by the same school of prophetic reformers, the decalogue pletion
of the
and exhortations in 5–11 were later joined. The provisions in 27 for the prophetic
public promulgation and enforcement of the law appear to belong to a later law-
stratum of the book. The entire legal section (5–28), however, was in book
the present form probably complete, or nearly so, before the Babylonian exile.
Its codes, therefore, represent the development of Israel's law under the influence of the great prophetic preachers and editors who lived and worked
between 750 and 600 B.C. To distinguish them from the earlier primitive
codes on the one side, and the later development of Israel's law on the other,
they may appropriately be designated as the *Deuteronomic* or *Prophetic
Codes* (technically represented by D). In them is found a large proportion
of the noblest and most enduring legislation in the Old Testament.

V

EZEKIEL AND THE HOLINESS CODE

The tendencies in the exile to develop written codes

THE promulgation of the Deuteronomic codes marked the beginning of the reign of the written law. Before that date oral laws and customs sufficed almost entirely for the needs of the people; but henceforth the authority of the written law steadily increased until it ultimately overshadowed *the word of the prophet and the counsel of the wise.* To this tendency the revolutionary experiences of the Babylonian exile gave a powerful impetus. The new conditions amid which the survivors of the Jewish race found themselves, suddenly transformed them into a literary people (cf. p. 13). Upon the work of the scribe depended the preservation of their laws and institutions; and closely bound up with these was the future of the race. The exile also gave its religious leaders new points of view and the changed conditions made new laws necessary. Deuteronomy contained few ceremonial laws; but in the minds of the exiled priests in Babylon the ritual occupied the position of commanding importance. Hence they proceeded to record the customary usages of the destroyed temple, to improve upon these where improvement was necessary and feasible, and thus to develop codes adapted to the needs of that restored Jewish community which was the object of their dreams.

Ezekiel's activity as a codemaker

The prophet Ezekiel clearly illustrates this tendency. Born a priest, probably trained at the temple and familiar with its institutions as well as with the recently promulgated Deuteronomic codes, he, together with other Jewish priests and nobles, was carried captive to Babylonia in 597 B.C. The first period of his residence in captivity was devoted to the work of preaching; but in 572 B.C., near the close of his ministry, he prepared the remarkable programme or code found in chapters 40–48 of his book. It is in the form of a detailed vision of the restored community and temple. Chapters 40–43 describe the new sanctuary on Mount Zion, 44–46 the ordinances to be observed in connection with it, while 47 and 48 give a picturesque account of the rehabilitation and allotment of the land of Israel.

His new and revolutionizing regulations

Many of the measurements and ceremonial laws of this code are undoubtedly reproductions of those of the pre-exilic temple, an institution with which Ezekiel was personally acquainted. He does not hesitate, however, to introduce entirely new regulations. The temple slaves of alien blood, who had formerly ministered at the sanctuary, are forever excluded (44[7, 8]). Also the Levites, the descendants of the priests of the local shrines outside Jerusalem, who, according to Deuteronomy 18[7, 8] were allowed to officiate at the temple, were now excluded from this privilege (44[13]) and assigned to the menial duties hitherto performed by the temple slaves. Only the sons of Zadok were permitted to approach Jehovah's altar and to offer sacrifices to him. Thus

36

Ezekiel for the first time establishes that sharp distinction between priest and Levite which was soon universally accepted; but in his code the high priest is simply the head of the priesthood and is not yet clad in special garments and invested with supreme authority as the civil and spiritual head of the community. Instead of the later elaborate ceremonial of the day of atonement on the tenth of the seventh month (Nu. 29[7-11]), Ezekiel ordains that twice each year—at the beginning of the first and sixth months—a rite of atonement be observed, but with a very different and much simpler sacrificial formula (45[18-20]).

It is not strange that later Jewish rabbis, confronted by these and other wide variations, found great difficulty in reconciling Ezekiel's code with their own theory of the origin of Israelitish law, and that they were inclined to regard it as a heretical. To the modern scholar Ezekiel is an invaluable index to the true history of the Old Testament legislation; for his work can be definitely dated. Evidently his code is the successor of the Deuteronomic and the precursor of those priestly codes which became the ultimate formative norm of later Judaism. He is one of the pioneers in the movement emanating from the exiles in Babylonia that defined religion in the terms of the ritual and aimed to develop a detailed series of laws regulating the life of the individual and, especially, the ceremonial services of the temple. *His place among Israel's lawgivers*

His code, as such, was never practically adopted by the Jewish race. For nearly two centuries more the Deuteronomic codes sufficed for the needs of the struggling community in Palestine. Much in Ezekiel's programme, as for example the allotment of the land, was theoretical, not practical. At the same time the principles that he emphasized, and most of the innovations that he advocated, were taken up by later priestly lawgivers and in modified and more practical form were incorporated in the law-book ultimately adopted by the Jews of Palestine. His primary aim in developing his code in this concrete and dramatic way, was to convince his contemporaries that Jehovah's people would certainly be restored to their native land, and to inspire them to prepare for the return. The later codes, as well as subsequent history, demonstrate that his higher prophetic purpose was realized. Thus he stands, not merely as the incarnation of the dominant spirit of the exile, but also as the man who, more than any other, shaped the life and thought of later Judaism. *His influence upon later Judaism*

Underlying all of Ezekiel's preaching and laws is the dominant conception of Jehovah's holiness. The arrangement of the temple, its ritual, the laws guarding the ceremonial purity of the priest, even the allotment of the land, these all are intended to guard the central sanctuary and the Holy One inhabiting it from coming again into contact with anything common or unclean. Furthermore, these elaborate regulations were intended to impress strongly upon the minds of his readers the supreme holiness of Jehovah and the corresponding obligation of his people to be holy. The vision of Isaiah (Is. 6) is here interpreted into the terms of both ritual and life. *His dominant idea: Jehovah's holiness*

The same conception and application reappear in the laws of Leviticus 17–26; and are so distinctive that this collection has been appropriately designated, and is now generally known as, the *Holiness Code* (technically

Points of contact between Ezekiel and the Holiness Code represented by P^h). The underlying thought that binds the group together is expressed in the words of Jehovah in Leviticus $22^{31\text{-}33}$, *Ye shall observe my commands and do them: I am Jehovah. And ye shall not profane my holy name; but I will be treated as holy among the Israelites. I am Jehovah who maketh you holy, who brought you out of the land of Egypt, to be your God: I am Jehovah* (cf. 19^2, $20^{7,\,8,\,26}$, $21^{6\text{-}8,\,15,\,23}$, $22^{9,\,16}$). A study of the individual laws demonstrates that, as in Ezekiel, both moral and ceremonial holiness is contemplated. The impressive refrain, *I am Jehovah*, is repeated forty-six times and is one of many common characteristics that distinguish these laws. The same expression is also found seventy-eight times in Ezekiel, and not once in the writings of his earlier contemporaries, Isaiah and Jeremiah. There are many other striking points of contact both in vocabulary and idiom. The unusual formula beginning, *Every man of the house of Israel* (Lev. $17^{3,\,8,\,10,\,13,\,15}$), is found nowhere else in the Old Testament except in Ezekiel, where it is very common (*e. g.*, Ezek. $14^{4,\,7,\,8}$, $44^{10,\,12}$). The social crimes especially prohibited in the Holiness Code (*e. g.*, 18^8, $20^{10\text{-}12}$, 17, $19^{13,\,15,\,36}$, 20^9, $21^{1\text{-}5}$),* are denounced by Ezekiel in terms almost identical (*e. g.*, $22^{10,\,11}$, $18^{7,\,8,\,12,\,16}$, $33^{15,\,25}$, 45^{10}, 22^7, $44^{25,\,20}$). A like emphasis is also laid on the sanctity of the temple (cf. Lev. 19^{30}, 20^3, 21^{12}, 23, 26^2 and Ezek. 5^{11}, 8^6, $23^{38,\,39}$). Both seek to guard the priesthood from all possible defilement. Thus in language, thought, and purpose, Ezekiel and the laws of the Holiness Code are bound together by closest ties.

Explanation of the points of likeness The points of contact are so many and so fundamental that they can be explained only on the assumption of a vital connection between the two. At the same time minor variations in vocabulary and representation indicate that Ezekiel was not the author of both. Thus, for example, the Holiness Code knows nothing of his distinction between the priests and Levites. It also sanctions, except in the case of the high priest (Lev. 21^{14}), the marriage of priests with widows, a practice which Ezekiel condemns (44^{22}). A detailed comparison of the two systems leads to the conclusion that both come from the same priestly circles and approximately the same date, but that Ezekiel was acquainted with the major portion of the laws in the Holiness Code.

Contents of Leviticus 17 and 18 In its present form the Holiness Code consists of ten or eleven groups of laws, which have evidently been disarranged at several points or else disturbed by insertions made by later priestly editors. The first group, $17^{3\text{-}16}$, includes a pentad of much expanded laws regarding the slaughter of animals and sacrifice. All except the last are introduced by the peculiar formula, *Every man of the house of Israel* ($^{3,\,8,\,10,\,13}$). The completion of this decalogue is perhaps to be found in $18^{3,\,4}$, a passage which contains a group of brief commands emphasizing the duty of faithful allegiance to Jehovah. The next section, $18^{6\text{-}30}$, embraces, as Professor Paton has pointed out,† two decalogues regarding purity in the social relations. Here, as in 19, the formula, *I am Jehovah*, marks the end of each pentad. The following indicates the method of classification:

---

* For a detailed comparison of vocabulary, literary style and teachings, cf. Carpenter and Battersby, *The Hexateuch*, I, 147–51.
† Jour. of Bib. Lit., 1897, Vol. XVI, 31 ff.

First Decalogue : Purity in Those Related through Parents and Children

First Pentad: Kinship of the First Degree, Leviticus 18[6, 7, 8, 9, 10].
Second Pentad: Kinship of the Second Degree, 18[11, 12, 13, 14, 15].

Second Decalogue : Purity in Remoter Relationship

First Pentad: Relationship through Marriage, 18[16, 17a, 17b, 18, 19].
Second Pentad: Outside the Family, 18[20, 21, 22, 23a, 23b].

The remaining verses of chapter 18 ([24-30]) contain a concluding exhortation; this, as a whole, is probably from the original editor of the code, but at several points is supplemented by a later priest.

Leviticus 19 contains a large group of laws regarding religious, moral, and ceremonial duties. Those in [2-8] have evidently been disarranged. They are in part parallel to the prophetic decalogue of Exodus 20[2-17]. The parallel is still more complete if the dislocated fragment in 24[15b-22] be combined with 19[2-8]. Possibly they represent the remnants of an original decalogue. Furthermore, if [35] be transferred to its logical position after [11a], two complete decalogues and one pentad of a third decalogue, are to be found in [9-18]. The end of each pentad is again marked by the formula, *I am Jehovah*. The analysis is as follows: The decalogues in Leviticus 19

First Decalogue : Duties to Others

First Pentad: Kindness to the Needy, 19[9a, 9b, 10a, 10b, 10c].
Second Pentad: Honesty in Business Relations, 19[11a, 35, 11b, 11c, 12].

Second Decalogue : Laws against Injustice

First Pentad: Toward Dependents, 19[13a, 13b, 13c, 14a, 14b].
Second Pentad: In Legal Matters, 19[15a, 15b, 15c, 16a, 16b].

Third Decalogue : Laws against Unkindness

First Pentad: In the Heart, [17a, 17b, 18a, 19a, 19b].

It is in this last pentad that the Old Testament legislation reaches its noblest expression: one of its commands, *Thou shalt love thy neighbor as thyself*, is exalted by Jesus to a position of transcendent authority. Remnants of the second pentad, which probably dealt with unkindness to the helpless, are perhaps to be found in 19[33, 34], *An alien . . . in your land ye shall not wrong. Thou shalt love him as thyself.* Leviticus 19[19] contains three laws against the mixing of dissimilar things. Duplicate versions of these are found in Deuteronomy 22[9-11]. In the same context, [5, 12], are found the remaining two laws of this pentad. One of them has, for some unknown reason, been removed from its natural connection in Leviticus 19 and is now found in Numbers 15[37-41]. This section has all the characteristics of the Holiness Code and was probably once a part of it. The second pentad of this decalogue is now to be found in [26-28]; but in [20-25] several incongruous laws regarding illicit relations between a free man and a betrothed slave and the eating of the fruit of young trees, have been introduced. The following appears to have been the original form of the laws:

Decalogue concerning Prohibited Practices

First Pentad: Mingling of Dissimilar Things (Dt. 22^5), Leviticus $19^{19b,}$ $^{19c, 19d}$, Numbers 15^{37-41}.

Second Pentad: Imitation of Heathen Practices, Leviticus $19^{26a, 26b, 27,}$ $^{28a, 28b}$.

The remainder of the chapter, $^{29-37}$, contains a composite of social and humane laws.

Analysis of Leviticus 20–25

Leviticus $20^{2-7, 27}$ prescribes the penalty to be imposed for apostasy and necromancy, while 20^{8-26} contains a group of laws regarding chastity and ceremonial purity which are closely parallel to those in 18. The former passage (20^{2-7}) prescribes the penalties; in 18 the crimes are simply prohibited. Each group also employs different formulas and follows slightly different systems of classification. The laws in 18 are simpler, more homogeneous, and cast in the decalogue and pentad form, facts which indicate that these laws are probably much older than their present setting. Leviticus 21^1–22^{16} contains the laws regarding the priests; 22^{21-32} defines the animals suitable for sacrifice. Most of Leviticus 23 is evidently from a later priest, but in $^{10-20, 39-42}$ are found certain early regulations regarding the observation of the feasts of unleavened bread, weeks, and tabernacles. As has already been noted (p. 39), the detached group of criminal laws in 24^{15b-22} evidently belong with 19. The rest of 24 is from a later priestly source. The original humane laws in 25 ($^{2b-7, 14, 17-22, 24, 25, 35-40a, 43, 47, 53, 55b}$) which aim through the institution of the Sabbatical and year of jubilee to relieve the unfortunate and needy, are also closely related to the other regulations of the Holiness Code. The many late priestly supplements are readily recognized.

Leviticus 26

The concluding chapter (26) emphasizes, in the form of a hortatory address, the fundamental duty of loyalty to Jehovah and his commands. In thought and spirit this chapter closely resembles the concluding exhortations of Deuteronomy. The evils that will follow disobedience are solemnly pointed out; and in $^{30-39}$ a vivid picture is given of the horrors of exile. This is followed in $^{40-45}$ by the prospect of a restoration, if the people repent. The promise, however, is not nearly so definite or detailed as that contained in Ezekiel 40–48. The Holiness Code also has its own concluding formula (^{46}) indicating clearly that it was once a complete and independent collection: *These are the statutes and judgments and laws which Jehovah made between himself and the Israelites on Mount Sinai by the hand of Moses.*

Real character of the Holiness Code

The concluding exhortations, as well as the many civil, criminal and humane laws, demonstrate that this remarkable code was more than a manual for the use of priests. Like Deuteronomy, it was evidently intended to be a book for the people. As in Deuteronomy, the penalties are few, the appeal is to the individual conscience, and, in many sections, the direct second person singular, *Thou*, is employed. In contrast with the later priestly codes, it has many other fundamental points of contact with the laws of Deuteronomy. It emphasizes the obligation to offer sacrifices only at Jerusalem and manifests the same uncompromising hostility to all heathen cults (17³⁻⁷, 19⁴, ³⁰, 20¹⁻⁸, 26¹). It makes no reference to the later sin-offerings and knows of only two kinds of animal sacrifice, the burnt-offering and the ordinary sacrifice. Its system of feasts is simple, corresponding closely to those in Deuteronomy and the early prophetic narratives. For these feasts no fixed date has yet been established. The spring feast is still simply a harvest festival and the later stern day of atonement is unknown.

In the Holiness Code the humane element is also very prominent. The spirit of the prophet pervades it. In this respect it is a worthy companion piece and sequel of Deuteronomy. At the same time the interest in the ritual is more marked and the point of view of the priest is constantly revealed. It is a remarkable blending of these two very different *motifs*. In subject-matter and aim it stands midway between the prophetic codes of Deuteronomy, and the priestly codes of Ezekiel and the later writers who place the emphasis chiefly upon the ceremonial. The blend-ing of pro-phetic and priestly ele-ments

In its original unity, before supplemented by the late priestly additions that were intended to bring it into conformity with the later point of view, the Holiness Code stands, also, in point of time between the Deuteronomic codes and that of Ezekiel. It bears the marks of the Babylonian exile; and yet there is everywhere apparent an intimate acquaintance with the life of the pre-exilic Judean state. Likewise, Ezekiel's sermons, delivered before the final destruction of Jerusalem in 586 B.C., reveal in language, ideas, and aims, an intimate familiarity with the majority of its laws. It is probable, therefore, that the original draft of this code was made between the first and final captivity (597–586 B.C.), a period in which the more enlightened leaders, like Jeremiah and Ezekiel, saw clearly that the state was doomed, and that Israel's laws and institutions, if they were to be preserved, must be put into written form. Its prob-able date

The presence of many duplicate versions of the same law, the primitive nature of certain of the regulations, the frequent points of contact with the early codes in Exodus 20²³–23¹⁹, and the pentad and decalogue structure of several groups of laws, strongly suggest that the work of the exilic editor was largely the work of a compiler, and that many of its enactments come from a much earlier period in Hebrew history. This is especially true of the simple decalogues in 17–19. Their structure indicates that they were originally intended to be orally transmitted. They are apparently the Judean counterparts of the Northern Israelitish *Judgments* and of the religious and humane laws in Exodus 20²³–23¹⁹. Their roots are probably to be traced to the Mosaic and nomadic periods of Israelitish history. In their pentad and decalogue form, however, they assume the settled agricultural life of Palestine. Furthermore, the majority of them reflect the ethical teachings of the prophets of the eighth century B.C. It is therefore probable that they were not promulgated before the latter part of that century. Some of them, as for example those in 17¹–18⁵, cannot be earlier than the age of Deuteronomy. The remainder of the original Holiness Code apparently The older ele-ments in the code records the standards and ceremonial usages in vogue in Judah during the half century immediately before the exile; although many of them doubtless reflect customs as old as the Hebrew race. Thus, as in the case of every Old Testament code, a majority of the laws are much older than the date of the collection in which they are at present found; hence, it may truly be said that the later Jewish traditions which aim to emphasize the antiquity of Israel's laws are not without a large and substantial basis in fact.

VI

THE PRIESTLY CODES

For at least two centuries after the fall of Jerusalem in 586 B.C., the in- Growth fluences that had led Ezekiel and the author or authors of the Holiness Code of later cere- to develop their legal systems, continued to bear abundant fruit. The result monial laws is a large body of heterogeneous regulations and traditional precedents, now scattered through Exodus, Leviticus and Numbers, but all sharing certain marked characteristics which distinguish them sharply from Israel's earlier laws. The first characteristic is that they all, with the exception of Numbers 27$^{1-11}$, 35 and 36, relate to ceremonial observances. Thus at once are revealed the point of view of the priest and the dominant interest of exilic and post-exilic Judaism. These priestly laws represent the bridge over which the Israelitish race passed from the highly ethical and spiritual religion of the pre-exilic prophets to the rigorous ritualism of the scribes and Pharisees.

Throughout, these laws assume the belief in one supreme Deity, worshipped Their peculiar point of view by his people at one central sanctuary. Though written, as most of them are, from the point of view of the wilderness, they ignore the unequivocal testimony of the earlier historical records, and assume that the institutions which developed in the later days of the kingdom or grew out of the changed conditions of the exile, were in full force in the age of Moses. In this belief they share again the peculiar point of view of later Judaism. Like the Chronicler (cf. Vol. II, pp. 27, 28), they have, in their passionate love for the temple and its ritual, lost the historical perspective, and project back on the barren canvas of the wilderness the priestly ideals which fill their minds.

Their vocabulary and conception of the ritual, as compared with those of Wide varia- tions from the earlier codes the pre-exilic lawgivers, have also undergone a fundamental transformation. Thus, for example, the earlier word for sacrificial gift (*minhah*), a word that signified both vegetable and animal offerings, is used fully ninety times, but always with the restricted meaning of *cereal-offering*. Likewise, the pre-exilic forms of sacrifice in which the individual offerers prominently participate, fall into the background; and in the later priestly codes practically all the sacrifices, with the exception of the sin-offering, are public and under the charge of the priests and Levites. Whole burnt-offerings, of which all or the greater part of the animal is consumed or given to the priestly representatives of Jehovah, take the place of those earlier sacrificial feasts in which only a small part was burnt and the major portion eaten by the offerer, his family and dependents, and the poor Levites. The ancient festivals cease to be joyous feasts closely connected with the harvests, and become solemn religious assemblies celebrated at fixed dates and with only slightly varying public sacrifices. Certain new festivals, like the day of atonement, and certain new offerings, like the sin-offering, appear in these later laws. All these new ideas and institutions are the outgrowth of the sense of guilt impressed by the exile upon the consciousness of the race. These increased forms and sacrifices indicate also an ardent desire to attain a ceremonial purity more worthy of the favor of the Holy One. The separation between the priesthood and the laity, slight indeed in the earliest period, is now complete; and the distinction between priest and Levite, first made by Ezekiel, is now absolute; each class of temple ministers, moreover, have defined for them in detail their rights and limitations.

Aims of the priestly law-givers   These radical distinctions evince the real animus of the later priestly lawgivers. Like Ezekiel and the authors of the Holiness Code, on the one hand, they were uplifted by an awful sense of the holiness and majesty of Jehovah; and on the other hand, like all their race after the great calamity of 586 B.C., they were crushed with a sense of national guilt. As individuals they were conscious of no great sins, but their race as a whole seemed to lie, rejected and polluted, under the dark shadow of Jehovah's displeasure. The prophetic doctrine of personal righteousness seemed inadequate to meet the needs of the situation. The priest, therefore, influenced by all the precedents of the past, by the example of the Babylonians and other contemporary nations and by the traditions of their own class, sought relief through the ritual. Forthwith they set to work to purge their ritual of its unworthy heathen elements, to elaborate it in such manner that it might prove adequate to the great need, to guard it by carefully formulated laws from all irregularity or perversion, and finally, so to establish its divine authority that the faithful observation of each regulation would be assured.

Evidence of gradual growth and different editors   Studied in the light of these common aims, the various priestly laws possess a real unity. At the same time the evidence indicates clearly that they come not from one but several hands, during a period of a century or two; for within the priestly codes themselves there are repetitions of particular laws in the same or different forms. Leviticus 6^8–7^{38}, for example, covers practically the same ground as chapters 1–5; and in some cases laws that appear to be late supplant or modify or supplement older regulations. The present structure of the priestly codes indicates, moreover, that they are made up of originally distinct, sometimes very loosely co-ordinated, groups of laws.

The priestly directions or teaching   Such a group is found in Leviticus 1–3, 5–7, 11–15, Numbers 5, 6, 15 and 19^{14-22}. It is distinguished from all other groups by the presence of such introductory or closing formulæ as: *This is the torah of the burnt-offering* (Lev. 6^9), or *of the cereal-offering* (Lev. 6^{14}), or *of the guilt-offering* (cf. also Lev. 6^{25}, 7^{11}, 11^{46}, 12^7, $14^{1, 54}$, 15^{32}, Nu. 5^{29}, 6^{21}, 19^{14}). This collection of laws is evidently a manual for the guidance of priests and worshippers in the discharge of their sacrificial obligations. It deals with the different kinds of sacrifice, the distinctions between clean and unclean, the rules of observance for priests and people, and the duties of those assuming the Nazirite vow. The majority of these laws are evidently based on *tôrôth* or decisions rendered by the priests (hence for the group the technical designation P^t). The frequently recurring phrase, *according to the ordinance* (e. g., Lev. 5^{10}, Nu. 15^{24}), also suggests that many of these laws simply reproduce established (possibly earlier documentary) regulations of the pre-exilic temple.

In language and theme the priestly directions are rather closely related Their origin both to each other and to the Holiness Code. They have been revised at and certain points and adapted to the priestly point of view; but in their oldest date form they were apparently associated with the pre-exilic tent of meeting, not with the late priestly dwelling or tabernacle. Furthermore, occasional traces of pentads strengthen the conclusion that this group of laws, like the Holiness Code, has as its nucleus certain pre-exilic priestly regulations. These earliest regulations have been supplemented by formularies of customs that had gradually grown up about the temple, and by rules of procedure given by older priests for the guidance of their younger colleagues and for worshippers. The changed conditions of the exile led to further revision and supplementing, until these priestly directions attained their present form. To date them exactly is impossible. The older pentads probably go back to the days of the two Hebrew kingdoms, and, in many cases, doubtless reflect still earlier customs. The final formulation of the laws as a whole cannot, however, be dated before the earlier part of the exile. They were probably joined to the other priestly codes at a considerably later date; for they have no organic connection with their context nor with the historical framework that furnishes the setting for most of the later laws.

The groundwork of the priestly codes (technically known as P^g) consists The ground-(1) of an historical introduction to the Old Testament laws as a whole (desig- work nated in Vol. I, pp. 43–48, as the *Late Priestly Narratives*), and (2) of a more of the priestly or less homogeneous group of laws that is adjusted to this framework. codes As has already been noted (Vol. I), the historical sections are very terse, indeed little more than genealogical lists, except where they expand to introduce a covenant like that of the sabbath (Gen. 1^1–2^{4a}), or an important legal institution like the rite of circumcision (Gen. 17). They trace Israel's history in outline to the settlement in Canaan; but they find their true culmination in the covenant and traditional legislation at Sinai. Sinai and the wilderness, therefore, furnish the setting for all the laws peculiar to this groundwork. The dwelling or tabernacle takes the place of the later temple, and all the laws intended for subsequent use centre about it. In the wilderness, apart from all people and things that might defile, the ideal ceremonial purity of the *congregation* and *camp* is set forth in carefully elaborated regulations.

To this groundwork belong the main body of the laws regarding the passover Its conin Exodus 12$^{1-13, \, 43-49}$, the detailed directions regarding the dwelling or tents tabernacle in 25–29, the law of the sabbath (35$^{2, \, 3}$), the consecration of the date priesthood (Lev. 9–10), the day of atonement (16), the sacred calendar (23$^{4-8, \, 23-25, \, 33-38}$), the lamps and showbread (24$^{1-9}$), the census at Sinai (Nu. 1$^{1-4}$), the Levites (3), the priestly benediction (6$^{22-27}$), the use of trumpets (10$^{1-8}$), and the duties and dues of the priests and Levites (18). The fact that the same technical terms, peculiar idioms, and characteristic ideas bind together these laws and their historical setting, suggests that they may have once constituted an independent literary unit. If so, they may, on the basis of the narrative sections, be approximately dated somewhere between 450 and 400 B.C. (cf. Vol. I, p. 47).

The supplemental priestly codes   What has been true of all legal codes was especially so in a period of intense literary activity such as this; the work of revision and supplementing in all likelihood began soon after the groundwork was complete. Whether the Holiness Code and the priestly directions were among the first additions cannot be definitely determined. Aside from these larger and older codes, the additions to the groundwork represent simply the continuation of the process that had already produced the earlier groups of priestly laws. These supplemental priestly codes, however, have their own peculiarities in vocabulary and thought. They are intended to fill up the gaps in the older system of laws and to define more definitely the method of procedure. In this respect they are the immediate precursors of the oral law of later Judaism now found in the Mishna; for traditional precedents, such, for example, as the story of Zelophehad's daughters in Numbers 27$^{1-11}$, here figure prominently, and are none other than earlier types of the halachic midrashim that became so popular with the later scribes. The tendency to make the ritual more elaborate is strong. Thus, an altar of incense, not previously known, is introduced; and the formal act of anointing, hitherto reserved for the consecration of the high priest, is now extended to the ordinary priests; the formula of blood-sprinkling, also, becomes more elaborate, and a secondary passover is added. These supplemental laws increase in many ways the income of the temple and priests; the tithe of the ground, for example, is extended to the herd, and the poll-tax becomes one-half instead of one-third of a shekel.

Their contents   The supplemental laws bulk large in the Pentateuch; but such is their prolixity and their reiteration of older regulations that their importance is far from proportionate to their volume. They mark the beginning of that intellectual, spiritual and literary deterioration which is still more in evidence in the Mishna and Talmud. To these supplemental codes belong the detailed and repetitious account of the preparation of the dwelling or tabernacle in Exodus 35–40, the law of the sin-offering (Lev. 4), the consecration of Aaron and his sons (8), the fiftieth year of jubilee (25$^{8-17, 23, 25-55}$), vows and consecrated gifts (27), the order of the tribes (Nu. 2), the census of the adult males (4), the dedication of the altar (7), heterogeneous ceremonial laws (8 and 9), purification with the ashes of the red heifer (19), the law of inheritance illustrated by the case of Zelophehad's daughters (27$^{1-11}$), the calendar of sacred seasons (28, 29), regulations regarding vows made by men and women (30), the laws of war (31), and the marriage of an heiress (36). In addition to these independent regulations, almost all the important earlier priestly laws contain supplemental sections from the hands of the late priestly scribes, who sought thus to bring the older into harmony with the later institutions.

Their origin and date   Most of the supplemental priestly laws bear on their face the evidence of their late origin; but a few of them, those for example regarding vows, probably reflect comparatively early usage. Obviously it is difficult to fix the date of these laws, for they clearly represent the growth of many years. Possibly some of them had already found a place in the law-book accepted about 400 B.C. by the Jewish community in Palestine (Neh. 10). It is probable, however, that the majority are later additions. The temple tax, for example, in the days of Ezra and Nehemiah was still one-third of a shekel (Neh. 10^{32}) and not one-half, as required by the supplemental law in Exodus 30$^{11\text{-}16}$. And, as has already been noted, the date of the great day of atonement must have been fixed later, for there is no suggestion in Ezra or Nehemiah of its having been observed on the tenth day of the seventh month. The fact that in Nehemiah 10^{37} only the tithe of the ground is required, as in the earlier priestly codes, likewise indicates that the definite supplemental law in Leviticus 37$^{30\text{-}33}$, which adds a tithe of the herd and of the flock, was not yet incorporated in the law of Moses. With most of these later regulations, however, the Chronicler was familiar. It is safe to say, therefore, that the priestly codes in their composite form were, with the possible exception of certain brief scribal additions, in existence and accepted as authoritative by the Jewish race at least as early as 250 B.C.

As is well known, the influences which in divine providence produced the priestly codes did not cease to be felt when the canon of the law was closed. Old institutions continued to develop and new ones to come into existence. Hundreds of legal questions not anticipated by the Old Testament laws arose, and the final decisions in time came to have binding authority. In most cases traditional precedents associated with Moses were developed, usually as a product of scribal imagination, to lend support to that authority. For centuries these were treasured and augmented in the rabbinical schools. Lest they should supplant the written law of the Pentateuch, they were at first preserved only in oral form; but at length their bulk defied the power of human memory. The scattering of the Jews after the destruction of Jerusalem in 70 A.D., also endangered their preservation. Accordingly by 200 A.D. they were committed to writing. The Mishna, which records the majority of them, itself in time failed to answer all the questions that changed conditions and rabbinic imagination suggested: about it in turn there grew up during the succeeding centuries a vast body of comments and traditional decisions, ultimately gathered together about 600 A.D., in the great treasury of Jewish thought and literature, the Babylonian Talmud. *His- tory of later Jewish law*

The priestly codes, in their final written form, stand at the middle point in a process of legal development that began in remote Semitic antiquity (cf. Frontispiece). For nearly two thousand years it can be traced in the life and literature of the Israelitish race. No one will maintain that the priestly codes represent the zenith of that development; it is rather to be found in the Deuteronomic and Holiness codes. In many ways the priestly laws represent a step backward to the more primitive stages when religion and religious duty were defined in the terms of the ceremonial. *Place of the priestly codes in the history of Is- raelit- ish law*

There are few institutions or rites in the priestly codes that were not in vogue among other Semitic peoples and especially the Babylonians. Both races had practically the same sacrificial terminology; the same kinds of vegetable and animal sacrifices were offered; victims a year old were preferred and they must be without blemish; arks, altars, temples, tables of showbread, and the paraphernalia of sacrifice were nearly identical. The distinctions between clean and unclean food, and the laws of ceremonial purity were shared *Strong influ- ence of com- mon Semitic institu- tions* in common. In almost every law of the priestly codes the influence of the inheritances from Israel's primitive past and of the Babylonian religion with which the exiled priests came into closest contact, is clearly reflected. Hence it was inevitable that the clear prophetic vision of God should often be obscured by the priesthood and the ritual, that the individual should become only a member of the congregation, and that forms strikingly similar to those of the peoples about should take the place of that personal worship which the prophets so fervently upheld.

The real value and significance of the priestly codes
And yet it must be remembered that the priestly laws are not antithetic to the older prophetic legislation. Both continued to exist side by side until they were united by a priestly editor. The priestly lawgivers assumed the ethical and personal teachings of the early codes as the basis upon which they reared their ritual and hierarchy. They also appreciated the firm hold that the ancient ritual had upon the great body of their nation. Though its origin was in a sense heathen and its influence often debasing, they could not expel it if they would. Accordingly they devoted themselves to singling out those older laws and customs that were adapted to the new conditions, to eliminating the debasing elements in the prevailing religious rites, and to giving the ritual as a whole a nobler and more spiritual meaning. History records the success of their efforts. Through the period of greatest peril and trial they preserved their race and religion intact within the wall of separation which they reared high about them. And though without the heathen raged, within that sacred enclosure the faithful—as the Psalms abundantly attest —found inward peace and joy in the presence of the Eternal Father.

PERSONAL AND FAMILY LAWS

PERSONAL AND FAMILY LAWS

A

PERSONAL RELATION AND CONDITION

I

PARENTS AND CHILDREN

§ 1. **Honor and Obedience Due Parents,** Ex. 21¹⁵, ¹⁷, Dt. 5¹⁶ [Ex. 20¹²],
Dt. 21¹⁸⁻²¹, 27¹⁶, Lev. 19³ᵃ, 20⁹

Primitive Codes

Ex. 21 ¹⁵He that striketh his father or his mother shall be put to death. Penalty
¹⁷He that curseth his father or his mother shall be put to death. for filial impiety

Personal Relation and Condition.—Israel's primitive laws contain no references to the king or state or even to judges; but the master who stands at the head of the household is frequently mentioned, Ex. 21⁵,⁶, 22⁸. He is regarded as the responsible and representative member of society. The earliest laws themselves deal chiefly with questions that concern the family. This characteristic is undoubtedly due to the fact that they embody usages and customary laws that come from the early nomadic stage when there was no organized state and when the family or tribe was the only social unit.

Throughout most of the period represented by the O.T., Israelitish society retained its original simple organization. At the head of the family was the father. Sharing with him the authority was his wife, if she was the mother of sons. Next in rank, but ever subject to their father, with whom they usually continued to live even after they had wives and children of their own, stood the sons. The daughters always occupied a very inferior position, being counted as little better than slaves until they were married and became mothers. Hired servants, either foreigners or freedmen who possessed little property but not yet reduced by poverty to slavery, are recognized in the laws. Much more numerous and important were the household slaves. Both foreigners and native Israelites were found in their ranks. Outside the family and regarded as wards of the community or state, were the aliens who had become permanent residents in the land of Israel.

§ 1 It is to the lasting glory of the O.T. legislators that they broke away from oriental tradition and demanded equal homage for both mother and father. The emphasis given to this law is doubtless due to the fact that the authority of the father was one of the cornerstones of early Israelitish society, and that obedience to the human parents was closely akin to obedience to the Divine Parent. Semitic law never went as far as the Roman, which gave to the father absolute power of life and death over his children. The Code of Hammurabi is still milder, for it not only aims to protect the son's right of inheritance even against the wishes of the father but also rules that:

§ 169 *If he has committed a grave crime against his father, which cuts off from sonship, for the first offence he shall pardon him. If he has committed a grave crime a second time, the father shall cut off his son from sonship.*

The old Sumerian laws, however, made slavery the penalty for a son who repudiated his father:

If a son has said to his father, You are not my father, he may brand him, lay fetters upon him, and sell him.

If a son has said to his mother, You are not my mother, one shall brand his forehead, drive him out of the city, and make him go out of the house.

The Babylonian, as well as the Hebrew father had the right to sell his children, if need be, as slaves, or to hire out his son and to take his wages.

Deuteronomic Codes

Reward of filial piety　　**Dt. 5** [16]Honor thy father and thy mother, as Jehovah thy God hath commanded thee; that thy days may be long, and that it may go well with thee, in the land which Jehovah thy God giveth thee.[a]

Procedure in the case of wilful disobedience　　**21** [18]If a man have a stubborn and rebellious son, who will not obey the voice of his father, or the voice of his mother, and, though they chastise him, will not give heed to them, [19]his father and his mother shall take hold of him, and bring him before the elders of his city, and to the gate of the place where he lives, [20]and they shall say to the elders of his city, This our son is stubborn and rebellious, he will not obey our voice; he is a spendthrift and a drunkard. [21]Then all the men of his city shall stone him to death; thus thou shalt put away the evil from thy midst, and all Israel shall hear, and fear.

Public condemnation　　**27** [16]Cursed be he who dishonoreth his father or his mother. And all the people shall say, So may it be.[b]

Holiness Code

Reiteration of the older law　　**Lev. 19** [3a]Ye shall fear each man his mother and his father. **20** [9]For every one that curseth his father or his mother shall be put to death; he hath cursed his father or his mother; his blood shall be upon his own head.

§ 2. Authority of Father over Unmarried Daughter, Nu. 30[3-5]

Supplemental Priestly Codes

Father able to annul even a vow made by his daughter　　**Nu. 30** [3]When a woman maketh a vow to Jehovah, and bindeth herself by a pledge, while she is still in her father's house, in her youth, and her father heareth her vow, and her pledge with which she hath bound herself, and her father saith nothing to her, then all her vows shall be valid, and every pledge with which she hath bound herself shall be valid. [5]But if her father express his disapproval of her on the day that he heareth, none of her vows or her pledges with which she hath bound herself shall be valid; and Jehovah will forgive her, because her father expressed his disapproval of her.

---

　　[a] Dt. 5[16] The variant in Ex. 20[12] reads, *Honor thy father and thy mother that thy days may be long upon the land which Jehovah thy God giveth thee.* Both contain the original brief command of the prophetic decalogue, supplemented by a statement of the blessing that will surely follow its faithful observance.
　　[b] Dt. 27[16] This verse comes from the later supplement to the book of Deuteronomy. It may, however, represent an old liturgical formula. The language of these curses, Dt. 27[14-26], is related to the *Judgments* in Ex. 21–22[20], and the Holiness Code.
　　§ 2 The phraseology of this section connects it with some of the latest additions to the O.T. It is not closely joined to its context, 29 and 31, but rather supplements the laws regarding vows in Lev. 27 and Nu. 6. It, however, probably reflects earlier usage and well illustrates the legal status of the unmarried Hebrew daughter, for a vow in ancient times was otherwise regarded as irrevocable.

II

THE MARRIAGE RELATION

§ 3. Relatives between whom Marriage is Illegitimate, Dt. 22³⁰, 27²⁰, ²², ²³, Lev. 18⁶⁻¹⁸, ²⁴, ²⁵

Deuteronomic Codes

Dt. 22 ³⁰A man shall not marry his father's wife and shall not uncover With a his father's skirt.[c] **27** ²⁰Cursed be he who lieth with his father's wife, step-mother because he hath uncovered his father's skirt. And all the people shall say So may it be.

²²Cursed be he who lieth with his half-sister, the daughter of his father, With a or the daughter of his mother. And all the people shall say, So may it be. half-sister

²³Cursed be he who lieth with his mother-in-law. And all the people With a shall say, So may it be. mother-in-law

Holiness Code

Lev. 18 ⁶None of you shall approach to any who are closely related to With him, to uncover their nakedness: I am Jehovah. ⁷The nakedness of thy an own or step-father, and the nakedness of thy mother, shalt thou not uncover; she is thy mother, mother; thou shalt not uncover her nakedness. ⁸The nakedness of thy own or half-father's wife shalt thou not uncover; it is thy father's nakedness. ⁹The sister nakedness of thy sister, the daughter[d] of thy mother, whether born at home, or away, her nakedness thou shalt not uncover.

¹⁰The nakedness of thy son's daughter or of thy daughter's daughter, With a their nakedness thou shalt not uncover; for their nakedness is thine own. grand-daugh-¹¹The nakedness of thy father's wife's daughter, begotten of thy father, who ter, is thy sister—her nakedness thou shalt not uncover. ¹²Thou shalt not un-daugh-cover the nakedness of thy father's sister; she is thy father's near kinswoman. ter-in-law, or ¹³Thou shalt not uncover the nakedness of thy mother's sister; for she is thy sister-mother's near kinswoman. ¹⁴Thou shalt not uncover the nakedness of thy in-law

---

Marriage Relation.—Since the family was the most important unit in ancient Semitic society, marriage was always carefully guarded. So completely was attention fixed on the interests of the family and clan that the parents always arranged the preliminaries, and the feelings and wishes of the contracting parties were rarely, if ever, consulted.

§ 3 This group of laws and its counterpart, Lev. 20¹¹, ¹², ¹⁴, ¹⁷, ¹⁹⁻²¹ are evidently intended primarily to guard the purity and peace of the family life. No distinction is made between relationship by marriage and by blood. The three capital offences are marriage with a step-mother or a daughter-in-law, or both a mother and her daughter, Lev. 20¹¹, ¹², ¹⁴, § 72. In none of these cases is the alliance between blood kinsmen.

The O.T. laws record the successive stages in the development of the moral conscious-ness of the nation in regard to marriage. The primitive laws are silent and the earliest narra-tives imply that the usage of the Hebrews was similar to that among the Egyptians and Per-sians, where marriage between brothers and sisters and in some cases between parents and children was not unknown. Thus according to Gen. 20¹², Abraham married his half-sister. If David's son Amnon had chosen to marry his half-sister Tamar, evidently the public opinion of his day would have approved the act, II Sam. 13¹³. Lot married two daughters according to the tradition in Gen. 19³⁰⁻³⁸; Jacob married two sisters; Moses' father married his own aunt, Ex. 6²⁰. The law of levirate marriage survived in the face of later public opinion. The desire to perpetuate the family and to keep intact its hereditary wealth, was stronger in the

---

c Dt. 22³⁰ Evidently a euphemism; enter into marital relations with a stepmother.

d Lev. 18⁹ A scribe has added, anticipating the detailed law in,¹¹ *the daughter of thy father or.*

Holiness Code

father's brother, thou shalt not approach his wife; she is thine aunt. ¹⁵Thou shalt not uncover the nakedness of thy daughter-in-law; she is thy son's wife; thou shalt not uncover her nakedness. ¹⁶Thou shalt not uncover the nakedness of thy brother's wife; it is thy brother's nakedness.

With both a mother and daughter or granddaughter or with two sisters
¹⁷Thou shalt not uncover the nakedness of a woman and her daughter; thou shalt not take her son's daughter, or her daughter's daughter, to uncover her nakedness; they are near kinswomen; it is unchastity. ¹⁸And thou shalt not take a woman as your wife in addition to her sister, to be her rival to uncover her nakedness, beside the other in her life-time. ²⁴Defile not yourselves in any of these ways, for in all these ways the nations, which I am casting out before you defiled themselves; ²⁵thus the land became defiled, and I visited its iniquity upon it and the land cast out its inhabitants.

§ 4. Marriage with a Captive, Dt. 21¹⁰⁻¹⁴

Deuteronomic Codes

Forms and limitations to be observed
Dt. 21 ¹⁰When thou goest forth to battle against thine enemies, and Jehovah thy God delivereth them into thy hands, and thou carriest them away captive, ¹¹and seest among the captives a beautiful woman, and thou hast a desire for her, and wouldest make her thy wife, ¹²then thou shalt bring her home to thy house; and she shall shave her head, and pare her nails; ¹³and she shall put off the garb of her captivity, and shall remain in thy house, and lament for her father and her mother a full month. After that thou mayest go in unto her, and be her husband, and she shall be thy wife. ¹⁴But if thou have no delight in her, then thou shalt let her go where she will; but thou shalt not in any case sell her for money, thou shalt not deal with her as a slave, because thou hast humbled her.

§ 5. Marriage with Aliens, Ex. 34¹²ᵃ, ¹⁵, ¹⁶, Dt. 7¹⁻⁴, Nu. 25⁶⁻¹³

Deuteronomic Codes

No intermarriage with native peoples
Ex. 34 ¹²ᵃTake heed ¹⁵not to make any alliance with the inhabitants of the land, lest, when they play the harlot after their gods and sacrifice to their gods and thou be invited, thou eat of their sacrifice; ¹⁶and lest, if

earlier period than the moral sense. The latter evidently developed rapidly under the preaching of the prophets, so that in Dt., and in the older decalogues preserved in the Holiness Code, it finds definite expression in laws which Ezek. makes the basis of one of his sermons, 22¹⁰, ¹¹.

§ 4 Female captives in war, like slaves, were adopted by the Israelitish community and family. Therefore the law provides for the marriage of Hebrews with them, simply stipulating that it shall not be done hastily and without consideration for the feelings of the captive. Having been raised to the position of a wife, she cannot again be sold as a slave. The Babylonian law also made the same provisions regarding female slaves, if they had borne children to the master. It further decreed, H. C. § 137, that if divorced the slave must be provided with means to support the children, and that when they had grown up she should have the equivalent of one son's share in her first husband's property and be free to marry the husband of her choice.

§ 5 The laws against intermarriage with foreigners cannot be traced back beyond the late prophetic codes. Indeed the supplemental editorial addition in Ex. 34¹⁵, ¹⁶ and in Dt. 7¹⁻⁴ are probably little, if at all, earlier than the Babylonian exile. The suggestive silence of the primitive codes is explained by the references in the earlier historical narratives where the marriage of kings like David, Solomon, and Ahab, and of private citizens like Samson and the mother-in-law of Ruth with foreigners, is a common practice, uncondemned by the earlier writers.

Non-intermarriage, however, was a corollary of Elijah's stern principle of non-alliance with foreigners. The Deuteronomic school first applied this principle rigidly to the life of the nation. The changed conditions of the Babylonian exile made non-intermarriage an absolute

Deuteronomic Codes

thou take their daughters as wives for thy sons, and their daughters play the harlot after their gods, thou also make thy sons play the harlot after their gods.

Dt. 7 ¹When Jehovah thy God shall bring thee into the land which thou art going in to possess, and shall clear away many nations before thee, the Hittites, the Girgashites, the Amorites, the Canaanites, the Perizzites, the Hivites, and the Jebusites, seven nations greater and mightier than thou, ²and when Jehovah thy God shall deliver them into thy hands and thou shalt smite them, then thou shalt completely destroy them^e without making any terms with them, or without showing any mercy to them; ³neither shalt thou make marriages with them; thou shalt not give thy daughter to his son, nor shalt thou take his daughter as a wife for thy son. ⁴For he will turn away thy son from following me to serve other gods so that the anger of Jehovah will be kindled against you, and he will quickly destroy thee.

[margin: Extirpation not intermarriage, the later law]

Priestly Codes

Nu. 25 ⁶Now, behold, one of the Israelites came and brought home to his kinsmen a Midianite woman in the sight of Moses and of all the congregation of the Israelites, while they were weeping at the door of the tent of meeting. ⁷And when Phinehas, the son of Eleazar, the son of Aaron the priest, saw it, he rose up from the midst of the congregation and took a spear in his hand, ⁸and went after the man of Israel into the large tent and thrust both of them through, the man of Israel and the woman, through the body. So the plague was stayed from the Israelites. ⁹And those who died of the plague were twenty-four thousand.

¹⁰And Jehovah spoke to Moses, saying, ¹¹Phinehas, the son of Eleazar, the son of Aaron the priest, hath turned away my wrath from the Israelites, in that he was jealous with the jealousy which I myself show among them, so that I did not consume the Israelites in my jealousy. ¹²Therefore say, 'Behold, I give to him my covenant of peace; ¹³and it shall be to him and his descendants after him the covenant of an everlasting priesthood; because he was jealous for his God and made atonement for the Israelites.'

[margin: A traditional precedent: death the penalty for intermarriage]

[margin: Reward of Phinehas' zeal]

§ 6. Marriage of Priests, Lev. 21⁷, ¹³⁻¹⁵

Holiness Code

Lev. 21 ⁷A priest^f shall not marry a woman who is a harlot or dishonored; nor shall he marry a woman who has been divorced from her husband; for a priest is consecrated to his God.

[margin: Not to marry an immoral woman]

---

essential, if the exiles were to preserve their racial identity. The records of Ezra 9, 10 and Neh. 13²³⁻²⁸ clearly indicate that the Jews of Palestine continued to intermarry with foreigners as late as 400 B.C. With the adoption of the priestly law they appear to have accepted the stricter rule in force among the Jews of the dispersion, so that from this time marital alliances with any outside the race were regarded as illegal. The late priestly precedent in Nu. 25⁶⁻¹⁵ was evidently intended to aid in enforcing this law and to trace it back to Moses, cf. Introd. p. 46. Marriage with resident aliens who had permanently identified themselves with the Jewish community was permitted even in the case of a priest's daughter, at least in the Holiness Code, Lev. 22¹², ¹³.

^e Dt. 7² Lit., *devote, put them under the ban, i. e.,* put them to death.

§ 6 In this concrete and effective way the later lawgivers impressed upon the minds the people through the symbolism of the ritual, moral as well as ceremonial obligations.

^f Lev. 21⁷ Heb *he*

Holiness Code

The high priest ¹³A high priest shall take a virgin as his wife. ¹⁴A widow, or a divorced woman, or a dishonored woman, or[g] a harlot, such he shall not take; but a virgin of his own father's kin shall he take as his wife,¹⁵ that he may not make his offspring dishonored among his father's kin: for I am Jehovah who sanctifieth him.

§ 7. Marriage after Seduction, Ex. 22¹⁶, Dt. 22²⁸, ²⁹

Primitive Codes

Seduction of a virgin Ex. 22 ¹⁶If a man entice a virgin who is not betrothed and lie with her, he must make her his wife by paying a dowry for her.

Deuteronomic Codes

A wife thus wedded never to be divorced Dt. 22 ²⁸If a man find a virgin who is not betrothed and take hold of her and lie with her, and they be caught in the act, ²⁹the man who lay with her shall give to the girl's father fifty shekels of silver; moreover she shall be his wife because he hath humbled her; he may not divorce her as long as he liveth.

§ 8. Levirate Marriage, Dt. 25⁵⁻¹⁰

Deuteronomic Codes

The family of a deceased man to be perpetuated by his brother Dt. 25 ⁵If brothers dwell together, and one of them die without having a son, the wife of the deceased shall not be married to a man outside the clan; her husband's brother shall go in unto her, and make her his wife, and perform the duty of a husband's brother to her. ⁶The first son whom she beareth shall succeed to the name of his brother who is dead, that his name may not become extinct in Israel.

Procedure if the surviving brother refuses to do his duty ⁷But if the man doth not wish to take his brother's wife, then she shall go up to the elders at the city gate and say, My husband's brother refuseth to perpetuate his brother's name in Israel; he will not perform the duty of a husband's brother to me.[h] ⁸Then the elders of his city shall call him, and speak to him; and if he stand, and say, I do not wish to take her, ⁹then his brother's wife shall come to him in the presence of the elders, and loose his sandal from off his foot, and spit in his face; and she shall speak forth and say, Thus shall it be done to the man who will not build up his brother's house. ¹⁰And his house shall be called in Israel, 'The house of him who hath his shoe loosed.'

---

[g] Lev. 21¹⁴ So Gk. The Heb. omits *or*.

§ 7 The prophetic lawgivers sought to guard against social immorality and the neglect of the marriage obligations by also imposing a definite marriage dowry and refusing divorce to the man who defied the laws of society. The amount fixed was fifty shekels in contrast to the thirty shekels usually paid for a slave.

§ 8 The aim of this law is to prevent the extinction of a family. Although recorded only in Dt., it is clearly an ancient institution, for it is assumed in the early Judean prophetic narrative of Gen. 38⁸, ¹⁴, ²⁶, and in the story of the marriage of Ruth and Boaz. The custom is not confined to the Hebrews, but is widely prevalent. The Hindu *Laws of Manu* enforce it in case the deceased leaves no issue of either sex. The same law is in force in Madagascar and among the Calchaquis of Brazil. The Hebrew version in Deuteronomy limits the law to cases where the deceased was living on the same estate with his brother and left no male heir.

[h] Dt. 25⁷ Cf. Ruth 4¹.

§ 9. Authority of a Husband over his Wife, Nu. 30⁶⁻⁸, ¹³⁻¹⁵

Supplemental Priestly Codes

Nu. 30 ⁶If a woman be married while her vows are upon her, or the rash Hus-band's power to an-nul any vow made by his wife utterance of her lips with which she hath bound herself, ⁷and her husband hear of it, and say nothing to her on the day that he heareth of it, then her vows shall be valid, and her pledges with which she hath bound herself shall be valid. ⁸But if her husband express his disapproval of her on the day that he heareth of it, then he rendereth her vow invalid, and the rash utterance of her lips, with which she hath bound herself; and Jehovah will forgive her. ¹³Every vow and every oath pledging some self-infliction[i] her husband may render valid or invalid. ¹⁴But if her husband say nothing to her for several days, then he hath rendered all her vows or all her pledges which rest upon her valid; he hath rendered them valid because he said nothing to her on the day that he heard of them. ¹⁵But if he render them null and invalid, after he hath heard of them,[j] he taketh her[k] iniquity upon himself.

§ 10. The Test of a Wife's Chastity and the Penalty for Unchastity, Dt. 22¹³⁻²¹, Nu. 5²⁹, ¹³ᵇ, ³⁰ᵃ, ¹⁴ᵇ, ³⁰ᵇ, ¹⁶, ¹⁷, ¹⁹, ²⁰, ²², ²⁵, ²⁶ᵇ, ²⁷ᵃ, ²⁸

Deuteronomic Codes

Dt. 22 ¹³If, after a man has married a wife and entered into marital Proced-ure in case of un-chas-tity relations with her, he turn against her, ¹⁴and frame against her shameful

---

§ 9 This law has many peculiarities and few points of contact with the original priestly legislation. It is more akin to the later rabbinical discussions, and, therefore, is probably a very late addition to the Pentateuch. It clearly illustrates the secondary place assigned to women by oriental custom: even in assuming religious obligations the wife must have the approval of her husband.

[i] Nu. 30¹³ Lit., *to afflict herself*, *i. e.*, some form of abstinence; usually fasting is intended, cf. Is. 58³, ⁵, Ps. 35¹³.

[j] 30¹⁵ *I. e.*, tries to annul her vows after he has tacitly endorsed them.

[k] 30¹⁵ Gk. and Sam., *his*.

§ 10 Among the Arabs to-day and in the villages of Palestine, the evidences of a bride's chastity are still displayed, cf. Buckhardt, *Arab Proverbs*, 117; *Bedouins*, I, 266. Although the absence of this evidence is not necessarily a positive proof of unchastity, the crude law of the nomad still accepts it as a sufficient cause for divorce. The law in Dt. 22¹³⁻²¹ clearly reflects exceedingly primitive usage. Possibly still more primitive—certainly more barbarous —is the ordeal proposed in Nu. 5 to satisfy the jealous suspicions of a husband regarding his wife's chastity. The duplication of parallel and yet distinctly variant phrases, the evidence of different points of view, and in general the prolixity of the present law reveal the presence here of two originally distinct laws; one proposing a test by ordeal to determine whether the suspected wife is guilty or innocent, the other outlining a method of punishing by ordeal a wife whose guilt is already established. The latter law is given under § 70, which deals with adultery.

The law of jealousy was probably introduced in Nu. 5 by one of the later priests. Similar rites were in vogue among many primitive peoples, *e. g.*, the Hindus, cf. *The Laws of Manu*, IX–XIV; the Greeks, cf. Frazer's *Pausanias' Description of Greece*, IV, 175 ff., 253 ff. Among the negroes of West Africa *the bitter water* (probably containing poisonous herbs) figures, cf. Ratzel, *Völkerkunde* II, 55, 349. In Japan an accused man is made to drink water in which paper inscribed with a certain character has been dipped. This is supposed to cause him pain until he confesses his guilt. Cf. Gray, *Numbers*, 44, 45 for additional illustrations.

Like all trials by ordeal, the injustice to the innocent is obvious. In the case of the guilty the appeal to superstitious fear undoubtedly often revealed the culprit. Probably this and the sacred lot are only two of the many similar rites which were in force among the early Hebrews. The Code of Hammurabi dealt with the problem much more simply and humanely: § 131 *If a man's wife has been accused by her husband, and has not been caught lying with another, she shall swear her innocence, and return to her house.*

An older custom, however, strikingly similar to the Hebrew law in that it provides for trial by ordeal, is found in the same code: § 132 *If a man's wife has the finger pointed at her on account of another, but has not been caught lying with him, for her husband's sake she shall plunge into the sacred river.*

Deuteronomic Codes

charges, and give her an evil name and say, I married this woman, and when I came near to her, I did not find in her the evidences that she was a virgin, ¹⁵then the father of the young woman and her mother shall take and bring evidences of the young woman's virginity to the elders of the city at the gate; ¹⁶and the young woman's father shall say to the elders, I gave my daughter to this man as wife, and he turned against her; ¹⁷and now see he hath framed shameful charges saying, 'I did not find in thy daughter the evidences that she was a virgin,' and yet these are the evidences of my daughter's virginity. Then they shall spread the garment before the elders of the city.   ¹⁸And the elders of that city shall take the man and punish him; ¹⁹and they shall fine him a hundred shekels of silver, and give them to the young woman's father because the man hath given an evil name to a virgin of Israel; and she shall be his wife; he may not divorce her as long as he liveth.

Penalty if the wife is guilty

²⁰But if it prove to be true that the evidences that the young woman was a virgin were not found, ²¹then they shall bring out the young woman to the door of her father's house, and the men of her city shall stone her to death because she hath committed a shameful act in Israel, in that she hath been a harlot in her father's house; thus shalt thou purge out the evil from thy midst.

Supplemental Priestly Codes

Trial by ordeal

Nu. 5 ²⁹This is the law of jealousy : If a wife who is subject to her husband turn aside and is defiled, ¹³ᵇand she remain undiscovered although she be defiled,[1] ³⁰ᵃor if the spirit of jealousy seize a man and he be jealous of his wife, ¹⁴ᵇeven though she be not defiled, ³⁰ᵇthen he shall set the woman before Jehovah and the priest shall execute upon her all this law : ¹⁶the priest shall bring her near, and set her before Jehovah; ¹⁷and the priest shall take holy water in an earthen vessel, and the priest shall take some of the dust that is on the floor of the dwelling and put it into the water.   ¹⁹Then the priest shall take oath of her, and shall say to the woman, If no man has lain with thee, and if thou hast not gone aside to uncleanness, while subject to thy husband, thou shalt be immune from this water of bitterness that causeth the curse.   ²⁰But if thou hast gone aside, while subject to thy husband, and defiled thyself, and some man has lain with thee besides thy husband, ²²when this water that causeth the curse shall go into thy bowels, it shall cause thy body to swell, and thy thigh to fall away.   And the woman shall say, So may it be ! So may it be !   ²⁵Then the priest shall take the cereal-offering of jealousy out of the woman's hand, and shall wave the cereal-offering before Jehovah, and bring it to the altar.ᵐ   ²⁶ᵇAfterward he shall make the woman drink the water.ⁿ   ²⁷ᵃAnd when he hath made her drink the water, if she be defiled and hath been unfaithful to her husband, the water that

---

[1] Nu. 5¹³ᵇ Fragments of the original law of jealousy are found in ¹³, ¹⁴. These have been gathered up and repeated by the editor in ³⁰. On the basis of ¹³ᵇ, ¹⁴, ³⁰ the original can be restored as above. Cf. Carpenter and Harford-Battersby, *Hexat.*, II, 192.
ᵐ Nu. 5²⁵ Possibly the last clause belongs to the duplicate narrative.
ⁿ Nu. 5²⁶ᵇ This clause is omitted in the Gk. and Syr.

Supplemental Priestly Codes

causeth the curse shall enter into her and become bitter, and her body shall swell, and her thigh shall fall away. ²⁸But if the woman have not defiled herself, but be innocent, then she shall be free and shall bear offspring.

§ 11. **Laws of Divorce** Gen. 2¹⁸, ²³, ²⁴, Ex. 21⁷⁻¹¹, Dt. 22¹⁸, ¹⁹, ²⁸, ²⁹, 24¹⁻⁴

Primitive Codes

Gen. 2 ¹⁸Then said Jehovah, It is not good for man to be alone; I will make a helper suited to him. ²³Then said the man, *{The natural basis and sanctity of the marriage relation}*

> This, now, is bone of my bone
> And flesh of my flesh.
> This one shall be called woman,
> For from man was she taken.

²⁴Therefore a man leaves father and mother and cleaves to his wife, so that they two become one flesh.

Ex. 21 ⁷If a man sell his daughter to be a slave, she shall not go free as do the male slaves. ⁸If she does not please her master, who hath espoused her to himself, then he may let her be redeemed; he shall have no power to sell her to a foreign people, seeing he hath dealt deceitfully with her. ⁹If he espouse her to his son, he shall deal with her as with a daughter. ¹⁰If he marry another wife, her food, her raiment, and her duty of marriage shall he not diminish. ¹¹If he do not these three things to her, then she may go out without having to pay any money. *{Rights of a Hebrew slave married to her master}*

Deuteronomic Codes

Dt. 22 *If a man shall charge his newly-wedded wife with unchastity and her innocence be established,* ¹⁸the elders of that city shall take the man and punish him; ¹⁹and they shall fine him a hundred shekels of silver and give them to the young woman's father because the man has given an evil name to a virgin in Israel; and she shall be his wife; he may not divorce her as long as he lives. *{Cases in which a wife may not be divorced}*

²⁸If a man findeth a young woman, who is a virgin but is not betrothed, and lay hands on her, and lie with her, and they be found, ²⁹then the man who lay with her shall give to the young woman's father fifty shekels of

---

§ 11 The inferior position of the wife was an established canon in the ancient Semitic world. Since she was conceived of as the possession of her husband, his right of divorcing her was taken for granted. Even the modern Arab has only to lead his wife to the door of his tent and tell her to go and the marriage relation is severed.

The Hebrew lawgivers sought, as did Hammurabi, to interpose barriers in the way of hasty divorce. To this end they emphasized the sanctity of the marriage relation; and protected the rights of the female slave who had been made her master's wife. They also required the husband to formulate in writing the reasons for divorcing his wife and to give her this document. No provision is made that she may secure redress if the charge is false or insufficient; possibly this was left to her family or clan. The time and formality required to draw up a written charge would in itself be a powerful deterrent. The further provision that a divorced wife could not be taken back by her former husband also prevented hasty action.

The Code of Hammurabi marks a still greater advance over the primitive Semitic usage in regard to marriage. Cf. Appendix III. It even goes so far as to provide that the husband must pay alimony in case the divorced wife was not unfaithful. More surprising still, it enacts (§ 142) that, for sufficient cause, the wife could repudiate her husband and take her marriage-portion and return to her father's home.

Deuteronomic Codes

silver, and she shall be his wife, because he hath humiliated her; he may not divorce her as long as he lives.

Process and limitations of divorce **24** ¹When a man taketh a wife, and marrieth her, if she find no favor in his eyes, because he hath found some indecency[o] in her, he shall write her a bill of divorce,[p] and deliver it into her hand, and send her out of his house. ²And when she departeth out of his house, she may go and become another man's wife. ³But if the second husband turn against her and write her a bill of divorce and deliver it into her hand, and send her out of his house, or if the second husband who took her to be his wife die, ⁴her first husband who sent her away may not take her again to be his wife[q] after she is defiled; for that is an abomination before Jehovah, and thou shalt not involve in guilt the land which Jehovah thy God is about to give thee as an inheritance.

III

MASTERS AND HIRED SERVANTS

§ 12. Rights of Hired Servants, Dt. 24¹⁴, ¹⁵, Lev. 19¹³ᵇ, 25⁶, 22¹⁰ᵇ

Deuteronomic Codes

Fair dealing with hired servants **Dt. 24** ¹⁴Thou shalt not oppress a hired servant who is poor and needy, whether he be one of thine own race, or of the resident aliens who are in thy land within thy town. ¹⁵On the same[a] day shalt thou pay him his wages before the sun goeth down; for he is poor and setteth his heart upon it, and let him not cry against thee to Jehovah, and thou be guilty of a crime.[b]

Holiness Code

Payment of wages **Lev. 19** ¹³ᵇThe wages of a hired servant shall not remain with thee over night until the morning.

---

[o] Dt. 24¹ Lit., *the nakedness of a thing.* The reference is probably to indecent or immodest action. The exact meaning of the term was the subject of much discussion and difference of opinion among the Rabbis, cf. the Mishna tractat, *Gittin.*

[p] 24¹ Lit., *a writ of cutting off.*

[q] 24⁴ The law seems to regard this second marriage as almost equivalent to adultery. It is closely connected with the teaching of Jesus in Mt. 5³².

§ 12 The spirit of justice and consideration that characterizes the O.T. laws is here especially prominent. The enactments aim simply to protect the rights of hired servants. This was necessary, since they were usually either poor or else foreigners, and therefore not possessed of the full rights of citizenship. In the later codes hired servants are always classed with aliens and excluded from the distinctively Israelitish religious privileges, indicating perhaps that at that time they were without exception foreigners. They were never adopted into the families of the Hebrews, as were the slaves, and therefore were not given the same rights. From Lev. 25⁵³ and Is. 21¹⁶ it appears that hired servants frequently engaged their services for a year. Is. 16¹⁴ makes the regular period three years—half that of a slave. From Dt. 24¹⁴, ¹⁵ and Job 14⁵, ⁶ it is evident that the contract might be by the day or month. The significant point is that it was always for a stipulated period and that, for the time fixed, the obligations of the servant were probably very similar to those of a slave.

[a] Dt. 24¹⁵ Heb., *înis.*

[b] Dt. 24¹⁵ Lit., *it be sin in thee.* The expression is peculiar to Dt.

Holiness Code

25 ⁶The sabbath of the land shall be for food for you; for thee and for thy male and female slave, and for thy hired servant and for the settler who resideth with thee. `Privileges`

22 ¹⁰ᵇA hired servant shall not eat of that which is holy.ᶜ `Limitations`

IV

SLAVES AND MASTERS

§ 13. Enslavement of Israelites and Resident Aliens, Lev. 25³⁹, ⁴⁰ᵃ, ⁴³⁻⁴⁶

Holiness Code

Lev. 25 ³⁹If thy fellow countryman become poor and sell himself to thee, thou shalt not make him serve as a slave. ⁴⁰ᵃAs a hired servant and as a settler shall he be to thee. ⁴³Thou shalt not rule over him with harshness, but thou shalt fear thy God. `Consideration for Hebrew slaves`

Supplemental Priestly Codes

Lev. 25 ⁴⁴Any male or female slave, whom ye may have, ye shall buy of the nations that are round about you. ⁴⁵You may also buy them of the descendants of the settlers who reside among you, and of their families that are with you, that have been begotten in your land; and they shall be your possession. ⁴⁶Ye may also make them an inheritance for your children after you, to hold as a possession; ye may make them serve as slaves forever; but over your kinsmen the Israelites ye shall not rule with harshness one over another. `Foreigners, but not Hebrews, to be held as slaves`

§ 14. Permanent Slavery, Ex. 21⁵, ⁶, Dt. 15¹⁶, ¹⁷

Primitive Codes

Ex. 21 ⁵If a slave shall definitely say, I love my master, my wife, and my children, I will not go free, ⁶then his master shall bring him before `The custom of piercing the ear`

ᶜ Lev. 22¹⁰ᵇ *I. e.*, parts of the offerings which the Heb. offerers and the priests were allowed to eat.

Slaves and Masters.—The institution of slavery may be traced to the earliest period of Semitic history. Some of the oldest Babylonian tablets relate to the sale of slaves. The laws regulating this ancient institution were most of them established ages before the Hebrews appeared on the horizon of history. It was one of the chief corner-stones of Semitic society. In general it represented not so much the oppression as the protection of the weak by the strong. It was the chief refuge of the poor, the weak and the unfortunate, for which antiquity otherwise made little provision. Since it was so common and apparently so natural, little stigma attached to it. The position and rights of slaves in the ancient East were far superior

---

§ 13 While slavery probably arose from the custom of taking captives in war, in later times it appears, in nine cases out of ten, to have been the result of poverty. It is assumed as an established institution by the O.T. lawgivers; they simply endeavored to ameliorate its harshness. The very late priestly writers endeavored to restrict it entirely to foreigners. The original Holiness Code, however, appears to have simply enjoined consideration in the treatment of Hebrew slaves.

§ 14 The mildness and comparative advantages of the Hebrew institution of slavery are vividly illustrated by these laws. The choice of liberty, however was not without its heavy restrictions, for individual freedom meant the abandonment of wife and children. Under this strong pressure many Israelites undoubtedly preferred to assume the permanent badge of slavery.

Primitive Codes

God,[a] and shall lead him to the door, or the door-post, and his master shall bore through his ear with an awl; and the man shall be his slave as long as he liveth.

Deuteronomic Codes

The later custom **Dt. 15** [16]If a slave says to thee, I will not go out from thee, because he loveth thee and thy household, and because he is contented with thee, [17]then thou shalt take an awl and thrust it through his ear into the door, and he shall be thy slave forever. Thou shalt also do the same in the case of thy female slave.

§ 15. Sale of Slaves, Ex. 21⁷, ⁸

Primitive Codes

Limitations of sale of female slaves **Ex. 21** [7]If a man sell his daughter to be a slave, she shall not go free as do the male slaves. [8]If she does not please her master, who hath espoused her to himself, he may let her be redeemed; only he shall have no power to sell her to a foreign people, seeing he hath dealt deceitfully with her.

§ 16. Manumission of Israelitish Slaves, Ex. 21²⁻⁴, ²⁶, ²⁷, Dt. 15¹²⁻¹⁵, ¹⁸, Lev. 25¹⁰

Primitive Codes

Release after six years **Ex. 21** [2]If a man[b] buy a Hebrew slave, he shall serve six years, but in the seventh year he shall go free without having to pay any ransom. [3]If

to those in Rome or in modern times. In Babylonia, as in Israel, slaves were carefully guarded by law and common interests, so that their lot was very similar to that of trusted family servants to-day. In the East obedience to authority has always been emphasized more than the idea of personal liberty. The individual attained his true glory not by standing alone, but as an integral part of an illustrious family or tribe or nation. Each in turn recognized his responsibility to the whole, and, therefore, cruel masters and disloyal slaves appear to have been comparatively rare. Faithful slaves enjoyed most of the privileges shown the children of the household, and often intermarried into the family. They were also sometimes made the heirs of childless masters, cf. Gen. 15².

[a] Ex. 21⁶ Probably to the family gods or penates placed in early times beside the door. Cf. Ex. 12⁷, and for a survival of the institution, Is. 57⁸. The parallel in Dt. omits the reference to the household god, but preserves the same primitive ritual. It probably symbolized the initiation of the slave into the worship of the household god, and, therefore, his complete admission into the family. This rite was a very common one in antiquity, especially among the Arabians, Lydians, Carthaginians and Mesopotamians.

§ 15 The reason for this law is found in the fact that female slaves apparently were always made the wives or concubines of the master or of some immediate member of his family and thereby were raised to a position above that of the ordinary slave.

[b] Ex. 21² Heb., *thou*, but in all other civil laws the third person is used. cf. Introd., p. 23. Evidently here the *thou* has been introduced by a scribe who was influenced by the use of the second person in ¹.

§ 16 In the old Babylonian society there does not appear to have been any provision for the release of slaves at the end of an appointed time. The O.T. law assumes that at the end of six years the Hebrew slave will have paid his debt or expiated the penalty which led to his enslavement. The Deuteronomic law goes further and urges that the master provide his manumitted slave with the means necessary to begin again his independent life. The account in Jer. 34 of the reluctant liberation of their slaves by the citizens, under the pressure of a siege, in order to win Jehovah's favor, and their shameless repudiation of their solemn promise when the crisis was over, indicate that this law was probably never strictly enforced. It embodied an ideal too high for the people as a whole to attain, and yet its presence even in the oldest codes is most significant. The later priestly codes substituted, in practice at least, the very different and less strenuous law that at the end of every forty-nine (7x7) years all slaves should be freed. While less just, it apparently gave greater promise of being enforced, for enforcement would depend not upon the action of individual masters at the end of six years of service, but

Primitive Codes

he came in single, he shall go out unmarried; if he be married, then his wife shall go out with him. ⁴If his master give him a wife and she bear him sons or daughters, the wife and her children shall be her master's, but the man shall go out by himself.

²⁶If a man smite the eye of his male slave or the eye of his female slave so that it is destroyed, he shall let him go free for his eye's sake. ²⁷And if he knock out a tooth of his male or female slave, he shall let him go free for his tooth's sake.

The indemnity for serious personal injury

Deuteronomic Codes

Dt. 15 ¹²If one of thine own race, a Hebrew man or a Hebrew woman, be sold to thee, he shall serve thee six years; then in the seventh year thou shalt let him go free. ¹³And when thou lettest him go free, thou shalt not let him go empty-handed; ¹⁴rather thou shalt furnish him liberally[c] from thy flock, and thy threshing-floor, and thy winepress; according as Jehovah thy God hath blessed thee thou shalt give to him.[d] ¹⁵And thou shalt remember that thou wast a slave in the land of Egypt, and that Jehovah thy God redeemed thee: therefore I now command thee to do this thing. ¹⁸It must not seem hard to thee, when thou lettest him go free, for to the value of double the hire of a hireling hath he served thee six years;[e] and thus Jehovah thy God will bless thee in all that thou doest.

Injunction to be generous to the liberated slave

Supplemental Priestly Codes

Lev. 25 ¹⁰Ye shall set apart as sacred the fiftieth year, and proclaim liberty throughout the land to all its inhabitants. It shall be a year of jubilee for you, and ye shall return each to his possession, and ye shall return each to his family.

Release for all Israelites in the year of jubilee

§ 17. Redemption of Israelitish Slaves, Lev. 25⁴⁷⁻⁵⁵

Supplemental Priestly Codes

Lev. 25 ⁴⁷If a foreigner or alien residing with thee become rich and thy fellow countryman become poor beside him and sell himself to the

Israelitish slaves to be redeemed from foreigners at any time

---

upon the united action of the community, so that any failure to observe it would be readily recognized. It was accompanied by the law that no Hebrew be enslaved (§ 4); hence in theory, at least, this late law was unnecessary when first promulgated. Cf. for the probable origin of the year of jubilee, note § 113.

[c] Dt. 15¹⁴ Lit. *surround with a necklace, i. e.,* load him down with treasures.

[d] Dt. 15¹⁴ In this deeply philanthropic law the older regulations of Ex. 21³, ⁴ regarding the children and wife acquired by the slave in servitude are ignored.

[e] Dt. 15¹⁸ *I. e.,* if a hired laborer had been engaged in his stead the expense would have been double the cost of the slave.

§ 17 This law reflects the impoverished and pitiable condition of the Jews which resulted from the Babylonian exile. Nehemiah found in his day that many had been sold as slaves to foreigners, and he states that he and his followers, according to their means, had redeemed their fellow Jews who had been enslaved. This law, with the exception of ⁴⁷, ⁵⁵ᶜ, which was original to the Holiness Code, probably comes from the general period of Nehemiah or soon after. It provides for the redemption of Jews from foreign masters, whenever the slave or his kinsmen could provide the necessary means. Naturally it could be enforced only within the jurisdiction of the Judean community in Palestine. It also emphasized the responsibility of procuring the liberation of an enslaved Jew whenever that was possible.

Babylonian usage suggested the principles underlying this late regulation. Cases are on record of Babylonian slaves buying their own freedom. A member of a noble family who

Supplemental Priestly Codes

foreigner or alien residing with thee, or to a descendant of the foreigner's family, ⁴⁸he may be redeemed after he has sold himself; one of his kinsmen may redeem him; ⁴⁹or his uncle, or his uncle's son may redeem him; or one of his near family kinsmen may redeem him; or, if he become rich, he may redeem himself. ⁵⁰And he shall reckon with his purchaser from the year that he sold himself to him to the year of the next jubilee; and the price of his release shall be according to the number of years of service on the same terms as a hired servant shall he be with him. ⁵¹If there are yet many years, in proportion to them shall he give back the price of his redemption out of the money for which he was bought. ⁵²And if there remain but a few years until the year of jubilee, then he shall reckon with him; according to the years of service still remaining shall he pay back the price of his redemption.ᶠ

To be treated kindly and released in the year of jubilee

⁵³As a servant hired by the year shall he be with him; thou shalt not look on quietly while he rules him harshly. ⁵⁴And if he be not redeemed in any of these ways, then he shall go free at the year of jubilee together with his children. ⁵⁵For to me the Israelites are servants; they are my servants whom I brought out of the land of Egypt: I am Jehovah your God.

§ 18. Reception of Fugitive Slaves, Dt. 23¹⁵, ¹⁶

Deuteronomic Codes

Protection and consideration

Dt. 23 ¹⁵Thou shalt not deliver to his master a slave who has fled from his master to thee. ¹⁶He shall dwell with thee in thy land, in the place which he shall choose within one of thy towns, where it pleaseth him best, without your oppressing him.

---

through some accident had been enslaved, could at any time be redeemed by that family and the master could not prevent it. In Persian times a member of the conquering race could not be legally enslaved. Cf. Johns' *Babylonian and Assyrian Laws, Contracts and Letters*, pp. 175, 176.

ᶠ Lev. 25⁵² *I. e.*, he shall multiply the price paid by the number of years yet remaining until the year of jubilee and divide it by the total number of years from the time of his enslavement to the next year of jubilee.

§ 18 This law was probably retained and emphasized by the prophetic lawgivers because, making it possible for slaves to escape from cruel masters, it tended to relieve their lot. In its origin it probably goes back to the nomadic period, when one tribe eagerly welcomed fugitives from a hostile tribe. It may also reflect the readiness of the Hebrews in later days to receive foreign additions to their ranks, since numbers were vitally necessary to their supremacy in the close competition which was always waged for the limited territory of Palestine. The flight of Shimei's slaves to Achish king of Gath, I Kgs. 2³⁹, illustrates what was probably a common practice.

Among the Hebrews themselves the enforcement of this law must have been beset with many complications. It is also counter to the laws of Hammurabi which are very explicit and strict on this point:

§ 16 *If a man has harbored in his house a male or female slave from a patrician's or plebeian's house, and has not caused the fugitive to leave on the demand of the officer of the slaves condemned to public forced labor, that householder shall be put to death.*
§ 17 *If a man has caught either a male or female runaway slave in the open field and has brought him back to his owner, the owner of the slave shall give him two shekels of silver.* § 18. *If such a slave will not name his owner, his captor shall bring him to the palace, where he shall be examined as to his past and returned to his owner.* § 19. *If the captor has secreted that slave in his house and afterward that slave has been caught in his possession, he shall be put to death.* § 20. *If the slave has fled from the hands of his captor, the latter shall swear to the owner of the slave and he shall be free from blame.*
The wide variations illustrate the very different estimates placed on the value of property and the diverse points of view of the two legal systems.

§ 19. Penalty for Injury Done to Slaves, Ex. 21[20, 21, 26, 27]

Primitive Codes

Ex. 21 [20]If a man strike his male or female slave with a stick so that he die at once, the master must be punished.   [21]If, however, the slave[g] survive a day or two the master shall not be punished, for it is his own loss.

[26]And if a man strike his male or female slave in the eye so as to destroy it, he shall let him go free for his eye's sake.   [27]And if he knock out a tooth of his male or female slave, he shall let him go free for his tooth's sake.

Fatal injury by master

Permanent injury

§ 20. Reparation for Injury Done to Slaves, Ex. 21[32]

Primitive Codes

Ex. 21 [32]If an ox gore a male or female slave, then thirty shekels of silver shall be given to their master, and the ox shall be stoned.

Injury by an ox

§ 21. Religious Privileges of Slaves, Dt. 12[17, 18], 16[10, 11], Ex. 12[43b, 44]

Deuteronomic Codes

Dt. 12 [17]Thou mayst not eat within thine own gates the tithe of thy grain or thy new wine, or thine oil, or the firstlings from thy herd or thy flock, nor any of thy vows which thou vowest, nor thy voluntary offerings, nor anything which thou presentest as a gift; [18]but thou shalt eat them before Jehovah thy God in the place which Jehovah thy God shall choose, together with thy son and thy daughter, and thy male and female slaves, and the Levite who is within thy city; and thou shalt rejoice before Jehovah thy God over all that thou hast acquired.

To share the tithes and the sacrificial feasts

16 [10]Thou shalt keep the feast of weeks to Jehovah thy God according to the measure of the voluntary offerings which thy hand shall present, in proportion as Jehovah thy God hath blessed thee.   [11]Thou and thy son and thy daughter, thy male and female slaves, and the Levite who dwelleth in thy town, and the resident alien, the fatherless and the widow who live with thee, shall rejoice before Jehovah in the place where Jehovah thy God shall choose to have his name dwell.

To share in feast of weeks

Priestly Codes

Ex. 12 [43b]This is the regulation regarding the passover: [44]Each man's slave, who is bought for money, after thou hast circumcised him, shall partake of the passover meal.

In passover feast

---

§ 19 These laws mark a distinct advance over current Semitic usage. The Code of Hammurabi simply protects the rights of masters and says nothing about the rights of slaves. Although under the Heb. laws the injury to a slave was not punished as severely as one to a free man or woman, it is exceedingly significant that it was punished at all. The distinction in the penalty is further illustrated by the law of Lev. 19[20] (cf. § 71), which provides that illicit intercourse with a betrothed female slave shall be punished, but not by death as in the case of free men and women.
  [g] Ex. 21[21] Supplying its implied subjects. In the original only the personal pronouns are used.
  § 20 The Code of Hammurabi further enacts that if a slave die as the result of an operation, the surgeon must give another slave to the master, § 219.
  § 21 Since slaves were regarded as regular and permanent members of an Israelitish family, they were accorded full religious privileges, whether aliens or Hebrews by birth.

V

ALIENS

§ 22. **Rights and Duties of Resident Aliens,** Ex. 22²¹ [23⁹], Dt. 24¹⁴, ¹⁷, ¹⁸, 1¹⁶, 27¹⁹, Lev. 25⁴⁷, ⁴⁸ᵃ, ⁵³, 19³³, ³⁴, 24²², Nu. 15²⁹, ³⁰, 35¹⁵, 15¹⁴⁻¹⁶, 9¹⁴

Primitive Codes

Justice and protection

Ex. 22 ²¹Thou shalt not wrong nor oppress a resident alien; for ye were resident aliens in the land of Egypt.

Deuteronomic Codes

Dt. 24 ¹⁴Thou shalt not oppress a hired servant who is poor and needy, whether he be one of thy fellow countrymen or one of thy resident aliens who are in thy land within thy gates. ¹⁷Thou shalt not pervert the justice due to the resident alien, or to the fatherless, nor take the widow's garment in pledge; ¹⁸but thou shalt remember that thou wast a slave in Egypt and that Jehovah thy God redeemed thee from there. Therefore I command thee to do this thing. 1 ¹⁶And I charged your judges at that time, saying, Hear the cases between your fellow countrymen, and judge righteously between a man and his fellow countryman and the alien who resideth with him.

Public condemnation of injustice

27 ¹⁹Cursed be the one who perverteth the justice due the resident alien, fatherless, and widow. And all the people shall say, So may it be!

Holiness Code

Not to hold permanently nor oppress a Hebrew slave

Lev. 25 ⁴⁷If an alien or the one living with thee become rich and thy fellow countryman become poor beside him, and sell himself to the alien or the one living with thee, or to a descendant of the alien's family, ⁴⁸ᵃ he may after he is sold be redeemed; one of his kinsmen may redeem him.ᵃ ⁵³As a hired servant year by year shall he remain with him; thou shalt not look on quietly while the resident alien rules him harshly.ᵇ

Aliens.—True to their early nomadic instincts, the Israelites were generous in their treatment of aliens who came to seek their protection and hospitality. They distinguished sharply, however, between a foreigner (*ben nekhar*), one who retained his allegiance to his own tribe or nation, the protection of which he therefore continued to enjoy, and the resident alien (*gêr*) who had taken up his permanent abode in and placed himself under the protection of an Israelitish tribe. Their attitude toward aliens also underwent great transformations in succeeding ages under the influence of the stirring political experiences through which they passed.

§ 22 The resident alien figures prominently in Israelitish legislation. Usually he was one who had been attracted by the tribe of his adoption either through intermarriage or trade, or to escape debt at home or the consequences of a crime, or simply impelled by a desire to better his condition. The Hebrews were always ready to welcome such, for it tended to increase their numbers and strength in warring Palestine where peace was won only by constant warfare.

Naturally the resident alien came without wealth or family support. Accordingly he was treated as a ward of the community and each succeeding code grants him greater rights and privileges. The Deuteronomic codes seek to insure to him not only justice but kindness, love and practical charity. In the Holiness and priestly codes, he is granted religious rites equal to those of the native Israelites, provided he submits to the rite of circumcision. With these comes equal responsibility in keeping Israel's law. Through this wide open door in later times foreign proselytes passed the high wall of separation and became identified with the Jewish community.

ᵃ Lev. 25⁴⁸ᵃ Vs. ⁵³ appears to have been the original sequel of ⁴⁷. Vss. ⁴⁸ᵃ, ᶠᶠ are later additions.

ᵇ Lev. 25⁵³ Lit., *rule harshly over him in thy sight.*

Holiness Code

19 ³³If an alien make his home with you in your land, ye shall do him no wrong. ³⁴ᵃThe alien who makes his home with you shall be to you as the native born among you. **24** ²²Ye shall have the same law for the resident alien as for the native born: for I am Jehovah your God. — *Equal rights with Israelites*

Priestly Codes

Nu. 15 ²⁹Ye shall have the same law for him who doeth anything unintentionally, for him who is native born among the Israelites, and for the alien who makes his home among them. ³⁰But whoever doeth anything defiantly,ᶜ whether he be native born or a resident alien, the same revileth Jehovah; that one shall be cut off from among his people.ᵈ **35** ¹⁵For the Israelites and for the foreigner and for the alien residing among them, there shall be six cities as a place of refuge; that every one who killeth any person unintentionally may flee to them. — *Resident aliens subject to same laws as the native Israelites*

15 ¹⁴If an alien reside among you, or if any one else be among you throughout your generations, and wish to present an offering made by fire of an odor pleasing to Jehovah, as ye do, so shall he do. ¹⁵There shall be but one statute for the assembly,ᵉ both for you and for the alien who resideth among you,ᶠ a statute forever throughout your generations; ye and the resident alien shall both be alike before Jehovah. ¹⁶There shall be one law and one regulation for you, and for the alien who resideth among you. — *To observe same sacrificial customs*

9 ¹⁴If an alien reside among you, and wisheth to keep the passover to Jehovah, according to the regulations governing the passover, and according to its ordinance, shall he do; ye shall have one statute, both for the resident alien, and for him who is native born. — *Also the passover regulations*

§ 23. Limitations and Rights of Foreigners, Dt. 15³ᵃ, 23²⁰ᵃ, 14²¹ᵃ, ᶜ, Ex. 12⁴³

Deuteronomic Codes

Dt. 15 ³ᵃOf a foreigner thou mayest exact [a loan even during the seventh year of release]. **23** ²⁰ᵃTo a foreigner thou mayest lend upon interest; but not to a fellow countryman. — *To pay interest at all times*

14 ²¹ᵃ,ᶜYe shall not eat of anything that dieth of itself, but thou mayest sell it to a foreigner. — *Allowed to eat unclean food*

Priestly Codes

Ex. 12 ⁴³And Jehovah said to Moses and Aaron, This is the ordinance of the passover: no foreigner shall eat of it. — *Excluded from passover feast*

ᶜ Nu. 15³⁰ Lit., *with a high hand.*
ᵈ Nu. 15³⁰ *I. e.*, placed under the ban, deprived of the privileges of the clan and driven from the tribe or community.
ᵉ Nu. 15¹⁵ *For the assembly* is missing in the Syr. and Lat., and may be a gloss or due to dittography.
ᶠ Nu. 15¹⁵ *Among you*, found in Gk., not in Heb.
§ 23 The Heb. word commonly used to designate an unnaturalized foreigner means lit., *stranger*, and was applied to gods, men and lands. It included all not identified by birth or choice or possession with Israel. Unlike the resident alien, the foreigner had no rights in the land. From the days of Moses everyone and everything foreign was viewed askance. The bitter experiences of the Babylonian exile deepened the feeling of hatred.

B

RIGHTS OF PROPERTY

§ 24. Restoration of Lost Property, Ex. 23⁴, ⁵, Dt. 22¹⁻⁴

Primitive Codes

Property even of enemy to be protected

Ex. 23 ⁴If thou meet thine enemy's ox or ass going astray, thou shalt surely bring it back to him again. ⁵If thou see the ass of him who hateth thee lying prostrate under its burden, thou shalt in no caseᵍ leave it in its plight; rather thou shalt, together with him, help it out.ʰ

Deuteronomic Codes

Later version of the above law

Dt. 22 ¹Thou shalt not see thy fellow Israelite's ox or his sheep going astray, and withhold thy helpⁱ from them; thou shalt surely bring them again to thy brother. ²And if thy fellow Israelite do not live near thee, or if thou do not know him, then thou shalt bring it home to thine house, and it shall be with thee until thy fellow Israelite seek after it; then thou shalt restore it to him again. ³Thus shalt thou do with his ass, and with his garment, and with every lost thing which belongeth to thy fellow Israelite, which he hath lost and thou hast found; thou mayst not withhold thy help. ⁴Thou shalt not see thy fellow Israelite's ass or his ox fallen down by the way and withhold thy help from them; thou shalt surely help him to lift them up again.

§ 25. Reparation for Damage or Loss of Property, Ex. 21²⁸⁻³⁶, 22⁷⁻¹⁵, Lev. 24¹⁸, ²¹ᵃ, 6¹⁻⁵

Primitive Codes

Damage resulting from one's carelessness

Ex. 21 ³³If a man open a cistern, or if a man dig a cistern but doth not cover it, and an ox or an ass fall into it, ³⁴the owner of the cistern shall make it good; he shall give money to the owners and the carcass shall be his. **22** ⁵If a man burn over a field or vineyard and let the fireʲ spread so that it

---

Rights of Property.—In the light of the later commercial habits of the Hebrews, it is interesting to note that their laws have comparatively little to say about property and property rights: only a few simple directions, evidently coming from the early nomadic period, survive. They probably sufficed, however, to guide judges in the more complicated cases that later arose. The Deuteronomic lawgivers were primarily interested in maintaining the rights of the needy and oppressed, while the authors of the priestly law were chiefly concerned with the development of the ritual, so that the reason for their silence is evident. Life and worship, not things, interested them.

§ 24 The high ethical note struck in the primitive codes, which enjoin kindness to an enemy, is astonishing (cf. § 115), especially as the Deuteronomic codes substitute, *fellow Israelite*.   The reason for the substitution is probably to make the law applicable to all cases.

ᵍ Ex. 23⁵ Restoring the corrupt Heb. with the aid of Gk. and Luc., which have retained the negative.

ʰ Ex. 23⁵ Following a reconstructed text suggested by the Gk. and Luc. and supported by the context.

ⁱ Dt. 22¹ Lit., *hide thyself.*

§ 25 The corresponding principles operative in the Bab. system are illustrated by the laws of Hammurabi found in Appendix IV. In general the penalties are much more severe in the Babylonian code.

ʲ 22⁵ At an early period the text of this verse was misunderstood and is generally misinterpreted. The current interpretation makes a domestic animal, instead of fire, that which destroys the vineyard. Slightly correcting the text the above reading is secured—a reading which is consonant with the context and especially ⁶.

Primitive Codes

devoureth a neighbor's field, out of the best of his own field, and the best of his own vineyard, shall he make restitution. ⁶If fire break out and catch in thorns so that the shocks of grain, or the standing grain, or the field are consumed, he that kindled the fire must make restitution.

21 ²⁸If an ox fatally gore a man or a woman, the ox shall be stoned, and its flesh shall not be eaten, but the owner of the ox shall be acquitted.^{k} ²⁹But if the ox was already in the habit of goring, and it hath been reported to its owner, and he hath not kept it in, with the result that it hath killed a man or a woman, the ox shall be stoned, and its owner shall also be put to death. ³⁰If a ransom is fixed for him, he shall give for the redemption of his life whatever amount is determined. ³¹Whether the ox hath gored a boy or a girl, this law shall be executed.

³²If the ox gore a male or female slave, thirty silver shekels shall be given to their master, and the ox shall be stoned.

³⁵If one man's ox hurt another's so that it dieth, then they shall sell the live ox, and divide the money received from it; they shall also divide the carcass between them. ³⁶Or if it be known that the ox was already in the habit of goring, and its owner hath not kept it in, he must pay ox for ox, and the carcass shall belong to him.

22 ¹⁴If a man borrow an animal from his neighbor, and it be hurt or die while its owner is not with it, the man must make restitution.^{l} ¹⁵If its owner be with it, the man need not make it good; being a hired animal, it came for its hire.

⁷If a man deliver to his neighbor money or personal property to keep, and it be stolen out of the man's house, if the thief be found, he shall make double restitution.^{m} ⁸If the thief be not found, then the master of the house shall come before God^n to prove whether or not he hath taken^o his neighbor's goods.

[margin notes: Fatal injury inflicted by a man's ox | Injury to a slave | Injury of one ox by another | Injury to an hired animal | Loss of money or personal property held in trust]

---

^{k} Ex. 21²⁸ Hammurabi's law, § 250, reads: *If a bull has gone wild and gored a man, and caused his death, there can be no suit brought against the owner.*

^{l} Ex. 22¹⁴ The Code of Hammurabi is much more explicit:

§ 244 *If a man has hired an ox, or an ass, and a lion has killed it in the open field, the loss falls on its owner.*

§ 245 *If a man has hired an ox and has caused its death, by carelessness, or blows, he shall restore ox for ox, to the owner of the ox.*

§ 246 *If a man has hired an ox, and has broken its leg, or cut its neck (?), he shall restore ox for ox, to the owner of the ox.*

§ 247 *If a man has hired an ox, and knocked out its eye, he shall pay to the owner of the ox half its price.*

§ 248 *If a man has hired an ox, and has broken its horn, cut off its tail, or torn its muzzle, he shall pay one-quarter of its price.*

§ 249 *If a man has hired an ox, and God has struck it, and it has died, the man that hired the ox shall make affidavit and go free.*

^{m} Ex. 22⁷ Cf. Hammurabi's Code:

§§ 102, 103 *If the merchant has given money, as a speculation, to the agent, who during his travels has met with misfortune, he shall return the full sum to the merchant. If, on his travels, an enemy has forced him to give up some of the goods he was carrying, the agent shall specify the amount on oath and shall be acquitted.*

^{n} Ex. 22⁸ Go to one of the sanctuaries or consult a priest that he may determine through the sacred oracle whether he is guilty or not. The analogy in the Code of Hammurabi is illuminating:

§ 106 *If an agent has taken money of a merchant, and his principal suspects him, that principal shall prosecute his agent, put him on oath before the elders, as to the money taken; the agent shall pay to the merchant threefold what he misappropriated.*

^{o} Ex. 22⁸ Lit., *put his hand to.*

The analogies to the Code of Hammurabi are especially close:

§ 120 *If a man has deposited his corn for safe keeping in another's house and it has suffered damage in the granary, or if the owner of the house has opened the store and taken the corn,*

Primitive Codes

Loss of animal held in trust

10 If a man deliver to his neighbor an ass, or an ox, or a sheep, or any beast, to keep, and it die or be hurt or be driven away without any one's having seen it, 11 an oath sworn by Jehovah shall be between both of them to decide whether or not the one hath taken his neighbor's property; the owner must accept it, and the other need not make restitution. 12 If it be stolen from him, he shall make restitution to its owner. 13 If the animal be torn in pieces, let him bring it as evidence; he need not make good that which was torn.

Procedure in breach of trust

9 In every case of breach of trust whether it concern ox, or ass, or sheep, or clothing, or any kind of lost thing of which one saith, This is it, the case of both parties shall come before God; he whom God shall condemn shall make double restitution to his neighbor.

Holiness Code

Injury to an animal

Lev. 24 18 He that smiteth a beast so that it dieth shall make it good, life for life. 21a And he that killeth a beast shall make it good.

Priestly Codes

General law regarding breach of trust or fraud

Lev. 6 1 Jehovah spoke thus to Moses,[p] 2 If anyone sin and break faith with Jehovah, by deceiving his neighbor in regard to a deposit, or a pledge, or by robbing or defrauding his neighbor,[q] 3 or if he have found something which was lost, and deny it and perjure himself, if by doing any one of these things a man hath sinned and so is guilty, 4 he shall restore that which he took by robbery, or the thing which he obtained by fraud, or the deposit which was entrusted to him, or the lost thing which he found, 5 or anything about which he swore falsely; he shall restore it in full and shall add to it a fifth more; he shall give it to its rightful owner on the day that he is found guilty.

§ 26. Theory of the Ownership of Land, Lev. 25²³

Supplemental Priestly Codes

All land held in trust for Jehovah

Lev. 25 23 The land shall not be sold in perpetuity; for the land is mine, and ye are resident aliens and settlers with me.

---

or has disputed the amount of the corn that was stored in his house, the owner of the corn shall declare on oath the amount of his corn, and the owner of the house shall return him double.

§ 124 *If a man has given on deposit to another, before witnesses, gold, silver, or any goods whatever, and his claim has been contested, he shall prosecute that man, and [the man] shall return double what he disputed.*

§ 125 *If a man has given anything whatever on deposit, and, where he has made his deposit, something of his has been lost, together with something belonging to the owner of the house, either by house-breaking or a rebellion, the owner of the house who is in default shall make good all that has been given him on deposit, which he has lost, and shall return it to the owner of the goods. The owner of the house shall look after what he has lost and recover it from the thief.*

§ 126 *If a man has said that something of his is lost, which is not lost, or has alleged a depreciation, though nothing of his is lost, he shall estimate the depreciation on oath, and whatever he has claimed he shall return double.*

[p] Lev. 6¹⁻⁵ Heb. 5²⁰⁻²⁴.

[q] Lev. 6² Intentionally or unintentionally.

§ 26 The theory of the ownership of the land comes from the very late priests and is akin to the idea, expressed in the same context ⁵⁵, that the Israelites are Jehovah's slaves.

§ 27. Conveyance of Real Property, Lev. 25¹⁵, ¹⁶, ³⁴

Supplemental Priestly Codes

Lev. 25 [15]According to the number of the years after the jubilee thou shalt buy land from thy neighbor, and according to the number of the crops until the next jubilee shall he sell it to thee. [16]If the number of the years be great, thou shalt increase its price, but if the number of years be small, thou shalt reduce its price, for it is the number of the crops that he selleth to thee.
Land only sold subject to re-version

[34]But the fields in the pasture land of the cities belonging to the Levites may not be sold, for it is their perpetual possession. No sale of Levitical pasture land

§ 28. Redemption of Hereditary Land, Lev. 25²⁴⁻²⁷, ²⁹⁻³²

Supplemental Priestly Codes

Lev. 25 [24]In all the land of our possession ye shall allow the land to be redeemed. [25]If thy fellow countryman become poor and sell some of his possession, his kinsman who is nearest to him shall come and redeem that which his brother hath sold. Right of kins-man to redeem land

[26]And if a man have no one to redeem it, and he become rich and find sufficient to redeem it, [27]then let him count the years since its sale and refund the value of the remainder [until the year of jubilee] to the man to whom he sold it; thus he may return to his possession. Of seller to re-deem it

[29]If a man sell a dwelling house in a walled city, he shall have the right of redeeming it for a whole year after it has been sold; for a year he shall retain the right of redemption. [30]Then if it is not redeemed within a year, the house that is in the walled city shall be assured in perpetuity to him who bought it, to him and his descendants; it shall not be released in the year of jubilee. [31]But the houses of the villages which have no walls around them, shall be reckoned as belonging to the fields of the country; the right of redemption shall be retained for them and they shall be released in the year of jubilee. [32]But in the case of the houses in the cities which belong to the Levites, the Levites shall have the perpetual right of redemption. Re-demp-tion of houses in walled cities

---

§ 27 This section like the preceding, appears to be a late priestly supplement to the older law of the sabbatical year. Cf. §§ 223, 224. There is no evidence that, in the long period preceding Nehemiah, the law of the year of jubilee, which provided that all land should revert to its hereditary owners, was known; and the proof that it was not in force is conclusive. The present enactment provides that all land shall be sold at a price, proportionate to the number of crops that can be raised on it before it must revert to its original owner.

§ 28 The law in ²⁵ is apparently a very old one and provides that in the case of a forced sale of hereditary land the nearest kinsman shall have the first right of buying it. Jer. 32⁷⁻¹⁵ contains an account of some land thus purchased by the prophet Jeremiah from his kinsman. The story of Naboth's vineyard, I Kgs. 21 also illustrates how carefully the hereditary rights were guarded. The later supplemental law, possibly reviving a primitive usage, provides that ancestral lands may be redeemed at any time.

§ 29. Reversion of the Hereditary Land, Lev. 25^{13, 28b, 31b, 33} [Nu. 36^{3, 4}]

Supplemental Priestly Codes

All
land
and
houses
in un-
walled
towns
to re-
vert
at the
jubilee

Lev. 25 ¹³In the year of jubilee ye shall return each to his possession. ^{28b}At the jubilee [a poor man's land] shall be released and he shall return to his possession. ^{31b}[Houses in villages without a wall] shall also be released at the jubilee. ³³If one of the Levites doth not^r redeem [his hereditary possession] the house that was sold in the city of their possession shall be released at the year of jubilee; for the houses in the cities of the Levites are their possession among the Israelites.

IV

RIGHTS OF INHERITANCE

§ 30. The Law of Primogeniture, Dt. 21¹⁵⁻¹⁷, 25^{5, 6}

Deuteronomic Codes

Double
right
of el-
dest son
inalien-
able

Dt. 21 ¹⁵If a man have two wives, the one beloved and the other hated, and both the one who is beloved and the one who is hated have born him children, and if the first-born son belong to her who is hated, ¹⁶on the day that he causeth his sons to inherit that which he hath, he shall not be allowed to give the right of the first-born to the son of the beloved wife to the exclusion of the eldest, the son of the one who is hated; ¹⁷but he shall acknowledge the first-born, the son of the one who is hated, by giving him a double portion^a of all that he hath, for he is the first product of his strength; the right of the first-born is his.

In case
of a
Levi-
rate
mar-
riage

25 ⁵If brothers live together, and one of them die, and have no son, the wife of the deceased shall not be married to a man outside the clan; her husband's brother shall go in to her, and make her his wife, and perform the duty of a husband's brother to her. ⁶Then the first son whom she bears shall succeed to^b the name of the deceased brother, that his name may not become extinct^c in Israel.

---

§ 29 The late priestly point of view is manifest in this law; it aimed to overthrow the prevailing usage, which insured a permanent title to a purchaser. The genesis of the late regulation and its connection with the condition of the returning exiles will be discussed in § 113. Nu. 36^{3, 4} contain the only other allusion in the Pentateuch to the year of jubilee, cf. § 32.

　　^r Lev. 25³³ The negative has been lost in the Heb. but is restored in the Lat., as the context demands.

　　Rights of Inheritance.—Customary usage had so established the rights of inheritance among the Israelites that detailed enactments were unnecessary. In the earlier times the property passed to the male heirs, and upon them devolved the obligation to support the mother and the unmarried sisters. If there were no sons, the father's brothers assumed the duties of parents and inherited the property of the deceased. The present laws simply deal with exceptional cases.

　　§ 30 This law was disregarded by David who appointed Solomon as his successor, even though he was not his oldest son, I Kgs. 1¹¹⁻¹³. For the Bab. usage cf. Appendix V.

　　^a Dt. 21¹⁷ Lit., *mouth of two.*
　　^b Dt. 25⁶ Lit., *stand upon.*
　　^c Dt. 25⁶ Lit., *be blotted out.*

§ 31. Rights of Daughters to Inherit, Nu. 27¹⁻¹¹

Supplemental Priestly Codes

Nu. 27 ¹There came near the daughters of Zelophehad, the son of Hepher, The the son of Gilead, the son of Machir, the son of Manasseh, of the families tradi-of Manasseh[d] the son of Joseph; and these are the names of his daughters : case Mahlah, Noah, Hoglah, Milcah, and Tirzah. ²And they stood before Moses and before Eleazar the priest, and before the princes and all the congregation, at the door of the tent of meeting, saying, ³Our father died in the wilderness, and he did not belong to those who conspired against Jehovah in the company of Korah; but he died in consequence of his own sin; and he had no sons. ⁴Why should our father's name disappear[e] from among his family because he had no son? Give us therefore an hereditary possession among our father's kinsmen. ⁵So Moses laid their case before Jehovah.

⁶Then Jehovah spoke thus to Moses, ⁷What the daughters of Zelophehad Ruling say is right, thou shalt surely give them an hereditary possession among that their father's kinsmen, and thou shalt transfer to them their father's inheri- inheritances tance. ⁸Moreover thou shalt speak thus to the Israelites, 'If a man die and shall have no son then ye shall transfer his inheritance to his daughter. ⁹And if pass to he have no daughter, then ye shall give his inheritance to his brothers. ¹⁰And kins-if he have no brothers, then ye shall give his inheritance to his father's men brothers. ¹¹And if his father have no brothers then he shall give his inheri- nearest tance to the nearest kinsman in his family, that he may possess it.' This shall be an established ordinance[f] for the Israelites, as Jehovah commanded Moses.

§ 32. Heiress to Marry within her Own Tribe, Nu. 36¹⁻¹²

Supplemental Priestly Codes

Nu. 36 ¹The heads of the father's houses of the family[g] of the sons of The Gilead, the son of Machir, the son of Manasseh, of the families of the sons tradi-of Joseph, came near and spoke before Moses[h] and before the princes, the case heads of the father's houses of the Israelites; ²and they said, Jehovah com-manded my lord to give the land by lot as an inheritance to the Israelites; and my lord was commanded by Jehovah to give the inheritance of Zelophe-

---

§ 31 It was only in the latest period of O.T. history that daughters were recognized as legal heirs, cf. § 30. The present tradition, which attributes the origin of the institution to Moses, is clearly one of the latest parts of the O.T., and is cited to give authority to this radical but just departure from long established usage. In the Code of Hammurabi definite provision was made for inheritance by daughters. Cf. Appendix V. In Job 42¹⁵ daughters are given equal rights with sons. The account of the carrying out of the traditional precedent in Nu. 27¹⁻¹¹ is recorded in the late priestly section of Josh. 17³⁻⁶, from which it is clear that the daughters were originally tribes.

[d] Nu. 27¹ *Of the families of Manasseh*, is probably secondary.

[e] Nu. 27⁴ Lit., *be taken away, withdrawn.*

[f] Nu. 27¹¹ Lit., *statute of an ordinance.*

§ 32 This traditional precedent is a supplement of the preceding. Its object is to render it impossible for ancestral property to pass from a clan.

[g] Nu. 36¹ It is possible that for *family* we should here read *families*, cf. 26³⁰.

[h] Nu. 36¹ Gk. adds, *and, before Eleazar the high priest.*

73

Supplemental Priestly Codes

had our brother to his daughters. ³If now they marry any of the sons of the other tribes of the Israelites, then their inheritance will be withdrawn from the inheritance of our fathers and will be added to the inheritance of the tribes to which their husbands belong; thus something will be taken away from the lot of our inheritance. ⁴When the jubilee of the Israelites shall come, then their inheritance will be added to the inheritance of the tribe to which their husbands belong; thus their inheritance will be withdrawn from the inheritance of the tribe of our fathers.ⁱ

Ruling that female heirs shall not alienate property from their clan

⁵Then Moses gave this command to the Israelites in accord with the word of Jehovah : The tribe of the sons of Joseph have spoken right. ⁶This is the thing which Jehovah doth command concerning the daughters of Zelophehad, They may marry whom they think best; only they shall intermarry in the family of their father's tribe, ⁷so that no inheritance of the Israelites shall pass from one tribe to another tribe; for the Israelites shall retain each the inheritance of the tribe of his fathers. ⁸Every daughter who cometh into possession of an inheritance of any tribe of the Israelites, shall become the wife of one of the family of her father's tribe, that the Israelites may possess each the inheritance of his father, ⁹and that no inheritance may pass from one tribe to another; for the tribes of the Israelites shall cleave each to his own inheritance.

The traditional precedent

¹⁰Even as Jehovah commanded Moses, so did the daughters of Zelophehad; ¹¹for Mahlah, Tirzah, Hoglah, Milcah, and Noah, the daughters of Zelophehad, were married to their father's cousins. ¹²They were married into the families of the sons of Manasseh the son of Joseph; and so their inheritance remained in the tribe of their father's family.

ⁱ Nu. 36⁴ This was probably added by a scribe who had in mind Lev. 25¹³⁻¹⁶.

CONSTITUTIONAL LAWS

CONSTITUTIONAL LAWS

A

POLITICAL ORGANIZATION

§ 33. Qualifications for Citizenship, Dt. 23¹⁻⁸

Deuteronomic Codes

Dt. 23 ¹No one who is wounded in the stones or hath his privy member Eu-
cut off may enter into the assembly of Jehovah.[a] ²No bastard shall enter nuchs and
into the assembly of Jehovah; even to the tenth generation none of his bas-
descendants shall enter into the assembly of Jehovah.   dis-

³No Ammonite or Moabite shall enter into the assembly of Jehovah; quali-
never even to the tenth generation shall one belonging to them enter into the Also
assembly of Jehovah, ⁴because they did not meet you with bread and water mon-
in the way,[b] when ye came forth from Egypt, and because they hired against ites and
thee Balaam the son of Beor from Pethor of Aram Naharaim,[c] to curse thee. ites
⁵Nevertheless Jehovah thy God would not hearken to Balaam; but Jehovah

---

Political Organization.—The life of the Hebrews before the exile was so simple that
few constitutional laws were necessary. Their political organization was not the result of
legislative enactments; it was rather the outgrowth of primitive institutions and an adaptation of these to new needs. The original unit of Hebrew as well as of all Semitic society was
the family. In time, by the natural processes of intermarriage and generation, this grew into
the clan and tribe. Theoretically all members of the clan or tribe were direct descendants of the
same ancestors; but as a matter of fact it contained in the past, as do Arab tribes to-day, many
aliens, admitted either through intermarriage or adoption or as slaves. Just as the head of
the family was the father, so the most powerful and representative elder was head of the clan
or tribe. As to-day, the sheik was usually chosen from a certain leading family; but he was
not necessarily succeeded by his oldest son. The ablest man, the one possessing the greatest
resources, whether in actual wealth or physical strength or intellectual acumen or personal
prestige and influence, was chosen by the members of the tribe as their leader in war, and
their arbiter in cases of dispute. It is important to note that his authority was not absolute;
it rested on common consent; he was but the servant of the tribal community. His counsel-
lors were the tribal chieftains and elders, who represented the different clans and families.

By almost unconscious stages the kingdom grew out of this simpler institution. In the
days of the Judges certain leaders successfully espoused a common cause. Because they
brought deliverance and protection their authority was recognized during their lifetime by a
local federation of tribes, but at their death the union was dissolved. When, however, the
energetic, able Philistines threatened the independence of all the Hebrew tribes, in desperation
they called one of their local chiefs, who had demonstrated in a war with the Ammonites his

---

[a] Dt. 23¹ This expression evidently means that he shall not share the religious privileges
of the temple. A reference to this law is found in Lam. 1¹⁰.

[b] Dt. 23⁴ According to the ancient Heb. tradition in Gen. 19³⁰⁻³⁸, the Ammonites and
Edomites were regarded as bastards. With deeper historical insight, a later editor traces
the exclusive attitude to the ancient hostility between the Hebrews and their vindictive neighbors across the Jordan. He may well have had in mind the cruel advantages which they took
at the time when Jerusalem was destroyed and the Jews were fugitives or in exile.

[c] Dt. 23⁴ᵃ Cf. Nu. 20¹⁹⁻²¹.

Deuteronomic Codes

thy God turned the curse into a blessing for thee, because Jehovah thy God loved thee.[d] ⁶Thou shalt never seek their peace nor their prosperity all thy days.

But not Edomites and Egyptians ⁷Thou shalt not abhor an Edomite, for he is thy kinsman; thou shalt not abhor an Egyptian,[e] because thou wast a resident alien in his land. ⁸The children of the third generation that are born to them may enter into the assembly of Jehovah.

§ 34. The Census, Nu. 1¹⁻³, 3¹⁴, ¹⁵, 4¹⁻³

Supplemental Priestly Codes

Census of those available for war **Nu. 1** ¹Jehovah gave this command to Moses in the Wilderness of Sinai, in the tent of meeting, on the first day of the second month, in the second year after they had come out of the land of Egypt: ²Take a census of all the congregation of the Israelites, by their families, by their fathers' houses, according to the number of the names, all the males, by their heads, ³from twenty years old and upward, all in Israel who are able to go forth to war, shalt thou and Aaron [f]number by their hosts.

Of the Levites **3** ¹⁴Jehovah also commanded Moses in the Wilderness of Sinai: ¹⁵Number the Levites by their fathers' houses, by their families, every male from a month old and upward shalt thou number them. **4** ¹Jehovah gave this command to Moses and Aaron: ²Take a census of the Kohathites from among the Levites, by their families, by their fathers' houses, ³from thirty years old and upward even to fifty years old, all who enter upon the service, to do the work in the tent of meeting.

§ 35. Division of the Land, Josh. 18²⁻¹⁰, Nu. 26⁵²⁻⁵⁶ [33⁵⁴]

Deuteronomic Codes

The late prophetic tradition regarding the original allotment of Canaan **Josh. 18** ²Since there remained among the Israelites seven tribes which had not yet divided their inheritance, ³Joshua said to the Israelites, How

ability to lead, to guide and represent them not only during his own life but at his death to transmit his authority to his descendants. Thus the Hebrew kingship came into existence. All its traditions were democratic. The king was deliberately chosen as the servant of the people. The only native precedents to shape its development were those connected with the earlier institution of the sheik. In time the immediate followers and supporters of the king grew into a nobility that in part took the place of the earlier tribal elders. The city organization also succeeded that of the clan; but the old tribal bonds never entirely disappeared, and the people always clung tenaciously to their popular rights in opposition to the despotic policies introduced by such rulers as Solomon and Ahab.

[d] Dt. 23⁴ᵇ, ⁵ Cf. Vol. I, § 98. The later editor who added these vss. evidently had before him the present composite narrative of Nu. 22, 23.

[e] Dt. 23⁷ The older hostile attitude toward the Egyptians has evidently disappeared, and the law reflects the later days when, before the exile, the Egyptians were the only allies of the Hebrews.

§ 34 The early Hebrews like the modern Arabs of the desert, regarded the taking of a census as displeasing to the Deity, cf. II Sam. 24, Vol. II, § 33. The earlier laws accordingly contain no regulations concerning it. Not until the Israelites had come into contact with the Babylonians and Persians did they formulate a definite census law. This was cast in the form of a legal precedent associated with Moses. Its theoretical and priestly character is obvious. It is one of the many very late traditional precedents by which the priestly schools aimed to establish on a Mosaic basis the institutions of their own day.

[f] Nu. 1³ This clause is probably a late addition.

§ 35 The tradition that the land of Canaan was originally divided among the Hebrew tribes

Deuteronomic Codes

long will you be remiss in taking possession of the land which Jehovah the God of your fathers hath given you? ⁴Appoint three men from each tribe and I will send them, and they shall arise and walk through the land, and mark it out for their inheritance; then they shall come to me. ⁵And they shall divide it into seven divisions for themselves. Judah shall remain in his territory on the south, and the house of Joseph shall remain in their territory on the north. ⁶And ye shall mark out the land into seven divisions, and bring the plan here to me. Then I will cast lots for you here before Jehovah your God. ⁷For the Levites have no portion among you, inasmuch as the priesthood of Jehovah is their inheritance; and Gad and Reuben and the half-tribe of Manasseh have received their inheritance on the east side of the Jordan, which Moses the servant of Jehovah gave them.

⁸So the men arose and departed. And Joshua gave this command to those who went to mark out the land: Go and walk through the land, and mark it out and come again to me; and I will cast lots for you here before Jehovah in Shiloh. ⁹So the men went and passed through the land and marked it out in a book by cities into seven divisions; then they came to Joshua to the camp at Shiloh. ¹⁰And Joshua cast lots for them in Shiloh before Jehovah. Thus Joshua there divided the land among the Israelites according to their divisions.

Supplemental Priestly Codes

Nu. 26 ⁵²Jehovah said to Moses, ⁵³Among these the land shall be apportioned as an inheritance according to the number of names. ⁵⁴To the large tribe thou shalt give a proportionately large inheritance, and to the smaller tribe thou shalt give a proportionately small inheritance, to each according to those who are numbered as belonging to it shall its inheritance be given. ⁵⁵Yet the land shall be divided by lot, according to the names of the tribes of their fathers they shall inherit. ⁵⁶According to the lot shall their inheritance be divided between the more numerous and less numerous tribes.

The later priestly version

§ 36. Respect Due Rulers, Ex. 22²⁸ᵇ

Primitive Codes

Ex. 22 ²⁸ᵇThou shalt not curse a ruler of thy people.ᵍ

Not to curse a ruler

by lot, comes from the comparatively late period when the actual process by which they became possessed of their final abiding place had long been forgotten. The original basis is apparently a later Judean prophetic story but this has been reversed by a Deuteronomic editor, so that in its final form it may here be classified with the Deuteronomic laws. Cf. Vol. I, § 117. The late priestly precedents in Nu. 25⁵²⁻⁵⁶, 33⁵⁴ were intended to guide the returning exiles in establishing their individual titles to the soil of Palestine. The version in Nu. 33⁵⁴ is simply an abbreviation of that in 25⁵²⁻⁵⁶.

§ 36 This brief law from the Ephraimite prophetic decalogue is linked with the command not to revile God. Evidently in the mind of the primitive lawgiver the civil rulers are regarded as the earthly representatives of the divine King.

ᵍ Ex. 22²⁸ᵇ Lit., *among thy people.*

§ 37. Qualifications and Duties of the King, Dt. 17¹⁴·²⁰

Deuteronomic Codes

Must be a native Israelite

Dt. 17 ¹⁴When thou comest to the land which Jehovah thy God is about to give thee, and shalt possess it, and shalt dwell in it, and shalt say to thyself, I will set over me a king as have all the nations that are round about me, ¹⁵be sure to set over thee as king him whom Jehovah thy God shall choose; one from among thy fellow Israelites shalt thou set over thee as king; thou mayst not put a foreigner over thee who is not a fellow Israelite.

Must avoid the crimes of Solomon

¹⁶Only he shall not provide many horses for himself, nor shall he cause people to return to Egypt in order that he may provide many horses, since Jehovah hath said to you, Ye shall never again return that way. ¹⁷Neither shall he take many wives for himself, lest his heart turn away; neither shall he collect for himself great quantities of silver and gold.

Must rule in accord with the Deuteronomic laws

¹⁸And when he sitteth upon his kingly throne he shall write for himself in a book a copy of this law which is in the charge of the Levitical priests;[h] ¹⁹and he shall have it always with him, and he shall read in it daily as long as he liveth, that he may learn to fear Jehovah his God, to take heed to observe all the words of this law and these statutes, ²⁰that his heart be not lifted up above his kinsmen, and that he turn aside from this command neither to the right nor to the left in order that he and his descendants may continue long to rule in the midst of Israel.

B

MILITARY REGULATIONS

I

ORGANIZATION OF THE ARMY

§ 38. Legal Age of Service, Nu. 26²ᵃ· ³ᵃ [1²· ³]

Priestly Codes

Twenty years and over

Nu. 26 ²ᵃTake a census of all the congregation of the Israelites, ³ᵃfrom twenty years old and upward, all in Israel who are able to go forth to war in Israel.

---

§ 37 These laws seek primarily to regulate those abuses which became most glaringly apparent in the reigns of Solomon and Ahab, cf. I Kgs. 10¹⁴–11¹³. They aim to maintain the original, simple, democratic ideal of the Hebrew kingship against the seductive and subversive influence which came in from the neighboring despotisms. In effect these regulations make the king a constitutional ruler, who stands in striking contrast to the tyrants who ruled in all the neighboring states. They also assume that primitive Hebrew conception of the king, as Jehovah's representative, responsible for all his acts to the Divine Sovereign, which was the historical and abiding basal idea of the theocracy.

[h] Dt. 17¹⁸ *I. e.*, in the central sanctuary. Cf. 31⁹, ²⁶.

Organization of the Army.—Except the royal body guard of six hundred in the days of David, cf. Vol. II, § 34, the Hebrews do not appear to have maintained a standing army. Throughout all their history their main defence was the militia, which was called out only in

§ 39. Exemptions from Military Service, Dt. 20¹ᵃ, ⁵⁻⁷. 24⁵, Nu. 1⁴⁸, ⁴⁹, 2³³

Deuteronomic Codes

Dt. 20 ¹ᵃWhen ye go out to fight against your foes, ⁵the officers shall speak to the people, saying, What man is there that hath built a new house but not dedicated it? let him go and return to his house, lest he die in the battle, and another man dedicate it. ⁶And what man is there that hath planted a vineyard, but not partaken of its fruit?ⁱ let him return to his house, lest he die in battle, and another man use its fruits.

⁷If there is any who is betrothed to a wife, but hath not married her, let him go and return to his house, lest he die in battle, and another man marry her.

24 ⁵When a man is newly married he shall not go out in the military service,ʲ neither shall any business be imposed upon him; he shall stay at home one year to attend to his household,ᵏ and shall give pleasure to his wife whom he hath married.

Those who have just completed a house or vineyard

A betrothed man

A newly married man

Supplemental Priestly Codes

Nu. 1 ⁴⁸For Jehovah spoke thus to Moses: ⁴⁹Only the tribe of Levi shalt thou not number, neither shalt thou take a census of them among the Israelites. **2** ³³So the Levites were not numbered among the Israelites, as Jehovah commanded Moses.

Levites

§ 40. Minor Officers, Dt. 20⁹, 11¹ᵃ, ¹³⁻¹⁵

Deuteronomic Codes

Dt. 20 ⁹When the officers have made an end of speaking to the people, they shall appoint commanders of the forces over the people.

1 ¹ᵃThese are the words which Moses spoke to all Israel, ¹³Take for your tribes men who are wise, intelligent, and known, that I may make them officers over you. ¹⁴And ye answered me, 'The thing which thou proposest to do is good.' ¹⁵So I took the heads of your tribes, men of wisdom and reputation, and made them officers over you, captains of thousands and captains of hundreds, and captains of fifties, and captains of tens, and officers according to your tribes.

Appointment

The Mosaic precedent

time of war and at the close of the campaign disbanded. Practically all able-bodied men over twenty years of age were eligible for military service. The king was the head of the army with experienced officers under him. The forces were divided into regiments, companies, and smaller bands of fifty and ten, commanded by officers chosen, probably, from the local tribes and cities represented.

§ 39 These laws strikingly illustrate the idealism of the Deuteronomic codes: the belief that Jehovah will deliver his people if they are loyal to him, is so strong that the humane principle is unhesitatingly applied to specific cases where forced service might bring especial discomfort. The humane laws also reveal the growing interest in the welfare of the individual that characterizes these later codes. First Mac. 3⁵⁶ states that Judas observed these laws; but otherwise there is no evidence that they were at other times practically enforced. In the very late priestly precedent, in Nu. 1 and 2, only the Levites are exempted from military service.

ⁱ Dt. 20⁶ Lit., *treated it as common, i. e.,* partaken of its fruit after the firstfruit had been set aside as sacred to Jehovah.

ʲ Dt. 24⁵ Lit., *host.*

ᵏ Dt. 24⁵ Lit., *for his house.*

§ 40 According to I Mac. 3⁵⁵, Judas Maccabus appointed on the battle-field the commanders of thousands, hundreds, fifties, and tens. This law is also substantiated by the later priestly precedent in Nu. 1⁴⁻¹⁶ which, like that in Dt. 1¹³⁻¹⁵, traces the custom back to Moses. It is probably very ancient. The commanders thus appointed were the tribal chieftains already familiar with war and leadership.

II

REGULATIONS GOVERNING THE ARMY IN THE FIELD

§ 41. Cleanliness of the Camp, Dt. 23⁹⁻¹⁴

Deuteronomic Codes

Each
man to
guard
against
pollut-
ing it

Dt. 23 ⁹When thou goest forth in a military campaign against thine enemies, thou shalt keep thyself from every evil thing. ¹⁰If there be among you anyone who is not clean as the result of an accident by night, then he shall go away outside the camp, he must not come inside the camp. ¹¹But when evening cometh on, he shall bathe himself in water; and when the sun is set he may come inside the camp. ¹²Thou shalt have a place also outside the camp, to which thou shalt go out; ¹³and thou shalt have a paddle¹ among thy weapons, and when thou sittest down outside thou shalt dig a hole with it, and shalt turn back and cover thy excrement, ¹⁴for Jehovah thy God ever goeth about in the midst^m of thy camp, to deliver thee and to give thine enemies into thy hands;^n therefore thy camp should be holy, that he may see no unclean thing in thee and turn away from thee.

§ 42. Manner of Attack, Dt. 20¹⁻⁴, ¹⁰⁻¹², Nu. 10⁹

Deuteronomic Codes

En-
cour-
age-
ment
to be
brave
and
trust in
God

Dt. 20 ¹When thou goest forth to battle against thine enemies, and seest horses and chariots, and a people more than thou, be not afraid of them; for Jehovah thy God is with thee, he who brought thee up from the land of Egypt. ²And when ye draw near to offer battle, the priest shall approach and speak to the people, ³and say to them, Hear O Israel, ye are drawing near this day to fight against your enemies; do not lose heart, fear not, nor tremble, neither be afraid because of them; ⁴for Jehovah your God is going with you, to fight for you against your enemies in order to deliver you.

Pre-
limi-
naries
preced-
ing the
attack

¹⁰When thou drawest near to a city to fight against it, proclaim peace to it.^o ¹¹And if it make a peaceful response and open its gates to thee, then shall all the people that are found in it be compelled to do forced labor for thee and serve thee. ¹²But if it make no peace with thee but offer battle against thee, then thou shalt lay siege against it.

---

§ 41 While this law was of practical hygienic value, the motive which gave rise to it was evidently religious and ceremonial. The simple anthromorphic conception of Jehovah in ¹⁴ suggests that this law in its present form comes from an early period. From I Sam. 21⁵ it may be inferred that the weapons of war, and probably the person of the warriors, were in ancient times solemnly consecrated. Cf. also II Sam. 1²¹. The priestly law of Nu. 5¹⁻⁴ states that in the traditional march through the wilderness all lepers were excluded from the camp. Every one ceremonially impure, either because of an issue, Lev. 15²,¹⁵, or from contact with a corpse, was also shut out; but these laws, though based upon the same principle as the former, make no reference to a military camp.

¹ Dt. 23¹³ Lit., *tent pin, i. e.,* that is something pointed or similar in form to a tent pin.

^m Dt. 23¹⁴ Lit., *going to and fro.* It means that Jehovah accompanied his people in all their campaigns.

^n Dt. 23¹⁴ Lit., *before thee.*

^o Dt. 20¹⁰ *I. e.,* give it a chance to surrender without being attacked.

§ 42 War is regarded as inevitable by the lawgivers. Their effort is to regulate as far as possible its barbarity and to prevent needless loss of life.

Priestly Codes

Nu. 10 ⁹When ye go to war in your land against the foe that oppresseth you, ye shall sound an alarm with the trumpets; and ye shall be remembered before Jehovah your God, and ye shall be saved from your enemies. *Call to battle*

§ 43. Division of the Booty, I Sam. 30²¹⁻²⁵

Primitive Codes

I Sam. 30 ²¹Now when David came to the two hundred men, who had been too faint to follow him, so that he had to leave them behind at the Brook Besor, they went out to meet David, and the people who were with him. And when they came near to the people, they saluted them. ²²Then all the wicked and base scoundrels among the men who went with David began to say, Because they did not go with us, we will not give them any of the spoils that we have recovered, except to each, his wife and his children, that he may take them away and depart. ²³But David said, Do not so, my brothers, after that which Jehovah hath given us, and after he hath preserved us and delivered the marauding band that came against us into our hand. ²⁴And who will give heed to you in this matter, for— *Origin of the law of equal distribution of booty*

As is the share of him who goeth down into battle,
So is the share of him who remaineth with the baggage.
They shall all share alike.

²⁵And from that time on he made it a statute and precedent in Israel to this day.

§ 44. Disposal of the Spoils and Captives, Dt. 20¹⁰, ¹²⁻¹⁸, 7¹, ², ¹⁶, ²²⁻²⁶, 20¹⁹, ²⁰, 21¹⁰⁻¹⁴, Nu. 31¹ᵃ, ², ³, ⁷⁻¹⁸, ²¹⁻³¹

Deuteronomic Codes

Dt. 20 ¹⁰When thou drawest near to a city to fight against it, proclaim peace to it. ¹²But if it make no peace with thee, but offer battle against thee, then thou shalt lay siege against it. ¹³And when Jehovah thy God delivereth it into thy hand, thou shalt put every male in it to the edge of the sword; ¹⁴but the women, and the little ones, and the animals, and all that is in the city, even all its spoil, shalt thou take to thyself as booty; and thou shalt eat the spoil of thine enemies, which Jehovah thy God hath given thee. *In the case of distant foes*

---

§ 43 This enactment, embedded in the early historical narratives, is especially interesting, for it illustrates one of the common ways in which a law came into existence. Cf. Introd., p. 12.
§ 44 It is a great relief to note that these laws enjoining the merciless destruction of the Canaanites and Midianites took form centuries after the conquest, and that the actual practice in the earlier day was far different. These laws also stand in striking contrast to the humane principles laid down by Amos, 1⁶, ¹³, and with the prevailingly philanthropic spirit of the codes in which they are found. The explanation lies in the fact that these later lawgivers are dealing not with present but past conditions, and are thinking not of the suffering of the innocent but of the glaring evils in Israel's character and religion which were directly traceable to the influence of the early Canaanitish inhabitants of the land, whom the Hebrews absorbed. These blood-thirsty laws were formulated in the days following the reaction of Manasseh when the true prophets of Jehovah were engaged in a death struggle with the old popular heathen cults. In essence they declare that it would have been better for Jehovah's people to have exterminated the evil, root and branch, than to have allowed it to remain a constant menace to Israel's true life and faith.

Deuteronomic Codes

[15]Thus shalt thou do to all the cities that are very far off from thee, which are not of the cities of these nations.

The peoples of Canaan

[16]But of the cities of these peoples, that Jehovah thy God giveth thee for an inheritance, thou shalt save alive nothing that breatheth; [17]but thou shalt utterly destroy[p] them, the Hittites, the Amorites, the Canaanites, the Perizzites, the Hivites, and the Jebusites, as Jehovah thy God hath commanded thee,[q] [18]that they may not teach you to do according to all their abominations, which they have done to their gods, and so ye sin against Jehovah your God. **7** [1]But when Jehovah thy God shall bring thee into the land which thou art going in to possess, and shall clear away many nations before thee, the Hittites, the Girgashites, the Amorites, the Canaanites, the Perizzites, the Hivites, and the Jebusites, seven nations greater and mightier than thou, [2]and when Jehovah thy God shall deliver them into thy hands and thou shalt smite them, then thou shalt completely destroy them without making any terms with them or without showing any mercy to them. [16]But thou shalt consume[r] all the peoples that Jehovah thy God shall deliver into thy power; thou shalt show them no pity; neither shalt thou serve their gods for that would be a snare to thee.

Gradual but complete extermination of both peoples and cults

[22]And Jehovah thy God will clear away those nations before thee little by little; thou mayst not consume them all at once, lest the wild beasts become too numerous for thee. [23]But Jehovah thy God will deliver them into thy hand and will throw them into great confusion, until they are destroyed. [24]And he will deliver their kings into thy hand, and thou shalt blot out their name from the earth;[s] no man will be able to stand before thee until thou hast destroyed them. [25]The graven images of their gods shall ye burn with fire; thou shalt not covet the silver or the gold that is on them, nor take it for thyself, lest thou be snared thereby, for it is an abomination to Jehovah thy God. [26]And thou shalt not bring an abomination into thy house, lest thou fall like it under the ban;[t] thou shalt utterly detest and abhor it, for it is placed under the ban.

Fruit trees to be spared even in war

20 [19]When thou shalt besiege a city a long time in making war against it in order to capture it, thou shalt not destroy its trees by wielding an ax against them; thou mayest eat of them, but thou shalt not cut them down; for is the tree of the field a man, that it should be besieged by thee?[u] [20]Only the trees which thou knowest are not fruit trees, thou mayst destroy and cut, that thou mayst build siege-works against the city that maketh war with thee, until it fall.

Permission to marry a female captive

21 [10]When thou goest forth to battle against thine enemies, and Jehovah thy God delivereth them into thy hands, and thou carriest them away captive [11]and seest among the captives a beautiful woman, and thou

---

[p] Dt. 20[17] Lit., *place under the ban, devote.*
[q] Dt. 20[17] *E. g.*, 7[2], Ex. 23[31-33].
[r] Dt. 7[16] Lit., *eat.*
[s] Dt. 7[24] The Heb. idiom is, *make their name to perish from under heaven.*
[t] Dt. 7[26] *I. e., be given up to destruction.*
[u] Dt. 20[19] Following the Gk. and Lat. in translating this clause as a question.

Deuteronomic Codes

hast a desire for her, and wouldst make her thy wife, [12]then thou shalt bring her home to thy house; and she shall shave her head and pare her nails, [13]and she shall put off the garb of her captivity and shall remain in thy house, and bewail her father and her mother a full month; after that thou shalt go in unto her, and be her husband, and she shall be thy wife. [14]But if thou have no delight in her, then thou shalt let her go where she will; but thou shalt not sell her in any case for money; thou shalt not deal with her as a slave, because thou hast humbled her.

Supplemental Priestly Codes

Nu. 31 [1a]Jehovah said to Moses, [2]Avenge the Israelites on the Midian- The ites; afterward thou shalt be gathered to thy father's kin. [3]Therefore Moses tradi- gave this command to the people: Equip men from among you for the war, priestly that they may go against Midian, to execute Jehovah's vengeance on Midian. dent [7]So they made war on Midian, as Jehovah commanded Moses, and slew every male. [8]They also slew the kings of Midian with the rest of their slain: Evi, Rekem, Zur, Hur, and Reba, the five kings of Midian; Balaam, too, the son of Beor, they slew with the sword.

[9]And the Israelites took captive the women of Midian with their little Dis- ones. And all their cattle, and all their flocks, and all their goods they took posal as booty. [10]But all their cities, in the places in which they dwelt, and all tives their enclosures they burnt with fire. [11]And they took all the spoil and all and the booty both of man and of beast. [12]And they brought the captives, and booty the booty and the spoil to Moses and Eleazar the priest, and to the congrega- tion of the Israelites at the camp in the plains of Moab, which are by the Jordan at Jericho.

[13]Then when Moses and Eleazar the priest, and all the princes of the More congregation, went forth to meet them outside the camp, [14]Moses was angry instruc- with the officers of the host, the captains of thousands and the captains of regard- hundreds, who came from the service of the war. [15]And Moses said to cap- them, Have you saved all the women alive? [16]Behold, these caused tives the Israelites, through the counsel of Balaam, to break faith with Jehovah booty in the affair of Peor, and so the plague was among the congregation of Jehovah. [17]Now therefore kill every male among the little ones, and kill every woman who has entered into marital relations. [18]But all the female children, who have not entered into marital relations, keep alive for your- selves.

[21]And Eleazar the priest said to the warriors who went to the battle, This De- is the statute of the law which Jehovah hath commanded Moses, [22]' Only the direc- gold, the silver, the brass, the iron, the tin, and the lead,—[23]every thing that tions re- may be put into the fire, ye shall put through the fire, that it may be clean; their it shall surely be purified by means of the water of impurity; and all that can cere- not be put into the fire you shall put through the water. [24]And ye shall wash purifi- your clothes on the seventh day, and shall be clean; and afterwards ye shall cation come into the camp.'

Supplemental Priestly Codes

Jehovah's portion of the spoil for the priests

²⁵Then Jehovah commanded Moses, ²⁶Make an estimate of the booty that was taken, both of man and of beast, thou, and Eleazar the priest, and the heads of the fathers' *houses* of the congregation, ²⁷and divide the booty into two parts; between the men skilled in war, who went out to battle, and all the congregation. ²⁸And levy a contribution for Jehovah upon the warriors who went out to battle : one in five hundred, of the persons, and of the oxen, and of the asses, and of the flocks : ²⁹take it from their half, and give it to

Portion of the Levites

Eleazar the priest, as a special contribution to Jehovah. ³⁰And from the Israelites' half thou shalt take one drawn out of every fifty, of the persons, of the oxen, of the asses, and of the flocks, *even* of all the cattle, and give them to the Levites who have charge of the dwelling of Jehovah. ³¹And Moses and Eleazar the priest did as Jehovah commanded Moses.

C

The Judiciary

§ 45. Appointment of Judges, Ex. 18¹³⁻²⁶, Dt. 16¹⁸ᵃ

Primitive Codes

Moses' work as judge

Ex. 18 ¹³Now Moses sat as judge to decide cases for the people, and the people stood about Moses from morning until evening. ¹⁴But when Moses' father-in-law saw all that he was doing for the people, he said, What is this thing that you are doing for the people? why are you sitting all alone while all the people stand about you from morning until evening? ¹⁵And Moses answered his father-in-law, Because the people keep coming to me to inquire of God. ¹⁶Whenever they have a matter of dispute, they come

---

The Judiciary.—In its method of administering justice the ancient East differed widely from the modern West. The most striking difference was the absence in the ancient East of any distinct judicial organization. Political, judicial and religious duties were often discharged by the same officials. In Egypt, Babylonia and Israel the judges to whom cases were referred were quite invariably either civil officers or priests. Every prominent public official, from the king himself to the local tribal elders, could thus be called upon to act as judges. The result was that justice often miscarried for lack of system and a responsible organization to attend to its execution. Also in Babylonia, Egypt, and ancient Israel, most cases were tried not before one but several associated judges. In Babylonia such a judicial body might consist of from four to twelve, among whom were often found civil officials, scribes, priests and elders. A similar mixed court was established at Jerusalem during the latter days of the monarchy.

In ancient Israel, however, ordinary cases were decided by the tribal or local elders assembled at the city gates, or else by the priests to whom the questions in dispute were referred at the local sanctuary and later at the temple at Jerusalem. Important cases could be carried to the king, as the ultimate authority, or later to the central court at Jerusalem, cf. § 47. It is not clear what determined the choice of a court. Probably much liberty was allowed to the individual litigants. If a crime was involved, the community or the local elders or the priests doubtless took the initiative, according to the nature of the offence.

In the ancient East the litigants each presented and pled his own case, although in preparing it he was free to utilize the services of friends or scribes. The plaintiff and defendant, in Babylonia at least, also produced their own witnesses, who were duly sworn and carefully examined. For a full and illuminating presentation of the facts regarding judges, law-courts and legal processes, cf. John's *Bab. and Assyr. Laws, Contracts and Letters*, pp. 80–112.

§ 45 The early Ephraimite prophetic account of Moses' activity as judge throws much light upon the origin of Israel's judiciary, cf. Introd., pp. 10, 11. The explicit law directing the establishment of local courts is comparatively late.

Primitive Codes

to me, that I may decide which of the two is right, and make known the
statutes of God, and his decisions.

¹⁷Then Moses' father-in-law said to him, This thing which you are doing His ex-
is not good. ¹⁸Both you and these people who are about you will surely ample
wear yourselves out, for the task is too heavy for you; you are not able to point-
perform it by yourself alone. ¹⁹Now hearken to me, I will give you good judges
counsel, so that God will be with you : You be the people's advocate with
God, and bring the cases to God, ²⁰and you make known to them the statutes
and the decisions, and show them the way wherein they must walk, and the
work that they must do. ²¹Moreover you must provide out of all the people
able, God-fearing, reliable men, hating unjust gain; and place such over them
to be rulers of thousands, rulers of hundreds, rulers of fifties, and rulers of
tens; ²²and let them judge the people at all times. Only every great matter
let them bring to you; but every small matter let them decide themselves; so
it will be easier for you, and they will bear the burden with you. ²³If you
do this thing and God so commands you, then you will be able to endure,
and all these people also will go back to their places satisfied. ²⁴So Moses
hearkened to the advice of his father-in-law, and did all that he had said.
²⁵And Moses chose able men out of all Israel, and made them heads over
the people, rulers of thousands, rulers of hundreds, rulers of fifties and rulers
of tens. ²⁶And they judged the people at all times; the difficult cases they
brought to Moses, but every small matter they decided themselves. ²⁷Then
Moses let his father-in-law depart, and he went his way to his own land.

Deuteronomic Codes

Dt. 16 ¹⁸ᵃJudges and officers shalt thou appoint according to thy tribes Local
in all the cities which Jehovah is about to give thee. judges

§ 46. **Duties of Judges**, Ex. 23⁶⁻⁸, Dt. 16¹⁸ᵇ⁻²⁰, 1¹⁶, ¹⁷, 27²⁵, 25¹, ², Lev. 19¹⁵ [35]

Primitive Codes

Ex. 23 ⁶Thou shalt not prevent justice being done to thy poor in his To ad-
cause. ⁷Keep aloofᵃ from every false matter.ᵇ Do not condemnᶜ the inno- ter jus-
cent nor him who hath a just cause. Do not vindicateᵈ the wicked. ⁸Thou tice to
shalt take no bribe, for a bribe blindeth the eyes of those who see and per- classes
verteth the cause of the righteous.ᵉ alike

---

§ 46 The strong emphasis which the prophets placed on justice, especially in the law-
courts, left its deep impress on Israel's laws. To insure justice to all alike was one of the
chief aims of the Deuteronomic codes.
The same lofty purpose actuated Hammurabi. This is illustrated by the drastic punishment which he directs to be inflicted upon a judge suspected of rendering a decision under
unjust influence:
§ 5 *If a judge has given a verdict, rendered a decision, granted a written judgment, and
afterward has altered his judgment, that judge shall be prosecuted for altering the judgment
he gave and shall pay twelvefold the penalty laid down in that judgment. Further, he shall be
publicly expelled from his judgment-seat and shall not return nor take his seat with the judges
at a trial.*
ᵃ Ex. 23⁷ Lit., *keep far away from.*
ᵇ Ex. 23⁷ *I. e.,* every crooked conspiracy to prevent justice.
ᶜ Ex. 23⁷ Lit., *do not slay.*
ᵈ Ex. 23⁷ So Gk. which has clearly preserved the original text.
ᵉ Ex. 23⁸ Or, *righteous matters.*

Deuteronomic Codes

Dt. 16 ¹⁸ᵇThe judges shall judge the people with righteous judgment. ¹⁹Thou shalt not prevent justice; thou shalt not show partiality;[f] neither shalt thou take a bribe, for a bribe blindeth the eyes of the wise and perverteth the words[g] of the righteous. ²⁰Justice and only justice[h] shalt thou follow, that thou mayst live and inherit the land which the Lord thy God giveth thee.

To be influenced only by the principles of justice

1 ¹⁶At that time[i] Moses said, I give your judges this charge, ' Hear the cases between your fellow countrymen, and judge righteously between a man and his neighbor, and the alien residing with him. ¹⁷Ye shall be impartial in judgment; ye shall give equal hearing to the weak and strong; ye shall not be afraid of any man; for the judgment is God's; and the case that is too difficult for you, bring to me and I will hear it.'

Public censure

27 ²⁵Cursed be he who taketh a bribe to condemn[j] an innocent person. And all the people shall say, So let it be.

Judge to witness corporal punishment

25 ¹If there be a controversy between men and they come for a decision, and judgment is pronounced upon them, with the result that the righteous is vindicated and the wicked condemned, ²and if the culprit deserveth to be beaten, then the judge shall make him lie down and be beaten in his presence with the number of blows corresponding to his crime.[k]

Holiness Code

To be absolutely impartial

Lev. 19 ¹⁵Ye shall do no injustice in rendering a judicial decision.[l] Thou shalt not show partiality to the poor nor have undue consideration for the powerful; but justly shalt thou judge thy neighbor.

§ 47. The Supreme Court of Appeal, Dt. 17⁸⁻¹¹

Deuteronomic Codes

Difficult cases to be referred to it

Dt. 17 ⁸If a question involve bloodshed or conflicting claims, or the plague of leprosy,[m]—questions of controversy within thy city too difficult for thee to decide,—then thou shalt set out and go up to the place which the Lord thy God shall choose; ⁹and thou shalt come to the Levitical priests, and to the judge who shall be officiating in those days; and thou shalt inquire; and they shall make known to thee the proper judicial sentence.

---

[f] Dt. 16¹⁹ Lit., *Know the faces of;* RV, *respect persons.*
[g] Dt. 16¹⁹ Lit., *words, statements.*
[h] Dt. 16²⁰ Lit., *Justice, justice.* The repetition intensifies the form of the command.
[i] Dt. 1¹⁶ The event referred to is recorded in Ex. 18. Cf. § 45.
[j] Dt. 27²⁵ Lit., *to slay.*
[k] Dt. 25² The law goes on to add that the blows inflicted must be limited to thirty-nine.
[l] Lev. 19¹⁵ The first command contained in the vs. is repeated in ³⁵.
§ 47 The O.T. furnishes no further information regarding the appointment and constitution of the central court at Jerusalem. In ancient times Moses, and later the Heb. kings (II Sam. 12¹⁻⁶, 15²), were the final arbiters in disputed questions. The tradition in Ex. 18 implies that Moses appointed a judicial body, somewhat similar to the one the existence of which is implied in Dt. 17⁸⁻¹¹. In II Chr. 19⁸⁻¹¹ the establishment of a central court of appeal, consisting of priests, Levites and the heads of the fathers' houses is attributed to Jehoshaphat. The late tradition may reflect historical facts, for the present law in Dt. implies that such a tribunal was in existence in the days of Josiah.
[m] Dt. 17⁸ Lit., *between blood and blood, between plea and plea, and between stroke and stroke,* i. e., criminal, civil, and ceremonial cases. The latter refers to a stroke, like a plague, especially leprosy, in connection with which the priests were expected to render a decision.

Deuteronomic Codes

[10]Thou shalt also act according to the tenor of the sentence which they Its de-
shall make known to thee from that place which Jehovah shall choose; and cisions
to be
thou shalt do exactly as they direct thee, [11]according to the tenor of the faithfully
instruction which they shall give thee, and according to the decision which exe-
they shall impart to thee, thou shalt do without departing from the sentence cuted
which they shall make known to thee, either to the right hand or to the left.

§ 48. Number of Witnesses Required to Convict, Dt. 19[15], 17[6], Nu. 35[30]

Deuteronomic Codes

Dt. 19 [15]One witness shall not stand up alone to testify against a man Two re-
for any crime, nor for any sin which he hath committed.[n] By the testimony quired
to con-
of two or three witnesses must a matter be established.   17 [6]On the testi- vict of
a crim-
mony of two or three witnesses shall a man be condemned to death; he shall inal
offence
not be put to death on the testimony of one witness.

Supplemental Priestly Codes

Nu. 35 [30]In every case of murder, the murderer shall be put to death
on the testimony of witnesses; on the testimony of but one witness shall no
one suffer death.

§ 49. Duties of Witnesses, Ex. 23[1-3] [20[16]], Dt. 5[20], 17[7], Lev. 19[16], 5[1]

Primitive Codes

Ex. 23 [1]Thou shalt not spread abroad a false report. Do not enter To tell
the
into a conspiracy with a wicked man to be an unrighteous witness. [2]Thou truth
shalt not follow the majority in doing what is wrong. Thou shalt not bear and
nothing
testimony in a case so as to pervert justice.[o] [3]Thou shalt not show par- but the
tiality to a poor man in his case. truth

Deuteronomic Codes

Dt. 5 [20]Thou shalt not bear false witness against thy neighbor. To take
the in-
17[7]The witnesses shall first raise their hands against a murderer to put itiative
him to death, and afterwards the hands of all the people. Thus thou shalt in the
execu-
purge away the evil from thy midst. tion of
a mur-
derer

---

§ 48 The eminent wisdom of this law, especially in capital offences, is obvious.
[n] Dt. 19[15] *I. e.*, a moral crime or some infringement of the ceremonial law.
§ 49 Prevarication is one of the most crying evils of the East. *A lie is the salt of a man* is
too often accepted as good ethics.   The Israelitish lawgivers strenuously sought to eliminate
this deadly menace to the purity of the courts.   The parties to a dispute were probably under
obligation to produce their witnesses, as in ancient Babylonia under Hammurabi:
§ 13 *If a man has not his witnesses at hand, the judge shall set him a fixed time not exceeding six months, and if within six months he has not produced his witnesses, the man has lied; he
shall bear the penalty of the suit.*
[o] Ex. 23[2] Following a corrected text.

Holiness Code

Not to repeat malign charges

Lev. 19 [16]Thou shalt not go about as a tale bearer among thy people; nor shalt thou seek the blood of thy neighbor:[p] I am Jehovah.

Priestly Codes

Not to conceal testimony

Lev. 5 [1]If anyone sin when under oath as a witness by failing to give information concerning what he hath seen or known,[q] he shall bear the consequences of his iniquity.

§ 50. Punishment of False Witnesses, Dt. 19[16-21]

Deuteronomic Codes

To suffer the penalty of the crime unjustly charged

Dt. 19 [16]If a malicious witness stand up against a man to accuse him of treason,[r] [17]then both the men who have the dispute shall stand before Jehovah, before the priests and the judges who shall be officiating in those days; [18]and the judges shall thoroughly investigate; and should it prove that the witness is a false witness, and hath testified falsely against his countryman, [19]then shall ye do to him as he purposed to do to his fellow countryman; thus thou shalt purge away the evil from thy midst, [20]that those who remain may heed and fear, and never again commit any such crime in thy midst. [21]And thou shalt not show pity;[s] life for life, eye for eye, tooth for tooth, hand for hand, foot for foot.

§ 51. Execution of Judicial Sentence, Dt. 25[2, 3]

Deuteronomic Codes

Judge to witness corporal punishment

Dt. 25 [2]If a culprit deserve to be beaten, the judge shall make him lie down and be beaten in his presence with the number of blows corresponding to his crime. [3]Forty blows may he inflict upon him, but no more, lest, if he add more blows than these, thy fellow countryman be held in contempt in thine eyes.

§ 52. Punishment for Contempt of Court, Dt. 17[12, 13]

Deuteronomic Codes

Refusal to accept sentence of supreme tribunal

Dt. 17 [12]Should a man act presumptuously, so as not to hearken to the priest who standeth to minister there before the Lord thy God, or to the

---

[p] Lev. 19[16] *I. e.*, by trying to bring a capital charge against him and probably also by false testimony in the courts.

[q] Lev. 5[1] Lit., *and heareth the voice of the oath, and is a witness whether he hath seen or known, if he do not give information.*

[r] Dt. 19[16] *I. e.*, against law and custom.

§ 50 The justice of the law is self-evident; the laxness of our modern legal usage is in unfortunate contrast to it.

[s] Dt. 19[21] Lit., *thine eye shall not show pity.*

§ 51 Punishment of the bastinado, as was common in Egypt, is evidently here contemplated. The law further voices the humane spirit of the Deuteronomic codes.

§ 52 The decision referred to is that of the central tribunal at Jerusalem. The severity of the punishment recalls Hammurabi's free use of the death penalty, or the barbarous severity of many of the old English laws. The law, however, was probably of the nature of a threat, for there is no evidence that it was actually enforced.

Deuteronomic Codes

judge, that man shall die. ¹³Thus thou shalt purge away the evil from Israel, that all the people may take heed, and fear, and never again act presumptuously.

§ 53. The Object of Cities of Refuge, Ex. 21¹²⁻¹⁴, Dt. 19¹⁻¹³, 4⁴¹⁻⁴³, Nu. 35⁹⁻¹⁵

Primitive Codes

Ex. 21 ¹²If a man strike another so that he die, the manslayer shall be put to death. ¹³If a man lie not in wait, but God deliver him into his hand, then I will appoint thee a place to which he may flee. ¹⁴If a man attack another maliciously to slay him by treachery, thou shalt take him from mine altar that he may be put to death.

Early law of altar-asylum

Deuteronomic Codes

Dt. 19 ¹When Jehovah thy God shall cut off the nations, whose land Jehovah thy God giveth thee, and thou shalt dispossess them, and shalt dwell in their cities, and in their houses, ²thou shalt set apart three cities for thyself in the midst of thy land, which Jehovah thy God is about to give thee as a possession. ³Thou shalt prepare the way, and divide the territory of thy land, which Jehovah thy God will let thee inherit, into three parts, that every manslayer may flee thither.

Three cities to be set aside as places of refuge

⁴And this is the rule in regard to the manslayer, who may flee thither and live : whoso killeth his neighbor accidentally without having been his enemy formerly, ⁵as for example when a man goeth into the forest with his neighbor to cut wood, and he swingeth the ax with his hand to cut down a tree,ᵗ and the head slippeth from the helve and striketh his neighbor, so that he die, the man shall flee to one of these cities and live; ⁶lest the avenger of blood pursue the manslayer, while he is enraged,ᵘ and overtake him, because the way is long, and take his life, although he did not deserve to die, since he was not formerly the dead man's enemy. ⁷Therefore I command that thou shalt set apart three cities. ⁸And if Jehovah thy God enlarge thy borders as he hath sworn to thy fathers, and give thee all the land which he promised to give to thy fathers, ⁹if thou shalt keep all this command to do it, which I command thee this day, in that thou love Jehovah thy God, and walk ever in his ways, then shalt thou add three other cities, besides these three, ¹⁰that innocent blood may not be shed in the midst of thy land, which Jehovah thy God giveth thee as an inheritance, and thus blood-guilt be upon thee.

For the deliverance of the innocent manslayer

¹¹But if any man hate his neighbor, and lie in wait for him, and attack

But not of the murderer

---

§ 53 The relentless Semitic law of blood revenge made a place of refuge for the innocent manslayer a necessity among the Hebrews. As among most ancient peoples, the altar-asylum was an established institution in Israel. The law in Ex. 21¹⁴ aims to guard against its abuse. When all the high places outside Jerusalem, with their altars, were abolished by the Deuteronomic law and the reform measures of Josiah, it became necessary to establish convenient cities of refuge. Apparently the towns selected were the sites of ancient shrines (cf. Josh. 20⁷, ⁸). thus comporting with the customs already fixed. Cf. also § 83.

ᵗ Dt. 19⁵ Lit., *his hand impelleth with the ax to cut down the tree.*
ᵘ Dt. 19⁶ Lit., *while his heart is hot.*

Deuteronomic Codes

The east-Jordan cities

him and strike him mortally so that he die, and the murderer flee to one of the cities of refuge, ^{12}the elders of his city shall send and bring him, and deliver him into the hand of the avenger of blood, that he may die. ^{13}Thou shalt have no mercy on him, but shall purge away the innocent blood from Israel, that it may go well with thee.

4 ^{41}Then Moses set apart three cities on the other side^v of the Jordan toward the sunrise, ^{42}that a manslayer who had slain his neighbor accidentally and without having been formerly his enemy might flee thither, and by fleeing to one of these cities might save his life: ^{43}Bezer in the wilderness on the table land for the Reubenites, Ramoth in Gilead for the Gadites, and Golan in Bashan for the Manassites.

Supplemental Priestly Codes

The later version of the law

Nu. 35 ^9Jehovah gave this command to Moses: ^{10}Speak thus to the Israelites, and say to them, 'When ye pass over the Jordan into the land of Canaan, ^{11}ye shall select as suitable for yourselves, cities to be cities of refuge for you, that the manslayer who killeth any person unintentionally may flee thither. ^{12}And the cities shall be a refuge from the avenger of blood, that the manslayer may not be put to death until he can stand before the congregation for judgment. ^{13}And the cities which ye shall give shall be for you six cities of refuge. ^{14}Ye shall set apart three^w cities beyond Jordan, and three cities shall ye set apart in the land of Canaan; they shall be cities of refuge. ^{15}These cities shall be a refuge for the Israelites and for the resident alien and the one who hath settled among them; that every one who hath killed another unintentionally may flee to them.'

D

POPULAR INSTRUCTION IN THE LAW

§ 54. Publishing the Law, Dt. 27^{1-4, 8}, Josh. 8^{30-32}

Deuteronomic Codes

Command to write the laws on plastered stones

Dt. 27 ^1Moses and the elders of Israel gave this command to the people: Keep all the commands which I lay upon you this day. ^2And

---

^v Dt. 4^{41} *I. e.*, on the east side.

^w Nu. 35^{14} Cf. for these cities, Josh. 20^{7, 8}.

Popular Instruction in the Law.—The zeal of the authors of the Deuteronomic codes led them to resort to very positive means to impress the new law upon the popular consciousness. Their methods were similar to those of the great prophets like Isaiah. Just as he wrote his central teaching during the years 737–735 B.C. on a tablet and set it up before the people, Is. 8^1, so the prophetic reformers of the days of Josiah decreed that the essentials of the law should be published before the eyes of the people. The method may be traced back at least as far as the days of the great Hammurabi. Primitive tablets were probably thus set up in Solomon's temple. Cf. Introd., p. 22. Doubtless the influence of the example of their Assyrian masters also affected the authors of Dt.

The public reading of the law by Josiah is recorded in II Kgs. 24^2. In the same way, a few years later, Baruch read certain of Jer.'s sermons to the people, Jer. 36^{10}.

Through the emphasis which the Deuteronomic lawgivers placed upon the instruction

§ 54 These passages in Dt. and Josh. are both later products of the Deuteronomic school.

Deuteronomic Codes

when ye shall pass over the Jordan to the land which Jehovah thy God is about to give thee, thou shalt set up great stones and plaster them with plaster; ³and thou shalt inscribe upon them all the words of this law, when thou hast passed over, that thou mayst go into the land which the Lord thy God giveth thee, a land abounding in milk and honey, as the Lord the God of thy fathers hath promised thee. ⁴And when ye are passed over Jordan ye shall set up these stones, which I command you this day, on Mount Ebal, and thou shalt plaster them over with plaster. ⁸And thou shalt inscribe upon the stones all the words of this law very plainly and carefully.

Josh. 8 ³⁰Then Joshua built on Mount Ebal an altar to Jehovah the God of Israel, ³¹as Moses the servant of Jehovah had commanded the Israelites, as it is written in the law of Moses, an altar of unhewn stones, upon which no one had set a tool. And they offered burnt-offerings on it to Jehovah, and sacrificed peace-offerings. ³²And he inscribed there upon the stones a copy of the law of Moses, which he had written in the presence of the Israelites. Execu-
tion of
the
com-
mand

§ 55. Public Reading of the Law, Dt. 31⁹⁻¹³, Josh. 8³³⁻³⁵

Deuteronomic Codes

Dt. 31 ⁹Moses wrote this law and delivered it to the priests the sons of Levi, who bore the ark of the covenant of Jehovah, and to all the elders of Israel. ¹⁰And Moses gave them this command: At the end of seven years, in the year fixed for the release, at the feast of tabernacles, ¹¹when all Israel come to see[a] the face of Jehovah thy God in the place which he shall choose, thou shalt read this law aloud before all Israel. ¹²Assemble the people, the men, the women and the children, as well as the aliens who reside within thy city, that they may hear, and learn, and fear Jehovah your God, and faithfully follow all the words of this law, ¹³and that their children who have not known may hear, and learn to fear Jehovah your God as long as ye live in the land which ye are going over the Jordan to possess. Com-
mand
public-
ly to
read
the law
in the
seventh
year

Josh. 8 ³³And all Israel with their elders, officers, and judges were standing on each side of the ark before the priests, the Levites, who carried the ark of the covenant of Jehovah—the resident alien as well as the native born—half of them in front of Mount Gerizim, and half of them in front of Mount Ebal, as Moses the servant of Jehovah had commanded them at the first, that they should bless the people of Israel. ³⁴And afterwards Joshua read all the words of the law, the blessing and the curse, according to all that is written in the book of the law. ³⁵There was not a word of all that Moses commanded, which Joshua did not read before all the assembly of Israel, and the women, and the little ones, and the resident aliens who were residing among them. First
public
reading

---

^q of children by their parents, they laid the foundation of the later educational system which was the strength and glory of Judaism. The decalogue structure of the primitive laws suggests, however, that catechetical instruction began in the earliest period of Israel's history. These varied methods of inculcating the fundamental principles of the law proved effective, as the later character of the Jewish race amply demonstrates.

^a Dt. 31¹¹ Slightly revising the Heb. text. Heb., *appear before.*

§ 56.   Instruction of Children, Dt. 6⁶⁻⁹, ²⁰⁻²⁵, [11¹⁸⁻²¹]

Deuteronomic Codes

Constantly to study and inculcate the law

Dt. 6 ⁶These words, which I command thee this day, shall be upon thy heart; ⁷and thou shalt impress[b] them upon thy children, and thou shalt talk of them when thou sittest in thy house, and when thou walkest by the way, and when thou liest down, and when thou risest up.   ⁸Thou shalt bind them as a reminder on thy hand, and have them as bands on thy forehead between thine eyes, ⁹and thou shalt mark them on the posts of thy house and on thy doors.

Historic reasons for keeping the law

²⁰When thy son asketh thee in the future, What mean the testimonies, and the statutes, and the judgments, which Jehovah our God hath commanded you ? ²¹then shalt thou say to thy son, We were Pharaoh's slaves in Egypt; but Jehovah brought us out of Egypt with a strong hand; ²²and Jehovah performed before our eyes great and destructive signs and wonders, upon Egypt, upon Pharaoh, and upon all his household; ²³and he brought us out from there, that he might bring us in to give us the land which he swore to our fathers.   ²⁴And Jehovah commanded us to act in accord with all these statutes, to fear Jehovah our God, that we might always prosper, and that he might preserve us alive, as at this day.   ²⁵We shall be righteous if we observe faithfully this command before Jehovah our God, as he hath commanded us.

---

§ 56 The earnest exhortations of Dt. 6⁶⁻⁹, ²⁰, ²¹ are repeated in slightly different form in 11¹⁸⁻²¹. These passages clearly reveal the educational aims of the Deuteronomic writers, who were powerfully influenced by the spirit and methods of the great prophets of the Assyrian period.

ᵇ Dt. 6⁷ Lit., *prick in.*

CRIMINAL LAWS

CRIMINAL LAWS

I

CRIMES AGAINST JEHOVAH

§ 57. **Worshipping Other Gods,** Ex. 34[14], 22[19], 23[13b], [20[3]], Dt. 5[7], 6[14], 8[19, 20], 30[17, 18], 11[16, 17, 26-28], 17[2-7]

Primitive Codes

Ex. 34 [14]Thou shalt worship no other God, for Jehovah, whose name is Jealous, is a jealous God[a]. Absolute loyalty

22 [19]Whoever sacrificeth to any god, except to Jehovah only,[b] shall be placed under the ban.[c] to Jehovah

23 [13b]Make no mention of the name of other gods, nor let it be heard on thy[d] lips.[e]

Crimes against Jehovah.—The distinctive teaching which Moses impressed upon the early Israelites appears to have been that Jehovah demanded the entire loyalty and devotion of his people. The command is imbedded in the oldest decalogue, and is always given the position of chief prominence and authority. It was the corner stone of Israel's civic and religious life. The common worship of the same God bound together the ancestors of the Hebrews wandering in the wilderness. The battle cry which rallied the people in the days of the judges, was, *Come up to the help of Jehovah against the mighty,* Jud. 5[20]. Loyalty to the God of the race was a stronger bond than even that of blood. Hence everything which tended to break down or weaken this bond was naturally regarded as treason.

When the Hebrews settled in Canaan and absorbed a large Canaanitish population and fell heir in time to the high places and institutions of the native races, the great struggle began between the more austere demand of the Jehovah worship and the invidious seductions of Canaanitish Baalism. When the latter in the days of Ahab and under the patronage of Jezebel threatened to win the day, Elijah appeared with his stern protest which at length found popular expression in the revolution of Jehu. When again under Manasseh the religious cults of Assyria and Babylonia gained the ascendency in Judah, the reformation which followed, under Josiah, was characterized by great severity. Apostasy, being treason, is, according to the Deuteronomic codes to be punished by death. The struggle between the Jehovah religion, as interpreted by the great prophets of the Assyrian period, and heathenism, was so intense that the most humane of all the O.T. lawgivers showed no mercy. The comparative absence of kindred laws in the priestly codes indicates that when they were formulated the exile had done its work and the great crisis was over; the loyalty of a majority of the nation was forever assured.

[a] Ex. 34[14] This primitive law, preserved in the early Judean prophetic narratives, is introduced by, *for.* This was clearly added by the later prophetic editor to connect it with his exhortations against making covenants with foreign peoples. Possibly [14b] is from the same hand. Cf. Dt. 4[24], 5[9], 6[15].

[b] Ex. 22[19] Or Sam. and Gk. A., *to another god.* These texts also leave out, *except to Jehovah only,* which may be a later explanatory gloss.

[c] Ex. 22[19] Cf. Josh. 6[17], 7 and Vol. I, § 110, note [b]. It sometimes has the meaning of, *utterly destroy.* In the earlier laws it probably meant the withdrawal of the protection of the tribe or nation and implied that Jehovah would execute the judgment, Dt. 20[16, 17].

[d] Ex. 23[13b] So Sam., supported by the rest of the vs. The Heb. has the pl.

[e] Ex. 23[13b] Lit., *heard out of thy lips.* The vs. in its present position in Ex. is probably secondary, but it may well represent an early Ephraimite duplicate of Ex. 34[14].

Deuteronomic Codes

Conse-
quences
of dis-
loyalty

Dt. 5 ⁷Thou shalt have no other gods[f] besides[g] me.

6 ¹⁴Ye shall not go after other gods,—the gods of the peoples that are round about you[h]—¹⁵for Jehovah thy God who is in the midst of thee is a jealous God; take heed lest the anger of Jehovah thy God be kindled against thee, and he destroy thee from off the face of the earth. **8** ¹⁹If thou shalt forget Jehovah thy God and shalt follow after other gods, and serve and worship them, I solemnly warn you this day that ye shall surely perish. ²⁰As the nations that Jehovah maketh to perish before you, so shall ye perish, because ye would not harken to the voice of Jehovah your God.

30 ¹⁷If thy heart is rebellious and thou dost not take heed but art drawn away, and worship other gods, and serve them, ¹⁸I declare to you this day, that ye shall surely perish; ye shall not enjoy long life in the land which thou art passing over the Jordan to go in to possess.[i]

11 ¹⁶Take heed to yourselves, lest your heart be deceived, and ye turn aside, and serve other gods, and worship them, ¹⁷and the anger of Jehovah be aroused against you, and he shut up the heavens, so that there shall be no more rain, and the land yield not its produce, and ye perish quickly from off the land which Jehovah is about to give you. ²⁶Behold, I set before you this day a blessing and a curse : ²⁷the blessing, if ye will heed the commands of Jehovah your God, which I command you this day; ²⁸and the curse, if ye will not heed the commands of Jehovah your God, but turn aside out of the way which I command you this day, in order to go after other gods, which ye have not known.

Proced-
ure in
punish-
ing dis-
loyalty
to Je-
hovah

17 ²If there be found in the midst of thee, within any of thy cities which Jehovah thy God is about to give thee, a man or a woman, who doeth that which is evil in the sight of Jehovah thy God, in transgressing his covenant, ³and hath gone and served other gods and worshiped them, or the sun, or the moon, or the host of heaven, which I have not commanded, ⁴and it be reported to thee and thou hast heard of it, then shalt thou investigate thoroughly, and if it prove to be true and be established that such abomination hath been committed in Israel, ⁵then thou shalt bring forth that man or woman, who hath done this evil, to thy gates, even the man or the woman; and thou shalt stone them to death. ⁶On the testimony of two or three witnesses shall he who is condemned be put to death. He shall not be put to death on the testimony of one witness. ⁷The hand of the witness shall first be raised against him to put him to death, and then the hands of all the people. Thus thou shalt purge the evil from thy midst.

---

[f] Dt. 5⁷ The Heb. may also be translated *god*. So Luc., Targ., and Gk. A.

[g] Dt. 5⁷ The duplicate of Ex. 20³. The Heb. expression which means lit. *in my face*, or *in my presence*, or *before my face*, is translated as above in accord with its obvious meaning in Gen. 28⁹, 31⁵⁰, Lev. 18¹⁸, where it signifies to have a rival. In Job 1¹¹, 21³¹, Is. 65³ it means *before* or *openly*. The command appears to demand that Jehovah's people shall give him the first place in their hearts, but also that they shall pay fealty to no other rival deity.

[h] Dt. 6¹⁴ The late prophetic addition in Ex. 23²⁴, ²⁵ repeats the injunctions of Dt. 6¹⁴ and 8¹⁹.

[i] Dt. 30¹⁷, ¹⁸ In view of their awkward connection with the context it seems probable that these vss. belong to a secondary section of the book of Dt.

§ 58. Apostasy, Dt. 13¹⁻¹⁸

Deuteronomic Codes

Dt. 13 ¹If there arise in the midst of thee a prophet, or one who dreams Death
dreams, and he give thee a sign or portent, ²and the sign or portent come to penalty for an
pass, in connection with which he spoke to thee, saying, Let us go after other apos-
gods which thou hast not known, and let us serve them; ³thou shalt not listen proph-
to the words of that prophet, or to that one who dreams dreams; for Jehovah et
your God is testing you to know whether ye love Jehovah your God with
all your heart and with all your soul.ʲ ⁴Ye shall follow Jehovah your God
and fear him, and keep his commands, and obey his voice, and ye shall serve
him, and remain true to him.ᵏ ⁵That prophet or that one who dreams dreams
shall be put to death, because, against Jehovah your God, who brought you
out of the land of Egypt and redeemed thee out of the condition of slavery,
he hath spoken treason,ˡ in order to draw thee aside out of the way in which
Jehovah thy God commanded thee to walk. Thus shalt thou purge away
the evil from thy midst.

⁶If thy brother, the son of thy mother, or thy son, or thy daughter, or the Even
wife of thy bosom, or thy friend, who is dear to thee as thy own soul, should for a
near
entice thee secretly, saying, Let us go and serve other gods, which neither relative
thou nor thy father hast known, ⁷certain of the gods of the surrounding friend
peoples, either near thee or far from thee, from one end of the earth to the
other,ᵐ ⁸thou shalt not yield nor listen to him, nor show pity to him, neither
shalt thou spare him, nor shalt thou hide him from justice, ⁹but thou shalt
surely kill him; thy hand shall be first raised against him to put him to death,
then the hands of all the people. ¹⁰And thou shalt stone him to death,
because he hath sought to draw thee away from Jehovah thy God, who
brought thee out of the land of Egypt when thou wast a slave. ¹¹Thus all
Israel shall hear and fear, and shall never again do any such wickedness as
this is in thy midst.

¹²If thou shalt hear this report regarding one of thy cities, which Jehovah An
is about to give thee in which to dwell: ¹³Certain fellows have gone out from apos-
tate
thy midst and have drawn away the inhabitants of their city, saying, ' Let city to
be de-
us go and serve other gods,' which ye have not known, ¹⁴then thou shalt stroyed
inquire and investigate, and carefully ascertain the facts. If it prove true with all
its in-
and be established that such an abomination hath been committed in thy habi-
tants
midst, ¹⁵thou shalt surely put the inhabitants of that city to the sword, de-
stroying it utterly and all that is in it.ⁿ ¹⁶And thou shalt gather all its spoil

§ 58 Religious impostors, sometimes doubtless self-deceived, have been from time im-
memorial, the bane of the East, which is always attentive to the *man of the spirit*. From the
days of Ahab, I Kgs. 22, until the days of Nehemiah these false prophets were not only mis-
leading the people, but also undermining the influence of the true men of God. In the days
of Jer. they appear to have been most common and active.
    ʲ Dt. 13³ᵇ·⁴ The sudden transition to the plural perhaps indicates that these vss. are a
later insertion. The Gk. has the plural in ³ᵃ. Possibly the variations are simply scribal
errors.
    ᵏ 13⁴ Lit., *cling to*.
    ˡ 13⁵ Or, *rebellion*.
    ᵐ 13⁷ The reference is primarily to the Assy. and Bab. cults which came in during the
days of Manasseh and the exile. The Heb. has the plural in the first part of the vs.
    ⁿ 13¹⁵ So Gk. The Heb. adds awkwardly, *and its cattle with the edge of the sword*.

Deuteronomic Codes

into the midst of its open space and shalt burn with fire the city and all its
spoil as a whole burnt-offering to Jehovah thy God; and it shall remain a
heap° forever, it shall never be rebuilt. ^{17}Let nothing of the devoted thing
cling to thy hand, that Jehovah may turn from his hot anger and show mercy
to thee, and that in his mercy he may make thee great, as he promised with
an oath to thy fathers, ^{18}if thou wilt listen to the voice of Jehovah thy God
by keeping all his commands which I am giving thee to-day and by doing
what is right in his sight.

§ 59. **Idolatry,** Ex. 34^{17}, 20^{23b}, $^{[4-6]}$, Dt. 5$^{8-10}$, 16^{21,22} 12$^{1-4}$ 7^5 27^{15}, 4$^{15-28}$,
Lev. 19^4, 26^1

Primitive Codes

Prohi-
bition
of mol-
ten
idols

Ex. 34 ^{17}Thou shalt make thee no molten gods.

Ex. 20 ^{23b}Gods of silver and gods of gold thou shalt not make for thyself.^{p}

Deuteronomic Codes

Of im-
ages of
all
kinds

Dt. 5 ^{8}Thou shalt not make for thyself a graven image,^{q} nor any likeness
of anything that is in heaven above, or that is on the earth beneath, or is in
the water under the earth; ^{9}thou shalt not worship them nor serve them;
for I, Jehovah thy God, am a jealous God, one who visits the iniquity of the
fathers upon the children and upon the third and fourth generations of
those who hate me, ^{10}but one who shows favor to thousands of those who
love me and keep my commandments.^{r}

Of all
heathen
symbols

16 ^{21}Thou shalt not plant an asherah,^{s} which thou shalt make of any kind
of tree, beside the altar of Jehovah thy God; ^{22}neither shalt thou set up a
pillar which Jehovah thy God hateth.

To de-
stroy
all hea-
then
shrines
and
sym-
bols

12 ^{1}These are the statutes and the judicial decisions which ye shall
faithfully observe in the land which Jehovah, the God of thy fathers hath
given thee as a possession, all the days that ye may live upon the earth. ^{2}Ye

---

° 13^{16} Lit., *a tel, i. e.*, a mound made by ruins.

§ 59 From their ancestors the Hebrews inherited the primitive custom of representing the
Deity in wood or stone. The oldest idols appear to have been sacred stones, in which the god
was supposed to dwell. In time these were cut into the shape of animals or human beings.
Micah's ephod, Judg. 17, the family god in David's home, I Sam. 19^{13}, the calves overlaid
with gold in the royal sanctuary of Northern Israel, and the silence of the earlier prophets all
indicate that idolatry was not absolutely forbidden by Israel's early teachers. Gradually,
however, as their conception of the Deity broadened and the evils inherent in idolatry became
apparent, the people began to view these popular symbols with suspicion. Hosea speaks
scornfully of the calf of Samaria, 10^5; by the time of Josiah idols were placed under the ban.

The commands of the successive codes record the development of the higher ideal.
First the expensive molten gods, probably made by foreign craftsmen and fashioned after
heathen models, were forbidden. Finally in the prophetic decalogue of Ex. 20 and Dt. 5 all
forms of idols are absolutely discarded. The law is made very explicit to eliminate all possibility of error.

^{p} Ex. 20^{23b} Heb., *for yourselves;* but the original form was probably in the singular as
in the following vs. The plural is apparently due to the influence of the plural in the later
addition in 20^{22}.

^{q} Dt. 5^8 The original command probably consisted simply of this first sentence. The rest
is explanatory and hortatory.

^{r} Dt. 5$^{8-10}$ The duplicate is found in Ex. 20$^{4-6}$.

^{s} Dt. 16^{21} *I. e.*, one of the sacred poles, reared probably as symbols of the sacred trees,
worshipped in ancient times.

Deuteronomic Codes

shall destroy all the places in which the nations, that ye shall dispossess, served their gods, upon the high mountains and upon the hills and under every green tree; ³and ye shall break down their altars, and dash in pieces their pillars, and burn their asherahs with fire; and ye shall hew down the graven images of their gods; and ye shall destroy their name out of that place. ⁴To Jehovah your God ye shall not do as they do[t].

7 ⁵Thus shall ye do to them: ye shall break down their altars, and dash in pieces their pillars, and hew down their asherahs, and burn their graven images with fire.

27 ¹⁵Cursed be the man who makes a graven or molten image, an abomination to Jehovah, the work of the hands of the craftsman, and setteth it up in secret. And all the people shall answer and say, So may it be. — Public condemnation

4 ¹⁵Take good heed to yourselves—for ye saw no manner of form in the day that Jehovah spoke to you in Horeb out of the midst of the fire[u]—¹⁶lest ye corrupt yourselves, and make for yourselves a graven image in the form of a statue, the likeness of male or female, ¹⁷the likeness of any beast that is on the earth, the likeness of any winged bird that flieth in the heavens, ¹⁸the likeness of anything that creepeth on the ground, the likeness of any fish that is in the water under the earth; ¹⁹and lest thou lift up thine eyes to heaven, and when thou seest the sun and the moon and the stars, even all the host of heaven, thou be drawn away and worship them, and serve these objects which Jehovah thy God hath allotted to all the peoples under the whole heaven. ²⁰But you Jehovah hath taken and brought forth from the iron furnace, out of Egypt, that you may be a people, his own inheritance, as you now are. ²¹Moreover Jehovah was angry with me because of you, and swore that I should not go over the Jordan and that I should not go in to that good land, which Jehovah thy God giveth thee as an inheritance; ²²but I must die in this land, I cannot go over the Jordan; but ye shall go over and possess that good land. ²³Take heed to yourselves, lest you forget the covenant of Jehovah your God, which he made with you, and make for yourselves a graven image in the form of anything which Jehovah thy God hath forbidden thee. ²⁴For Jehovah thy God is a devouring fire, a jealous God! — Reasons why the Israelites should have no idols

²⁵When children, and children's children shall be born, and ye shall have been long in the land, and shall corrupt yourselves, and make a graven image in the form of anything, and shall do that which is evil in the sight of Jehovah thy God, to provoke him to anger, ²⁶I call heaven and earth to witness against you this day, that ye shall soon perish completely from the land which ye are going over the Jordan to possess; ye shall not remain many years upon it, but shall be completely destroyed. ²⁷Jehovah will also scatter you among the peoples, and only a small number of you shall be left among the nations, among whom Jehovah shall lead you away. ²⁸And there ye shall serve gods, the work of men's hands, wood and stone, which neither see nor hear nor eat nor smell. — Exile the penalty for idolatry

---

[t] Dt. 12⁴ *I. e.*, worship him at the same places and with the same rites.
[u] Dt. 4¹⁵ This and the following vss. also belong to a later stratum in the Deuteronomic codes.

Holiness Code

Jeho-
vah,
not
idols,
the
true
object
of wor-
ship

Lev. 19 ⁴Turn not to idols,ᵛ nor make for yourselves molten gods : I am Jehovah your God.

26 ¹Ye shall make you no idols, nor shall ye erect for yourselves a graven image or a pillar, nor shall ye set up any figured stone in your land, to bow down to it : for I am Jehovah your God.

§ 60. **Sorcery and Divination,** Ex. 22¹⁸, Dt. 18⁹⁻¹⁴, Lev. 18³, ²⁴, 20²³, ²⁷, 19²⁶ᵇ, ³¹, 20⁶

Primitive Codes

Death
for the
sorcer-
ess

Ex. 22 ¹⁸A sorceress shall not live.ʷ

Deuteronomic Codes

No
form of
hea-
then
super-
stition
to be
toler-
ated

Dt. 18 ⁹When thou comest into the land which Jehovah thy God is about to give thee, thou shalt not learn to imitate the abominations of these nations. ¹⁰There shall none be found with thee who maketh his son or his daughter to pass through the fire, or who obtaineth oracles by lot, or a diviner,ᵃ or one who observeth omens,ᵇ or a sorcerer, ¹¹or a charmer, or a medium,ᶜ or a wizard, or a necromancer. ¹²For whoever doeth these things is an abomination to Jehovah; and because of these abominations Jehovah thy God is driving them out before thee. ¹³Thou shalt be perfect with Jehovah thy God. ¹⁴For these nations, that thou shalt dispossess, give heed to those who practice augury and to diviners; but as for thee, Jehovah thy God hath not permitted thee so to do.

Holiness Code

To
avoid
all hea-
then
cus-
toms

Lev. 18 ³Ye shall not imitate the customs of the land of Egypt, in which ye dwelt, nor the customs of the land of Canaan, whither I am bringing you; neither shall ye follow their established usages. ²⁴Defile not yourselves in any of these ways, for in all these ways have the nations which I am casting out from before you defiled themselves. **20** ²³And ye shall not follow the established usages of the nations,ᵈ which I am casting out before you; for they did all these things; therefore I abhorred them.

Death
to all
medi-
ums
and
wizards

²⁷A man or a woman who is a medium or a wizard shall surely be put

---

ᵛ Lev. 19⁴ Or, *do not regard unreal gods;* lit., *unreal thing.* The later priestly writers frequently use this contemptuous term as a synonym of idol.

§ 60 In I Sam. 28⁹ it is stated that Saul drove out the wizards and mediums from his kingdom, but in his last extremity Israel's first king is represented as resorting to one of the representatives of the occult arts. The better sense of Israel's prophets and lawgivers revolted against these survivals of a heathen past, as did also the more enlightened leaders of Assyria and Greece. The sorceress with her evil craft probably represents these cults in the primitive codes; but in Dt. they are all classed together and placed under the ban of divine disapproval.

ʷ Ex. 22¹⁸ R. V., *thou shalt not suffer a sorceress to live,* but the above trans. is supported by the Heb., and the fact that the second person is not used in the context of the civil decalogues, cf. Introd., p. 23.

ᵃ Dt. 18¹⁰ The exact form of divination is not known. Possibly it was by examining the form of the liver of sacrificial animals, as among the Babylonians and many ancient peoples.

ᵇ Dt. 18¹⁰ Probably the flight of birds.

ᶜ Dt. 18¹¹ Gk., *ventriloquists,* cf. I Sam. 28.

ᵈ Lev. 20²³ So Sam., Gk., Syr. and Targ. Heb., *nation.*

Holiness Code

to death; ye shall stone them[e]; they shall be responsible for their own death.

19 ²⁶ᵇYe shall not practise augury or divination.

³¹Turn ye not to those who are mediums or wizards; seek them not out to be defiled by them : I am Jehovah your God.

20 ⁶Against the person who turns to those who are mediums or wizards, to practise apostasy[f] with them, I will indeed set my face, and I will cut him off from among his people.

§ 61. **Sacrifice of Children to Heathen Gods,** Dt. 12²⁹⁻³¹, 18¹⁰ᵃ, Lev. 18²¹ᵃ, 20²·⁵

Deuteronomic Codes

Dt. 12 ²⁹When Jehovah thy God shall cut off the nations from before Not to thee, which thou art going in to dispossess, and thou hast dispossessed imitate them and dwellest in their land, ³⁰take heed to thyself that thou be not en- hideous snared after them, when they have been destroyed from before thee, and that rite thou inquire not after their gods, saying, How do these nations serve their gods? even so will I do likewise. ³¹Thou shalt not do thus to Jehovah thy God; because every abomination which Jehovah hateth have they done to their gods; for even their sons and their daughters do they burn in the fire to their gods. **18** ¹⁰ᵃNone who maketh his son or his daughter to pass through the fire shall be found with thee.

Priestly Codes

Lev. 18 ²¹ᵃAnd thou shalt not give any of thy offspring to make them Death pass through the fire to Molech. **20** ²Moreover, thou shalt say to the the Israelites, Any one of the Israelites or of the aliens who reside in Israel, who penalty giveth of his offspring to Molech, shall surely be put to death; the people of the land shall stone him.[g] ³I will also turn against[h] that man and will cut him off from among his people; because he hath given of his offspring to Molech, to defile my sanctuary and to profane my holy name. ⁴And if the people of the land do at all shut their eyes to that man's doings, when he giveth of his offspring to Molech, and fail to put him to death, ⁵then I will turn against that man and his family, and will cut him off, and all from among their people who follow after him to practice apostasy[i] with Molech.

ᵉ Lev. 20²⁷ So Gk. Heb., *they shall be stoned.*
ᶠ Lev. 20⁶ Lit., *play the harlot after, i. e.,* be disloyal to Jehovah.
§ 61 Human sacrifice was apparently a common practice among the ancient inhabitants of Palestine. The many skeletons of children found in the temple precincts of the ruins at Gezer and Taanach and the frequent allusions to it in the O.T. confirm this conjecture. The ancient Hebrews shared the Canaanitish belief that every first-born child belonged to the Deity. In the times of calamity the first impulse in the minds of the people was to win Jehovah's favor by human sacrifice, Mi. 6⁷. When heathen influence was strong, as in the days of Ahaz and Manasseh, the same barbarous practice came into vogue. In the valley of Hinnom to the south of Jerusalem the Hebrews had been wont *to burn their sons and their daughters in the fire,* Jer. 7³¹, ³², 19⁵, Ps. 106³⁷, ³⁸. These references suggest, however, that the crime was committed in the later days only in the name of Baal or Molech (or Milk, *King*). The expression, *to make to pass through the fire,* appears to refer to the same rite, probably designating some peculiar form of human sacrifice.
ᵍ Lev. 20²ᵇ This seems to be taken from the Holiness Code.
ʰ Lev. 20³ Heb., *set my face against.* So in ⁵.
ⁱ Lev. 20⁵ Lit., *play the harlot;* as elsewhere, ceremonial rather than social crimes are evidently in the mind of the author.

§ 62. **Blasphemy,** Ex. 22²⁸ᵃ [20⁷], Dt. 5¹¹, Lev. 19¹², 18²¹ᵇ, 24¹⁵ᵇ. ¹⁶, ¹⁰.¹³, ²³

Primitive Codes

Not to revile God

Ex. 22 ²⁸ᵃThou shalt not revile God.

Deuteronomic Codes

Not to misuse his name

Dt. 5 ¹¹Thou shalt not invoke the name of Jehovah thy God falsely,ʲ for Jehovah will not hold him guiltless who taketh his name falsely.

Holiness Code

Not to profane it

Lev. 19 ¹²Ye shall not swear by my name falsely, so as to profane the name of thy God: I am Jehovah.

18 ²¹ᵇThou shalt not profane the name of thy God: I am Jehovah.

Penalty for blasphemy

24 ¹⁵ᵇWhoever curseth his God shall bear the consequences of his sin. ¹⁶And he who blasphemeth the name of Jehovah, shall surely be put to death; all the congregation shall surely stone him; the resident alien, as well as the native, when he blasphemeth the Name, shall be put to deathᵏ.

Supplemental Priestly Codes

A traditional case

Lev. 24 ¹⁰The son of an Israelitish woman, whose father was an Egyptian, went out among the Israelites;ˡ and the son of the Israelitish woman and a man of Israel strove together in the camp, ¹¹and the son of the Israelitish woman blasphemed the Name and reviled; and they brought him to Moses. And his mother's name was Shelomith, the daughter of Dibri, of the tribe of Dan. ¹²And they put him in prison until Jehovah's will should be disclosed to them.

Public stoning the penalty

¹³Then Jehovah commanded Moses, Lead him who hath reviled outside the camp; and let all who heard him lay their hands on his head; then let all the congregation stone him. ²³So Moses spoke to the Israelites, and they led him who had reviled outside the camp and stoned him. Thus the Israelites did as Jehovah commanded Moses.

§ 63. **False Prophecy,** Dt. 18¹⁸⁻²²

Deuteronomic Codes

Death the penalty

Dt. 18 ¹⁸A prophet like Moses will I raise up to them from time to time from their fellow countrymen; I will put my messages in his mouth, and he shall speak to them all that I command him. ¹⁹And if any one will not give heed to my words which he shall speak in my name, I will exact punishment of him. ²⁰But the prophet who shall presume to deliver a message in my name, which I have not commanded him to deliver, or shall speak in the name of other gods, that prophet shall die.

ʲ Dt. 5¹¹ Cf. Ex. 23¹ *Take up a false report,* Nu. 23⁷, Ps. 15³, 81², 16⁴, 24⁴, *He who hath not lifted up his soul to falsehood or sworn deceitfully.* Also Is. 5¹⁸, Ezek. 12²⁴, 13⁶⁻⁹. The idiom seems to mean to desecrate the name of God by swearing to what is not true, or by cursing another, or in connection with any form of sorcery or witchcraft.
ᵏ Lev. 24¹⁶ᵇ Evidently a scribal addition, for it has an expression, *congregation,* not found in the Holiness Code and is but a duplicate of ¹⁶ᵃ.
ˡ Lev. 24¹⁰⁻¹³, ²³ A precedent introduced by a late priestly editor.
§ 63 Cf. note § 50.

Deuteronomic Codes

^{21}And if thou shalt think to thyself, How shall we recognize the message   Test of
which Jehovah hath not spoken? ^{22}then know that if a prophet speak in   true proph-
the name of Jehovah, and the prediction be not fulfilled, follow not, nor   ecy
come to pass, that it is a prediction which Jehovah hath not spoken. The
prophet hath spoken it presumptuously; thou need not be afraid of him.

§ 64. Desecration of Sacred Things, Lev. 19^30b, 22^3b, Nu. 18^22, 3^38b, 4^17-20
Lev. 7^20, 21

Holiness Code

Lev. 19 ^{30b}Reverence my sanctuary : I am Jehovah.   Temple

22 ^{3b}If^{m} any man among yourselves or your descendants^{n} approach the   Exclu-sion of
holy things which the Israelites have consecrated to Jehovah, having his   all but
uncleanness upon him, that one shall be cut off from my presence : I am   the priests
Jehovah.

Priestly Codes

Nu. 18 ^{22}Henceforth the Israelites shall not come near the tent of meeting,
lest they bear the consequences of their sin and die.

Supplemental Priestly Codes

Nu. 3 ^{38b}The stranger that cometh near the dwelling shall be put to death.   Death

4 ^{17}And Jehovah spoke thus to Moses and Aaron, ^{18}Cut ye not off the   the penalty
tribe of the families of the Kohathites from among the Levites; ^{19}but thus do
to them, that they may live and not die, when they approach the most holy
things : Aaron and his sons shall go in, and appoint each of them to his
service and to his burden; ^{20}but they shall not go in to see the holy things
even for a moment, lest they die.

Priestly Codes

Lev. 7 ^{20}One who eateth of the flesh of the peace-offerings which belong   Penalty
to Jehovah, having his uncleanness upon him, shall be cut off from his people.   for pol-luting
^{21}And when any one toucheth an unclean thing, the uncleanness of man, or   sacred food
an unclean beast, or any unclean swarming creature,^{o} and eateth of the
flesh of the sacrifice of peace-offerings, which belong to Jehovah, that one
shall be cut off from his people.

§ 65. Labor on the Sabbath, Ex. 34^21, 23^12 [20^8-11], Dt. 5^12-15, Lev. 19^3b [20a], 26^2a,
Ex. 35^2, 3, 31^13b-17, Nu. 15^32,36

Primitive Codes

Ex. 34 ^{21}Six days thou shalt work, but on the seventh day thou shalt   Rest from all labor
rest; in plowing time and in harvest thou shalt rest.

§ 64 These laws are peculiar to the exilic and post-exilic codes in which the sanctity of
holy things is especially emphasized.
     ^{m} Lev. 22^{3b} A scribe has appended, *Say to them.*
     ^{n} Lev. 22^{3b} Lit., *throughout your generations;* this is evidently a gloss.
     ^{o} Lev. 7^{21} So the Gk., Syr., and San., Heb., *detestable thing.*
     § 65 In the oldest codes the sabbath rest is simply enjoined for social and humane reasons.
Nor until it was made a religious institution by later Judaism, was labor on that day punished

Primitive Codes

23 [12]Six days thou shalt do thy work, but on the seventh thou shalt rest, that thine ox and thine ass may have rest, and that the son of thy female slave and the resident alien may be refreshed.

Deuteronomic Codes

Consecrated to rest for working beast and man

Dt. 5 [12]Observe the sabbath day to keep it holy, as Jehovah thy God commanded thee. [13]Six days thou shalt labor, and do all thy work; [14]but the seventh day is a sabbath to Jehovah thy God; in it thou shalt do no work, thou, nor thy son, nor thy daughter, nor thy male or female slave, nor thine ox, nor thine ass, nor any of thy cattle, nor the alien who resideth within thy city, that thy male and female slave may rest as well as thou. [15]Thou shalt also remember that thou wast a slave in the land of Egypt and that Jehovah thy God brought thee out from there by a mighty hand and an outstretched arm; therefore Jehovah thy God commanded thee to keep the sabbath day.[p]

Holiness Code

To be faithfully kept

Lev. 19 [3b]Ye shall keep my sabbaths: I am Jehovah your God.[q]
26 [2a]Ye shall keep my sabbaths and reverence my sanctuary.

Priestly Codes

Death to one who labors on Jehovah's day

Ex. 35 [2]Six days shall work be done;[r] but on the seventh ye shall have a day consecrated to Jehovah, a sabbath of complete rest;[s] whoever doeth any work in it shall be put to death. [3]Ye shall kindle no fire in any of your dwellings on the sabbath.

Supplemental Priestly Codes

Sabbath the sign of the covenant between Jehovah and his people

Ex. 31 [13b]Ye shall surely keep my sabbaths, for it is a sign between me and you throughout your generations; that ye may know that I am Jehovah who am sanctifying you.[t] [14]Ye shall keep the sabbath, therefore, for it is holy to you; every one who profaneth it shall surely be put to death; for whoever doeth any work in it, that one shall be cut off from among his people. [15]Six days shall work be done,[u] but on the seventh day is a sabbath of complete rest, holy to Jehovah; whoever doeth any work on the sabbath, shall surely be put to death. [16]Therefore the Israelites shall keep the sabbath, by observing the sabbath throughout their generations, as a perpetual covenant. [17]It is a sign between me and the Israelites forever, for in six days Jehovah made heaven and earth, and on the seventh day he rested and was refreshed.[v]

A traditional precedent

Nu. 15 [32]While the Israelites were in the wilderness, they found a man gathering sticks on the sabbath. [33]And those who found him gathering

---

as a crime. The traditional precedent of Nu. 15[32-36] is one of the latest additions to the Pentateuch. Cf. notes §§ 210, 217.

[p] Dt. 5[12-15] The version of Ex. 20[8-11] is nearly identical.

[q] Lev. 19[3b] This injunction is repeated in [20a].

[r] Ex. 35[2] Gk. and Sam., *shalt thou work.*

[s] Ex. 35[2] Or, cf. 16[23] and 31[15], *a day holy to Jehovah, a sabbath of solemn rest.*

[t] Ex. 31[13b], While these vss. have many of the idioms and ideas of the Holiness Code, they abound in the expressions peculiar to the later additions to the priestly codes. For an attempt to distinguish the earlier nucleus, cf. § 217.

[u] Ex. 31[15] Gk., *shalt thou work.*

[v] Ex. 31[17] Cf. Gen. 2[1, 3].

Supplemental Priestly Codes

sticks brought him to Moses and Aaron and to all the congregation. ³⁴And they put him in confinement, because it had not been clearly explained what should be done to him. ³⁵Then Jehovah said to Moses, The man shall surely be put to death; all the congregation shall stone him outside the camp. ³⁶So all the congrégation led him outside the camp, and stoned him to death, as Jehovah commanded Moses.

II

CRIMES AGAINST THE STATE

§ 66. Bribery, Ex. 23⁸, Dt. 16¹⁹ᵇ, 27²⁵

Primitive Codes

Ex. 23 ⁸Thou shalt take no bribe, for a bribe blindeth those who see, and perverteth the cause of the righteous. Pro-
hibition

Deuteronomic Codes

Dt. 16 ¹⁰ᵇThou shalt not take a bribe, for a bribe blindeth the eyes of the wise and subverteth the cause of the righteous.

27 ²⁵Cursed be he who taketh a bribe to condemn an innocent person. And all the people shall say, So let it be. Public
con-
demna-
tion

§ 67. Perverting Justice, Ex. 23¹⁻³, ⁶, ⁷, Dt. 16¹⁹ᵃ, ²⁰, Lev. 19¹⁵ ⁽³⁵ᵃ⁾

Primitive Codes

Ex. 23 ¹Thou shalt not spread abroadᵃ a false report. Do not enter into a conspiracy withᵇ a wicked man to be an unrighteous witness. ²Thou shalt not follow the majority in doing wrong. Thou shalt not bear testimony in a case,ᶜ so as to pervert justice. ³Thou shalt not show partiality to a poor man in his cause. ⁶Thou shalt not prevent justice being done to thy poor in his cause. ⁷Keep aloof from every false matter; and do not condemn the innocentᵈ or him who has a just cause. Do not vindicateᵉ a wicked man. Not to
thwart
justice
either
as wit-
ness or
judge

Deuteronomic Codes

Dt. 16 ¹⁹ᵃThou shalt not pervert justice. Thou shalt not show partiality. ²⁰Justice, and only justice shalt thou follow, that thou mayest live and inherit the land which Jehovah thy God giveth thee. Abso-
lute im-
partial-
ity

Crimes against the State.—Since in most criminal offences Jehovah or else, as in murder, the family of the slain was regarded as the plaintiff, few misdemeanors were classed in Heb. law as crimes against the state. They were limited simply to those acts which endanger the integrity of the public tribunals.

ᵃ Ex. 23¹ Lit., *take up*. The same word is used in Ex. 20⁷.
ᵇ Ex. 23¹ Lit., *put thy hand with*.
ᶜ Ex. 23² Omitting the clause, *to turn aside after the majority*, which is apparently a verbal repetition of the preceding clause. Gk., *so as to pervert justice*.
ᵈ Ex. 23⁷ Lit., *slay*.
ᵉ Ex. 23⁷ Following the obviously superior reading of the Gk. and Sam.

Holiness Code

Lev. 19 ¹⁵Ye shall do no injustice in rendering a judicial decision. Thou shalt not show partiality to the poor nor have undue consideration for the powerful; but justly shalt thou judge thy neighbor.

§ 68. **Perjury,** Dt. 5²⁰ [Ex. 20¹⁶], Dt. 19¹⁶⁻²¹, Lev. 19¹²

Deuteronomic Code

Prohibition

Punishment to correspond to the nature of the false testimony

Dt. 5 ²⁰Thou shalt not bear false witness against thy neighbor.

19 ¹⁶If a malicious witness stand up against a man to accuse him of treason, ¹⁷then both the men who have the dispute shall stand before Jehovah, before the priests and the judges who shall be officiating in those days; ¹⁸and the judges shall thoroughly investigate, and should it prove that the witness is a false witness, and hath testified falsely against his fellow countryman, ¹⁹then shall ye do to him, as he had purposed to do to his fellow countryman; thus shalt thou purge away the evil from thy midst.   ²⁰And those who remain shall hear and fear, and never again do any such evil in thy midst. ²¹Thou shalt show no pity; life for life, eye for eye, tooth for tooth, hand for hand, foot for foot.

Holiness Code

Lev. 19 ¹²Ye shall not swear by my name falsely, so as to profane the name of thy God : I am Jehovah.

§ 69. **Deliberate Defiance of the Law,** Dt. 17¹², ¹³, Nu. 15³⁰, ³¹

Deuteronomic Codes

Death the penalty

Dt. 17 ¹²Should a man act so presumptuously as not to hearken to the priest who standeth to minister there before Jehovah thy God, or to the judge, that man shall die; thus thou shalt purge away the evil from Israel, ¹³so that all the people may hear, and fear, and never again act presumptuously.

Priestly Codes

Nu. 15 ³⁰A person who acts wilfully, whether he is a native or a resident alien, the same blasphemeth Jehovah; and that one shall be cut off from among his kinsmen.   ³¹Because he hath despised the word of Jehovah and hath broken his command, that one shall utterly be cut off; he shall bear the consequences of his iniquity.

---

§ 68 Here the penalty enjoined in the Deuteronomic codes and that of Hammurabi is substantially the same:
§ 3 *If a man has borne false witness in a trial, or has not established the statement that he has made, if that case be a capital trial, that man shall be put to death.* § 4. *If he has borne false witness in a civil law case, he shall pay the damages in that suit.*
§ 69 The law in Dt. 17¹², ¹³ deals simply with a case which had been decided by the central tribunal at Jerusalem.

III

CRIMES AGAINST MORALITY AND DECENCY

§ 70. **Adultery,** Dt. 5¹⁸ [Ex. 20¹⁴], Dt. 22²²⁻²⁴, Lev. 18²⁰, 20¹⁰,
Nu. 5¹²ᵇ, ¹³ᵃ, ᶜ, ¹⁵, ¹⁸, ²¹, ²³, ²⁴, ²⁶ᵃ, ²⁷ᵇ, ³¹

Deuteronomic Codes

Dt. 5 ¹⁸Thou shalt not commit adultery. Pro-
hibition

22 ²²If a man be found lying with a married woman, they shall both of Death them die, the man who lay with the woman and the woman; thus shalt thou the
penalty purge away the evil from Israel.

²³If a man find in the city a young woman who is a virgin betrothed to Also in a husband, and lie with her, ²⁴then ye shall bring them both out to the gate case of
a be- of that city and stone them to death, the damsel because she did not cry out, trothed although she was in the city, and the man because he hath seduced his virgin neighbor's wife; thus shalt thou purge away the evil from thy midst.

Holiness Code

Lev. 18 ²⁰Thou shalt not enter into illicit intercourse with thy neighbor's Later wife to defile thyself with her. prohi-
bition

20 ¹⁰If a man commit adulteryᶠ with his neighbor's wife, the adulterer as well as the adultress shall be put to death.

Priestly Codes

Nu. 5 ¹²ᵇIf a man's wife turn asideᵍ and is unfaithful to him, ¹³ᵃ,ᶜ and a Proced- man enter into illicit relations with her and it be hid from her husband, and ure in
case of there be no witness against her and she be not caught in the act, ¹⁵then the a sus-
pected man shall take his wife to the priest, and shall bring an offering for her, the wife tenth part of an ephah of barley meal; he shall pour no oil upon it nor put frankincense on it, for it is a cereal-offering of jealousy, a memorial cereal-offering, bringing iniquity to remembrance. ¹⁸Then the priest shall place the woman before Jehovah, and loosen the hair of the woman's head, and put in her hands the memorial cereal-offering, which is the cereal-offering of jealousy, and the priest shall hold in his hand the water of bitterness which causeth the curse.

²¹Then the priest shall make the woman swear with the oath of execration, The
oath of

---

§ 70 Most primitive people dealt very severely with the crime of adultery. Thus the execra-
tion code of Hammurabi decrees that:
   § 129 *If a man's wife be caught lying with another, they shall be strangled and cast into the water. If the wife's husband would save his wife, the king can save his servant.*
   The aim in all these laws was clearly to preserve intact the integrity and purity of the family and clan. The laxness of public opinion and modern laws in dealing with this most hideous of crimes, which condemns families and individuals to lives of unspeakable pain and ignominy, stands in disgraceful contrast to the attitude of the ancients who classed it with murder.
   ᶠ Lev. 20¹⁰ A scribe has added by mistake, *with another man's wife, even he who committeth adultery.*
   ᵍ Nu. 5¹²ᵇ Cf. note § 10 for the reasons for the analysis here presented. This law is one of the earlier sections of the priestly codes, but it evidently reproduces a very primitive custom.

Priestly Codes

and the priest shall say to the woman, Jehovah make you an execration and an oath among thy people, when Jehovah causeth thy thigh to fall away, and thy body to swell. ²³Then the priest shall write these execrations in a book, and he shall wipe them off into the water of bitterness, ²⁴and he shall make the woman drink the water of bitterness that causeth the curse, so that the water that causeth the curse may enter into her and become bitter. ²⁶ᵃThe priest shall also take a handful of the cereal-offering, as its memorial-offering, and burn it upon the altar. ²⁷ᵇThus the woman shall become an execration among her people. ³¹The man shall be free from guilt, but that woman must bear her own guilt.

§ 71. Illicit Intercourse, Lev. 19²⁰⁻²²

Holiness Code

Proced-
ure
in the
case of
a be-
trothed
female
slave

Lev. 19 ²⁰If any man lieth carnally with a woman, who is a slave, betrothed to another man, but who has in nowise been redeemed nor given her freedom, there shall be a judicial inquiry, but they shall not be put to death,ʰ because she was not free.

Priestly Codes

Lev. 19 ²¹The man shall bring his guilt-offering to Jehovah, to the entrance of the tent of meeting, a ram as a guilt-offering; ²²and the priest shall make atonement for him with the ram of the guilt-offering before Jehovah for his sin which he hath committed; then the sin which he hath committed shall be forgiven him.

§ 72. Unlawful Marriage, Dt. 22³⁰, 27²⁰, ²², ²³, Lev. 18⁶⁻¹⁸, 20¹¹, ¹², ¹⁴, ¹⁷, ²⁰, ²¹

Deuteronomic Codes

With
step-
mother

Dt. 22 ³⁰A man shall not marry his father's wife, and shall not uncover his father's skirt.

Public
con-
demna-
tion of
incest

27 ²⁰Cursed be he who lieth with his father's wife, because he hath uncovered his father's skirt.   And all the people shall say, So may it be.
²²Cursed be he who lieth with his half-sister, the daughter of his father, or the daughter of his mother.   And all the people shall say, So may it be.
²³Cursed be he who lieth with his mother-in-law.   And all the people shall say, So may it be.

Holiness Code

With a
mother
or
sister

Lev. 18 ⁶None of you shall approach any who are closely related to him, to uncover their nakedness: I am Jehovah.   ⁷The nakedness of thy father and the nakedness of thy mother, shalt thou not uncover; she is thy mother;

ʰ Lev. 19²⁰ Or, *he shall be examined, but he shall not die.*
§ 72 The Hammurabi code is in part parallel to the O.T. laws:
§ 157 *If a man, after his father's death, has lain in the bosom of his mother, they shall both of them be burnt together.*
§ 158 *If a man, after his father's death, be caught in the bosom of his step-mother, who has borne children, that man shall be cut off from his father's house.*

Holiness Code

thou shalt not uncover her nakedness. ⁸The nakedness of thy father's wife shalt thou not uncover: it is thy father's nakedness. ⁹The nakedness of thy sister, the daughter of thy mother,ⁱ whether born at home or away, her nakedness thou shalt not uncover.

¹⁰The nakedness of thy son's daughter or of thy daughter's daughter, their nakedness thou shalt not uncover, for their nakedness is thine own. ¹¹The nakedness of thy father's wife's daughter, begotten of thy father, who is thy sister, her nakedness thou shalt not uncover. ¹²Thou shalt not uncover the nakedness of thy father's sister; she is thy father's near kinswoman. ¹³Thou shalt not uncover the nakedness of thy mother's sister, for she is thy mother's near kinswoman. ¹⁴Thou shalt not uncover the nakedness of thy father's brother, thou shalt not approach his wife, she is thine aunt. ¹⁵Thou shalt not uncover the nakedness of thy daughter-in-law;ʲ she is thy son's wife; thou shalt not uncover her nakedness. ¹⁶Thou shalt not uncover the nakedness of thy brother's wife; it is thy brother's nakedness. ¹⁷Thou shalt not uncover the nakedness of a woman and her daughter; thou shalt not take her son's daughter, or her daughter's daughter, to uncover her nakedness; they are thy near kinswomen; it is unchastity. ¹⁸And thou shalt not take a woman as your wife in addition to her sister, to be her rival, to uncover her nakedness, beside the other in her lifetime.

[Marginal notes: With a grand-daughter, ter, aunt, daughter-in-law, or sister-in-law]

Lev. 20 ¹¹A man who lieth with his father's wife has uncovered his father's nakedness; both of them shall surely be put to death; they shall be responsible for their own death. ¹²And if a man lies with his daughter-in-law, both of them shall surely be put to death; they have done what is unnatural; they shall be responsible for their own death.

[Marginal notes: With both a mother and daughter, ter, or grand-daughter, ter, or two sisters]

¹⁴And if a man taketh a wife and her mother, it is unchastity; they shall be burnt with fire, both he and they, that there may be no unchastity among you. ¹⁷And if a man shall take his sister, whether his father's daughter, or his mother's daughter,ᵏ he hath uncovered his sister's nakedness; he shall bear the consequences of his iniquity. ²⁰And if a man shall lie with his uncle's wife, he hath uncovered his uncle's nakedness; they shall bear the consequences of their sin; they shall die childless. ²¹And if a man shall take his brother's wife, it is impurity; he hath uncovered his brother's nakedness; they shall be childless.

[Marginal note: Penalties for different forms of incest]

§ 73. Sodomy, Lev. 18²², 20¹³

Holiness Code

Lev. 18 ²²Thou shalt not lie with a man, as with a woman; it is an abomination.

[Marginal note: Prohibition]

ⁱ Lev. 18⁹ Cf. § 3 noted.
ʲ Lev. 18¹⁵ The corresponding law of Hammurabi reads: § 155. *If a man has betrothed a maiden to his son and his son has known her, and afterward the man has lain in her bosom, and been caught, that man shall be strangled and she shall be cast into the water.*
ᵏ Lev. 20¹⁷ The Heb. adds a supplemental note providing for the punishment of both, *and see her nakedness, and she see his nakedness, it is a disgrace; and they shall be cut off in the sight of the children of their people.* Lev. 20¹⁹ *And thou shalt not uncover the nakedness of thy mother's sister, nor of thy father's sister, for he who does this has made naked his near kin; they shall bear the consequences of their iniquity* is also an awkward gloss differing in style from the context.
§ 73 For the origin of the term sodomy, cf. Gen. 19⁴⁻⁸. In antiquity it was apparently a common crime.

Holiness Code

Death the penalty

20 ^{13}If a man lieth with a man, as with a woman, both of them have committed an abomination; they shall surely be put to death; they shall be responsible for their own death.

§ 74. **Bestiality,** Ex. 22^{19}, Dt. 27^{21}, Lev. 18$^{23-25}$, 20$^{15, 16}$, 18^{19}, 20^{18}

Primitive Codes

Ex. 22 ^{19}Whoever lieth with a beast shall surely be put to death.

Deuteronomic Codes

Death the penalty

Dt. 27 ^{21}Cursed be he who lieth with any manner of beast. And all the people shall say, So may it be.

Holiness Code

Later prohibitions

Lev. 18 ^{23}And thou shalt not lie with any beast to defile thyself with it, nor shall any woman stand before a beast, to lie down to it; it is unnatural. ^{24}Defile not yourselves in any of these ways for in all these ways the nations, which I am casting out before you, defiled themselves; ^{25}thus the land became defiled and I visited its guilt upon it and the land cast forth its inhabitants.

20 ^{15}If a man lieth with a beast, he shall surely be put to death and ye shall slay the beast. ^{16}And if a woman approach any beast to lie down with it, thou shalt kill the woman and the beast; they shall be put to death; their blood shall be upon them.

18 ^{19}Thou shalt not approach a woman to uncover her nakedness as long as she is impure through her monthly uncleanness.

20 ^{18}If a man shall lie with a woman having her sickness and shall uncover her nakedness,^{1} both of them shall be cut off from among their people.

§ 75. **Prostitution,** Dt. 23$^{17, 18}$, Lev. 19^{29}, 21^{9}

Deuteronomic Codes

Prohibition of temple prostitutes

Dt. 23 ^{17}None of the Israelitish women or men shall become a temple prostitute.^{m} ^{18}Thou shalt not bring the hire of a harlot or the wages of such a dog into the house of Jehovah thy God for any vow, for both these are an abomination to Jehovah thy God.^{n}

Holiness Code

Penalty for a priest's daughter

Lev. 19 ^{29}Profane not thy daughter by making her a harlot, lest the land fall into harlotry, and the land become full of unchastity.

21 ^{9}If the daughter of a priest profaneth herself by playing the harlot, she profaneth her father; she shall be burnt with fire.

---

^{1} Lev. 20^{18} The Heb. adds what is probably a supplemental gloss, *he has laid bare her fountain and she has uncovered the fountain of her blood.*

^{m} Dt. 23^{17} The current rendering, *sodomite* is incorrect.

^{n} Dt. 23$^{17, 18}$. Heb., 23$^{18, 19}$.

§ 76. Indecent Assault, Dt. 25$^{11, 12}$

Deuteronomic Codes

Dt. 25 ^{11}When men strive with one another, and the wife of the one Penalty draweth near to deliver her husband from the one who is attacking him, and mutila- putteth forth her hand, and taketh him by his private members, ^{12}thou shalt cut off her hand; thou shalt show no pity.

§ 77. Interchange of the Dress of the Sexes, Dt. 22^5

Deuteronomic Codes

Dt. 22 ^{5}A woman shall not wear any article pertaining to a man, neither Prohi- shall a man put on a woman's garment, for whoever doeth these things is an bition abomination to Jehovah thy God.

§ 78. Unnatural Mixtures, Dt. 22$^{9-11}$, Lev. 19^{19}

Deuteronomic Codes

Dt. 22 ^{9}Thou shalt not sow thy vineyard with two kinds of seed, lest the Prohi- whole be forfeited° to the sanctuary, the seed which thou hast sown, and the in case increase of the vineyard. ^{10}Thou shalt not plough with an ox and an ass to- of seed gether. ^{11}Thou shalt not wear stuff made of mixed wool and linen.

Holiness Code

Lev. 19 ^{19}Ye shall keep my statutes. Thou shalt not let thy cattle breed In case with a different kind. Thou shalt not sow thy field with two kinds of seed, of ani- and thou shalt not wear a garment of mixed goods. mals

§ 79. Kidnapping, Ex. 21^{16}, Dt. 24^7

Primitive Codes

Ex. 21 ^{16}He that stealeth a man, and selleth him, or if he still be found Death in his hand, the thief shall surely be put to death. the penalty

Deuteronomic Codes

Dt. 24 ^{7}If a man be found stealing any of his fellow Israelites, and he treat him as a slave or sell him, then that thief shall die; thus shalt thou purge away the evil from thy midst.

---

§ 76 This is the one case in which the Heb. law countenances the mutilation of the culprit. The aim is to prevent by the severity of the judgment all immodest acts of which the present case is a type.

° Dt. 22^9 Lit., *become sacred.*

§ 79 The Code of Hammurabi is equally severe in punishing this heinous crime: § 14. *If a man has stolen a child, he shall be put to death.* § 15. *If a man has induced either a male or female slave from the house of a patrician or plebeian to leave the city, he shall be put to death.*

§ 80. **Covetousness**, Dt. 5²¹ [Ex. 20¹⁷]

Deuteronomic Codes

Prohi-
bition

Dt. 5 ²¹Thou shalt not covet thy neighbor's wife, neither shalt thou desire thy neighbor's house, his field, or his male or female slave, his ox, or his ass, or anything that is thy neighbor's.

§ 81. **Lying**, Lev. 19¹¹ᵇ

Holiness Code

Prohi-
bition

Lev. 19 ¹¹ᵇYe shall not lie to one another.

IV

CRIMES AGAINST THE PERSON

§ 82. **Dishonoring Parents**, Ex. 21¹⁵, ¹⁷ [20¹², Dt. 5¹⁶, 21¹⁸⁻²¹, 27¹⁶, Lev. 19³ᵃ, 20⁹]

Primitive Codes

Penalty
in ex-
treme
cases

Ex. 21 ¹⁵He that striketh his father or his mother shall be put to death. ¹⁷He that curseth his father or mother shall be put to death.

§ 83. **Murder**, Ex. 21¹²⁻¹⁴, ²⁰, ²¹, Dt. 5¹⁷ [Ex 20¹³], Dt. 19¹¹⁻¹³, Lev. 24¹⁷, ²¹ᵇ, Gen. 9⁵, ⁶, Nu. 35¹⁴⁻³⁴

Primitive Codes

Penalty
accord-
ing to
intent

Ex. 21 ¹²If a man strike another so that he die, the manslayer shall be put to death. ¹³If a man lie not in wait, but God deliver him into his hand, then I will appoint thee a place to which he may flee. ¹⁴If a man attack

---

§ 80 The original injunction probably read, simply, *thou shalt not covet;* the different codes have variously expanded it, in defining its application. Ex. 20¹⁷ reads, *Thou shalt not covet thy neighbor's house, thou shalt not covet thy neighbor's wife, nor his male or female servant, nor his ox, nor his ass, nor anything that is thy neighbor's.* Like the law of love in Lev. 19, it is one of the few enactments which define, as did Jesus, individual responsibility for the motives as well as the resulting acts.

§ 81 This law is in striking contrast to the oriental attitude toward telling the truth, which is expressed by the popular proverb, *A lie is the salt of a man.*

§ 82 For the additional laws under this head cf. § 1. The Deuteronomic codes provide that the parents must present to the elders of the city a formal charge against their son, and then that the community stone him to death. The Holiness Code simply reiterates the injunction of the primitive codes. For the corresponding regulations in the Code of Hammurabi, cf. note § 1. It also enacts that: § 195. *If a son has struck his father, his hands shall be cut off.*

§ 83 The Heb. laws aimed thoroughly to protect the innocent, as well as to punish the guilty. Each succeeding law sought more carefully to correct the abuses incidental to the pervading law of blood revenge and to guard only those who had committed unintentional murder. At the same time the responsibility for punishing a murderer is left not with the state but with the relatives of the slain. Cf. note § 53 for a discussion of the cities of refuge and Josh. 20⁷, ⁸ for the late priestly list of these cities. The detailed law in Nu. 35¹⁴⁻³⁴ is introduced in a very late priestly section, which, contrary to the earlier priestly codes, Nu. 18²⁰, ²⁴, assigns forty-eight cities to the Levites. The linguistic evidence also indicates that it is one of the latest additions to the O.T., cf. note § 160.

Primitive Codes

another maliciously to slay him by treachery, thou shalt take him from my altar, that he may be put to death.

^{20}If a man strike his male or female slave with a stick so that he die at once, the master must be punished. ^{21}If, however, the slave survive a day or two, the master shall not be punished, for it is his own loss. *In case of slaves*

Deuteronomic Codes

Dt. 5 ^{17}Thou shalt not kill.

19 ^{11}If any man hate his neighbor, and lie in wait for him, and attack him and strike him mortally so that he die, and the murderer flee into one of the cities of refuge, ^{12}the elders of his city shall send and bring him and deliver him into the hand of the avenger of blood, that he may die. ^{13}Thou shalt have no mercy on him, but thou shalt purge away the innocent blood from Israel, that it may go well with thee. *No altar-asylum for the guilty*

Holiness Code

Lev. 24 ^{17}He that smiteth any man mortally shall surely be put to death. ^{21b}He that killeth a man shall be put to death. *Life for life*

Priestly Codes

Gen. 9 ^{5}Surely your own blood will I require; from every beast will I require it, and at the hand of every man, even at the hand of every man's brother, will I require the life of man. ^{6}He that sheds man's blood, by man shall his blood be shed, for in the image of God made he man.

Supplemental Priestly Codes

Nu. 35 ^{14}Ye shall set apart three cities beyond the Jordan, and three cities shall ye set apart in the land of Canaan; they shall be cities of refuge. ^{15}These six cities shall be for refuge for the Israelites and for the resident alien and the one who hath settled among them, that every one who hath killed another unintentionally may flee to them. *Cities of refuge*

^{16}But if he smote him with an iron weapon, so that he died, he is a murderer; the murderer shall surely be put to death. ^{17}If he smote him with a stone such as can be held in the hand, whereby a man may die, so that he died, he is a murderer; the murderer shall surely be put to death. ^{18}Or if he smote him with a weapon of wood such as can be held[p] in the hand, whereby a man may die, so that he died, he is a murderer; the murderer shall surely be put to death. ^{19}The avenger of blood shall himself put the murderer to death; when he meeteth him, he shall put him to death. ^{20}If he pushed him through hatred, or hurled anything[q] at him insidiously, so that he died, ^{21}or in enmity smote him with his hand, so that he died, he who smote him shall surely be put to death; he is a murderer; the avenger of blood shall put the murderer to death, when he meeteth him. *Laws to be applied in case of intentional murder*

---

p Nu. 35^{18} So Gk. and Sam.
q Nu. 35^{20} So Gk. Heb. omits, *anything*.

Supplemental Priestly Codes

In case of accidental homicide

²²But if he pushed him inadvertently and not out of enmity, or hurled at him anything without lying in wait, ²³or cast at him, without seeing him, any stone whereby a man may die, so that he died, and he had not been his enemy nor sought his harm, ²⁴then the congregation shall judge between the smiter and the avenger of blood according to these ordinances. ²⁵Thus the congregation shall rescue the manslayer from the hand of the avenger of blood, and the congregation shall send him back to his city of refuge, whither he had fled, that he may dwell therein until the death of the high priest, who was anointed with the holy oil. ²⁶But if the manslayer shall at any time go beyond the border of his city of refuge, whither he fled, ²⁷and the avenger of blood find him without the border of his city of refuge, and the avenger of blood slay the manslayer, he shall not be guilty of blood, ²⁸because he should have remained in his city of refuge until the death of the high priest; but after the death of the high priest the manslayer may return to his own land.

Safeguards of justice and order

²⁹These shall serve as a statute and regulative ordinance for you throughout your generations in all your dwellings. ³⁰In every case of murder the murderer shall be put to death on the testimony of witnesses; on the testimony of but one witness, however, shall no one suffer death. ³¹Moreover ye shall take no ransom for the life of a murderer who is guilty of death, but he shall surely be put to death. ³²And ye shall take no ransom for him who hath fled to his city of refuge, that he may return to dwell in the land, until the death of the highʳ priest. ³³So ye shall not pollute the land wherein ye dwell,ˢ for blood especially polluteth the land, and no expiation can be made for the land for the blood that is shed therein but by the blood of him who shed it. ³⁴So yeᵗ shall not defile the land which ye inhabit, in the midst of which I dwell; for I, Jehovah, dwell in the midst of the Israelites.

§ 84. **Assault,** Ex. 21¹⁵, ¹⁸, ²⁶, ²⁷, Dt. 27²⁴, Lev. 24¹⁹

Primitive Codes

Penalty if victim is a parent

Ex. 21 ¹⁵He that striketh his father or his mother shall surely be put to death.

For injury inflicted in a fight

¹⁸If men contend and one strike the other with a stone or a club,ᵘ and he do not die, but is confined to his bed, then, if he rise again, and can walk out supported on his staff, the one who struck him shall be acquitted; only he must pay for the loss of the other man's time until he is thoroughly healed.

Injury to a slave

²⁶If a man strike his male or female slave in the eye, so as to destroy it, he shall let him go free because of the loss of his eye. ²⁷If he knock out his

---

ʳ Nu. 35³² So Gk., Sam., and Syr. The Heb. omits, *high*.
ˢ Nu. 35³³ So Gk., Sam., and Syr. The Heb. has no verb.
ᵗ Nu. 35³⁴ So Gk., Sam., and Syr. The Heb. has, *thou shalt*.
ᵘ Ex. 21¹⁸ Or, *fist*. So Gk.; but the Targs. interpret, *club*, and this is best supported by the context.
§ 84 For the corresponding detailed laws of Hammurabi cf. Appendix VI. In both the Heb. and Bab. systems the *lex talionis* is still in force, although the tendency to substitute a milder penalty is apparent, and always when the victim is a slave.

Primitive Codes

male or female servant's tooth, he shall let him go free because of the loss of his tooth.

Deuteronomic Codes

Dt. 27 ²⁴Cursed be he that smiteth his neighbor in secret. And all the people shall say, So may it be.

Public condemnation

Holiness Code

Lev. 24 ¹⁹If a man disfigureth his neighbor, as he hath done, so shall it be done to him.

Penalty for mutilation

§ 85. Personal Injury, Ex. 21²⁸⁻³², ²²·²⁵

Primitive Codes

Ex. 21 ²⁸If an ox fatally gore a man or woman, the ox shall be stoned and its flesh shall not be eaten, but the owner of the ox shall be acquitted. ²⁹But if the ox was already in the habit of goring, and it hath been reported to its owner and he hath not kept it in, with the result that it hath killed a man or a woman, the ox shall be stoned and its owner also shall be put to death. ³⁰If a ransom is fixed for him, he shall give for the redemption of his life whatever amount is determined. ³¹Whether the ox hath gored a boy or a girl, this law shall be executed.ᵛ ³²If the ox gore a male or female servant, thirty silver shekels shall be given to their master and the ox shall be stoned.

Penalty if inflicted by an animal

²²If men strive together and hurt a pregnant woman so that she hath a miscarriage and yet no harm to her result, he shall be fined, as the woman's husband shall determine,ʷ and he shall pay for the miscarriage. ²³But if any harm follow, then thou shalt give life for life, ²⁴eye for eye, tooth for tooth, hand for hand, foot for foot, ²⁵branding for branding, wound for wound, stripe for stripe.ˣ

If inflicted upon a pregnant woman

§ 86. Rape, Dt. 22²⁵⁻²⁷

Deuteronomic Codes

Dt. 22 ²⁵If a man find a young woman who is betrothed in the field and the man force her and lie with her, then simply the man who lay with her shall die, ²⁶but thou shalt do nothing to the young woman; the young woman hath committed no sin worthy of death, for this case is as when a man attacketh his neighbor and slayeth him, ²⁷for he found her in the field, the betrothed young woman cried out, but there was none to save her.

Death penalty for the guilty man

---

§ 85 The laws of Hammurabi are very similar:
§ 251 *If a man's ox be a gorer, and has revealed its evil propensity as a gorer, and he has not blunted its horn or shut up the ox, and then that ox has gored a free man and caused his death, the owner shall pay half a mina of silver.* § 252. *If it be a slave that has been killed, he shall pay one third of a mina of silver.*
ᵛ Ex. 21³¹ Lit., *according to this judgment* (or *ruling*) *shall it be done to him.*
ʷ Ex. 21²² Slightly correcting the text as suggested by Budde. The present Heb. construction is very doubtful. It may possibly be translated, *as the judges determine.*
ˣ Ex. 21²²⁻²⁵ For the somewhat similar laws of Hammurabi, cf. Appendix VI, §§ 209–214.

§ 87. Seduction, Ex. 22¹⁶, ¹⁷, Dt. 22²⁸, ²⁹

Primitive Codes

Penalty **Ex. 22** ¹⁶If a man entice a virgin, who is not betrothed and lie with her, he must make her his wife by paying a dowry for her. ¹⁷If her father refuse absolutely to give her to him, he shall pay money equivalent to the dowry of young girls.

Deuteronomic Codes

The later law **Dt. 22** ²⁸If a man find a virgin, who is not betrothed, and take hold of her, and lie with her, and they be caught in the act, ²⁹then the man who lay with her shall give to the girl's father fifty shekels of silver; moreover she shall be his wife, because he hath humbled her; he may not divorce her as long as he lives.

§ 88. Wronging the Defenceless, Ex. 22²¹⁻²⁴, Dt. 24¹⁴ᵃ, 27¹⁸, ¹⁹, Lev. 19¹⁴, ³³

Primitive Codes

Aliens, widow, and orphans **Ex. 22** ²¹Thou shalt not wrong nor oppress a resident alien, for ye were aliens residing in the land of Egypt.ʸ ²²Ye shall not afflict any widow or fatherless child. ²³If thou afflict them at all and they cry to me, I will surely hear their cry; ²⁴and my wrath shall be aroused, and I will slay you with the sword, so that your wives shall be widows and your children fatherless.

Deuteronomic Codes

Hired servants **Dt. 24** ¹⁴ᵃThou shalt not oppress a hired servant who is poor and needy.

Blind **27** ¹⁸Cursed be the one who maketh the blind wander out of the way. And all the people shall say, So may it be.

Public condemnation ¹⁹Cursed be the one who perverteth the justice due the resident alien, fatherless, and widow. And all the people shall say, So may it be.

Holiness Code

Deaf, blind, and aliens **Lev. 19** ¹⁴Thou shalt not curse the deaf, nor put a stumbling block before the blind; but thou shalt fear thy God: I am Jehovah. ³³And if an alien make his home with youᶻ in your land, ye shall do him no wrong.

§ 89. Slander, Ex. 23¹ᵃ, Lev. 19¹⁶

Primitive Codes

Prohibition **Ex. 23** ¹ᵃThou shalt not spread abroad a false report.

Holiness Code

Lev. 19 ¹⁶Thou shalt not go about as a tale bearer among thy people; nor shalt thou seek the blood of thy neighbor: I am Jehovah.

---

§ 88 Cf. note § 106.
ʸ Ex. 22²¹ This vs. is in part duplicated in 23⁹, *Thou shalt not oppress a resident alien, for ye know how a resident alien feeleth, since ye were aliens residing in the land of Egypt.*
ᶻ Lev. 19³³ So Gk., Sam., and Syr. Heb., *thee.*
§ 89 The Heb. codes suggest no definite penalty for this pernicious crime. Hammurabi's Code, however, is grimly definite:
§ 127 *If a man has caused the finger to be pointed at a votary, or a man's wife, and has not justified himself, that man shall be brought before the judges, and have his forehead branded*

V

CRIMES AGAINST PROPERTY

§ 90. Theft, Ex. 22¹⁻⁴ [20¹⁵], Dt. 5¹⁹, 23²⁴, ²⁵, Lev. 19¹¹ᵃ, 6²·⁷

Primitive Codes

Ex. 22 ¹If a man shall steal an ox or a sheep, and kill or sell it, he shall Penal-
restore five oxen for one ox and four sheep for one sheep. ⁴If the theft be ties
found in his hand alive, whether it be ox, or ass, or sheep, he must pay
twice its value. ³ᵇIf he have nothing, then he shall be sold to pay for what
he hath stolen.

²If the thief be found breaking in and be struck down so that he die, In case
the one who striketh him is not guilty of murder. ³ᵇIf the sun hath risen, killed
the one who striketh him is guilty of murder; he must make restitution.

Deuteronomic Codes

Dt. 5 ¹⁹Thou shalt not steal.

23 ²⁴When thou comest into thy neighbor's vineyard, thou mayest eat of Prohi-
grapes thy fill at thine own pleasure, but thou shalt not put any in thy vessel. bition
²⁵When thou comest into thy neighbor's standing grain, thou mayest gather tion of
the heads with thy hand,ᵃ but thou shalt not putᵇ a sickle to thy neighbor's natural
standing grain. prod-
ucts

Holiness Code

Lev. 19 ¹¹ᵃThou shalt not steal.

Priestly Codes

Lev. 6 ²If any one sin and break faith with Jehovah, by deceiving his Repa-
neighbor in regard to a deposit or a pledge, or by robbing or defrauding his ration
neighbor, ³or if he hath found something which was lost and deny it and per- things
jure himself, if by doing any one of these things ⁴a man hath sinned, and so or ob-
is guilty, he shall restore that which he took by robbery, or the thing fraud-
which he obtained by fraud, or the deposit which was entrusted to him, or ulently
the lost thing which he found, ⁵or anything about which he swore falsely;
he shall restore it in full, and shall add to it a fifth more; he shall give it to
its rightful owner on the day when he is found guilty. ⁶He shall also bring
to the priest his guilt-offering for Jehovah, a ram without blemish out of the

---

Crimes against Property.—As has been noted in the Introd., p. 25, one of the fundamental differences between the O.T. and Bab. codes is that, while the Code of Hammurabi is
prodigal of human life, the Heb. laws carefully guard it; but in regard to property the emphasis is reversed. For the detailed Bab. laws regarding crimes against property cf. Appendix VII.

The relatively slight attention given in the O.T. to the rights of property is one of the
many lines of evidence proving that the interests and ambitions of the early Israelites lay
rather in national and religious than in material realms.

ᵃ Dt. 23²⁵ Cf. Mt. 12¹. Lk. 6¹ for the action of Jesus' disciples, which was in accord with
this ancient law.
ᵇ Dt. 23²⁵ Lit., *move.*

Priestly Codes

flock, according to thy valuation, as a guilt-offering.   ⁷Then the priest shall make atonement for him before Jehovah, and he shall be forgiven for whatever he may have done to incur guilt.

§ 91. Land Stealing, Dt. 19¹⁴, 27¹⁷

Deuteronomic Codes

Prohibition

Dt. 19 ¹⁴Thou shalt not remove thy neighbor's landmark, which they of former generations have set, in thine inheritance which thou shalt inherit, in the land which Jehovah thy God giveth thee as a possession.

Public condemnation

27 ¹⁷Cursed be he that removeth his neighbor's landmark.   And all the people shall say, So may it be.

§ 92. False Weights and Measures, Dt. 25¹³⁻¹⁶, Lev. 19³⁵⁻³⁷

Deuteronomic Codes

Prohibition of dishonesty in business

Dt. 25 ¹³Thou shalt not have in thy bag diverse weights,[c] a great and a small.   ¹⁴Thou shalt not have in thy house diverse measures,[d] a great and a small.   ¹⁵A perfect and just weight shalt thou have; a perfect and just measure shalt thou have, that thou mayest live long in the land which Jehovah thy God giveth thee.   ¹⁶For all who do these things, even all who do unrighteously, are an abomination to Jehovah thy God.

Holiness Code

Honesty in all social and business relations

Lev. 19 ³⁵Ye shall do no unrighteousness in judgment, or with rule, or with weight, or with measure.   ³⁶Just balances, just weights, a just ephah, and a just hin shall ye have: I am Jehovah your God, who brought you out of the land of Egypt.   ³⁷Ye shall therefore observe all my statutes and all my ordinances, and do them: I am Jehovah.

---

§ 91 Boundary stones among the Babylonians, as well as the Hebrews, marked the limits of estates, and to move them was the usual mode of stealing land.   The references in the prophetic and wisdom books indicate that the crime was a common one in Israel, cf. Hos. 5¹⁰, Pr. 22²⁸, 23¹⁰, Job 24².   The Babylonians, Greeks and Romans placed the boundary stones under the protection of the gods, and regarded them as sacred.   The Roman law provided that those who attempted to move them might be slain (Dron. Hal. ii, 74).

The law of Dt. 27¹⁷ recalls the curses of the ancient Bab. kings upon those who removed their neighbor's landmarks, cf. John's, *Bab. and Assyr. Laws, Contracts and Letters*, 191.

§ 92 These laws aim to counteract the common oriental custom of cheating in trade. When the weights used were ordinary stones, the temptation to steal was strong and its detection   difficult.

c Dt. 25¹³ Lit., *a stone and a stone, i. e.,* stones of different size.   Cf. Am. 8⁵ and Pr. 20²³.

d Dt. 25¹⁴ Lit., *two different ephahs.*   Cf. Am. 8⁵, Mi. 6¹⁰ and Ezek 45¹⁰.

HUMANE LAWS

HUMANE LAWS

I

KINDNESS TOWARDS ANIMALS

§ 93. The Threshing Ox, Dt. 25[4]

Deuteronomic Codes

Dt. 25 [4]Thou shalt not muzzle the ox when it treadeth out the grain.　Profit
sharing

§ 94. Wild Animals, Ex. 23[11], Lev. 25[5-7]

Primitive Codes

Ex. 23 [11]The seventh year thou shalt let the land rest and lie fallow, Object
that the poor of thy people may eat; and what they leave the wild beasts of the
shall eat.　In like manner thou shalt do with thy vineyard and thy olive- ical
yard.

Humane Laws.—Although the majority of the laws included under this head have
already been classified elsewhere, they are here grouped together as a basis for the comprehensive study of the most distinctive element in the O.T. codes.　A comparison of the O.T.
laws with the still earlier Code of Hammurabi or the contemporary Assyrian, Egyptian or
Phœnician systems reveals far more points of analogy than difference.　All assume very much
the same characteristic oriental institutions, such as the kingly form of government, slavery,
the secondary place of woman, and ceremonial worship, centring about certain sanctuaries
cf. Introd., p. 6.　To these humane laws, however, the other legal systems of antiquity present
few parallels.　They represent the high-water mark of Heb. legislation.　In them the teachings
of the prophets, who preached not only justice but consideration for the needy and love to all
men, find concrete expression.　Like the prophets, who inspired them, they rise far above the
sordid standards of their age and anticipate at many points the perfect teachings of the divine
Prophet of Nazareth.　Most of the O.T. laws have been superseded by others better adapted
to the changed conditions of to-day, but these humane laws, in spirit, if not in actual form,
have been incorporated in our modern systems or else remain lofty ideals towards which civilization is slowly but surely moving.

It is natural that the majority of them should be found in the Deuteronomic codes, which
have been most directly touched by the spirit and lofty teachings of the prophets of the Assyrian period, cf. Introd., p. 31.　The hortatory form of many of them also reveals the powerful
influence of the prophets.　In most of these laws no distinct penalty is prescribed in case the
given command is not obeyed.　Often the appeal is simply to the individual conscience, and
Jehovah is recognized as the only judge who can execute.　Sometimes, when great self-denial
is required to keep a given law, as for example, the remission of interest to the needy, the
promise is added that God will give prosperity to those who obey.　Elsewhere the people are
warned lest they incur Jehovah's displeasure by disobedience.　Frequently the appeal is to
the national sense of gratitude because of the great deliverance from Egypt.　Thus at almost
every point they reveal the spirit of the inspired prophet in the heart of the lawgiver.　Like
the teachings of Jesus they emphasize not merely the external act but the motive in the soul
of man.　Above the brutal despotism and inhuman cruelty and selfish materialism of their
age, they rise as beacon lights, guiding the human race on to the great social and philanthropic
movements of to-day.

§ 93 This and the kindred laws of Dt. represent the earliest recognition and formulation
of man's duty to the animal world over which he is called to rule.　They voice that profound
love for all of God's creatures which filled the heart of the Christ and which is the essence of
true religion.

Holiness Code

Lev. 25 ⁵That which groweth of itself of thy harvest thou shalt not reap, and the grapes of thy undressed vine thou shalt not gather; it shall be a year of complete rest for the land. ⁶The sabbath produce of the land shall be food for you; for thee, for thy male and female slave, for thy hired servant, and for the settler who resides with thee, ⁷and for thy cattle and the beasts that are in thy land shall all the produce be for food.

§ 95. Beasts of Burden, Ex. 23¹²ᵃ, ᵇ

Primitive Codes

Sabbath rest

Ex. 23 ¹²ᵃ, ᵇSix days shalt thou do thy work, and on the seventh day thou shalt rest, that thine ox and thine ass may have rest.

§ 96. The Mother and her Young, Ex. 34²⁶ᵇ, Dt. 22⁶, ⁷, Lev. 22²⁸

Primitive Codes

Consideration for the maternal relation

Ex. 34 ²⁶ᵇThou shalt not seethe a kid in its mother's milk.

Deuteronomic Codes

Dt. 22 ⁶If a bird's nest chance to be before thee in the way, in any tree or on the ground, with young ones or eggs, and with the mother sitting upon the young or upon the eggs, thou shalt not take the mother with the young; ⁷thou shalt surely let the mother go, but the young thou mayest take for thyself, that it may be well with thee, and that thou mayest live long.

Holiness Code

Lev. 22 ²⁸[When an animal is offered to Jehovah], whether it be a cow or ewe, ye shall not kill both it and its young on the same day.

II

CONSIDERATION FOR THE UNFORTUNATE

§ 97. In Taking Pledges, Dt. 24¹⁰, ¹¹

Deuteronomic Codes

To regard a poor man's feelings

Dt. 24 ¹⁰When thou lendest thy neighbor any kind of loan, thou shalt not go into his house to take a pledge from him. ¹¹Thou shalt stand without, and the man to whom thou dost lend shall bring out the pledge to thee.

---

§ 96 The exact principle underlying these three kindred laws is not clear. Possibly it is an ancient superstition, but apparently it is a sentimental reason. The same reward is urged for observing the injunction in Dt. 22⁶, ⁷, as the command to children to honor parents, 5¹⁶. In all of these cases the sanctity of the parental relation is evidently prominent in the minds of the lawgivers.

Consideration for the Unfortunate.—Hammurabi in the epilogue to his code, cf. Introd., p. 5, and in the evident purpose manifest in his laws to protect the widows and orphans, anticipates some of these regulations, but he nowhere reveals that delicate and chivalrous consideration for the feelings of the needy, which divines and guards against all acts which would inflict unnecessary pain on those whom the strong should protect.

§ 98. Return of Garments Taken in Pledge, Dt. 24¹², ¹³

Deuteronomic Codes

Dt. 24 ¹²In the case of a poor man, thou shalt not sleep with his pledge; ¹³thou shalt surely restore to him the pledge at sunset, that he may sleep in his garment and bless thee; thus thou wilt be counted righteous before Jehovah thy God.

To avoid thought- less cruelty

§ 99. Not to Take a Millstone in Pledge, Dt. 24⁶

Deuteronomic Codes

Dt. 24 ⁶No man shall take the mill or the upper millstone as a pledge, for thereby he taketh a man's life as a pledge.

Not to take a neces- sity

§ 100. Moderation in Inflicting the Bastinado, Dt. 25², ³

Deuteronomic Codes

Dt. 25 ²If a culprit deserves to be beaten, the judge shall make him lie down to be beaten in his presence with the number of blows corresponding to his crime. ³Forty blows he may inflict upon him, but no more, lest, if he add more blows than these, thy fellow countryman be held in contempt in thine eyes.

To guard against unjust cruelty

§ 101. Exemption of Relatives of Criminals from Punishment, Dt. 24¹⁶

Deuteronomic Codes

Dt. 24 ¹⁶Fathers shall not be put to death with their children, and children shall not be put to death with their fathers; each man shall be put to death simply for his own crime.

To spare the inno- cent

§ 102. Precautions against Accident, Dt. 22⁸

Deuteronomic Codes

Dt. 22 ⁸When thou buildest a new house, thou shalt make a parapet for thy roof, that thou bring not blood upon thy house, in case any man should fall from it.

To guard public safety

§ 99 The millstone was needed each day in grinding the grain for the use of the family, especially where poverty made an abundant supply of food impossible.

§ 101 In the ancient East the family often shared a father's fate, even when they were entirely innocent, cf. Dan. 6²⁴, Esth. 9¹³, ¹⁴, Herod. iii, 119. At least in the case of extreme offences, the same custom was in vogue in early Heb. history, cf. Josh. 7²⁴, ²⁵, II Sam. 21¹⁻⁹. It was the outgrowth of the primitive Semitic conception of the family as a closely knit social unit. The juster principle of individual responsibility was recognized, however, by Amaziah in dealing with the conspirators who slew his father. II Kgs. 14⁶, and that precedent may well be the basis of the present law.

III

TREATMENT OF DEPENDENT CLASSES

§ 103. Hired Servants, Dt. 24¹⁴, ¹⁵, Lev. 19¹³ᵇ

Deuteronomic Codes

To deal kindly and justly with hired servants

Dt. 24 ¹⁴Thou shalt not oppress a hired servant who is poor and needy, whether he be of thy own race, or of the resident aliens who are in thy land within thy city. ¹⁵On the same day thou shalt pay him his wages before the sun goeth down, for he is poor, and setteth his heart upon it; and let him not cry against thee to Jehovah, and thou be guilty of a crime.

Holiness Code

Lev. 19 ¹³ᵇThe wages of a hired servant shall not remain with thee all night until the morning.

§ 104. Slaves, Ex. 23¹²ᵃ, ᶜ, 21², Dt. 15¹²⁻¹⁵, Lev. 25³⁹, ⁴⁰ᵃ, ⁴³

Primitive Codes

To give rest and ultimate freedom to slaves

Ex. 23 ¹²ᵃ, ᶜSix days shalt thou do thy work, and on the seventh day thou shalt rest, that the son of thy handmaid and the resident alien may be refreshed.

21 ²If a man buy a Hebrew slave, he shall serve six years, but in the seventh year he shall go free without having to pay any ransom.

Deuteronomic Codes

To give liberally to a freed slave

Dt. 15 ¹²If one of thy own race, a Hebrew man or a Hebrew woman, be sold to thee, he shall serve thee six years; then in the seventh year thou shalt let him go free. ¹³And when thou lettest him go free, thou shalt not let him go empty-handed; ¹⁴rather thou shalt furnish him liberally from thy flock, and thy threshing-floor, and thy winepress; according as Jehovah thy God hath blessed thee thou shalt give to him. ¹⁵And thou shalt remember that thou wast a slave in the land of Egypt, and that Jehovah thy God redeemed thee; therefore I now command thee to do this thing.

Holiness Code

To be considerate of Hebrews

Lev. 25 ³⁹If thy fellow countryman become poor and sell himself to thee, thou shalt not make him serve as a slave. ⁴⁰ᵃAs a hired servant and as a settler shall he be to thee. ⁴³Thou shalt not rule over him with harshness, but thou shalt fear thy God.

---

§ 103 Cf. note § 12. The supreme justice and present day applicability of the principle underlying this law are obvious.
§ 104 Cf. note § 16 and the additional laws under the same sections; cf. also note § 13.

§ 105. Captives, Dt. 21¹⁰·¹⁴

Deuteronomic Codes

Dt. 21 ¹⁰When thou goest forth to battle against thine enemies, and To re-
Jehovah thy God delivereth them into thy hands, and thou carriest them gard
away captive, ¹¹and seest among the captives a beautiful woman, and thou ings
has a desire for her, and wouldst make her thy wife, ¹²then thou shalt bring rights
her home to thy house, and she shall shave her head, and pare her nails, ¹³and of a
she shall put off the garb of her captivity and shall remain in thy house, and wife
bewail her father and her mother a full month. After that thou shalt go in
unto her, and be her husband, and she shall be thy wife. ¹⁴But if thou have
no delight in her, then thou shalt let her go where she will; but thou shalt
not in any case sell her for money, thou shalt not deal with her as a slave,
because thou hast humbled her.

To regard the feelings and rights of a captive wife

§ 106. The Defenceless, Ex. 22²¹⁻²⁴, Dt. 24¹⁷, ¹⁸, 27¹⁸, ¹⁹, Lev. 19¹⁴

Primitive Codes

Ex. 22 ²¹Thou shalt not wrong nor oppress a resident alien, for ye were Not to
aliens residing in the land of Egypt. ²²Ye shall not afflict any widow or wrong
fatherless child. ²³If thou afflict them at all, and they cry to me, I will surely widows
hear their cry, ²⁴and my wrath shall be aroused, and I will slay you with the or or-
sword, so that your wives shall be widows and your children fatherless.

Not to wrong aliens, widows or orphans

Deuteronomic Codes

Dt. 24 ¹⁷Thou shalt not pervert the justice due the resident alien, or
the fatherless, nor take a widow's garment as a pledge; ¹⁸but thou shalt remember that thou wast a slave in Egypt, and that Jehovah thy God redeemed
thee from there; therefore I command thee to do this thing.

27 ¹⁸Cursed be the one who maketh the blind wander out of the way. Or the
And all the people shall say, So may it be. ¹⁹Cursed be the one who per- blind
verteth the justice due the resident alien, fatherless, and widow. And all
the people shall say, So may it be.

Holiness Code

Lev. 19 ¹⁴Thou shalt not curse the deaf, nor put a stumblingblock Or
before the blind; but thou shalt fear thy God: I am Jehovah.

deaf

§ 107. The Poor, Ex. 23⁶, Dt. 15⁷⁻¹¹, Lev. 25³⁵

Primitive Codes

Ex. 23 ⁶Thou shalt not prevent justice being done to thy poor in his Not to
cause.

Not to wrong him

---

§ 105 Cf. also note § 4.
§ 106 Among most ancient peoples, resident aliens had no legal rights and were therefore the objects of every form of injustice. This evil the Heb. lawgivers strenuously sought
to correct. Widows and orphans were unable to defend themselves from those who might
wrong them, and had no strong protectors. Accordingly they also were especially guarded
by benign provisions.
§ 107 The Israelitish race have always shown most remarkable and commendable loyalty
to its poorer members. This significant fact in history is doubtless due largely to the influence of these laws.

Deuteronomic Codes

Not to refuse a loan to the poor

Dt. 15 ⁷If there be with thee a poor man, one of thy fellow countrymen, in any of thy cities in thy land which Jehovah thy God giveth thee, thou shalt not be hardhearted, nor shut thy hand from thy poor brother; ⁸but thou shalt surely open thy hand to him, and shalt lend him sufficient for his need as he wanteth. ⁹Beware lest this base thought come in thy heart, The seventh year, the year of release, is at hand, and thou turn a deaf ear to thy poor brother,[a] and thou give him nothing; and he cry to Jehovah against thee, and thou be guilty of a crime.[b] ¹⁰Thou shalt surely give to him, and thy heart shall not be sad when thou givest to him, because for this Jehovah thy God will bless thee in all thy work, and in all that thou undertakest to do. ¹¹For the poor will never cease to be in the land; therefore I command thee, Thou shalt surely open thy hand to thy brother, to thy needy, and to thy poor in thy land.

Holiness Code

To support the poor

Lev. 25 ³⁵If thy fellow countryman become poor and fall into poverty with thee, thou shalt support him, and he shall live with thee.

IV

PHILANTHROPIC PROVISIONS FOR THE NEEDY

§ 108. **Leaving the Gleanings,** Dt. 24¹⁹⁻²², Lev. 19⁹, ¹⁰ [23²²]

Deuteronomic Codes

To leave a part of all natural products for the needy

Dt. 24 ¹⁹When thou reapest thy harvest in thy field, and hast forgot a sheaf in thy field, thou shalt not go again to bring it; it shall be for the resident alien, for the fatherless, and for the widow, that Jehovah thy God may bless thee in all the work of thy hands. ²⁰When thou beatest thy olive-tree, thou shalt not go over the boughs again; it shall be for the resident alien, for the fatherless, and for the widow. ²¹When thou gatherest the grapes of thy vineyard, thou shalt not glean it after thee; it shall be for the resident alien, for the fatherless, and the widow. ²²Thou shalt remember that thou wast a slave in the land of Egypt; therefore I command thee to do this thing.

---

[a] Dt. 15⁹ Lit, *thy eye be evil against.*
[b] Dt. 15⁹ Lit, *it be sin to thee,* cf. also 23²¹, 24¹⁵.
Philanthropic Provisions for the Needy.—It is from the social rather than the strictly legal point of view that these regulations are formulated. Some of them anticipate the principles assumed by modern socialism. They do not aim primarily to protect the rights of property or vested interests, but to define and facilitate the discharge of the obligations of society to its individual and needy members. They start with the assumption that those who have control of natural resources have certain duties to perform toward those less favored. They also seek by definite institutions to insure the more equable distribution of the products of the land.

Holiness Code

Lev. 19 ⁹When ye reap the harvest of your land, thou shalt not entirely reap the corners of thy field, neither shalt thou gather the gleanings of thy harvest. ¹⁰And thou shalt not glean thy vineyard, neither shalt thou gather the scattered fruit of thy vineyard; thou shalt leave them for the poor and for the resident alien : I am Jehovah your God.ᶜ

§ 109. Sharing Offerings, Dt. 16¹¹, ¹² [¹³, ¹⁴], 26¹¹

Deuteronomic Codes

Dt. 16 ¹¹When thou keepest the feast of weeks, thou shalt be joyful before Jehovah thy God, together with thy son and daughter and male and female slave and the Levite, who is within thy city, and the resident alien, and the fatherless, and the widow, who are among thee, at the place in which Jehovah thy God shall choose to have his name dwell. ¹²And thou shalt remember that thou wast once a slave in Egypt, and observe these statutes. *[side note: To share the sacrificial meals with the needy]*

26 ¹¹Thou shalt rejoice in all the good which Jehovah thy God hath given to thee and thy house, together with the Levite and the alien in the midst of thee.

§ 110. Distribution of the Tithe, Dt. 14²⁸, ²⁹, 26¹², ¹³

Deuteronomic Codes

Dt. 14 ²⁸At the end of every three years thou shalt bring out all the tithe of thine increaseᵈ in that year and shalt deposit it within thy city. ²⁹That the Levite, because he hath no portion nor inheritance with thee, and the resident alien, and the fatherless, and the widow, who are in thy city, may come and eat and be satisfied, in order that Jehovah thy God may bless thee in all the work to which thou puttest thy hand.ᵉ *[side note: To give triennial tithe to the needy and dependent]*

26 ¹²When thou hast made an end of tithing all the tithe of thy produce in the third year, which is the year of tithing, thou shalt give it to the Levite, to the resident alien, to the fatherless, and to the widow, that they may eat within thy city, and be filled. ¹³And thou shalt say before Jehovah thy God, I have put awayᶠ the consecrated things out of my house, and have also given them to the Levite, and to the resident alien, to the fatherless and to the widow, just as thou hast commanded me; I have not transgressed any of thy commands, neither have I forgotten them.

ᶜ Lev. 19¹⁰ Lev. 23²² is an exact repetition of 19⁹, ¹⁰ᵇ. It has no connection with its context and its presence is probably due to a later editor or to a scribal error.

§ 109 The rejoicing at the chosen sanctuary in Jerusalem on the occasion of the harvest festivals included the slaughter of sacrificial animals and a general merrymaking, cf. note § 140. The aim of the law is to provide that all the dependent members of the community may have a part in these festivities, even as the people had had before the days of Josiah's reformation, at the ceremonies in connection with the local shrines. Dt. 16¹³, ¹⁴ repeats the same injunctions in connection with the feast of tabernacles, cf. § 214.

ᵈ Dt. 14²⁸ *I. e., from thy private granaries.*
ᵉ Dt. 14²⁹ Lit., *work of thy hand which thou doest.*
ᶠ Dt. 26¹³ Lit., *I have exterminated.*

§ 110 Two out of every three years the tithe of all that the ground produced was carried to Jerusalem and eaten by the offerer and his dependents, cf. § 151; but on the third year it was stored up in the different towns to be given to the dependent members of the community as their individual needs required.

§ 111. Remission of Interest to the Poor, Ex. 22²⁵, Dt. 23¹⁹, ²⁰, Lev. 25³⁵⁻³⁸

Primitive Codes

To take no interest from the poor

Ex. 22 ²⁵If thou lend money to any of my people with thee who is poor, thou shalt not be to him as a creditor, neither shall ye demand interest of him.

Deuteronomic Codes

To take no interest from a Hebrew

Dt. 23 ¹⁹Thou shalt not lend on interest to thy fellow countryman: interest on money, food or on anything that is lent on interest. ²⁰To a foreigner thou mayest lend on interest; but to thy fellow countryman thou shalt not lend on interest, that Jehovah thy God may bless thee in all that thou undertakest to do, in the land to which thou art going to possess it.

Holiness Code

From a poor Hebrew

Lev. 25 ³⁵If thy fellow countryman become poor, and fall into poverty with thee, thou shalt support him, and he shall live with thee. ³⁶Take of him no interest or usury, but fear thy God, that thy fellow countryman may live with thee. ³⁷Thou shalt not give him thy money on interest, nor give him thy food for usury. ³⁸I am Jehovah your God, who brought you forth out of the land of Egypt, to give you the land of Canaan, and to be your God.

§ 112. Rest and Remission of All Interest on the Seventh Year, Ex. 23¹⁰, ¹¹, Dt. 15¹⁻¹⁰, Lev. 25¹⁻⁷, ²⁰⁻²²

Primitive Codes

To share natural products with the poor

Ex. 23 ¹⁰Six years thou shalt sow thy land, and shalt gather in its increase. ¹¹The seventh year thou shalt let the land rest and lie fallow, that

---

§ 111 The spirit, if not the literal form of these laws are still universally applicable. Their background is an exceedingly simple organization. Until the Babylonian exile forced the Israelites into the great currents of the world's trade, they remained simple farmers and shepherds, who despised the Canaanitish traders in their midst. Loans, therefore, were not made for commercial purposes but under the pressure of dire necessity. To exact interest from a poor man was to force him or his family into slavery. This inevitable result Nehemiah bitterly condemns, although he and his friends had been accustomed to make loans on interest, Neh. 5.

Also in the ancient East the rate of interest was usually exorbitant. In Babylonia it was at one time limited to 20 per cent. In Assyria 25 per cent per annum was not uncommon; in Egypt the legal rate was limited to 30 per cent, or 33⅓ in case the loan was in grain. Like Nehemiah, the exiles and the later Jews, who engaged in commerce, did not hesitate to demand interest. Evidently the aim of these laws, as is definitely stated in the earliest and latest versions, was simply to protect the poor Israelites from unjust exactions, for to withhold a loan entirely would be more harmful than to demand a moderate rate of interest.

§ 112 Cf. also note § 16, and for the laws regarding the liberation of slaves on the seventh year, § 104. It is significant that this law is found in the primitive as well as the Holiness Code. It implies the agricultural stage and, therefore, cannot be dated earlier than the settlement in Canaan. It represents the application of the sabbath principle of one period of rest in every seven to the cycle of the years. It is also made applicable to the land as well as to men and animals. The author of the Holiness Code, in Lev. 26³⁴, ³⁵, regards the exile as the enforced period of rest for the land. This statement confirms the inference from Jer. 34 that the law of the sabbatical year, both in its command to let the land lie fallow and to liberate all Heb. slaves at the end of six years, was, at least before the exile, largely disregarded. Second Chr. 36²¹ bears similar testimony. Until the days of Nehemiah the Judean community continued to treat it as an ideal too high to be realized, until, in the covenant solemnly established in behalf of the people, they promised that *on the seventh year they would leave the land uncultivated and refrain from the exaction of any debt*. Josephus avers that it was kept in the days of Alexander the Great, *Antiq.* XI, 8⁶. I Mac. 6⁴⁹, ⁵³ suggests that in the Greek period it had become a regular institution. Even Tacitus was acquainted with the law, *Hist.* 5⁴, and the Mishna *Shebe'th* states that only in Palestine was it fully observed.

Primitive Codes

the poor of thy people may eat; and what they leave the wild beasts shall eat.
In like manner thou shalt do with thy vineyard and thine oliveyard.

Deuteronomic Codes

Dt. 15 ¹At the end of every seven years thou shalt make a release.ᵍ To re-
²And this is the nature of the release : every creditor shall remit that which mit all
he hath lent to his neighbor; he shall not exact it of his neighbor or fellow
countryman, because Jehovah's release hath been proclaimed. ³Of a foreigner thou mayest exact it; but whatever of thine is with thy fellow countryman let thy hand release. ⁴Nevertheless there shall be no poor with thee, for
Jehovah will surely bless thee in the land which Jehovah thy God giveth
thee to possess as an inheritance, ⁵if only thou diligently hearken to the voice
of Jehovah thy God, to observe to do all this commands which I command
thee this day. ⁶For Jehovah thy God will bless thee, as he promised thee;
and thou shalt lend to many nations, but thou shalt not borrow; and thou
shalt rule over many nations, but they shall not rule over thee.

⁷If there be with thee a poor man, one of thy fellow countrymen, in any of To loan
thy cities in thy land which Jehovah thy God giveth thee, thou shalt not be readily
hardhearted, nor shut thy hand from thy poor brother; ⁸but thou shalt surely poor
open thy hand to him, and shalt surely lend him sufficient for his need as the
he wanteth. ⁹Beware lest this base thought come in thy heart, The seventh year
year, the year of release, is at hand, and thou turn a deaf ear to thy poor fore the
brother, and thou give him nothing, and he cry to Jehovah against thee, and release
thou be guilty of a crime. ¹⁰Thou shalt surely give to him, and thy heart
shall not be sad when thou givest to him; because for this Jehovah thy God
will bless thee in all thy work, and in all that thou undertakest to do.

Holiness Code

Lev. 25 ¹Jehovah said to Moses on Mount Sinai, ²Speak to the Israelites and say To
to them, 'When ye have come to the land which I give you, the land share
shall rest for a sabbath to Jehovah. ³Six years thou shalt sow thy field, and seventh
six years thou shalt prune thy vineyard, and gather in its produce; ⁴but the rest the
seventh year shall be a sabbath of complete rest for the land, a sabbath to natural
Jehovah; thou shalt neither sow thy field nor prune thy vineyard. ⁵That which ucts
groweth of itself of thy harvest thou shalt not reap, and the grapes of thy un- the
dressed vine thou shalt not gather; it shall be a year of complete rest for the needy
land. ⁶And the sabbath produce of the land shall be food for thee; for thee,
for thy male and female slave, for thy hired servant, and for the settler who
resideth with thee, ⁷and for thy cattle and the beasts that are in thy land shall
all the produce be for food. ²⁰And if ye say, What shall we eat in the seventh year? behold, we may not sow or gather in our produce; ²¹then I will
command my blessing upon you in the sixth year, and it shall bring forth
produce for three years. ²²And ye shall sow the eighth year, but eat of the
old stores; until the produce of the ninth year comes in, ye shall eat
of the old stores.'

ᵍ Dt. 15¹ The word comes from a Heb. verb meaning, *to fling down, let drop.*

§ 113. Restoration of Property and Freedom in the Year of Jubilee,
Lev. 25⁸⁻¹⁶, ²³, ⁴⁰ᵇ⁻⁴²

Priestly Codes

To proclaim rest and release in the fiftieth year

Lev. 25 ⁸Thou shalt count seven sabbaths of years, for seven times seven years; and there shall be the equivalent of seven sabbaths of years,[h] that is, forty-nine years. ⁹Then thou shalt sound a loud horn on the tenth day of the seventh month; on the day of atonement shall ye sound a horn through[i] all your land. ¹⁰And ye shall set apart as sacred the fiftieth year, and proclaim liberty throughout the land to all its inhabitants; it shall be a year of jubilee for you, and ye shall return each to his possession, and ye shall return each to his family. ¹¹A jubilee shall that fiftieth year be for you; ye shall not sow or reap that which groweth of itself in it, nor gather in the fruit of the undressed vines, ¹²for it is a jubilee; it shall be holy to you; ye shall eat its produce directly from the field.

To restore all hereditary property

¹³At this year of jubilee ye shall return each to his possession. ¹⁴And if thou sell any land to thy neighbor, or buy it of thy neighbor, ye shall not wrong each other. ¹⁵According to the number of the years after the jubilee thou shalt buy land from thy neighbor, and according to the number of the crops *until the next jubilee* shall he sell it to thee. ¹⁶If the number of years be great, thou shalt increase its price, but if the number of years be small, thou shalt reduce its price, for it is the number of the crops that he selleth to thee. ²³The land shall not be sold in perpetuity; for the land is mine, and ye are resident aliens and settlers with me.

To release all Hebrew slaves

⁴⁰ᵇIf thy fellow countryman sell himself to thee as a slave, he shall serve with thee to the year of jubilee; ⁴¹then he shall be released by thee, together with his children, and he shall return to his own family, and to the possession of his fathers shall he return. ⁴²For they are my servants, whom I brought from the land of Egypt; they shall not be sold as slaves.

---

h Lev. 25⁸ Lit., *days*.
i Lev. 25⁹ Lit., *cause to pass through*.
§ 113 The twenty-fifth chapter of Lev. presents many different problems. To the law in regard to the sabbatical year. ¹⁻⁷, ¹⁷⁻²², and the injunctions not to take interest from a poor Israelite or to treat him harshly, if he has fallen into a condition of slavery, ³⁵⁻⁴⁰ᵃ, ⁴³, ⁴⁷, ⁵³, ⁵⁵ᵇ, the laws regarding the year of jubilee have been so added that they frequently interrupt the context. The first group of laws, ¹⁻⁷, ¹⁹⁻²², appears to belong to the Holiness Code. It is doubtful whether or not this code originally contained any reference to the year of jubilee. The pre-exilic writers are without exception silent even where, as for example, in Is. 5 and Mi. 2, we would expect a reference to it, were they acquainted with it. Moreover two of the chief regulations regarding the year of jubilee: the rest of the land and the freeing of Heb. slaves, are antithetic to the earlier law which prescribed the seventh instead of the fiftieth year. The passage, therefore, relating to the year of jubilee would seem to be a later priestly addition, which aimed by generous concessions, so to soften the strenuous demands of the older law that the principle might gain popular acceptance. There is no evidence, however, that the attempt succeeded; in fact the Rabbis admit that this law was never observed.
    The regulations regarding the right of redeeming hereditary estates is clearly based on an ancient and long established custom, cf. § 28; but in the present form it is adapted to the law of the year of jubilee and is bound up with the decree that all hereditary lands must at that time revert to their original owners. This custom is not without precedent in the ancient world. Many Aryan peoples thus periodically redistributed their land among the heads of the families. Strabo states that the Dalmatians reassigned their lands every eight years. In certain village communities in Russia the custom has continued to the present. For additional illustrations cf. Maine, *Village Communities*, p. 81 f., Driver and White, *Leviticus*, p. 100. The earliest allusion, however, in the O.T. to any such institution, is found in Ezek. 46¹⁷, where land given by the prince is to revert to him *in the year of release*. Whether the prophet refers to an already established institution or possibly here gives a suggestion which

132

V

KINDLY ATTITUDE TOWARD OTHERS

§ 114. Reverence for the Aged, Lev. 19³²ᵃ

Holiness Code

Lev. 19 ³²ᵃThou shalt rise up before the hoary head, and honor the person of an old man.

To honor the aged

§ 115. Love for Neighbors, Ex. 23⁴, ⁵, Lev. 19¹⁷, ¹⁸

Primitive Codes

Ex. 23 ⁴If thou meet thine enemy's ox or ass going astray, thou shalt surely bring it back to him again. ⁵If thou see the ass of him who hateth thee lying prostrate under its burden, thou shalt in no case leave it in its plight, rather thou shalt, together with him, help it out.ʲ

To do to an enemy as ye would have him do to you

Holiness Code

Lev. 19 ¹⁷Thou shalt not hate thy fellow countryman in thy heart; thou shalt warn thy neighbor and not incur sin on his account.ᵏ ¹⁸Thou shalt not take vengeance, nor bear a grudge against the members of thy race; but thou shalt love thy neighbor as thyself: I am Jehovah.

To love thy neighbor as thyself

§ 116. Love for Resident Aliens, Dt. 10¹⁸ᵇ, ¹⁹

Deuteronomic Codes

Dt. 10 ¹⁸ᵇJehovah so loveth the resident alien that he giveth to him food and raiment. ¹⁹Love then the resident alien; for ye were once resident aliens in the land of Egypt.

To love the alien

---

was later developed into the law of the year of jubilee cannot be definitely determined. On the whole, the exile, with its changed conditions, inspiring new regulations and experiments, as Ezek.'s elaborate program testifies, appears to furnish the background and date of the law of the year of jubilee.

    Kindly Attitude toward Others. — In these laws, which relate to inner motives and feelings, the Heb. lawgivers almost attain to the N.T. ideal. In the brief command in Lev. 19¹⁸ᵇ Jesus found the epitome of all O.T. legislation regarding man's duty to his fellowmen. He, however, raised it above its narrower Israelitish setting and made it of universal application. A suggestion of that broader application is found in the noble command in Dt. 10¹⁹ to love the foreigners residing in the land of Israel.

    ʲ Ex. 23⁵ Slightly correcting the Heb. text.
    ᵏ Lev. 19¹⁷ *I. e.*, by failing to warn him and by cherishing hatred toward him.

LAWS DEFINING OBLIGATIONS TO JEHOVAH

LAWS DEFINING OBLIGATIONS TO JEHOVAH

I

NATIONAL OBLIGATIONS

§ 117. To Abstain from Apostasy and Idolatry, Ex. 34[14, 17] [20[1-5, 23b]], Dt. 5[7, 8] [9, 10], 6[14, 15], 27[15]], Lev. 26[1]

Primitive Codes

Ex. 34 [14]Thou shalt worship no other god, for Jehovah, whose name is Jealous, is a jealous God. [17]Thou shalt make thee no molten gods. — Loyal worship

Deuteronomic Codes

Dt. 5 [7]Thou shalt have no other gods besides me. [8]Thou shalt not make for thyself a graven image.

Holiness Code

Lev. 26 [1]Ye shall make no idols, nor shall ye erect for yourselves a graven image or a pillar, nor shall ye set up any figured stone in your land to bow down to it; for I am Jehovah your God. — No idols of any kind

§ 118. To Abstain from Heathen Rites, Ex. 22[19], Dt. 12[29-31], 14[1, 2] [18[9]], Lev. 18[3], 19[27, 28] [20[23]]

Primitive Codes

Ex. 22 [19]Whoever sacrificeth to any god, except to Jehovah shall be placed under the ban. — None of the prevailing heathen customs

---

Laws Defining Obligations to Jehovah.—In this group of laws the prophetic principles, that underlie and characterize the O.T. legislation, come most prominently to the front. Many of them belong more properly with the prophetic addresses than with Israel's laws, cf. Vol. III, where the great prophetic addresses attributed to Moses are introduced in their chronological setting. These commands like the humane laws, illustrate the true genius of Israel's legal system. Above all duties they placed the obligations of the nation and individual to the Divine King. In each code, but especially in the Deuteronomic codes, which reflect most fully the influence of the prophets, these primary commands are constantly reiterated.

Failure to keep them is in a few cases, as for example, apostasy, which was regarded as treason, punished by definite and extreme penalties; but ordinarily the appeal is simply to the conscience of the nation and the individual. These laws are most of them in fact exhortations rather than ordinances to be enforced by human courts of justice. Jehovah is himself alone the plaintiff, judge and executioner.

§ 117 Only the typical regulations are here introduced. Cf. for the additional laws, §§ 57-59.

§ 118 Cf. notes §§ 60, 61, and the same sections for the laws which are not repeated here.

Deuteronomic Codes

Dt. 12 ²⁹When Jehovah thy God shall cut off the nations from before thee, which thou art going in to dispossess, and thou hast dispossessed them, and dwellest in their land; ³⁰take heed to thyself that thou be not ensnared after them, when they have been destroyed from before thee; and that thou inquire not after their gods, saying, How do these nations serve their gods? even so will I do likewise. ³¹Thou shalt not do thus to Jehovah thy God; for every abomination which Jehovah hateth, have they done to their gods; for even their sons and their daughters do they burn in the fire to their gods.

14 ¹Ye are the children of Jehovah your God; ye shall not cut yourselves,ᵃ nor make any baldness between your eyes for the dead. ²For thou art a people holy to Jehovah thy God, and Jehovah hath chosen thee to be a people for his own possession, out of all peoples that are upon the face of the earth.

Holiness Code

Lev. 18 ³Ye shall not imitate the customs of the land of Egypt, in which ye dwelt, nor the customs of the land of Canaan, whither I am bringing you; neither shall ye follow their established usages.

19 ²⁷Ye shall not round off the corners of your hair, nor shalt thou disfigure the corners of thy beard. ²⁸Ye shall not make any incisions in your skin for the dead; nor shall ye tattoo any marks upon you:ᵇ I am Jehovah.

§ 119. To Abolish Heathen Shrines, Ex. 34¹², ¹³, 23²⁴, ²⁵ᵃ, Dt. 12², ³, 7⁵, ²⁵

Deuteronomic Codes

All paraphernalia of heathen worship to be destroyed

Ex. 34 ¹²Take heed to thyself, lest thou make a covenant with the inhabitants of the land to which thou art going, lest it be for a source of corruptionᶜ in thy midst: ¹³but ye shall break down their altars, and dash in pieces their pillars, and cut down their asherahs.

23 ²⁴Thou shalt not bow down to their gods, nor serve them, nor imitate their customs; but thou shalt tear them down completely, and break in pieces their pillars, ²⁵ᵃand serve Jehovah thy God.

Dt. 12 ²Ye shall destroy all the places in which the nations, which ye shall dispossess, served their gods, upon the high mountains and upon the hills and under every green tree; ³and ye shall break down their altars, and dash in pieces their pillars, and burn their asherahs with fire; and ye shall hew down the graven images of their gods; and ye shall destroy their names out of that place.

7 ⁵But thus shall ye do to them: ye shall break down their altars, and dash in pieces their pillars, and hew down their asherahs, and burn their

---

ᵃ Dt. 14¹ This custom was in vogue among the Hebs. even in the exile, cf. Jer. 16⁶, 41⁵.
ᵇ Lev. 19²⁸ All these marks doubtless indicated consecration to a special deity.
ᶜ Ex. 34¹² Lit., *be for a snare.*
§ 119 The commands in Ex. 34¹², ¹³ and 23²⁴, ²⁵ᵃ interrupt their context and reveal the characteristic words and phrases of the Deuteronomic editor, who probably gave them their present position.

Deuteronomic Codes

graven images with fire. ²⁵The graven images of their gods shall ye burn with fire; thou shalt not covet the silver or the gold that is on them, nor take it for thyself, lest thou be corrupted thereby, for it is an abomination to Jehovah thy God.

§ 120. To Preserve the Law, Dt. 4²

Deuteronomic Codes

Dt. 4 ²Ye shall not add to the words which I command you, neither shall ye take anything from it, that ye may keep the commands of Jehovah your God which I command you.

§ 121. To Study and Remember the Law, Dt. 6⁶, ⁷, 11¹⁸ᵃ [¹⁹]

Deuteronomic Codes

Dt. 6 ⁶These words which I command thee this day, shall be upon thy heart; ⁷and thou shalt impress them upon thy children, and shalt talk of them when thou sittest in thy house, and when thou walkest by the way, and when thou liest down, and when thou risest up.

11 ¹⁸Therefore ye shall lay up these my words in your heart and in your soul.

Constant inculcation of the principles of the law

§ 122. To Wear Constant Reminders of the Law, Dt. 6⁸, ⁹, 22¹² [11¹⁸ᵇ·²⁰], Nu. 15³⁷⁻⁴¹

Deuteronomic Codes

Dt. 6 ⁸Thou shalt bind the [words of Jehovah] as a reminder on thy hand, and have them as bands on thy forehead between thine eyes, ⁹and thou shalt write them on the posts of thy house and on thy doors.

22 ¹²Thou shalt make for thyself tasselsᵈ on the four corners of the coveringᵉ with which thou coverest thyself.ᶠ

Ever-present reminders of the law

Holiness Code

Nu. 15 ³⁷Jehovah gave this command to Moses: ³⁸Speak to the Israelites, and bid them make for themselves tassels on the borders of their garmentsᵍ throughout their generations, and that they put upon the tassel of each cor-

---

§ 121 Cf. also § 56. Dt. 11¹⁹ is a duplicate of 6⁷.
§ 122 Cf. also § 56. Dt. 11¹⁸ᵇ is a duplicate of 6⁸ and 11²⁰ of 6⁹.
ᵈ Dt. 22¹² Lit., *twisted cords*, as in I Kgs. 7¹⁷. In later times these were made of eight threads of white wool and were tied at regular intervals in four double knots.
ᵉ Dt. 22¹² *I. e.*, the outer shawl or mantle, the modern *abaye*, to the four corners of which the tassels were fastened.
ᶠ Dt. 22¹² The meaning of these symbols is explained in the following passage from Nu. 13³⁹.
ᵍ Nu. 15³⁸ᵇ The brief section here introduced appears from its language and spirit to have been taken from the Holiness Code. It is also closely parallel to Ezek. 6⁹. It probably reflects an old custom, which appears to be assumed as well as known in Dt. 22¹². The Asiatics pictured on the early Egyptian monuments wear tassels, so that the custom may have been introduced by the ancestors of the Hebs.

Holiness Code

ner a cord of blue;[h] ³⁹and it shall serve you as a tassel, that ye may look upon it, and remember all the commands of Jehovah, and do them, and that ye do not follow your own inclinations and desires[i] in accordance with which ye used to play the harlot;[j] ⁴⁰that ye may remember and do all my commands, and be consecrated[k] to your God. ⁴¹I am Jehovah your God, who brought you out of the land of Egypt, to be your God : I am Jehovah your God.

§ 123. **To Follow Its Commands,** Dt. 5¹, ³², ³³, 6¹⁻³, ¹⁶, ¹⁷, 7¹¹, ¹², 8¹, ⁵⁻¹⁴, 10¹², ¹³, 11¹, ⁸, ⁹, ²⁶⁻³², 26¹⁶, ¹⁷, 27¹⁰, ²⁶, 4⁵, ⁶, 30¹⁵, ¹⁶, Lev. 18⁴, ⁵, ²⁶, 19¹⁹ᵃ, ²⁷, 20⁸, ²², 25¹⁸, ¹⁹

Deuteronomic Codes

The duty of heeding Jehovah's commands

Dt. 5 ¹Moses summoned all Israel, and said to them, Hear, O Israel, the statutes and the ordinances which I speak in your ears this day, that ye may learn them, and take heed to do them. ³²Ye shall take heed to do[l] as Jehovah your God hath commanded you; ye shall not turn aside to the right or to the left. ³³Ye shall do all that Jehovah your God hath commanded you, that ye may live, and that it may be well with you, and that ye may live long in the land which ye shall possess.

6 ¹Now this is the command, the statutes, and the ordinances, which Jehovah your God commanded to teach you, that ye might do them in the land which ye go over to possess; ²that thou mightest fear Jehovah thy God, to keep all his statutes and his commands, which I command thee, together with thy son, and thy son's son, all the days of thy life; and that thou mayst live long. ³Hear therefore, O Israel, and take heed to do it, that it may be well with thee, and that ye may become exceedingly many, as Jehovah the God of thy fathers hath promised thee, in a land abounding in milk and honey.

Of keeping faithfully each of them

¹⁶Ye shall not test Jehovah your God as ye tested him at Massah.[m] ¹⁷Ye shall diligently keep the commands of Jehovah your God, and his testimonies and his statutes, which he hath commanded thee.

7 ¹¹Thou shalt therefore keep the commands, and the statutes, and the ordinances, which I command thee this day, to do them. ¹²And if ye hearken to these ordinances, and keep and execute them, Jehovah thy God will keep with thee the covenant and the mercy which he promised by oath to thy fathers.

8 ¹All the command which I command thee this day shall ye take heed to do, that ye may live and become numerous, and go in and possess the land which Jehovah promised by oath to your fathers.

---

[h] Nu. 15³⁸ *I. e.*, the threads with which the tassels were fastened to the mantle.
[i] Nu. 15³⁹ Lit., *heart and eyes.*
[j] Nu. 15³⁹ The Heb. text is exceedingly awkward. The reference is evidently to some form of apostasy.
[k] Nu. 15⁴⁰ Lit., *holy.*
§ 123 The multiplicity of these injunctions illustrates the emphasis put upon **the law,** and especially the written law, from the days of Josiah.
[l] Dt. 5³² Lit.. *to walk in the way.* So also in ³³.
[m] Dt. 6¹⁶ Cf. Ex. 17², ⁷.

Deuteronomic Codes

⁵Know, then, in thy heart, that as a man disciplineth his son, so Jehovah thy God disciplineth thee. ⁶And thou shalt keep the commands of Jehovah thy God, to walk in his ways, and to fear him. ⁷For Jehovah thy God is bringing thee into a good land, a land of watercourses, of fountains and springs, flowing forth in vales and hills; ⁸a land of wheat and barley, and vines and fig-trees and pomegranates; a land of olive trees and honey; ⁹a land wherein thou shalt eat bread without scarcity, in which thou shalt lack nothing; a land whose stones are iron, and out of whose hills thou mayst dig copper. ¹⁰And thou shalt eat and be full, and thou shalt bless Jehovah thy God for the good land which he hath given thee. ¹¹Beware lest thou forget Jehovah thy God, in not keeping his commands, and his ordinances, and his statutes, which I command thee this day: ¹²lest, when thou hast eaten and art satisfied, and hast built beautiful houses, and art dwelling in them; ¹³and when thy herds and thy flocks become numerous, and thy silver and thy gold is plentiful, and all that thou hast is multiplied, ¹⁴then thy heart be filled with pride,ⁿ and thou forget Jehovah thy God, who brought thee forth out of the land of Egypt, out of the house of bondage.

10 ¹²And now, Israel, what doth Jehovah thy God require of thee, but to fear Jehovah thy God, to walk in all his ways, and to love him, and to serve Jehovah thy God with all thy heart and with all thy soul, ¹³and keep the commands of Jehovah, and his statutes, which I command thee this day for thy good?

11 ¹Therefore thou shalt love Jehovah thy God, and keep his charge, and his statutes, and his ordinances, and his commands at all times.

⁸Therefore ye shall keep all the command which I command thee this day, that ye may be strong, and go in and possess the land, which ye are going over to possess; ⁹and that ye may live long in the land which Jehovah promised by oath to give to your fathers, and to their descendants, a land abounding in milk and honey.

²⁶See, I set before you this day a blessing and a curse: ²⁷a blessing, if ye will hearken to the commands of Jehovah your God, which I command you this day; ²⁸and the curse, if ye shall not hearken to the commands of Jehovah your God, but turn aside out of the way which I command you this day, in order to go after other gods, which ye have not known. ²⁹And when Jehovah thy God shall bring thee into the land which thou art going to possess, thou shalt set the blessing upon Mount Gerizim and the curse upon Mount Ebal.ᵒ ³²And ye shall give heed to all the statutes and the ordinances which I set before you this day.

26 ¹⁶This day Jehovah thy God commanded thee to do these statutes and ordinances; thou shalt, therefore, keep and do them with all thy heart, and with all thy soul. ¹⁷Thou hast caused Jehovah to say this day that he will be thy God, and that thou wilt walk in his ways and keep his statutes, and his commands, and his ordinances, and hearken to his voice. **27** ¹⁰Thou

ⁿ Dt. 8¹⁴ Lit., *thy heart be lifted up.*
ᵒ Dt. 11²⁹ Vss. ³⁰, ³¹ are here omitted, since they add only a local geographical coloring.

Deuteronomic Codes

shalt therefore obey the voice of Jehovah thy God, and do his commands, and his statutes, which I command thee this day. ²⁶Cursed be he that confirmeth not the words of this law to do them.

Reward of obedience
4 ⁵Behold, I have taught you statutes and ordinances, even as Jehovah my God commanded me, that ye should do so in the midst of the land which ye are going in to possess. ⁶Keep, therefore, and do them; for this is your wisdom and your understanding[p] in the sight of the peoples that shall hear all these statutes, and say, Surely this great nation is a wise and understanding people.

30 ¹⁵See, I have set before thee this day life and prosperity, and death and calamity; ¹⁶in that I command thee this day to love Jehovah thy God, to walk in his ways, and to keep his commands and his statutes and his ordinances, that thou mayst live and become numerous, and that Jehovah thy God may bless thee in the land which thou art going in to possess.

Holiness Code

Reiterated injunctions to keep the divine commands
Lev. 18 ⁴Mine ordinances shall ye execute, and my statutes shall ye keep, to follow them: I am Jehovah your God. ⁵Ye shall therefore keep my statutes, and mine ordinances; which if a man do he shall live by them: I am Jehovah. ²⁶Keep my statutes and mine ordinances and let neither the native born nor the alien residing among you do any of these abominable things.

19 ¹⁹ᵃYe shall keep my statutes. ²⁷Ye shall observe all my statutes, and all mine ordinances, and do them: I am Jehovah.

20 ⁸Ye shall keep my statutes, and do them: I am Jehovah who sanctifieth you. ²²Ye shall therefore keep all my statutes, and all mine ordinances, and do them, that the land, whither I bring you to dwell, may not cast you forth.

25 ¹⁸Ye shall execute my statutes and keep my ordinances and do them; ¹⁹then ye shall dwell in the land securely, and the land shall yield its fruit and ye shall eat your fill and dwell in it securely.

§ 124. **To Make No Heathen Alliances,** Ex. 34¹², ¹³ ⁽¹⁵, ¹⁶⁾, 23³¹ᵇ⁻³³, Dt. 7¹⁻⁴

Deuteronomic Codes

No truce with heathen peoples
Ex. 34 ¹²Take heed to thyself, lest thou make a covenant with the inhabitants of the land to which thou art going, lest it be a source of corrup-

---

[p] Dt. 4⁶ *I. e.*, evidence of your wisdom and insight.

§ 124 In the earlier days of Israel's history alliances with other nations were common and only a few of the more zealous prophets protested, even though alliances in the ancient Semitic world meant the recognition of the gods of the allied peoples. From the days of the exile the principles proclaimed by Elijah and the expostulations of Hos., Is. and Jer. were reinforced by the painful outcome of the alliance with Egypt, so that the doctrine of no alliances gained popular acceptance, at least among the Jews of the dispersion. Cf. also note § 44.

Deuteronomic Codes

tion in thy midst; [13]but ye shall break down their altars, and dash in pieces their pillars, and cut down their asherahs.[q]

23 [31b]I will deliver the inhabitants of the land into thy power; and thou shalt drive them out before thee. [32]Thou shalt make no covenant with them nor with their gods. [33]They shall not dwell in thy land, lest they make thee sin against me; for if thou serve their gods, it will surely be a source of corruption to thee.

Dt. 7 [1]When Jehovah thy God shall bring thee into the land which thou art going to possess, and shall clear away many nations before thee, the Hittites, the Girgashites, the Amorites, the Canaanites, the Perizzites, the Hivites, and the Jebusites, seven nations greater and mightier than thou, [2]and when Jehovah thy God shall deliver them into thy hands and thou shalt smite them, then thou shalt completely destroy them without making any terms with them or showing any mercy to them. [3]Neither shalt thou make marriages with them; thy daughter thou shalt not give to his son, nor shalt thou take his daughter as a wife for thy son. [4]For he will turn away thy son from following me, that they may serve other gods; thus will the anger of Jehovah be aroused against you, and he will destroy thee quickly.

No intermarriages with heathen peoples

§ 125. To Be a Holy Nation, Ex. 22^{31a}, 19^{6a}, Dt. 7^{6} [$14^{2, 21c}$], 18^{13}, $26^{18, 19}$, $28^{9, 10}$, Lev. 19^{2}, 20^{26} [7]

Primitive Codes

Ex. 22 [31a]Ye shall be holy men to me.

Deuteronomic Codes

Ex. 19 [6a]Ye shall be to me a kingdom of priests, and a holy nation.

Israel's unique choice and mission

Dt. 7 [6]Thou art a people holy to Jehovah thy God; Jehovah thy God hath chosen thee out of all the peoples that are on the face of the earth to be to him a peculiar people.[r]

18 [13]Thou shalt be perfect[s] with Jehovah thy God.

26 [18]And Jehovah hath caused thee to say this day that thou wilt be to him a peculiar people, as he hath promised thee, and that thou shouldst keep all his commands; [19]and that he will set thee high above all nations

---

[q] Ex. $34^{12, 13}$ The language of a Deuteronomic editor is clearly apparent in this section. So also in 23^{31b-33}.

§ 125 The conception of Jehovah's holiness, and its corollary the holiness of his people is exceedingly prominent in the literature just before the exile, cf. Introd., pp. 37, 38. In the Holiness Code it becomes the chief basis of ethics. Its origin is not entirely clear. Undoubtedly Is. gave a great emphasis to the doctrine, cf. Is. 6. The oldest expression of it in the legal literature is probably found in Ex. 22^{31a}, in connection with the ceremonial command not to eat any flesh that is torn by beasts in the field, although by some this vs. is regarded as a later addition because the law is cast in the plural rather than in the second person singular, as in the oldest decalogue. The striking passage, Ex. 19^{6a}, probably comes from a late prophetic editor, cf. Vol. I, note § 75.

[r] Dt. 7^{6} Dt. $14^{2, 21}$ are duplicates of this vs.

[s] Dt. 18^{13} *I. e.*, without physical, but especially moral blemish

Deuteronomic Codes

which he hath made, as a praise, and a name, and an honor; and that thou mayst be a people holy to Jehovah thy God as he hath promised.

28 ⁹Jehovah will establish thee as a people holy to himself, as he hath sworn to thee, if thou wilt keep the commands of Jehovah thy God, and walk in his ways. ¹⁰And all the peoples of the earth shall see that thou dost bear the name[t] of Jehovah; and they shall be afraid of thee.

Holiness Code

Lev. 19 ²Ye shall be holy, for I Jehovah, your God, am holy.

20 ²⁶Ye shall be holy to me, for I, Jehovah, am holy and have separated you from the peoples that ye may be mine.

II

INDIVIDUAL OBLIGATIONS

§ 126. **Reverence,** Dt. 5²⁹, 6²⁴, 8⁶ [4¹⁰, 6², ¹⁰⁻¹³, 10¹²⁻²⁰, 13¹⁴, 14²³, 17¹⁹, 31¹², ¹³], Lev. 19³²ᵇ [25¹⁷ᵇ]

Deuteronomic Codes

To walk humbly before God

Dt. 5 ²⁹Oh, that there were such a heart in them that they would fear me, and keep all my commands at all times, that it might be well with them, and with their children forever !

6 ²⁴Jehovah commanded us to do all these statutes, to fear Jehovah our God, for our good at all times, that he might preserve us alive, as to-day.

8 ⁶Thou shalt keep the commands of Jehovah thy God, to walk in his ways and to fear him.

Holiness Code

Lev. 19 ³²ᵇThou shalt fear thy God : I am Jehovah.

§ 127. **Gratitude,** Dt. 6¹⁰⁻¹², 8¹⁰, ¹⁹

Deuteronomic Codes

To remember the source of all blessings

Dt. 6 ¹⁰When Jehovah thy God shall bring thee into the land which he promised by oath to thy fathers, Abraham, Isaac, and Jacob, to give thee, great and attractive cities, which thou hast not built, ¹¹and houses full of

---

t Dt. 28¹⁰ Lit., *art called by.*

Individual Obligations.—In these commands the national and individual obligations are closely blended.

§ 126 The lawgivers, like the sages, declared that an attitude of genuine reverence and piety toward God was essential to all right thinking and doing. In nearly a score of passages confined to the Deuteronomic and Holiness codes, they emphasize the fundamental importance of the attitude, not of cringing terror, but of fear inspired by a true appreciation of the divine character—a fear which keeps its possessor from all acts of wilful disobedience and guides him in the way of intelligent, loyal service.

CEREMONIAL LAWS

CEREMONIAL LAWS

A

SACRED OBJECTS AND SHRINES

I

THE ARK AND TENT OF MEETING OR DWELLING

§ 132. **The Ark,** Nu. 10³³ᵃ, ᶜ, ᵉ, ³⁵, ³⁶, Dt. 10¹⁻⁵, 31²⁴⁻²⁶, Ex. 25¹⁰⁻²²

Primitive Codes

Nu. 10 ³³ᵃ, ᶜ, ᵉAs the Israelites journeyed, the ark of Jehovah went before them to seek out a halting place for them. ³⁵And whenever the ark started, Moses would say,

> Arise, O Jehovah,
> And let thine enemies be scattered;
> And let those who hate thee flee before thee.

Symbol of Jehovah's protecting presence

Sacred Objects and Shrines.—The tendency to associate the gods with certain places and objects was universal in antiquity, and still holds its sway in certain parts of the Orient. Something concrete and objective was required to make the faith of the worshippers real and personal. Among the primitive Semites, as among all early peoples, the most common sacred objects were springs, trees and stones, for each aroused the wonderment and awe of primitive man, and suggested the special presence of a deity. The water gushing from the barren rock was a never-ending miracle, which also brought life and refreshment to thirsty man. The tree, springing likewise from the dark, seemingly lifeless earth, was regarded as a symbol of the life-giving power of the god. Hence sacred trees, or their symbols, the asherahs or poles, were found beside nearly every ancient Semitic shrine.

The dwellers in the wilderness or in rocky Palestine also saw in the great stones—solid, immovable, defying storm and change through the centuries—the abiding-place of the deity. Sometimes the basis of the belief appears to have been the unusual form or character of the stone. Meteoric stones, like the sacred one at Mecca, naturally attracted the attention of early man. On their face they bore the evidence of their unique origin. If they had been seen to fall, a blazing ball of fire from heaven, their divine character was at once established. If a special revelation was given beside some stone, as, for example, in the tradition of Jacob at Bethel, the stone forever afterward was regarded as sacred. In Phœnicia and ancient Canaan there were many such *bethels, houses of god,* stones in which the deity was thought to dwell. In many cases a sanctuary grew up about the sacred stone, as at Bethel and Mecca; thus many of the ancient temples appear to have come into existence.

§ 132 Sacred arks were in common use among the ancient Semitic peoples. Among the Babylonians they were made in the shape of ships, and were carried in the sacred processions. They were used for the transportation of the images of the gods on both land and water. The ship of the Babylonian god Nabu was also provided with a captain and crew. Often in later times these ships or arks were richly adorned and studded with precious stones.

It is only in one of the latest priestly sources, where the tendency to idealize is strong, that the Hebrew ark is represented as covered with gold. In the Deuteronomic code it is simply a box of acacia wood. Probably the true dimensions are represented by the later tradition; about four feet long by two and one-fourth in width and depth. In the oldest sources it is called the *ark of Jehovah* or the *ark of God,* and was evidently regarded as the abiding-place of the Deity. Whether or not this belief was originally due to the fact that it contained two sacred stones—possibly meteoric in character—can never be determined. It has also been urged that it once contained an image of the god worshipped by the ancestors of the Hebrews. A later, and yet comparatively early tradition asserts that it was the repository of

149

Primitive Codes

³⁶And when it rested he would say,

> Return, O Jehovah,
> To the ten thousands of thousands of Israel.

Deuteronomic Codes

Repository of the two tablets of the law

Dt. 10 ¹At that time Jehovah said to me, Hew thee two stone tablets like the first, and come up to me in the mountain, and make an ark of wood.ᵃ ²And I will write on the tablets the words that were on the first tablets which thou didst brake, and thou shalt put them in the ark. ³So I made an ark of acacia wood and hewed two stone tablets like the first and went up into the mountain, having the two tablets in my hand. ⁴And he wrote upon the tablets, in the same writing as before, the ten wordsᵇ which Jehovah spoke to you in the mountain out of the midst of the fire in the day of the assembly. And Jehovah gave them to me. ⁵Then I turned and came down from the mountain, and put the tablets in the ark which I had made; and there they are as Jehovah commanded me.ᶜ

Of the written law

Dt. 31 ²⁴When Moses had made a final end of writing the words of this lawᵈ in a book, ²⁵he gave this command to the Levites, who bore the ark of the covenant of Jehovah: ²⁶Take this book of the law and put it beside the ark of the covenant of Jehovah your God, that it may be there as a witness against you.ᵉ

Priestly Codes

Form and dimensions of the ark

Ex. 25 ¹⁰They shall make an ark of acacia wood : two cubits and a half shall be its length, and a cubit and a half its width, and a cubit and a half its height. ¹¹And thou shalt overlay it with pure gold, both within and without, and thou shalt make on the top of it round about a projecting rim

---

the two tablets of the law. Accordingly in the Deuteronomic source it was called the *ark of the covenant of Jehovah* and in the priestly, *the ark of the testimony*. In the days of the settlement in Canaan, however, the ark figures in its original rôle as the abiding-place of the Deity and, therefore, in popular thought, as the invincible palladium which would bring victory to the Hebrews, I Sam. 4–6, cf. Vol. II, § 4. On the whole the earliest allusions to the ark favor the conclusion that it was an empty throne supported and guarded by cherubim. The base was a wooden chest, which could be easily transported. This implication is strongly supported both by the use of arks among other Semitic peoples and by the late priestly tradition in Ex. 25²². For further data, cf. Dibelius, *Die Lade Jahves*.

The history of the ark is only imperfectly recorded. There are no strong reasons for doubting the testimony of the early traditions, which trace its origin back to the period of the wilderness. Borne by the Hebrews in their advance to Canaan, it appears to represent in primitive thought the transfer of Jehovah from Sinai to Canaan, where he subsequently dwells with his people. After various experiences, it at last found a resting place in David's capital and became the central object of Solomon's temple. Possibly it was carried away by the Egyptian invader, Shishak, or survived until the destruction of the temple in 586 B.C., but more probably, in the damp climate of Palestine, it in time decayed and fell to pieces. The surprising fact is that the late priestly school revived and glorified the traditions of this symbol which came from the half-heathen past, and gave it a central place in their idealized history. Cf. for a possible explanation note § 134.

ᵃ Dt. 10¹⁻³ These vss. are practically a repetition of the early Judean narrative of Ex. 34¹⁻⁴, except that the latter contain no reference to the ark. Probably the original primitive code contained brief directions for the making of the ark, for which a late editor substituted the priestly version.

ᵇ Dt. 10⁴ᵃ This is a repetition of Ex. 34²⁸ᵇ.

ᶜ Dt. 10¹⁻⁵ These vss. evidently belong to one of the later passages of Dt.

ᵈ Dt. 34²⁴ *I. e.*, the original Deuteronomic law.

ᵉ Dt. 31²⁴⁻²⁶ These vss. are a later variant of 31⁹⁻¹³.

Priestly Codes

of gold. ^{12}And thou shalt cast for it four rings of gold and put them on its four feet, there shall be two rings on each side of it. ^{13}And thou shalt make poles of acacia wood, and overlay them with gold. ^{14}And thou shalt put the staves into the rings on the sides of the ark, in order with these to carry the ark. ^{15}The poles shall be left in the rings of the ark; they shall not be taken from it. ^{16}And thou shalt put the law^f into the ark which I shall give. ^{17}And thou shalt make a cover of^g pure gold: two and a half cubits long, and a cubit and a half wide. ^{18}And thou shalt make two cherubim^h of gold—of beaten work shalt thou make them—at the two ends of the cover. ^{19}And thou shalt fasten a cherub to each end; on the cover thou shalt fasten the cherubim at its two ends. ^{20}And the cherubim shall hold their wings spread out on high, so that they will overspread the cover with their wings, while they face each other; the faces of the cherubim shall be turned toward the cover.

^{21}And thou shalt place the cover upon the ark; and in the ark thou shalt put the law that I shall give thee. ^{22}And there I will meet with thee, and I will commune with thee from over the cover; from the place between the two cherubim which are upon the ark of the law I will make known to thee all the commands which I will give through thee to the Israelites.

Its use according to later tradition

§ 133. The Original Tent of Meeting, Ex. 33$^{5-11}$

Primitive Codes

Ex. 33 ^{5}Jehovah said to Moses, Say to the Israelites, 'Ye are a wilful people; if I go up into the midst of thee for one moment, I shall consume thee, therefore put off thy ornaments from thee, that I may know what to do to thee.' ^{6}So the Israelites despoiled themselves of their ornaments from Mount Horeb onward, *and with these Moses made a tent.*

Origin of the tent

^{7}Now Moses used to take the tent and pitch it outside the camp at some distance from the camp, and he called it the tent of meeting, And whenever anyone wished to consult Jehovah, he would go out to the tent of meeting,

Its use in the Wilderness

---

^{f} Ex. 25^{16} Lit., *testimony*, the late priestly collective term for the law.
^{g} Ex. 25^{17} The traditional translation is, *mercy-seat*, but the Heb. word comes from a root meaning *to cover*. The fact that this word usually has a symbolic and theological signification, is the basis of the current translation.
^{h} Ex. 23^{18} The cherubim, like the colossi which guarded the Assyrian and Babylonian palaces or the bulls overlaid with gold in the sanctuaries of Dan and Bethel in the days of Jeroboam I, were symbolic of strength, the wings of a bird, of swift flight, and the faces of men, of intelligence. All these elements belonged to the common Semitic symbolism of the age.
§ 133 As has already been shown in Vol. I, note § 79, the older prophetic and the late priestly narratives give two distinct pictures of the tent of meeting. According to the early Ephraimite prophetic account of Ex. 33$^{5-11}$, it is small and stands outside the camp at a distance, and is in charge of Moses' attendant Joshua; but according to the priestly tradition in Ex. 35–40 and Nu. 2 it is an exceedingly elaborate structure, stands in the midst of the camp, and may be entered only by the sons of Aaron. The allusions in the earlier version indicate that it was originally preceded by an account of its construction; but the late priestly editor of Ex. has left it out, because he was chiefly interested in the later detailed tradition of its form and structure, now found in Ex. 35–40.
That there was some simple portable tent for the ark, and that the sacred stones used in casting the lot were kept in connection with it seem exceedingly probable in the light of the testimony of the comparatively early traditions. To this tent the people would naturally resort to determine the divine will through Moses. These facts appear to be the basis of the familiar later tradition of the dwelling or tabernacle.

Primitive Codes

which was outside the camp. ⁸And whenever Moses went out to the tent, all the people would rise and stand, every man at his tent door, and look after Moses until he had gone into the tent. ⁹And when Moses had entered into the tent, the pillar of cloud would descend and stand at the door of the tent, while Jehovah spoke with Moses. ¹⁰And whenever the people saw the pillar of cloud standing at the door of the tent, every man stood up and worshipped, each at his tent door. ¹¹Thus Jehovah used to speak with Moses face to face, as a man speaks to his friend. Then he would return to the camp; but his attendant Joshua, the son of Nun, a young man, did not leave the tent.

§ 134. The Post-Exilic Conception of the Tent of Meeting or Dwelling, Ex. 25¹⁻⁹, 26¹⁻³³

Priestly Codes

Material for the dwelling

Ex. 25 ¹Jehovah said to Moses, ²Command the Israelites that they take for me a special offering; from every man whose heart maketh him willing ye shall take my offering. ³And this is the special offering which ye shall take from them : gold, silver, brass, ⁴violet, purple, and red cloth, fine linen, goats' hair, ⁵rams' skins dyed red, Egyptian leather, acacia wood, ⁶oil for the light, spices for the anointing oil, and for the sweet incense, ⁷onyx stones and precious stones for the ephod and for the breastplate. ⁸And let them make me a sanctuary, that I may dwell among them. ⁹Exactly as I show thee the plan of the dwelling and of all its furniture, even so shall ye make it.

Its curtains

26 ¹Moreover thou shalt make the dwelling with ten curtains; of fine twined linen, and violet, and purple, and red cloth, with cherubim the work of the skilled artisans shalt thou make them. ²The length of each curtain shall be twenty-eight cubits, and the width of each curtain four cubits : all

---

§ 134 Careful biblical students have long recognized the idealistic elements in this priestly tradition, first current in certain Jewish circles eight centuries after the days of Moses. In general character it is parallel to the Chronicler's idealized and glorified accounts of the days of David and Solomon and the pre-exilic temple. Cf. Vol. I, pp. 22–28. Gold and silver and gorgeous fabrics take the place of the plain wood, and goats' hair cloth which the desert life alone affords. Moses' attendant Joshua and the simple customs of the earlier age and narratives are supplanted by a highly developed priesthood and ritual. The institutions and ceremonial ideas of the post-exilic age are again projected back into the primitive life of the wilderness, that their origin and authority may be traced to Moses, the traditional fountain of all law. The plan and furnishings of the dwelling are also modelled after those of the pre-exilic and post-exilic temple, simply being adapted to the supposed conditions of the wilderness wanderings. Throughout, that centralization of all worship into one sanctuary, which did not come until the days of Josiah, § 140, is assumed.

It is not strange that there are occasional discrepancies. The conclusions of modern architects that a structure constructed on the plan here outlined would not bear its own weight is probably correct. To transport it a vast caravan of wagons and oxen would have been required. The complete absence of all reference to it in the pre-exilic literature, and the presence instead of the simple and very different tent of meeting, and many other convincing data confirm the conclusion that this account of the dwelling or tabernacle came from the minds of the late Jewish priests, familiar with the second temple.

The value of this elaborate description is insignificant compared with that of many other sections of the legal literature. In the past more attention has been devoted to it than it really deserves—often to the neglect of noble ethical laws, which possess a permanent value. The account of the dwelling and its furnishings and rites is important chiefly because it is an indirect picture of the second temple and of its institutions. The repetitious sections in Ex. 31¹⁻¹¹, 35–40, which simply tell in the same language of the execution of the commands to build the dwelling, have not been reproduced.

the curtains shall have the same measure. ³Each set of five curtains shall be joined to each other. ⁴And thou shalt make loops of violet on the edge of the outer curtain in the first set; and likewise shalt thou do with the edge of the outer curtain in the second set.[i] ⁵Fifty loops shalt thou make on the one curtain, and fifty loops shalt thou make on the edge of the curtain that is in the second set;[j] the loops shall be opposite one another. ⁶And thou shalt make fifty clasps of gold, and join the curtains to each other with the clasps, that the dwelling may be one whole.

⁷Furthermore thou shalt make curtains of goats' hair for a tent over the dwelling; eleven curtains shalt thou make for that purpose. ⁸The length of each curtain shall be thirty cubits, and the width of each curtain four cubits; the eleven curtains shall have the same measure. ⁹Thou shalt join five curtains by themselves, and the other six curtains by themselves, and the sixth curtain in the forefront of the tent thou shalt lay double. ¹⁰Moreover thou shalt make fifty loops on the edge of the outer curtain in the first set, and fifty loops on the edge of the outer curtain in the second set.[k] ¹¹And thou shalt make fifty clasps of brass, and put the clasps into the loops, and thus join the tent together, that it may be one whole. ¹²And as for the excess[l] which remaineth of the curtains of the tent, the half curtain which remaineth, shall hang over the rear of the dwelling. ¹³And the cubit on both sides, the excess length of the curtains of the tent, shall hang over both sides of the dwelling to cover it. ¹⁴Thou shalt also make a protecting covering for the tent of rams' skins dyed red, and a protecting covering of Egyptian leather[m] above.

Outer covering

¹⁵Moreover thou shalt make the boards for the dwelling of acacia wood standing upright. ¹⁶Ten cubits shall be the length of each[n] board, and a cubit and a half the width of each board. ¹⁷Each board shall have two tenons mortised to each other; thus shalt thou make all the boards of the dwelling. ¹⁸Thou shalt make the boards for the dwelling, twenty boards for the south side[o] facing southward. ¹⁹And thou shalt make forty sockets of silver under the twenty boards; two sockets under each board for its two tenons; ²⁰and for the second side of the dwelling, facing northward,[p] twenty boards, ²¹with their forty sockets of silver; two sockets under each board. ²²And for the rear of the dwelling westward thou shalt make six boards. ²³And two boards shalt thou make for the corners of the dwelling at the rear. ²⁴They shall be of equal size[q] beneath, and likewise they shall be of equal

Supporting timbers

---

[i] 26⁴ Or, *on the edge of the one curtain at the end, at the place of joining* . . ., *at the second place of joining.*

[j] 26⁵ Or, *that is, at the second place of joining.*

[k] 26¹⁰ Or, *edge of the outer curtain at the place of joining,* . . . *that is outermost at the second place of joining.*

[l] 26¹² Lit., *Overhanging part.*

[m] 26¹⁴ The exact meaning of the word is uncertain. It is probably of Egyptian derivation. The current translation, *seal skins*, is very doubtful.

[n] 26¹⁶ So Luc. and Syr.

[o] 26¹⁸ Luc., *north side.*

[p] 26²⁰ Luc. *south side.*

[q] 26²⁴ Heb., *twins.* The meaning may be that these corner boards are securely fastened to the adjoining boards of both the side and rear walls.

Priestly Codes

size^r at the top even to the first ring; thus shall they both be made; they shall form the two corners. ²⁵So there shall be eight boards with their sockets of silver, sixteen sockets; two sockets under each board.

Connecting bars

²⁶Moreover thou shalt make bars of acacia wood; five for the boards on the one side of the dwelling, ²⁷and five bars for the boards on the other side of the dwelling, and five bars for the boards on the rear of the dwelling, facing westward. ²⁸The middle bar which holds the boards shall pass through from end to end. ²⁹And thou shalt overlay the boards with gold, and make their rings of gold as holders for the bars; and thou shalt overlay the bars with gold. ³⁰So thou shalt erect the dwelling according to its plan, as it was showed thee on the mountain.

Veil between the holy and most holy place

³¹Furthermore thou shalt make a veil of violet, purple, and red cloth and fine twined linen; with cherubim, the work of the skilled artisan shalt thou^s make it. ³²Thou shalt hang it upon four pillars of acacia overlaid with gold; their hooks shall be of gold, upon four sockets of silver. ³³And thou shalt hang the veil under the clasps, and thou shalt bring in thither, within the veil, the ark of the testimony; thus the veil shall serve you as a partition between the holy place and the most holy.

§ 135. Furnishings of the Dwelling, Ex. 25²³⁻⁴⁰, 27¹⁻⁸ [Nu. 8⁴], Ex. 30¹⁷⁻²¹, ¹⁻⁶, 26³⁴⁻³⁷

Priestly Codes

Table of show-bread

Ex. 25 ²³Moreover thou shalt make a table^t of acacia wood: two cubits long, a cubit wide, and a cubit and a half high. ²⁴Thou shalt overlay it with pure gold, and make thereon a crown of gold round about. ²⁵Thou shalt also make for it a border of a handbreadth round about; and thou shalt make a golden crown for its border round about. ²⁶Then thou shalt make for it four rings of gold, and fasten the rings at the four corners that are on its four feet. ²⁷Close by the border shall the rings be, as holders for the staves whereby the table is borne. ²⁸And thou shalt make the staves of acacia wood, and overlay them with gold; with them shall the table be borne. ²⁹Thou shalt also make for it dishes, and cups, and flagons, and bowls with which the libation is poured out; of pure gold shalt thou make them. ³⁰And thou shalt set showbread upon the table before me continually.

Golden candle-stick

³¹Moreover thou shalt make a candlestick of pure gold; of beaten work shalt thou make^u the candlestick, even its base and its shaft; its cups, and^v its gourds, and its flowers shall be of one piece with it.^w ³²And there shall

---

r 26²⁴ So Sam. and Luc. Heb., *entire.*
s 26³¹ So Luc. and Syr. Heb., *shall he make it.*
§ 135 The diagram on the opposite page suggests the general plan and arrangements of the dwelling and its surrounding court.
t 25²³ Luc., *of pure gold and acacia wood.*
u 25³¹ So Luc., Sam. and Syr. Heb., *shall be made.* A briefer description of the candlestick is also given in Nu. 8⁴.
v 25³¹ So Luc. Heb., *its cups, its gourds and its flowers,* i. e., its cuplike ornaments consisting of gourds and flowers.
w 25³¹ Lit., *shall come forth from it.* Cf. also Nu. 8⁴.

Priestly Codes

be six branches going out from its sides: three branches of the candlestick from each side. ³³There shall be three cups made like almond-blossoms on each branch, consisting of a gourd and a flower; so for the six branches springing from the candlestick; ³⁴and on the candlestick four cups made like almond-blossoms, its gourds and flowers; ³⁵and a gourd under each pair of branches, of one piece with it, soᵃ for the six branches springing from the candlestick. ³⁶Their gourds and their branches shall be one piece with it; the whole a single piece of beaten work of pure gold. ³⁷Thou shalt also make its lamps, seven; and thouᵇ shalt set up its lamps that they may give light over against it. ³⁸And its snuffers and the snuffdishes, shall be of pure gold. ³⁹Of a talent of pure gold thouᶜ shalt make it, with all these vessels. ⁴⁰And see that thou make them after their plan, which was shown thee on the mountain.

27 ¹Thou shalt make the altar of acacia wood, five cubits long, and five cubits wide; the altar shall be square and its height shall be three cubits. ²And thou shalt make the horns for it on the four corners; the horns shall be of one piece with it; and thou shalt overlay it with brass. ³And thou shalt make its pots for taking away its ashes, and its shovels and its basins, and its flesh-hooks, and its firepans; all its vessels shalt thou make of brass. ⁴And thou shalt make for it a grating of network of brass; and upon the net shalt thou make four brazen rings at the four corners. ⁵And thou shalt put it under the ledge round the altar, that the net may reach half way up the

Sacri-ficial altar and its uten-sils

ᵃ 25³⁵ So Luc.   The Heb. omits, *so*.
ᵇ 25³⁷ So Luc.   Heb., *he shall*.
ᶜ 25³⁹ So Luc.   Heb., *shall he make it*.

NORTH

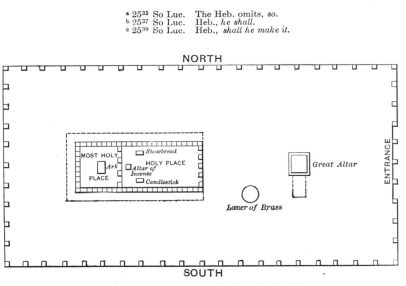

SOUTH

PLAN OF THE DWELLING AND ITS COURT

Priestly Codes

altar. ⁶Thou shalt also make staves for the altar, staves of acacia wood, and overlay them with brass. ⁷And in carrying it, its staves shall be put into the rings, and the staves shall be upon the two sides of the altar. ⁸Hollow, with planks shalt thou make it; as it was shown to thee on the mountain shalt thou make it.

Supplemental Priestly Codes

Ex. 30 ¹⁷Jehovah also gave this command to Moses, ¹⁸Thou shalt make a laver of brass, with its base of brass, to be used for washing. Thou shalt put it between the tent of meeting and the altar, and thou shalt put water in it, ¹⁹so that Aaron and his sons may wash their hands and their feet in it; ²⁰whenever they enter the tent of meeting, they shall wash with water, that they die not; or whenever they come near the altar to minister, to burn an offering made by fire to Jehovah. ²¹So they shall wash their hands and their feet, that they die not. This shall be statute forever[d] for them, even for him and his descendants throughout their generations.

Altar of incense

30 ¹Moreover thou shalt make an altar upon which to burn incense; of acacia wood shalt thou make it. ²A cubit shall be its length, and a cubit its width; it shall be square; and its height shall be two cubits; its horns shall be of one piece with it. ³And thou shalt overlay it with pure gold, its top, and the sides round about, and its horns; and thou shalt make on it a rim[e] of gold round about. ⁴And two golden rings shalt thou make for it under its rim, upon its two ribs;[f] upon the two sides of it thou shalt make them; and they shall serve[g] as holders for the staves with which to carry it. ⁵And thou shalt make the staves of acacia wood, and overlay them with gold. ⁶And thou shalt put it before the veil that is by the ark of the testimony, before the cover that is over the testimony, where I will meet with thee.

Order of arrangement

Ex. 26 ³⁴And thou shalt put the cover upon the ark of the testimony in the most holy place. ³⁵And thou shalt set the table without the veil, and the candlestick opposite the table on the south side of the dwelling; and thou shalt put the table on the north side. ³⁶Moreover thou shalt make a screen for the door of the tent, of violet, purple, and red cloth, and fine twined linen, embroidered work. ³⁷And thou shalt make for the screen five pillars of acacia wood, and overlay them with gold; their hooks shall be of gold; and thou shalt cast five sockets of brass for them.

---

d 30²¹ Or, *perpetual regulation.*
e 30³ *Border* or *crown.*
f 30⁴ *Upon its two ribs,* is possibly secondary, a marginal note from 25¹².
g 30⁴ Luc. and Sam. Heb., *it shall be.*

§ 136. Court of the Dwelling, Ex. 27⁹⁻¹⁹

Priestly Code

Ex. 27 ⁹Thus shalt thou make the court of the dwelling : for the southern Plan court there shall be hangings of fine twined linen a hundred cubits long on a and dimen-side; ¹⁰and its pillars shall be twenty, and their sockets twenty, of brass; sions the hooks of the pillars and their fillets shall be of silver. ¹¹And likewise for the north side[h] the hangings shall be a hundred cubits in length, and its pillars twenty, and their sockets twenty, of brass; the hooks of the pillars and their fillets, of silver. ¹²And along the width of the court on the west side shall be hangings of fifty cubits; their pillars ten, and their sockets ten. ¹³And the court on the east side facing eastward shall be fifty cubits wide. ¹⁴The hangings for the one side shall be fifteen cubits, their pillars three, and their sockets three. ¹⁵And for the other side there shall be hangings of fifteen cubits; their pillars three, and their sockets three. ¹⁶And for the gate of the court there shall be a screen of twenty cubits, of violet, and purple, and red cloth, and fine twined linen, embroidered work; their pillars four and their sockets four. ¹⁷All the pillars of the court round about shall be filleted with silver; their hooks also shall be of silver, but their sockets of brass. ¹⁸The length of the court shall be a hundred cubits, and the width fifty cubits, and the height five[i] cubits.[j] ¹⁹All the utensils of the dwelling for all its service, and all its pins, and all the pins of the court, shall be of brass.

II

ALTARS AND TEMPLES

§ 137. Ancient Altars and Places of Sacrifice, Ex. 20²⁴⁻²⁶ [Dt. 27⁵⁻⁷]

Primitive Codes

Ex. 20 ²⁴An altar of earth shalt thou make for me, and shalt sacrifice on Direc-it thy burnt-offerings, and thy peace-offerings, thy sheep, and thine oxen; in tions regard-ing con-

§ 136 This description is so much condensed that the meaning is not always clear. struc-
h 27¹¹ So Luc. and Sam. The Heb. inserts, *long*. tion
i 27¹⁸ So Sam. Heb., *five hundred.* Luc., *one hundred everywhere, and its width one* and *hundred everywhere.* use
j 27¹⁸ A scribe has added by mistake from ¹⁶, ¹⁷, *of fine twined linen, and their sockets of brass.*

§ 137 This primitive law, reproduced with slight abridgement and variations in Dt. 27⁵⁻⁷ reflects vividly the primitive usage and point of view. The command not to hew with an iron instrument the stone used as an altar, probably finds its ultimate basis in the early belief that the *numen* or spirit of the deity dwelt in the rock upon which the blood of the sacrifice was poured, and that a blow might drive it away. Cf. I Kgs. 18³¹, ³², Josh. 8³¹, I Sam. 14³²⁻³⁴. It also reveals the earliest conception of sacrifice: the blood poured out upon the rock in which the spirit of the god resided established the bond between the deity and his subjects, who presented and also shared in the sacrifice, cf. note § 195. The ritualistic injunctions remained in force long after the naïve, primitive ideas that suggested them had yielded to a broader faith.

The variant version in Dt. reads: ⁵*There thou shalt build an altar for Jehovah thy God, an altar of stones; thou shalt swing no iron tool over them.* ⁶*Thou shalt build the altar of Jehovah thy God of unhewn stones; and thou shalt offer burnt-offerings on it to Jehovah thy God.* ⁷*And thou shalt sacrifice peace-offerings, and shalt eat there; and thou shalt rejoice before Jehovah thy God.*

Primitive Codes

every place, where I record my name,ᵃ I will come to thee and I will bless thee. ²⁵But if thou make me an altar of stone, thou shalt not build it of hewn stones; for if thou swing an iron tool over it, thou hast polluted it. ²⁶Thou shalt not ascend by steps to mine altar,ᵇ that thy nakedness may not be uncovered before it.

§ 138. Solomon's Temple, I Kgs. 6²⁻⁶, ⁸, ⁹, ¹⁵⁻³⁵

Temple Records

Dimensions

I Kgs. 6 ²The length of the temple which King Solomon built for Jehovah was sixty and its breadth twenty cubits, and its height thirty cubits. ³And the porch before the large room of the temple was twenty cubits wide, corresponding to the width of the temple, and ten cubits deep before the temple. ⁴And for the temple he made windows with narrowed frames.

Side-chambers

⁵And around against the wall of the temple he built wings, both around the larger room and the inner room, and made side-chambers round about. ⁶The lower side-chamber was five cubits broad, and the middle six cubits broad, and the third seven cubits broad; for on the outside he made offsets around about the temple in order not to make an inset into the walls of the temple. ⁸The entrance into the lower side-chambers was on the south side of the temple. And one could go up by winding stairs into the middle story, and from the middle into the third. ⁹So he built the temple and finished it; and he covered the temple with cedar.

Interior decorations

¹⁵And he built the walls of the temple within with boards of cedar, from the floor of the temple to the rafters of the ceiling, overlaying them on the inside with wood; and he covered the floor of the temple with boards of cypress. ¹⁶And he built off the back twenty cubits from the innermost part of the temple with boards of cedar from the floor to the rafters; he built it within for an inner room, even for the most holy place. ¹⁷And the temple, that is the large room before the inner room, was forty cubits long. ¹⁸And there was cedar in the interior of the temple, carving in the form of gourds and open flowers; all was cedar, no stone was seen. ¹⁹And he prepared an inner room in the interior of the temple in order to place there the ark of the covenant of Jehovah. ²⁰And the inner room was twenty cubits long and twenty cubits broad and twenty cubits high. And he overlaid it with pure gold. And he made an altar of cedar wood ²¹before the inner room, and he overlaid it with gold. ²²And the whole temple was overlaid with gold, until all the temple was finished. ²⁹And he carved all the walls of the house round about with carved figures of cherubim and palm trees and opening flowers, both in the inner and outer rooms. ³⁰And the floor of the temple he overlaid with gold.

The cherubim

²³ᵃAnd in the inner room he made two cherubim of olive wood. ²⁶The height of the one cherub was ten cubits, and so was that of the other—²³ᵇeach

---

ᵃ Ex. 20²⁴ Lit., *cause my name to be remembered, i. e.,* at each of the many sacred places, where according to tradition Jehovah had revealed himself, as, for example, at Bethel.
ᵇ Ex. 20²⁶ *I. e.,* the approach was to be by a natural incline.
§ 138 The account of Solomon's temple is here reproduced from Vol. II, pp. 181-6, that it may be possible to make a complete study of this important institution. For the variations from the Heb. text, cf. Vol. II, notes under § 51. For the plans cf. opp. page.

Temple Records

ten cubits high. ²⁴And one wing of the cherub measured five cubits, and the other wing of the cherub also five cubits—ten cubits from the extremity of one wing to the extremity of the other. ²⁵And the other cherub also measured ten cubits : both the cherubim were of the same measurement and form. ²⁷And he set up the cherubim in the inner room of the temple, and the wings of the cherubim were stretched forth, so that the wing of the one touched the one wall, while the wing of the other cherub touched the other wall, and their wings touched one another in the middle of the temple ²⁸and he overlaid the cherubim with gold.

³¹And the door of the inner room he made with folding doors of olive Door of wood; the pilasters formed a pentagonal. ³²And on the two doors of olive the in-wood he carved carvings of cherubim and palm trees and opening flowers, room and he spread the gold over the cherubim and the palm trees.

³³So also he made for the door of the large room posts of olive wood, four square, ³⁴and two folding leaves of cypress wood : the two leaves of the one door were folding, and the two leaves of the other door were folding. ³⁵And he carved cherubim and palm trees and opening flowers, and overlaid them with gold applied evenly to the carving.

§ 139. Ornamentations and Furnishings of Solomon's Temple, I Kgs. 7¹³⁻⁴⁴, II Chr. 4¹, ⁷, ⁸ [3¹⁵⁻¹⁷, 4²⁻⁶, ⁸, 5¹, Jer. 52²¹⁻²³]

Temple Records

I Kgs. 7 ¹³Then King Solomon sent and brought Hiram-abi from Tyre. The ¹⁴He was the son of a widow of the tribe of Naphtali, an Aramean worker in pillars at the brass; and he was gifted with skill, understanding, and knowledge to carry en-on all kinds of work in brass. And he came to King Solomon and did all trance his work. ¹⁵For he cast the two pillars of brass for the porch of the temple. Eighteen cubits was the height of one pillar, and its circumference measured twelve cubits; the thickness of the pillar was four fingers—it was hollow. And the second pillar was similar. ¹⁶And he made two capitals of molten brass, to set upon the tops of the pillars; the height of the one capital was five cubits, and the height of the other capital was five cubits. ¹⁷And he made two nets (woven work, festoons, chain-work) for the capitals which were on the top of the pillars; a net for the one capital, and a net for the other capital. ¹⁸ᵇAnd he made the pomegranates; and two rows of pomegranates in brass were upon the one network, ²⁰ᵇand there were two hundred pomegranates—two rows around about the one capital. ¹⁸ᶜAnd he did the same to the other capital.   ¹⁹And the capitals that were upon the top of the pillars in the porch were of lily-work—four cubits. ²⁰ᵃAnd there were capitals above also upon the two pillars, in connection with the bowl-shaped part of the pillar which was beside the network. ²¹And he set up the pillars at the porch of the temple : and he set up the pillar at the right and called it Jachin; and he set up the pillar at the left and called it Boaz. ²²And upon the top of the pillars was lily-work. So was the work of the pillars finished.

²³And he made the molten sea ten cubits in diameter from brim to brim, Molten and five cubits high, and its circumference measured thirty cubits. ²⁴And sea

Temple Records

under its brim on the outside were gourds which encircled it, for thirty cubits, encircling the sea on the outside; the gourds were in two rows, cast when it was cast. ²⁶And it was a handbreadth thick; and its brim was wrought like the brim of a cup, similar to the flower of a lily. It held about sixteen thousand gallons. ²⁵It stood upon twelve oxen, three looking toward the north, and three looking toward the west, and three looking toward the south, and three looking toward the east; and the sea was set down upon them, and all their hinder parts were turned inward.

Movable brazen stands ²⁷And he made the ten stands of brass; each stand was four cubits long, four cubits broad, and three cubits high. ²⁸And the stands were made as follows : they had border-frames, and the border-frames were between the upright supports; ²⁹and on the border-frames that were between the upright supports were lions, oxen, and cherubim; and upon the upright supports likewise; and above and beneath the lions and oxen and cherubim was bevelled work. ³⁰ᵃAnd every stand had four wheels of brass and axles of brass. ³²And the four wheels were underneath the border-frames; and the axles and the wheels were cast as a part of the stand. And the height of each wheel was a cubit and a half. ³³And the construction of the wheels was like that of a chariot wheel : their axles, their felloes, their spokes, and their hubs, were all cast. ³⁴And at the four corners of each stand were four shoulder-pieces; the shoulder-pieces were cast as part of the stand. ³⁵And in the top of the stand was a round opening, half a cubit high, and on the top of the stand were its stays and its border-frames. ³⁶And on the flat surface of the stays and border-frames, he engraved cherubim, lions, and palm trees, according to the space on each, with wreaths round about. ³⁰ᵇAnd the four corners had shoulder-pieces : beneath the bowl the shoulder-pieces were cast, with wreaths at the side of each. ³¹And its opening within the shoulder-pieces was a cubit and more : and its opening was round after the form of a pedestal (a cubit and a half) and also upon its opening were gravings, and its border-frames were square, not round. ³⁷Thus he made the ten stands : all of them had one casting, and were of the same measure and form.

Position of the stands with their lavers ³⁸And he made ten lavers of brass; a laver contained three hundred and twenty gallons, and each laver measured four cubits; and on each one of the ten stands was a laver. ³⁹And he set the stands, five on the right side of the temple and five on the left side of the temple; and he set the sea on the right side of the temple eastward toward the south.

Altar of brass **II Chr. 4** ¹Moreover he made an altar of brass—twenty. cubits long, and twenty cubits broad, and ten cubits high.

Candlesticks ⁷And he made the ten candlesticks of gold according to the directions concerning them; and he set them in the temple, five on the right hand and five on the left. ⁸He made also ten tables, and placed them in the temple, five on the right side and five on the left. And he made a hundred golden bowls.

Completion of the work **I Kgs. 7** ⁴⁰And Hiram made the lavers and the shovels, and the bowls. So Hiram completed all the work that he wrought for King Solomon in the temple of Jehovah : ⁴¹the two pillars and the two bowl-shaped capitals that were on the top of the pillars, ⁴²and the four hundred pomegranates for

Temple Records

the two networks to cover the two bowl-shaped capitals that were on the top of the pillars, ⁴³and the ten stands and the ten lavers on the stands, ⁴⁴and the one sea with the twelve oxen under the sea.

§ 140. **The Later Law of the One Sanctuary**, Dt. 12¹⁰⁻¹⁸, 16⁵, ⁶, Lev. 17³⁻⁵, ⁷
[Dt. 12¹⁻¹², ¹⁹⁻²¹, ²⁶⁻²⁸, 14²²⁻²⁷, 15¹⁹, ²⁰, 31¹⁰, ¹¹]

Deuteronomic Codes

Dt. 12 ¹⁰When ye shall have crossed the Jordan, and dwell in the land which Jehovah your God hath given you as an inheritance, and he shall have given you rest from all your enemies round about, so that ye dwell in safety; ¹¹then to the place, where Jehovah your God shall choose to have his name dwell, ye shall bring all that I command you : your burnt-offerings, and your sacrifices, your tithes, and the special gifts of your hand, and all your choice votive-offerings which ye vow to Jehovah. ¹²And ye shall rejoice before Jehovah your God, together with your sons, your daughters, your male and female slaves, and the Levite who dwells in your city, for he hath no portion nor inheritance with you. Centralization of all the ceremonial religious life at Jerusalem

¹³Take heed not to offer thy burnt-offerings in every place that thou seest; ¹⁴but in the place which Jehovah shall choose in one of thy tribes, there thou shalt offer thy burnt offerings, and there thou shalt do all that I command thee. No offerings to be made elsewhere

¹⁵Yet thou mayest to thy heart's desire kill and eat flesh within any of thy cities, according as Jehovah thy God hath blessed thee : the unclean and the clean may eat of it, as of the gazelle and as of the hart. ¹⁶Only ye shall not eat of the blood; thou shalt pour it out upon the earth as water. Animals killed for food

¹⁷Thou mayest not eat within thy gates the tithe of thy grain of thy new wine, or of thine oil, or of the firstlings of thy herd or of thy flock, or any of thy votive-offerings which thou vowest, nor thy voluntary-offerings, nor the special gifts of thy hand; ¹⁸but thou shalt eat them before Jehovah thy God in the place which Jehovah thy God shall choose, together with thy son, thy daughter, thy male and female slaves, and the Levite who dwelleth in thy city; and thou shalt rejoice before Jehovah thy God over all which thou hast attained. Special offerings

16 ⁵Thou mayest not sacrifice the passover in any of thy cities, which Jehovah thy God giveth thee ⁶but at the place in which Jehovah thy God shall choose to have his name dwell, there thou shalt sacrifice the passover Passover feast

§ 140 The higher religious and ethical teachings of the great prophets of the Assyrian period and the evils, which became glaringly apparent in the reactionary reign of Manasseh, when heathenism had full sway, revealed clearly to the later prophets and priests who formulated the Deuteronomic and Holiness codes, the impossibility of developing the pure worship of Jehovah at the high places throughout the land. Cf. Introd., pp. 32, 33. Too many heathen traditions and debasing customs still clung to those ancient shrines. At Jerusalem under the direction of the more enlightened prophets and priests the higher ideals could be more favorably inculcated. The present laws prescribe this revolutionizing change in the national worship; with one stroke all the local festivals and cults are forbidden and all the formal religious life of Judah is centred in Jerusalem. The change marks in many ways, one of the most radical religious reformations recorded in human history.

Deuteronomic Codes

in the evening as the sun goes down, at the fixed time when thou camest
forth from Egypt.

Holiness Code

Every
animal
slain to
be pre-
sented
at the
temple

Lev. 17 ³If there be any man of the house of Israel who killeth an ox, or
lamb, or goat, either within the camp or without the camp,ᶜ ⁴and doth not
bring it to the entrance of the tent of meeting, to present it as an offering
to Jehovah before the dwelling of Jehovah, blood-guilt shall be imputed to that
man; he hath shed blood; and that man shall be cut off from among his
people, ⁵in order that the Israelites may bring their sacrifices which they are
wont to sacrifice in the open field, to Jehovah, at the entrance of the tent of
meeting, to the priest, and sacrifice them as sacrifices of peace-offerings to
Jehovah. ⁷And they shall no more offer their sacrifices to the satyrs, which
they faithlessly worship.ᵈ This shall be an everlasting statute for them throughout their generations.

III

EZEKIEL'S TEMPLE PLAN

§ 141. The Outer Gates and Court, Ezek. 40⁴⁻²⁷

Ezekiel's Code

Intro-
duction:
the
proph-
et's
vision

Ezek. 40 ¹In the twenty-fifth year of our captivity, in the beginningᵃ
of the year, in the tenth day of the month, in the fourteenth year after the

---

ᶜ Lev. 17³ This law of one central sanctuary stands at the beginning of the Holiness Code,
A later priestly editor has added clauses here and there to adapt it to its present context,
which assumes the point of view of the Wilderness, and is concerned with the tent of meeting.
ᵈ Lev. 17⁷ Lit., *after which they play the harlot.*
Ezekiel's Temple Plan.—Excepting the brief appendix, 29¹⁷⁻²¹, this plan of the restored
temple and of its service represents Ezekiel's closing work. It is dated in the year 572 B.C.,
twenty-five years after he was carried a captive to Babylon, and fourteen years after the fall
of Jerusalem. The plan reveals at every turn the two great influences that had come into
Ezekiel's life. The first was his acquaintance with the structure and institutions of the pre-
exilic temple, in close connection with which he, as the son of a priest, had been reared. In his
general plan of the temple proper he appears to have followed that of Solomon, cf. § 138, although
there are variations in the detailed measurements. The other prominent influence is that
of the Babylonian life and civilization amidst which he had lived for twenty-five years. This
influence is most evident in the great guarded gateways and thick walls with which he in imagination encircles his sanctuary. Like most of the Babylonian temples, that of Ezek. is,
indeed, a small city in itself, with many surrounding edifices for the uses of the priests and
the ritual; and all is encircled by high walls which render it an almost invincible fortress.
For the general type of oriental temples that he had in mind cf. the opposite page. Thus the
prophet, in this concrete way, emphasized the holiness of the God who was to dwell in this sacred
citadel, and the necessity of guarding Israel's Holy One from all that was ceremonially defiling,
cf. Introd., pp. 37, 38.
The Heb. text of Ezek. 40–48 is exceedingly corrupt. The original descriptions were
often obscure; when these were not fully understood, scribal errors were sure to creep in. Mis-
takes are also especially easy where detailed measurements and similar recurring formulas are
common. In many cases the Gk. has undoubtedly preserved better readings. In the description of the temple and its adjuncts the Gk. version differs so widely from the Heb. and is
so consistent with itself that it is probable that they each represent independent recensions,
and present two distinct plans of the temple. In general the Heb. text has here been followed, except where it is obviously in error and the Gk. in the right. The accompanying plans
of the gateways and temple enclosure will facilitate the understanding of the text, cf. p. 164.
ᵃ 41¹ As in Lev. 25⁹ the sacred new year began in the seventh year of the Babylonian or
secular calendar, *i. e.*, in September.

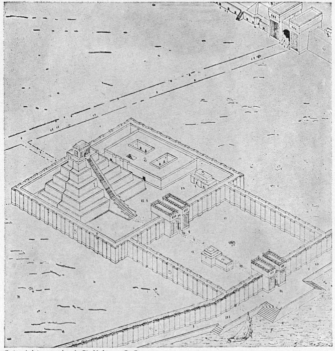

From "Explorations in Bible Lands During the Nineteenth Century."

A Babylonian Temple (Nippur)

An Egyptian Temple (Luxor)

ORIENTAL TEMPLES

Ezekiel's Code

city was taken, on that very day, the hand of Jehovah was laid upon me, and he brought me [2]in an inspired vision[b] to the land of Israel, and set me down upon a very high mountain,[c] on which was a city-like building toward the south.[d] [3]Thither he brought me, and there was a man whose appearance was like the appearance of bronze, with a flaxen line and a measuring reed in his hand; and he was standing in the gateway. [4]And the man said to me, Son of man, behold with thine eyes, and hear with thine ears, and give heed[e] to all that I shall show thee; for, in order that thou shouldst be shown it wert thou brought hither; declare all that thou seest to the house of Israel.

[5]There was a wall encircling a temple, and in the man's hand a measuring reed six cubits long, each cubit being equal to a cubit and a handbreadth[f] and he measured the thickness of the building, one reed; and the height one reed. Encir-
cling
wall

[6]Then he came to the east gateway and went up its steps and measured the threshold of the gate one reed wide.[g] [7]And each guard-room was one reed long, and one reed broad; and between the guard-rooms were spaces[h] of five cubits; and the threshold of the gate at the vestibule of the gate on the inner side was one reed.[i] [9]Then he measured the vestibule of the gate, eight cubits, and its jambs, two cubits; and the vestibule of the gate was on the inner side. [10]And the guard-rooms of the east gate were three on each side; all three were of the same dimensions; and the posts were on both sides. [11]And he measured the breadth of the entrance to the gateway, ten cubits; and the width[j] of the gate, thirteen cubits; [12]and there was a sill one cubit wide, before the guard-rooms on each side; and the guard-rooms, six cubits on both sides.[k] East
outer
gate-
way

[13]And he measured the gate from the outer wall of the one guard-room to the outer wall[l] of the other, twenty-five cubits wide; door opposite door. [14]He also measured the vestibule,[m] twenty[n] cubits; and the court reached to the jambs, round about the gateway. [15]And from the front of the gateway at the entrance to the front of the inner vestibule of the gate were fifty cubits. Dimen-
sions
of the
gate-
way

---

[b] 40[1], [2] Lit., *vision of God*, following the superior Gk. and Syr. The Heb. adds, *thither* at the end of [1] and repeats the verb, probably from [3].

[c] 40[2] Cf for the same idea, Is. 2[2], Mi. 4[1].

[d] 40[2] Or Gk., *opposite;* but according to 21[2] the prophet came from the north. The temple buildings referred to were also along the southern slope of the temple hill.

[e] 40[4] Heb., *set thy heart upon.*

[f] 40[5] Ezekiel's long cubit was probably about 21 inches. Herodotus (I. 178) states that the royal Babylonian cubit was three digits longer than the ordinary cubit.

[g] 40[6] So Gk. In the Heb. a scribe has by mistake repeated the last clause.

[h] 40[7] These were the niches, three on each side of the passage way, for the guards and Levites, cf. I Kgs. 14[28], II Chr. 12[11].

[i] 40[7] Some Heb. texts add the following gloss which contradicts [9] and is practically unintelligible, *He measured also the vestibule of the gate on the inner side, one reed.* This is not found in the Gk. The error is probably due to the fact that the scribe started to copy [9] entire.

[j] 40[11] The Heb. reads, *the length of the gate thirteen cubits,* but this contradicts [15], [21]. Either this is a gloss or else the text should be slightly revised so as to read as above.

[k] 40[12] The meaning possibly is that these barriers or sills before the guard-rooms were six cubits long and one in height and thickness.

[l] 40[13] Following the Gk.

[m] 40[14] Restoring the text as the context demands. The latter part of the vs. is very doubtful and obscure. The Gk. has an entirely different reading.

[n] 40[14] So Gk. Heb., *60*, but the Gk. is supported by the other measurements in the Heb.

Ezekiel's Code

¹⁶And the guard-rooms and their jambs had windows,° within the gate round about, and likewise the vestibule^p had windows round about within; and on each jamb were palm-trees.

Outer court

¹⁷Then he brought me into the outer court, and there were chambers and a pavement made round about the court; thirty chambers were upon the pavement. ¹⁸And the pavement was on the side of the gateways; it

° 40^{16} Or, *latticed.*
^p 40^{16} The Heb. text is corrupt; a scribe has apparently confused the Heb. word for *vestibule* with the similar word for *arch.*

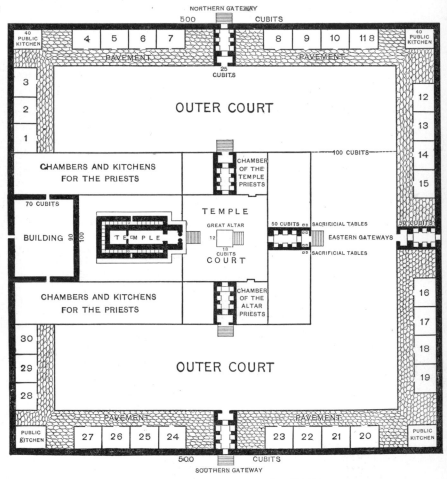

GENERAL PLAN OF EZEKIEL'S TEMPLE

164

Ezekiel's Code

corresponded to the length of the gateways, that is, the lower pavement. 19 Then he measured the breadth from the front of the lower gate to the front of the inner court without, one hundred cubits on the east and on the north.

North outer gateway

20 And the north gateway of the outer court, he measured its length and breadth. 21 And there were three guard-rooms on each side; and its jambs and its vestibules[q] corresponded to the measurement of the first gate; its length was fifty cubits, and its breadth twenty cubits. 22 And its windows and its vestibule[q] and its palm trees measured the same as those of the east gate; and seven steps led up to it; its vestibule was within.[r] 23 And there was a gate to the inner court opposite the north gate, corresponding to the one on the east;[s] and he measured from gate to gate one hundred cubits.

South gateway

24 And he led me toward the south; and he measured its guard-rooms[t] and its jambs and its vestibule; they were of the same dimensions as the others. 25 And there were windows in it and in its vestibule round about corresponding to the other windows; the length was fifty cubits, and the breadth twenty-five cubits. 26 And seven steps led up to it, and its vestibule[u] was within; and it had palm-trees, one on each side of its jambs. 27 And there was a gate to the inner court on the south; and he measured from gate to gate toward the south a hundred cubits.

§ 142. The Inner Court, Ezek. 40[28-47a]

Ezekiel's Code

South inner gate way

Ezek. 40 28 Then he brought me to the inner court at the south gateway; and he measured the south gateway; it measured the same as the others; 29 its guard-rooms, and posts and vestibule were of the same dimensions as the preceding; and there were windows in it and in its vestibule round about; it was fifty cubits long and twenty-five cubits wide.[v] 31 And its vestibule faced the outer court; and there were palm-trees beside its posts; and the ascent to it had eight steps.

East inner gateway

32 And he brought me to the east side of the inner court; and he measured the gateway; it measured the same as the others; 33 and its guard-rooms and posts and vestibules were of the same dimensions as the preceding; and there were windows in it and in the vestibule round about; it was fifty cubits long and twenty-five cubits wide. 34 And its vestibule faced the outer court; and there were beside its palm-trees posts, one on each side; and the ascent to it had eight steps.

North inner gateway

35 Then he brought me to the north gateway; and he measured the gateway; it measured the same as the others. 36 And its guard-rooms and posts and vestibules were of the same dimensions as the preceding; and there were

---

[q] 40[21, 22] Standard Heb. text, *arches*.
[r] 40[22] So Gk. Heb., *before them*.
[s] 40[23] The Heb. has simply, *to the east*.
[t] 40[24] So Gk. The Heb. omits, *and its guard-rooms*.
[u] 40[26] Translating as in [22].
[v] 40[29] The Gk. omits [30]. A scribe adds in the Heb. different dimensions, *Its vestibule round about was twenty-five cubits long and five cubits wide.* These, however, are impossible.

Ezekiel's Code

windows in it and in the vestibule round about; it was fifty cubits long and twenty-five cubits wide.   ³⁷And its vestibule faced the outer court; and there were beside its palm-trees posts, one on each side; and the ascent to it had eight steps.

Sacrificial
tables   ³⁸And there was a chamber with its opening into the vestibule of the gateway;ʷ there they washed the burnt-offering.   ³⁹And in the vestibule of the gateway were two tables on each side, on which were slain the burnt-offerings and the sin-offerings and the guilt-offerings.   ⁴⁰And outside the entrance to the gateway on the north, were two tables.   ⁴¹There were four within and four without the gateway : eight tables, upon which the burnt-offerings were slain.   ⁴²There were also four tables for the burnt-offering, of hewn stone, each a cubit and a half long, and a cubit and a half broad, and a cubit high; on which they laid the instruments wherewith the burnt-offerings and the sacrificial animals were slain, ⁴³and projections, one handbreadth in length, were fastened within round about.   And over the tables were protecting roofs to keep off the rain and the hot sun.ᵃ

Chambers for
the
acting
priests   ⁴⁴He brought me outside the gate and into the inner court, and there were two chambers on the inner court,ᵇ one by the north gate, facing the south, the other by the south gate facing the north.   ⁴⁵And he said to me, This chamber, which faces the south, is for the priests, who have charge of the temple; ⁴⁶and the chamber which faces the north is for the priests who have charge of the altar; they are the sons of Zadok, those of the sons of Levi who may come near to Jehovah to serve him.   ⁴⁷ᵃAnd he measured the court, a hundred cubits wide, and a hundred cubits broad—a perfect square.

§ 143. The Great Altar, Ezek. 40⁴⁷ᵇ, 43¹³⁻²⁷

Ezekiel's Code

Dimensions   **Ezek. 40** ⁴⁷ᵇThe altar was in front of the temple.   **43** ¹³And these are the measurements of the altar in cubits of a cubit and a handbreadth : the base shall be a cubit high, one cubit wide, with a border around its edge about a span wide; and this shall be the height of the altar : ¹⁴from the foundation baseᶜ to the lower ledge shall be two cubits, and the width one cubit; and from the smaller ledge to the greater ledge shall be four cubits, and the width one cubit.   ¹⁵And the altar hearthᵈ shall be four cubits high; and above the hearthᵉ shall be four horns, one cubit high.   ¹⁶And the altar

---

ʷ 40³⁸ Following a text slightly corrected by the aid of the Gk. and in accord with the demands of the architectural plan.   Heb., *by the posts, the gates*.   This chamber was probably* one of the niches or guard-rooms.   The Heb. reads, *a chamber and its door with jambs at the gateways*.   Probably the eastern gateway is the one here intended, although the context suggests the one on the north.

ᵃ 40⁴³ So Gk.   Heb., *and on the tables was the flesh of the oblation*.

ᵇ 40⁴⁴ So Gk.   The Heb. text is exceedingly corrupt.   The Heb. also reads, *east*, in the last line instead of *south gate*, as the context strongly demands.

§ 143   The general plan of the great altar was probably modelled closely after that of Solomon and is especially valuable, since for some reason the description of the latter has fallen out of the text of I Kgs. 6.   The diagram opposite will suggest the form of Ezekiel's altar.

ᶜ 43¹⁴ Lit., *base of the earth; of the earth* may be a scribal error.   Gk., *from the top of the base*.

ᵈ 43¹⁵ So Gk., Syr. and Lat.

ᵉ 43¹⁵ Again following the Gk.

Ezekiel's Code

hearth shall be twelve cubits square. ¹⁷And the ledge shall be fourteen cubits square; and the border about it shall be half a cubit; and the base one cubit wide round about. Its steps shall face the east.

¹⁸Then he said to me, O man, thus saith the Lord Jehovah : ' These are the regulations for the altar in the day when it is completed, " In order that burnt-offerings may be offered and blood sprinkled on it, ¹⁹thou shalt give[f] to the priests the Levites who are of the family of Zadok, who approach to serve me," saith the Lord Jehovah, " a young bullock as a sin-offering.[g] ²⁰And they[h] shall take some of its blood, and put it on the four horns, and on the four corners of the ledge, and on the border round about; thus shall they cleanse it and make atonement for it. ²¹They shall also take the bullock of the sin-offering, and it shall be burnt in the appointed place outside the temple. ²²And on the second day they shall offer a male goat without blemish as a sin-offering, and shall cleanse the altar, as they cleansed it with the bullock. ²³When they have made an end of cleansing it, they shall offer a young bullock and a ram from the flock without blemish. ²⁴And they shall present them before Jehovah, and the priests shall sprinkle salt upon them[i] and they shall offer them as a burnt-offering to Jehovah. ²⁵Seven days shalt thou provide daily a goat as a sin-offering;[j] they shall also provide a young bullock, and a ram from the flock, without blemish. ²⁶For seven days shall they make atonement for the altar and purify and consecrate it. ²⁷At the end of these days, on the eighth day and thereafter, the priests shall present your burnt-offerings and your peace-offerings upon the altar;[k] and I will accept you," saith the Lord Jehovah.'

Consecration of the altar

f 43¹⁹ The regular form of the religious commands. The community, not Ezek., is addressed. He himself was one of the Levitical priests to which reference is made.
g 43¹⁹ The sin-offering, as elsewhere in the priestly laws is not for moral but ceremonial defilement cf. note § 204.
h 43²⁰ So Gk. The Heb. has the second person singular throughout this and the following vss., except in ²², ²⁵. The Gk. evidently has the original reading and the variations are due to a scribe who was influenced by Ex. 29³⁶, Lev. 18¹¹ where the second person singular is used.
i 43²⁴ *I. e.*, the food for the Deity was prepared as an ordinary meal.
j 43²⁵ So the Gk. and the marginal reading of the Heb.
k 43²⁷ Cf. for the similar ceremony in the priestly codes, Ex. 29¹⁰⁻²⁰ § 162.

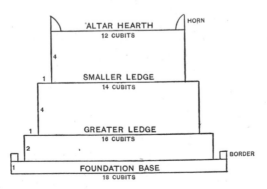

§ 144. The Temple Proper, Ezek. 40[48]–41[4, 15b-26]

Ezekiel's Code

Porch

Ezek. 40 [48]Then he brought me to the porch of the temple, and measured the jambs of the porch on each side,[l] five cubits in thickness, and the width of the gate was fourteen cubits and the pillars of the gate were three cubits thick on each side. [49]The dimensions of the porch were twenty by twelve[m] cubits; and the ascent was by ten steps;[n] and there were pillars by the jambs on each side.

Main hall

41 [1]Then he brought me to the hall of the temple and measured the jambs, six cubits broad on each side.[o] [2]And the breadth of the entrance was ten cubits; and the sides of the entrance were five cubits on each side; and he measured its length, forty cubits, and its width, twenty cubits.

Most holy place

[3]Then went into the inner room and measured the jambs of its entrance, two cubits; and the entrance, six cubits; and the side-walls[p] of the entrance, seven cubits on each side.[q] [4]And he measured its length, twenty cubits, and its breadth, twenty cubits, before the hall of the temple. And he said to me, This is the most holy place.

Interior decorations of the temple

[15b]And the hall of the temple, and the inner room and its porch were paneled,[r] [16]and the windows latticed[s] and covered.[t] And the galleries round about on their three stories, opposite the threshold, were ceiled with wood round about, from the ground up to the windows,[u] [17]and from the

§ 144 Cf. the description and plan of Solomon's temple, § 138. The plan below will indicate the general form of Ezek.'s temple.

[l] 40[48] Following the fuller and obviously better preserved Gk. reading.

[m] 40[49] So Gk. Heb., *eleven*.

[n] 40[49] Again the Gk. has retained the original reading.

[o] 41[1] So Gk. A scribe has added to the Heb., *the breadth of the tabernacle.*

[p] 41[3] So Gk.

[q] 41[3] This last clause is preserved only in the Gk.

[r] 41[15b] Following the Gk. supported by the context.

[s] 41[16] An exceedingly doubtful vs., cf. I Kgs. 6[4, 15], 7[4].

[t] 41[16] Transferring this clause from the end of the vs. where it interrupts the sense.

[u] 41[16] Or, *roof*, changing the text slightly.

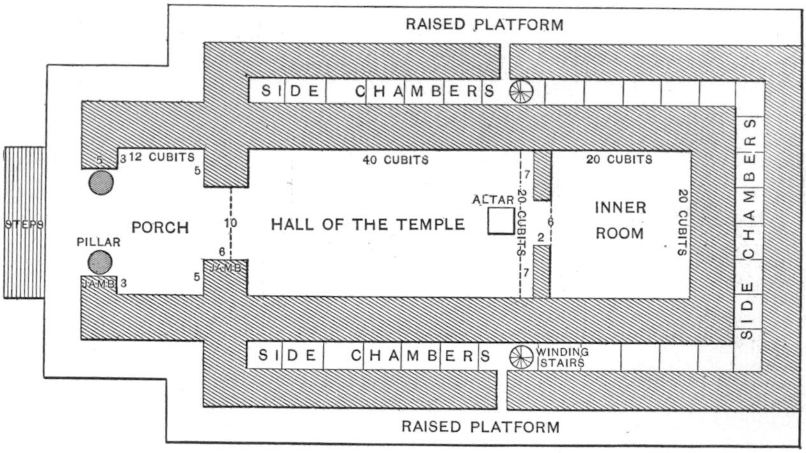

Ezekiel's Code

door to the inner room and without. And on all the wall round about within and without were drawings[v] [18]and carved cherubim and palm-trees, there being a palm-tree between every two cherubim. And each cherub had two faces; [19]the face of a man turned toward the palm-tree on the one side, and the face of a young lion turned toward the palm-tree on the other side; they were carved on all the temple round about. [20]From the ground to the top of the door were carved cherubim and palm-trees. The wall of the hall of the temple had[w] [21]pilasters. And before the holy place was something that looked like [22]an altar of wood,[x] three cubits high, and two cubits in thickness and two cubits in width; and its corners, and its base and walls were of wood. And he said to me, This is the table that stands[a] before Jehovah. [23]And the base of the temple and the holy place had two doors. [24]And each door had turning leaves; two for each door. [25]Cherubim and palm-trees were carved on them, as on the walls;[b] and there was a threshold[c] in front of the porch without. [26]And there were closed windows and palm-trees on both sides of the porch; thus were the side-chambers of the temple and the thresholds.

§ 145. The Side-Chambers, Ezek. 41[5-15a]

Ezekiel's Code

Ezek. 41 [5]Then he measured the thickness of the wall of the temple, six cubits; and the width of the side-chambers, four cubits, round about the temple on every side. [6]And the side-chambers were in three stories, one above another, and thirty in each story; and there were abatements all around the walls of the temple that the side-chambers might be fastened to them and not in the walls of the temple. [7]And the side-chambers became wider as they went up higher and higher,[d] for the temple grew narrower higher and higher up round about the temple;[e] and there was an ascent[f] from the lowest story to the highest by the middle story. [8]And I also saw that the temple had a raised platform round about; the foundations of the side-chambers were a full reed in height, that is, six great cubits. [9]The thickness of the outer wall of the side-chambers, was five cubits; and the space left between the side-chambers that belonged to the temple [10]and the outer chambers was twenty[g] cubits wide round about the temple on each side. [11]And the doors of the side-chambers were toward the open space, one door toward

Plan and dimensions

---

v 41 17 Lit., *measured.*
w 41 20 The Heb. repeats, *hall of the temple.*
x 41 22 So Gk.
a 41 22 Restoring the word demanded by the context and suggested by the Gk.
b 41 25 A scribe has added to make the sense clear, *on the doors of the hall of the temple.*
c 41 25 The meaning of this word is doubtful; *projecting roof* and *cornice* has been suggested.
d 41 7 This vs. is very doubtful. The above translation is based upon two plausible emendations. The idea clearly is that the upper chambers were larger because the outer walls of the temple receded.
e 41 7 The Heb. adds, *therefore there was width to the temple above.*
f 41 7 Correcting a slight error in the Heb.
g 41 10 Or *twenty-five cubits,* cf. [11].

Ezekiel's Code

Dimen-
sions
of the
western
build-
ing and
temple

the north and another door toward the south; and the width of the open space of the platform was five cubits round about. ^{12}And the building that faced the enclosure on the west was seventy cubits wide; and the wall of the building was five cubits thick round about, and its length ninety cubits. ^{13}So he measured the temple, a hundred cubits long; and the enclosure, and the building, with its walls, a hundred cubits long; ^{14}also the width of the front of the temple, with the eastern enclosure was one hundred cubits. ^{15a}And he measured the length of the building in front of the rear enclosure, its galleries on both sides, one hundred cubits.

§ 146. Chambers and Kitchens for the Priests, Ezek. 42$^{1-14}$, 46$^{19-24}$

Ezekiel's Code

Plan
and di-
men-
sions

Ezek. 42 ^{1}Then he brought me forth into the outer court on the north; and he brought me to the chamber which faced the enclosure and the building on the north. ^{2}One hundred cubits was its length on the north side,^{h} and the width was fifty cubits. ^{3}Opposite the space of twenty cubits^{i} which belonged to the inner court, and the raised platform which belonged to the outer court, was a gallery on each side in three tiers. ^{4}And in front of the chambers was a passage-way to the inner court, ten cubits wide and one hundred^{j} cubits long; and their doors were on the north. ^{5}The upper chambers were smaller, for the galleries took away from these, more than from the lower and the middle chambers in the building; ^{6}that is, they were in three stories, and had no pillars like the pillars of the outer courts; therefore the upper was smaller than the lowest and middle chambers. ^{7}And the outer wall by the side of the chambers along the outer court in front of the chambers was fifty cubits long; ^{8}that is, the length of the chambers in the outer court was fifty cubits, while in front of it was one hundred cubits. ^{9}Below these chambers was the entry on the east side, as one approached them from the outer court; ^{10}at the beginning^{k} of the outer wall on the south, in front of the enclosure and the building, were chambers, ^{11}with the passage-way before them; they were similar^{l} to the chambers on the north; of the same length and width, the same exits and arrangements, and with their doors on the south. ^{12}There was a door at the beginning of the passage-way, directly in front of the wall on the east, as one approached them.

Their
use

^{13}Then said he to me, the north and south chambers are the sacred chambers, where the priests who approach Jehovah shall eat the most holy things; there they shall deposit the most holy things, the cereal-offering, and the sin-offering, and the guilt-offering, for the place is holy.^{m}

---

§ 146 Cf. the general plan p. 164. It is impossible to determine definitely from the description just what was the plan and arrangement of these chambers of the priests.
^{h} 42^{2} Slightly correcting the Heb.
^{i} 42^{3} Cf. 41^{10}.
^{j} 42^{4} So Gk. Heb., *one*.
^{k} 42^{10} Following a slightly corrected text, cf. ^{12}.
^{l} 42^{11} Slightly emending the text.
^{m} 42^{13} The following vs. ^{14} is evidently a scribal insertion from 44^{19}.

Ezekiel's Code

46 [19]Then he brought me through the entry, which was at the side of the Kitch-
gate, into the priests' sacred chamber on the north; and there was a place ens
on the extreme western side. [20]And he said to me, This is the place where priests
the priests shall boil the guilt-offering and the sin-offering, and bake the and
cereal-offering, so as not to bring them out into the outer court, thereby people
making the people sacred.[n] [21]Then he brought me into the outer court, and
made me pass by the four corners of the court; and there in each corner of
the court was a court. [22]In the four corners of the court there were small[o]
courts forty cubits long and thirty cubits wide; these four in the corners were
of the same size. [23]And there was a row of stones[p] round about each of the
four, and places for boiling were constructed beneath the row of stones round
about. [24]Then he said to me, These are the houses where the ministers
of the temple shall boil the sacrifice of the people.

§ 147. Sanctity of the Temple and Land Consecrated by Jehovah's Presence, Ezek. 42[15]–43[12]

Ezekiel's Code

Ezek. 42 [15]Having finished the measurement of the inner temple he Total
brought me by way of the east gate, and measured it round about. [16]He area of
measured on the east side five hundred cubits,[q] with the measuring reed temple
round about. [17]He measured on the north side five hundred cubits[r] by the cincts
measuring reed round about. [18]He measured on the south side five hundred pre-
cubits by the measuring reed. [19]Then he turned to the west side and measured five hundred cubits by the measuring reed. [20]He measured it on the
four sides; and[s] it had a wall round about, five hundred cubits in length
and five hundred cubits in width, to separate between the sacred and the
common.

43 [1]Then he brought me to the east gate. [2]And behold the glory of the Vision
God of Israel came from the east; and his voice was like the sound of many of Je-
waters; and the earth shone with his glory. [3]And the vision which I saw hovah
was like[t] that which I saw when he[u] came to destroy the city; and the visions
were like that which I saw by the River Chebar; and I fell on my face. [4]Then
the glory of Jehovah came into the temple by the east gate. [5]And the Spirit
took me up, and brought me into the inner court; and, behold, the glory of
Jehovah filled the temple.

---

[n] 46[20] The belief that contact with sacred things rendered those touched also sacred and
therefore unfit for certain ordinary occupations was one of the fundamental beliefs of Semitic
antiquity, cf. 42[1-13], 44[19]. Lev. 6[18, 27].
[o] 46[22] So Gk. and Syr. The Heb. text is doubtful; possibly it may be rendered *inclosed*.
[p] 46[23] Or possibly, *colonnade*.
§ 147 This section reveals the religious purpose which actuated Ezek. in developing this
elaborate description of the temple.
[q] 42[15] So Gk. Heb., reeds.
[r] 42[17] Heb., *reeds*, but this is clearly due to a scribal error, cf. the plan and the data in
40[13, 15, 19, 33, 47]. The same error is repeated in [18, 19].
[s] 42[20] So Gk. and Syr. The Heb. omits the *and*.
[t] 43[3] Following the Gk.
[u] 43[3] Heb., *I*, but the context demands *he*, cf. 1 and 10.

Ezekiel's Code

Temple sanctified by Jehovah's presence

⁶Then I heard one speaking to me from the temple, as One stood by me. ⁷And he said to me, O man, this is the place of my throne, and the place for the soles of my feet, where I will dwell in the midst of the Israelites forever. And the house of Israel, they and their kings, shall no more defile my holy name^v with their idolatry^w and with the corpses of their kings ⁸by placing their thresholds by my threshold, and their door-posts beside my door-post, with only a wall between me and them, thus defiling my holy name by the abominations which they have committed; therefore I have destroyed them in mine anger. ⁹Now let them put away their idolatry, and the corpses of their kings, far from me, that I may dwell in the midst of them forever.

Ezekiel's commission

¹⁰Do thou, O man, show the house of Israel the temple, its appearance and its pattern,^x ¹¹that they may be ashamed of all that they have done, describe to them the temple and its construction, its exits and its entrances and its form, and make known to them all its ordinances and laws; and write it down in their sight, that they may take heed to perform all its forms and ordinances. ¹²This is the law of the temple: on the top of the mountain its whole territory shall be sacred. Behold, this is the law of the temple.

B

SACRED OFFICIALS

I

IN THE PRE–EXILIC HEBREW STATE

§ 148. **Call of the Tribe of Levi,** Ex. 32²⁵⁻²⁹, Dt. 10⁸

Primitive Codes

Zeal of the Levites and its reward

Ex. 32 ²⁵Now when Moses saw that the people had thrown off all restraint (since Aaron had given them the reins, to become an object of derision

---

^v 43⁷ The Heb. adds, *in the high place.*
^w 43⁷ Heb., *whoredom.*
^x 43¹⁰, ¹¹ Reconstructing the obviously corrupt Heb. with the aid of the Gk.
    Sacred Officials in the Pre-exilic Hebrew State.—According to the most primitive Semitic thought and usage the head of the family was also its priest. As society became more complex, the chief priest of the tribe was the sheik, and of the nation the king. Thus the earliest rulers of the city states of ancient Babylonia and Assyria were still the heads of the national religion, and as such were subject to certain ceremonial restrictions, as for example the refraining from certain acts on the seventh day. Among the Egyptians, the Ethiopians and the Sabeans the king was also the chief priest of the nation. Many of the more modern illustrations of the same institution might be cited; the Mikado of Japan is perhaps the most familiar example.
    The original idea underlying these wide-spread institutions seems to have been that the god or gods chose certain men to represent them. The archaic Babylonian sign for king pictures the hand of the god resting upon the head of the man thus chosen and commissioned.

Primitive Codes

among their enemies), ²⁶Moses stood in the gate of the camp and said, Whoever belongeth to Jehovah, come to me. And all the sons of Levi came together to him. ²⁷Then he said to them, Thus saith Jehovah the God of Israel, 'Let each man gird his sword on his thigh, and pass back and forth from gate to gate in the camp, and let each man kill his brother, and each man his friend, and each man his kinsman.' ²⁸And the sons of Levi did according to the injunction of Moses, and there fell of the people that day about three thousand men. ²⁹And Moses said, Consecrate yourselves to-day to the service of Jehovah (for every man was against his son and against his brother) that he may now bestow a blessing upon you.

Sometimes the primitive priest-king was conceived of as related to the gods; sometimes the bond or kinship was thought of as established by contact with the blood of the sacrificial animal which he slew in behalf of the tribe or nation. The same rite of anointing with oil (probably symbolizing the fat of the sacrifice) was employed in consecrating both king and priest. Thus the idea of the Messiah, the anointed, who represented both the god and the nation, was innate in earlier Semitic thought.

Hebrew history furnishes many suggestions regarding the origin of the priesthood. Even down to the days of the exile, the head of the family performed the sacrifice, cf. § 140. Gideon offers a burnt-offering on the altar which he rears, Judg. 6²⁶. Saul on the battle-field builds an altar on which the warriors slay their booty, I Sam. 14^{34, 35}. Only the stricter ceremonialism of a later age condemned his offering a burnt-offering on the eve of battle, I Sam. 10⁹. King Solomon sacrificed as the chief priest of the nation at the dedication of the temple, I Kgs. 8^{5, 62-64}. Three times each year he also offered the sacrifice in behalf of the nation, I Kgs. 9²⁵.

In time, however, the ceremonial and other restrictions placed upon the chief priest of the nation limited the free exercise of the kingly functions. Among some early peoples the chief ruler was shorn of all real military and civil power, and became only the head of the national cult. Other kings, like David and Solomon, appointed certain royal priests and conferred upon them the priestly functions which originally belonged to the head of the nation. Priests like Zadok, and those appointed by Jeroboam I of Northern Israel at the royal sanctuaries of Dan and Bethel, were officers of the king and undoubtedly at first were supported by royal revenues. Thus arose in Israel, as among other Semitic peoples, the distinct class of priests whose duty it was to attend to the details of the sacrificial ritual.

§ 148 The origin and functions of the sons of Levi appear to have been somewhat similar and yet different from those of the priests of the royal sanctuaries. The references to the sons of Levi in the earliest sources are unfortunately rare. The ancient oracle in Gen. 49⁵⁻⁷ speaks in condemnation of some act of vengeance committed by them, because *their anger was fierce and their wrath cruel.* The consequence was that *they were divided in Jacob and scattered in Israel.*

The act thus indicated is probably the basis of the story in Gen. 34, cf. Vol. I § 41. As in Gen. 49, the sons of Simeon are associated with those of Levi. The deed which elicited the rebuke attributed to Jacob, 34³⁰, was their pitiless zeal in slaying the Canaanites with whom their clansmen had just made a close alliance. Their motive was probably that *jealousy for Jehovah,* which would tolerate no alliances with heathen peoples—the same jealousy that inspired Elijah in later times. A similar spirit is revealed in the Northern Israelitish account of their bloody zeal in slaying their idolatrous kinsmen, cf. above. The story comes from a period when the prophetic conscience had been aroused to condemn the golden calves, long regarded as legitimate by the Northern Israelites; but it is only one of several illustrations of their devotion to the religion of Jehovah. This zeal was probably derived from their great clansman Moses. It naturally explains why they early suffered such a great disaster at the hands of the incensed Canaanites that the few who survived were scattered and went forth to find homes and a precarious existence among the other Hebrew tribes. Their jealousy for Jehovah, their relationship to the great leader Moses, and the fact that they had no tribal home nor unity also furnish a probable explanation of why they early became attached to the various shrines throughout the land of Israel.

The ancient story in Judg. 17 and 18 furnishes a vivid and almost contemporary picture of this process. Micah the Ephraimite, having established a family sanctuary with ephod and oracle, first appointed his son as its priest. But when a wandering Levite came by chance from Bethlehem in Judah, Micah at once engaged him, by the payment of a definite sum each year, to stay and *be a father and priest* to the Ephraimite household, 17¹⁰. Later the Danites stole the priest and paraphernalia of the shrine and so this Levite, Jonathan the grandson of Moses, 18³⁰, became the head of the priesthood of the famous sanctuary at Dan.

Thus it would appear that in this natural way the sons of Levi, the scattered clansmen of Moses, became the guardians of many of Jehovah's oracles and local shrines. It was also natural that in time the title, *son of Levi,* should be applied to all who belong to this class, whatever may have been their ancestry, so that like the terms, *sons of the prophets* or *sons of Korah,* it simply designated the members of a caste or guild.

Deuteronomic Codes

Conse-
cration
of the
Levites

Dt. 10 ⁸At that time[a] Jehovah set apart the tribe of Levi, to bear the ark of the covenant of Jehovah, to stand before Jehovah to minister to him,[b] and to bless in his name, even to the present day.

§ 149. **Duties of the Sons of Levi,** Dt. 33⁸ᵃ· ¹⁰, 21⁵ᵇ [18⁵], 17⁸⁻¹³, 31²⁵· ²⁶, 24⁸, 26¹⁻⁴, 20²⁻⁴

Primitive Codes

To ren-
der de-
cisions
and
offer
sacri-
fices

Dt. 33 ⁸ᵃOf Levi Moses said,

Thy Thummim and thy Urim[c] are for thy holy one.[d]
¹⁰They show Jacob thy judgments, *O Jehovah,*
And Israel thy instruction,
They bring to thy nostrils the savor of sacrifice,
And whole burnt-offering to thine altar.

Deuteronomic Codes

To act
as tem-
ple
minis-
ters

Dt. 21 ⁵ᵇJehovah thy God hath chosen the priests the sons of Levi to minister to him, and to bless in the name of Jehovah. And according to their sentence shall every dispute and case of assault[e] be decided.

To act
as
judges
in the
court
of final
appeal

17 ⁸If a case involving bloodshed or conflicting claims, or the plague of leprosy[f]—subjects of dispute within thine own city—be too difficult for thee to decide, then thou shalt set out and go up to the place which Jehovah thy God shall choose; ⁹and thou shalt come to the Levitical priests, and the judge who shall be in office in those days;[g] and thou shalt inquire, and they shall make known to thee the judicial decision. ¹⁰And thou shalt act according to the tenor of the sentence, that they shall make known to thee from the place which Jehovah shall choose; and thou shalt do exactly as they direct thee: ¹¹according to the tenor of the instruction which they give thee,

---

[a] Dt. 10⁸ This vs. originally once followed ⁵, which tells of Moses' descent from Horeb with the ten words. It implies the incident recorded in Ex. 20²⁵⁻²⁹ and possibly a fuller account, now lost, of the call of the tribe of Levi at that time, cf. also 18⁵.

[b] Dt. 10⁸ *I. e.*, to serve as priests, cf. I Sam. 16²¹.

§ 149 The story of the young Levite, who was employed by Micah the Ephraimite, Judg. 17, 18, as well as the references in I Sam. to the activity of Eli and his sons, would seem to indicate that originally the sons of Levi were simply the guardians of the sacred objects like the ark and the Urim and Thummim and, later, of the local shrines; and that the sacrifices were slain by the individual offerers or by the heads of the family or tribe, or by a seer like Samuel, I Sam. 9¹³. As guardians of the sacred objects, the Levites also became the interpreters of the divine oracles and therefore judges. Their functions thus appear from the first to have been somewhat different from those of the sons of Zadok to whom Solomon in time delegated his rights and duties as chief priest of the nation; although in early times the distinction between the seer and Levite and royal priest were not very clearly defined.

[c] Dt. 33⁸ᵃ The meaning of the vs. is obscure. The *Thummim and Urim*, always written elsewhere *Urim and Thummim*, Ex. 28³⁰, Lev. 8⁸, Ezra 2⁶³ and I Sam. 14⁴¹ were used in determining the lot. The two words apparently mean, *perfections and lights.* What the objects were and how they were used is only a matter of conjecture. From I Sam. 14⁴¹, ⁴², it may perhaps be inferred that they were stones and that the way they fell decided the lot.

[d] Dt. 33⁸ᵃ The reference appears to be to the tribe of Levi and their fidelity, possibly at the occasion recorded in Ex. 32²⁵⁻²⁹, although the subsequent context has led some scholars to maintain that Moses is intended.

[e] Dt. 21⁵ Lit., *stroke.* This statement is interjected into the midst of the law regarding an undetected murder, in the ceremonial purification of which the Levitical priests also participate.

[f] Dt. 17⁸ Lit., *If there arise a case too hard for thee in judgment, between blood and blood, between plea and plea, and between stroke and stroke.*

[g] Dt. 17⁹ Cf. note § 47.

Deuteronomic Codes

and according to the decision which they shall impart to thee, shalt thou do, without departing from the sentence which they shall make known to thee, either to the right or to the left. ¹²But should a man be so presumptuous as not to heed the decision of the priest who standeth there before Jehovah thy God, or of the judge, that man shall die; thus thou shalt put away the evil from Israel, ¹³in order that all the people may heed and fear, and never again act presumptuously.

24 ⁸Guard carefully against the plague of leprosy in that thou faithfully observe and follow all the directions which the Levitical priests give you. According to the commands which I gave them shall ye carefully do. {To take charge of cases of leprosy}

26 ¹When thou shalt come into the land which Jehovah thy God is about to give thee as an inheritance, and shalt possess it, and dwell therein, ²thou shalt take a part of the first of all the fruit of the ground, which thou shalt bring in from thy land that Jehovah thy God giveth thee; and thou shalt put it in a basket, and thou shalt go to the place in which Jehovah thy God shall choose to have his name dwell. ³And thou shalt come to the priest who shall be officiating in those days, and say to him, I declare this day to Jehovah thy God, that I have come to the land which Jehovah promised by oath to our fathers to give us. ⁴Then the priest shall take the basket out of thy hand, and set it down before the altar of Jehovah thy God. {To present the first fruits to Jehovah}

20 ²When ye draw near to offer battle, the priest[h] shall approach and speak to the people ³and say to them, Hear O Israel, ye are drawing near this day to fight against your enemies; do not lose heart, fear not, nor tremble, neither be afraid because of them; ⁴for Jehovah your God is going with you to fight for you against your enemies in order to deliver you. {To encourage the people on the eve of battle}

§ 150. Prohibition Against the Levites Holding Property, Dt. 18¹ᵃ, ᵇ, ² [10⁹]

Deuteronomic Codes

Dt. 18 ¹ᵃ, ᵇThe Levitical priests, even all the tribe of Levi, shall have no portion nor inheritance with Israel. ²And they shall have no inheritance among their kinsmen; Jehovah is their inheritance, as he hath declared to them.[i] {No inheritance}

---

[h] Dt. 20² As has already been noted, § 42, war was regarded by the Hebrews as a sacrament. Sacrifices were also offered before the battle, I Sam. 7⁹, ¹⁰, 13⁹, ¹⁰. The common idiom for declaring war was to *consecrate a war*, Is. 13³, Mi. 3⁵, Jer. 6⁴, 22⁷. The presence of the priests is therefore assured, although the present custom is mentioned nowhere else.

§ 150 This law was doubtless intended to anticipate exactions by the priestly judges and to prevent the alienation of temple property for private ends.

[i] Dt. 18² The passage here referred to is not found in the O.T. although the same idea is repeatedly expressed, cf. Josh. 13¹⁴, ³³, 18⁷, Nu. 18¹⁰ᵇ, Ezek. 44²⁸.

§ 151. **Means of Support of the Sons of Levi**, Dt. 18¹ᵃ, ᶜ, ³⁻⁸, 14²², ²³, ²⁷, 12¹⁹, 16¹⁰⁻¹⁴, 14²⁸, ²⁹ [12¹¹, ¹², ¹⁷, ¹⁸]

Deuteronomic Codes

Certain parts of the offerings — **Dt. 18** ¹ᵃ, ᶜThe Levitical priests, even all the tribe of Levi, shall eat the offerings made by fire to Jehovah,ʲ and of that which belongeth to him. ³And this shall be the priests' due from the people, from those who offer a sacrifice whether it be ox or sheep : they shall give to the priests the shoulder and the two cheeks and the stomach. ⁴The firstfruits of thy grain, of thy new wine, and of thine oil, and the first of the fleece of thy sheep thou shalt give him; ⁵for Jehovah thy God hath chosen him and his sons out of all thy tribes, to stand to minister in the name of Jehovah forever.

Rights of priests from local sanctuaries — ⁶And if a Levite cometh from any of thy townsᵏ in all Israel, where he resideth, and cometh with a whole-hearted desireˡ to the place which Jehovah shall choose; ⁷then he shall minister in the name of Jehovah his God, as do all his brethren the Levites, who serve Jehovah there. ⁸They shall have like portions to eat,ᵐ besides that which cometh from the sale of his patrimony.

Portions of the annual tithe — **14** ²²Of all the produce of thy seed thou shalt take a tenth of all that groweth in the field each year; ²³and before Jehovah thy God, in the place in which he shall choose to have his name dwell thou shalt eat the tithe of thy grain, of thy new wine, and of thine oil, and of the first-born of thy herd and of thy flock; that thou mayst learn to fear Jehovah thy God always. ²⁷Also thou shalt not forget the Levite who dwelleth within thy town, for he hath no portion nor inheritance with thee. **12** ¹⁹Take heed not to forget the Levite as long as thou livest in thy land.

A share in the feast of weeks — **16** ¹⁰Thou shalt keep the feast of weeks to Jehovah thy God according to the measure of the voluntary offerings which thy hand shall present in proportion as Jehovah thy God hath blessed thee. ¹¹Thou and thy son and thy daughter, thy male and female slaves, and the Levite who dwelleth in thy town, and the resident alien, the fatherless and the widow, who live with thee, shall rejoice before Jehovah, in the place where Jehovah thy God shall choose to have his name dwell. ¹²And thou shalt remember that thou wast a bondman in Egypt; and thou shalt observe and do these statutes.

---

§ 151 The income of the pre-exilic Levitical priests appears to have been very precarious, depending upon the wealth and importance of the shrine with which they were connected, and the generosity of the individual offerers. Dt. 18⁸ implies that certain of them had family possessions, but the passage is not entirely clear, and it is definitely stated elsewhere that the Levites were to have no inheritance, § 160. They are repeatedly classed with the resident alien, the fatherless, and the widow. As their numbers increased, their necessities probably compelled some of them to take up other occupations. In the Jewish community which Nehemiah found in Palestine, still living under the Deuteronomic law, the Levites had not received their portions and had gone to work in the fields, Neh. 13¹⁰. It was the uncertainty, however, and their inability to collect their dues, rather than the insufficiency, which made the support of the pre-exilic priests so unsatisfactory.

ʲ Dt. 18¹ *I. e.*, all offerings, a part of which was burnt as Jehovah's portion. The term occurs sixty-two times in the priestly and only once in the Deuteronomic codes.

ᵏ Dt. 18⁶ Lit., *gates*.

ˡ Dt. 18⁶ Lit., *with all the desire of his soul*.

ᵐ Dt. 18⁶⁻⁸ This provision was for the ministers of the ancient shrines, outside Jerusalem, which had been declared illegal by the Deuteronomic law. Second Kgs. 23⁸ states that Josiah destroyed all these high places in Judah and brought their priests to Jerusalem. Vs. ⁹ adds, however, that *the priests of the high places did not come up to the altar of Jehovah in Jerusalem, but ate unleavened bread among their kinsmen*.

Deuteronomic Codes

¹³Thou shalt keep the feast of tabernacles seven days, after thou hast gathered in the output of thy threshing-floor and thy wine-press. ¹⁴And thou shalt rejoice in thy feast, together with thy son and thy daughter, and thy male and female slaves, and the Levite, the resident alien, the fatherless, and the widow who live with thee. *In the feast of tabernacles*

14 ²⁸At the end of every three years thou shalt bring out all the tithe of thine increase in that year and shalt deposit it within thy city, ²⁹that the Levite, because he hath no portion nor inheritance with thee, and the resident alien, the fatherless, and the widow, who are in thy city, may come, and eat and be satisfied in order that Jehovah thy God may bless thee in all the work to which thou puttest thy hand. *Part of the triennial tithe*

§ 152. Slaves of the Sanctuary, Josh. 9²⁶, ²⁷

Primitive Codes

Josh. 9 ²⁶Joshua saved the Gibeonites from the hand of the Israelites so that they did not slay them. ²⁷And Joshua made them at that time hewers of wood and drawers of water, for the congregation, and for the altar of Jehovah (as they are to this day) in the place which he should choose. *Fate of the Gibeonites*

II

SACRED OFFICIALS IN EZEKIEL'S HIERARCHY

§ 153. Duties of the Levites and Priests, Ezek. 44

Ezekiel's Code

Ezek. 44 ¹Then he took me back to the outer eastern gate of the sanctuary, and it was closed. ²Then he[a] said to me, This gate shall remain closed; it shall not be opened, and none shall enter by it; for Jehovah the God of Israel hath entered by it, therefore it shall remain closed. ³As for the prince he may sit therein[b] to eat bread in the presence of Jehovah; he shall enter by the vestibule of the gate, and by the same way shall he go out. *Sanctity of the eastern gate*

---

§ 152 Captives of war were in ancient times dedicated to the Deity in gratitude for the victories gained. Upon them fell the menial services in the sanctuaries. In Babylon and Egypt they also cultivated the lands or herded the flocks belonging to the temples. The Chronicler in his list of the returned refers to a class called the *nethinim* or temple slaves. Ezek., however, reversed the ancient usage, cf. § 153. For the setting of the above passage from Josh. cf. Vol. I, § 113.

§ 153 Ezekiel not only adopts many of the existing regulations regarding the priesthood, but he also introduces not a few innovations which reappear in the later priestly codes. He provides that the foreign slaves be kept out of the sanctuary. Their former duties he assigns to the Levites, who had ministered before Josiah's reformation at the high places outside Jerusalem. He knows nothing about the sons of Aaron, but he distinctly stipulates that the sons of Zadok, the Levitical priests of the Jerusalem temple, shall perform the more important acts of sacrifice.

Ezekiel also defines more rigorously the ceremonial limitations of the priesthood and directs that they have an increased and definite portion of the offering. Thus at every point his enactments mark the transition from the earlier Deuteronomic to the more complex later priestly regulations.

a 44² The Heb. adds, *Jehovah.*
b 44³ So Gk., Syr., and Lat. The Heb. repeats, *prince.*

Ezekiel's Code

Of the entire temple

⁴Then he took me by way of the north gate to the front of the temple; and I looked and behold, the glory of Jehovah filled the temple. And I fell on my face. ⁵And Jehovah said to me, O man, give heed, see with thine eyes and hear with thine ears all that I tell thee regarding the regulations of the temple of Jehovah and all its laws,ᶜ and observe carefully how to enter the temple by all of the exits of the sanctuary. ⁶Say to the rebellious, even to the house of Israel, ' Thus saith the Lord Jehovah, "Enough of all your abominations, O house of Israel, ⁷in that ye have brought foreigners, neither consecrated in heart nor flesh,ᵈ to be in my sanctuary to profane it,ᵉ when ye offered me bread, fat and blood; thus yeᶠ have broken my covenant, withᵍ all your abominations ! ⁸And ye have not taken charge of my holy things but ye have set them as keepersʰ in charge of my sanctuary." '

Duties of the Levitical priests from the ancient sanctuaries

⁹Therefore thus saith the Lord Jehovah, ' No foreigner, consecrated neither in heart nor flesh,ⁱ of all the foreigners who are among the Israelites, shall enter my sanctuary. ¹⁰But those Levites who went far from me, when Israel went astray, who went astray from me after their idols,ʲ shall bear their guilt. ¹¹Yet they shall be ministers in my sanctuary, having oversight at the gates of the temple, and ministering in the temple, they shall slay the burnt-offering and the sacrifice for the people, and they shall stand before them and minister to them. ¹²Since they were wont to minister to them before their idols, and were a stumbling-block of iniquity to the house of Israel; therefore I have taken a solemn oathᵏ against them,' is the oracle of the Lord Jehovah, ' and they shall bear their guilt. ¹³And they shall not approach me to act as priests to me, so as to come near any of my sacred things, or to those which are most sacred; but they shall bear their shame and the punishment for the abominations which they have committed; ¹⁴I will make them responsible for the care of the temple, for all its service, and for all that shall be done therein.

Duties of the sons of Zadok

¹⁵But the priests the Levites, the sons of Zadok,ˡ who took charge of my sanctuary when the Israelites went astray from me, shall come near to me to minister to me, and they shall stand before me to offer to me fat and blood,' is the oracle of the Lord Jehovah. ¹⁶ 'They shall enter my sanctuary, and they shall approach near to my table to minister to me, and they shall keep my charge. ¹⁷When they enter the gates of the inner court, they shall wear linen garments, but they shall have on no wool while they are officiating in the gates of the inner court and in the temple.ᵐ ¹⁸They shall have linen

---

ᶜ 44⁵ *I. e.*, the proper rules for entering the temple with offerings.
ᵈ 44⁷ Lit., *uncircumcised, i. e.*, with no true religion.
ᵉ 44⁷ The Heb. adds, but the Gk. omits, *my temple.*
ᶠ 44⁷ So Gk., Syr. and Lat. Heb., *they.*
ᵍ 44⁷ So Gk. Heb., *to.*
ʰ 44⁸ So Gk. The reference is to foreign attendants at the pre-exilic temple, cf. § 152, Ezra 8²⁰, Neh. 7⁶⁰.
ⁱ 44⁹ This is the prototype of the Greek tablet found on the temple arch in 1870 by M. Clermont-Ganneau, which reads, *No stranger shall come within the balustrade and enclosure around the temple; whoever is caught will be himself responsible for his death, which will follow.*
ʲ 44¹⁰ *I. e.*, the priests of the local shrines outside Jerusalem.
ᵏ 44¹² Lit., *lifted up my hand* (in taking the oath).
ˡ 44¹⁵ The Zadok who succeeded Abiathar as the head of the Jerusalem priesthood in the days of Solomon, I Kgs. 2²⁷, ³⁵.
ᵐ 44¹⁷ Slightly correcting the Heb.

Ezekiel's Code

turbans upon their heads and linen breeches on their loins; they shall not gird themselves with anything that causeth sweat.^{n} ^{19}But when they go forth to the outer court to the people,^{o} they shall put off the garments in which they were officiating, and lay them in the sacred chambers; and they shall put on other garments, that they may not sanctify the people^p with their garments. ^{20}Neither shall they shave their heads, nor suffer their hair to grow long; they shall cut off their hair. ^{21}None of the priests shall drink wine, when they enter the inner court. ^{22}Neither shall they marry a widow nor a divorced woman, but only Israelitish virgins or the widow of a priest.

^{23}And they shall teach my people the difference between the sacred and As the common, and instruct them how to discern between the unclean and guardians of the clean. ^{24}And in a controversy they shall act as judges, judging it ac- the cording to my ordinances. And they shall keep my laws and my statutes and in all my appointed feasts; and they shall maintain the sanctity of my sab- ritual baths.

^{25}And they shall not approach a dead person to defile themselves; except Cere- in the case of a father, or a mother, or a son, or a daughter, or brother, or monial unmarried sister.^{q} ^{26}And after his defilement,^{r} a priest shall be given purity seven days. ^{27}And on the day that he goeth into the inner court,^{s} to min- ister in the sanctuary, he shall offer his sin-offering,' is the oracle of the Lord Jehovah.

^{28}And they shall have no^t inheritance; I am their inheritance; and ye Means shall give them no possession in Israel; I am their possession. ^{29}They shall of sup- eat the cereal-offering, and the sin-offering, and the guilt-offering; and every devoted thing^u in Israel shall be theirs. ^{30}And the best of all the firstfruits of every thing, and every contribution of every thing, of all your contribu- tions, shall belong to the priest; ye shall also give to the priests the best of your dough, that a blessing may rest on thy household. ^{31}The priests shall not eat of any thing that dieth a natural death or hath been mangled, whether it be bird or beast.

---

^{n} 44^{18} This last clause may be secondary. The meaning of the Heb. is not certain.
^{o} 44^{19} So Gk. The Heb. repeats, *to the court.*
^{p} 44^{19} The idea that sanctity, as well as ceremonial uncleanness, could be communicated by contact was firmly fixed in the Heb. mind. Cf. Lev. 6$^{18,\ 27}$, Josh 7^{12}.
^{q} 44^{25} The reason was probably to prevent interruptions in the sacrificial service.
^{r} 44^{26} So Syr. In the Heb. a scribe has confused two similar words, so that the vs. now begins, *after he is cleansed.*
^{s} 44^{27} So Gk. A Heb. scribe has added by mistake, *into the sanctuary.*
^{t} 44^{28} So Lat. and the demands of the context. The negative has been lost in the Heb.
^{u} 44^{29} *I. e.*, those things placed under the ban or dedicated to Jehovah.

§ 154. Duties of the Princes, Ezek. 45⁹⁻¹⁷, ²¹⁻²⁵, 46¹⁻¹⁵

Ezekiel's Code

To regulate weights and measures

Ezek. 45 ⁹Thus saith the Lord Jehovah, Enough, O princes of Israel! Put away violence and oppression, and practice justice and righteousness! Free my people from your robberies, is the oracle of the Lord Jehovah. ¹⁰Ye shall have just balances, and a just ephah, and a just bath. ¹¹The ephah[v] and the bath[w] shall be of one measure; the bath shall contain the tenth part of a homer, and the ephah the tenth part of a homer; the homer shall be the standard of measurement. ¹²And the shekel shall be twenty gerahs; five shekels shall be valued as five shekels[x], and ten as ten, and your maneh shall be fifty shekels.

To provide material for sacrifices

¹³This is the contribution that ye shall offer: the sixth part of an ephah out of every homer of wheat; and ye shall give the sixth part of an ephah out of every homer of barley; ¹⁴and the fixed proportion of oil,[a] shall be the tenth part of a bath out of every cor, the cor being ten baths;[b] ¹⁵and one lamb out of a flock of two hundred, from all the families[c] of Israel, as a cereal-offering, and a burnt-offering, and peace-offerings, to make atonement for them, saith the Lord Jehovah. ¹⁶All the people of the land shall contribute to this special gift for the prince in Israel. ¹⁷And it shall be the prince's part to give the burnt-offerings, and the cereal-offerings, and the libations at the feasts, and on the new moons, and on the sabbaths, at all the feast days of the house of Israel: he shall prepare the sin-offering, and the cereal-offering, and the burnt-offering, and the peace-offerings, to make atonement for the house of Israel.

Also for the stated offerings

²¹In the first month, on the fourteenth day of the month, ye shall observe the feast[d] of the passover; seven days unleavened bread shall be eaten. ²²On that day the prince shall provide for himself and for all the people of the land a bullock as a sin-offering; ²³and during the seven days of the feast he shall provide a burnt-offering for Jehovah, seven bullocks and seven rams without blemish; and a male goat daily as a sin-offering. ²⁴And he shall provide a cereal-offering, an ephah to a bullock, and an ephah to a ram, and of oil a hin to an ephah. ²⁵In the seventh month, on the fifteenth day of the month, at the feast, shall he do the same during the seven days, for the sin-offering, the burnt-offering, the cereal-offering, and for the oil.

Offerings for the sabbaths

46 ¹Thus saith the Lord Jehovah, The east gate of the inner court shall be shut during the six working days; but on the sabbath day, and on the day of the new moon it shall be open. ²And the prince shall enter from

---

§ 154 The Exile, as a matter of fact, and Ezek. by formal enactment reversed the relations between the priesthood and monarchy, so that the Jerusalem priests were no longer merely appendages of the royal court, but the central figures in the state; the chief functions of the prince was simply to provide certain stated offerings in the temple service.

v 45¹¹ This was a dry measure and contained about 36 or 37 litres, cf. Appendix IX.
w 45¹¹ The bath was a liquid measure, and contained about 8 gallons or 36 or 37 litres.
x 45¹¹ So Gk. A
a 45¹⁴ A scribe has added from Dt. 14, *of the bath of oil.*
b 45¹⁴ So Gk. The Heb. adds, *a homer, for ten baths are a homer.*
c 45¹⁵ So Gk. Heb., *from the well-watered.*
d 45²¹ Transferring the word, *feast,* and slightly correcting the Heb.

Ezekiel's Code

without by the vestibule of the gate, and shall stand by the door-post of the gate; and the priests shall prepare his burnt-offering and his peace-offerings, and he shall worship at the threshold of the gate, and then go out; but the gate shall not be shut until evening. ³And the people of the land shall worship at the door of that gate before Jehovah on the sabbaths and on the new moons. ⁴And the burnt-offering which the prince shall offer to Jehovah on the sabbath day shall be six lambs without blemish and one ram without blemish; ⁵the cereal-offering being an ephah to a ram, and for the lambs as he is able to give, and of oil a hin to an ephah.

⁶And on the day of the new moon it shall be a young bullock without blemish and six lambs, and a ram, without blemish; ⁷and he shall prepare a cereal-offering, an ephah for the bullock, and an ephah for the ram, and for the lambs as he is able, and of oil a hin to an ephah. *For the new moon*

⁸And when the prince shall enter, he shall go in by the vestibule of the gate, and he shall go forth by the same way. ⁹But when the people of the land shall come before Jehovah in the feast days, he who enters by the north gate to worship shall go out by the south gate; and he who enters by the south gate shall go out by the north gate; none shall return by the gate at which he came in, but shall go out straight ahead. ¹⁰The prince shall go in with them, when they go in, and go out, when they go forth. *Manner of entrance and exit*

¹¹And on the feast days and the festivals the cereal-offering shall be an ephah to a bullock, and an ephah to a ram, and for the lambs as he is able to give, and of oil a hin to an ephah. ¹²And when the prince shall prepare a voluntary-offering, a burnt-offering or peace-offerings as a voluntary-offering to Jehovah, the east gate shall be opened for him, and he shall present his burnt-offering and his peace-offerings, as he doth on the sabbath day; then he shall go out; and after he has gone out the gate shall be shut. *On the special feast days*

¹³And he[e] shall provide daily a lamb a year old without blemish as a burnt-offering to Jehovah;[f] each morning shall he provide it. ¹⁴And he shall provide as a cereal-offering with it each morning the sixth part of an ephah, and the third part of a hin of oil, to moisten the fine meal, as a cereal-offering to Jehovah by a perpetual ordinance. ¹⁵Thus shall he provide the lamb, and the cereal-offering, and the oil, each morning, as a regular burnt-offering.

---

[e] 46¹³⁻¹⁴ So Gk., Syr., and Lat. The Heb. has in these vss. the second person singular, although in ¹⁵, *they*, is used. The context supports the reading, *he*, throughout.
[f] 46¹⁴ So Gk. The Heb. adds, *continually*.

§ 155. Apportionment of the Land to the Temple, Levites, City, Prince, and Tribes, Ezek. 45¹⁻⁸, 46¹⁶⁻¹⁸, 47 [48]

Ezekiel's Code

To the
temple
and its
minis-
ters

Ezek. 45 ¹When ye allot the land as inheritance, ye shall offer as a special gift[g] to Jehovah, a sacred portion of the land, five thousand cubits long, and twenty[h] thousand cubits wide; it shall be sacred throughout its entire extent. ³And out of this area shalt thou measure off a space twenty-five thousand cubits long and ten thousand cubits wide, and on it shall the sanctuary, the most holy,[i] stand. ⁴It is a holy portion of the land; it shall belong to the priests who are the ministers in the sanctuary, who draw near to minister to Jehovah; and it shall be a place for their houses, and an open space for the sanctuary. ²Out of this a square of five hundred cubits shall be

---

§ 155 The question of the reassignment of the territory of Canaan was a prominent one in the minds of the priestly exiles in Babylonia. As a matter of fact the land about Jerusalem never passed out of the possession of the Jewish survivors of the great catastrophe of 586 B.C. This fact must have been known to Ezek. and his associates. His plan of apportionment, like many other elements in his program, must, therefore, be regarded as an ideal rather than a practical basis for reorganization. It aims concretely to emphasize the necessity of carefully protecting the temple, the abode of the Holy One, from all defiling contact with the outside world. The priests, the Levites, the prince and the different tribes all represent successive ranks of guardians about the sanctuary. Provision is also made for the priests and Levites proportionate to their importance in the new Jewish state.

The accompanying diagram will illustrate Ezek.'s plan of allotment given in 48. Since this chapter simply gives these details, in Ezek.'s repetitious style, it has not been reproduced in the present text.

g 45¹ Lit., *offer an oblation.*

h 45¹ So Gk. Heb., *ten.* The standard of measure is not given, but it is in all probability the cubit. The total area would contain between forty and fifty square miles.

i 45³ Restoring the Heb. with the aid of the Gk. This space corresponded to the common pasture grounds about every ancient Heb. village. Heb., *and a sanctuary for the sanctuary.* Gk., *houses set aside* or *assigned for their sanctification.*

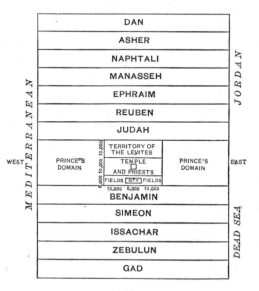

Ezekiel's Code

for the sanctuary, with an open space fifty cubits wide around it.ʲ ⁵And a space twenty-five thousand cubits long and ten thousand wide shall belong to the Levites, the ministers of the temple; their possession shall it be for cities in which to dwell.ᵏ

⁶And as the possession of the city, ye shall assign a space five thousand cubits wide, and twenty-five thousand long, beside the sacred reservation; it shall belong to the whole house of Israel. ⁷And the prince shall have the space on both sides of the sacred reservation and the possession of the city, facing the sacred reservation and the possession of the city, on the west and on the east, and of the same length as one of the portions of the tribes, from the west border to the east border ⁸of the land. It shall be his possession in Israel; and the princesˡ of Israel shall no more oppress my people, but shall give the land to the house of Israel according to their tribes. *(To the city and prince)*

46 ¹⁶Thus saith the Lord Jehovah, If the prince make a gift to any of his sons, out of his inheritance,ᵐ it shall belong to his sons; it is their possession by inheritance. ¹⁷But if he make a gift out of his inheritance to one of his servants, it shall be his to the year of release; then it shall revert to the prince; but as for his inheritance, it shall belong to his sons. ¹⁸Moreover the prince shall not take of the people's inheritance so as to deprive them by force of their possession; he shall give an inheritance to his sons out of his own possession, that none of my people be scattered from his possession. *(His right to alienate landed property)*

47 ¹Then he brought me to the door of the temple and there was water issuing from under the threshold of the temple eastward—the temple faced the east—and the water came downⁿ on the south side of the temple,ᵒ to the south side of the altar. ²Then he brought me out by the way of the north gate, and led me around outside to the eastern outer gate; and there water was flowing on the south side. *(Stream issuing from the temple)*

³As the man went forth eastward with the line in his hand, he measured a thousand cubits, and he caused me to pass through waters, ankle-deep. ⁴Again he measured a thousand cubits, and caused me to pass through waters, knee-deep. Again he measured a thousand cubits, and caused me to pass through waters, hip-deep. ⁵Afterward he measured a thousand cubits; and it was a river through which I could not pass, for the waters were deep enough to swim in, a river that could not be forded. *(Its increasing volume)*

⁶And he said to me, Seest thou, O man? Then he brought me back to the bank of the river. ⁷Now when I had returned, there on the bank of the river were very many trees on both sides. ⁸Then he said to me, These waters issue forth toward the eastern region, and shall descend to the Arabah; and they shall go to the Dead Sea into the salt waters;ᵖ which waters shall *(Its fertilizing effect)*

ʲ 45² This vs. evidently belongs here.
ᵏ 45⁵ So Gk. The Heb. makes no sense.
ˡ 45⁸ So Gk. Heb., *my princes.*
ᵐ 46¹⁶ So Gk. Heb., *it is his inheritance.*
ⁿ 47¹ So Gk., Syr., and Lat. In the Heb. a scribe has added from the first part of the vs., *from under.*
ᵒ 47¹ Ezek. probably has in mind one of the characteristic rivers of Palestine, which, like one branch of the Jordan, flows from its rocky source a full-fledged stream. Also in ancient times a spring issued from the temple mount, cf. *Letter of Aristeas,* and Is. 8⁶.
ᵖ 47⁸ Following a corrected text.

Ezekiel's Code

be made fresh. [9]Every living creature which swarmeth, in every place whither the river[q] cometh, shall live; and the fish shall be very many.[r] [10]Fishers shall stand by it from Engedi even to En-eglaim; it shall be a place for the spreading of nets; its[s] fish shall be like[t] the fish of the Great Sea, exceeding many. [11]But its marshes and pools shall not be made fresh; they shall be left for salt.[u] [12]And by the bank of the river on both sides shall grow every kind of tree which furnisheth food; their leaves shall not wither, neither shall their fruit fail; every month they shall bear fresh fruit, for their waters issue from the sanctuary, and their fruit shall be for food and their leaves for healing.

Distribution of land among the tribes

[13]Thus saith the Lord Jehovah, This is the border, whereby ye shall allot the land according to the twelve tribes of Israel.[v] [14]Ye shall share it equally, for I swore to give it to your fathers, and this land shall fall to you as your inheritance.

Its northern border

[15]And this is the border of the land on the north: From the Great Sea[w] by[x] Hethlon, to the entrance of[a] [16]Hamath, as far as Zedad, Berothah, and Sibraim,[b] which is between the border of Damascus and Hamath; and to Hazerenon,[c] which is on the border of Hauran; [17]thus the border shall run from the sea to Hazarenon[d], so that the territory of Damascus is on the north on the border of Hamath.[e] This is the northern border.

Eastern border

[18]On the east: Between Hauran, Damascus and Gilead and the land of Israel, shall be the Jordan; from the northern border to the eastern sea shall ye measure. This is the eastern border.

Southern border

[19]On the south: From Tamar as far as the waters of Meriboth-kadesh, to the brook of Egypt, and to the Great Sea. This is the southern border. [20]On the west: The Great Sea from the southern border to a point opposite the entrance of Hamath. This is the western border.

Principle of allotment

[21]Thus ye shall divide this land among yourselves according to the tribe of Israel. [22]Ye shall allot it as an inheritance for yourselves and the aliens residing among you, who have begotten children among you; and they shall be reckoned with you as the native-born among the Israelites; they shall be assigned a portion with you among the tribes of Israel. [23]And ye shall give the alien his portion in the land in which he dwells, saith the Lord Jehovah.

---

q 47⁹ So Gk. Heb., *rivers.*

r 47⁹ In the Heb. the first part of the vs. is repeated, through a scribal error in the latter part.

s 47¹⁰ Again following the superior reading of the Gk., Syr. and Lat.

t 47¹⁰ Following the Syr. in omitting the awkward and very late, *after their kinds.*

u 47¹¹ *I. e.,* that the natives may there gather salt.

v 47¹³ A scribe has added the clause, *Joseph two portions.* It interrupts the context. It was probably suggested by 48⁵· ⁶.

w 47¹⁵ *I. e.,* the Mediterranean.

x 47¹⁵ *In the direction of* is clearly a gloss in the Heb., for Hethlon is probably to be identified with the present Heitela near the shore of the Great Sea.

a 47¹⁵ Following the Gk. order.

b 47¹⁶ The reading and identification of these places are exceedingly doubtful.

c 47¹⁷ So ¹⁷ and 48¹, Nu. 34⁹. Heb., *Hatticon.*

d 47¹⁷ Reconstructing the corrupt Heb. with the aid of 48¹.

e 47¹⁷ The Heb. is obscure. Cornill would emend so as to read, *From Hazar-enon, which is on the border between the territories of Hauran and Damascus; the Jordan is the boundary between Gilead and the land of Israel.*

D

THE POST-EXILIC HIERARCHY

§ 156. Traditions Regarding the Origin of the Hierarchy, Nu. 3⁵⁻¹⁰ [17¹⁻¹¹, Ex. 28¹]

Priestly Codes

Nu. 3 ⁵Jehovah spoke thus to Moses, ⁶Bring the tribe of Levi near, and set them before Aaron the priest, that they may minister to him. ⁷They shall obey his orders and have charge of the whole congregation before the tent of meeting, to perform the service of the dwelling. ⁸They shall also care for all the furniture of the tent of meeting, and have charge of the Israelites, to perform the service of the dwelling. ⁹Thou shalt give the Levites to Aaron and to his sons; they shall be wholly given to him in behalf of the Israelites. ¹⁰Thou shalt also appoint Aaron and his sons to have charge of their priestly office; the layman who comes near shall be put to death. *(margin: Call and commission of the tribe of Levi)*

The Post-Exilic Hierarchy.—The fall of the Judean state in 586 B.C. and the long subjection to foreign masters which followed left the priests the one ruling class in Judaism. With the fall of the monarchy, civil as well as religious authority passed to the priests. The growing importance of the ritual also added to the prominence of the priesthood. The result was that from the days of Ezra and Nehemiah their numbers and duties and income rapidly increased. Their organization was also more highly developed. At the head of the hierarchy stood the high priest, with at times almost royal authority. Next in rank were his kinsmen and immediate associates the priests who were designated in the priestly codes as the *sons of Aaron*. Like the sons of Zadok in Ezek.'s hierarchy, note § 153, they were doubtless for the most part the descendants of the Levitical priests, who had served at the pre-exilic Jerusalem temple, cf. below. The distinction between them and the Levites, the descendants of the priests of the pre-exilic sanctuaries outside of Jerusalem, was sharply defined, and the Levites were allowed to perform only the menial duties in connection with the temple.

§ 156 The historical origin of the priesthood and of the later distinction between the priests and Levites has already been traced, cf. introd. under § 148. Later priestly tradition, however, following its natural tendencies, cf. Introd., p. 10, connected this origin directly with Moses. According to Nu. 3⁵⁻¹⁰, as Jehovah's herald, he proclaimed at Sinai the unique priestly prerogatives of the sons of Aaron and the dependent position of the Levites. Their choice is arbitrary and final, cf. also Ex. 28 and 29⁹. The tradition in Nu. 17¹⁻¹¹ also contains an account of a miraculous sign confirming the choice of Aaron, Vol. I, § 93.

No clear traces of this late priestly belief that Aaron was the ancestral father of the legitimate priesthood can be found in the pre-exilic literature. It is not certain that his name occurred at all in the original early Judean prophetic narratives. In the Ephraimite section, Ex. 32, when the idolatrous northern cults at Bethel and Samaria are indirectly condemned, Aaron directs the making of the golden calf. Elsewhere in the northern traditions, Joshua ministers at the tent of meeting, Ex. 33¹¹. The priests in charge of the pre-exilic Jerusalem temple were appointees of David and Solomon. Ezek. recognizes only the sons of Zadok and knows nothing of the sons of Aaron. The late title *son of Aaron* apparently included the Zadokites, and probably certain other priestly clans. Its origin is doubtful, but it seems to represent a compromise with the exclusive position set forth by Ezek. The Zadokites continued, however, to hold the chief offices, and later apparently again came into prominence as the party of the Sadducees.

I

THE LEVITES

§ 157. Legal Age of Service, Nu. 8[23-26]

Very Late Supplemental Priestly Codes

From twenty-five to fifty

Nu. 8 [23]Jehovah said to Moses, [24]This is that which concerneth the Levites: From twenty-five years old and upward they shall go in to fulfil their service in the work of the tent of meeting. [25]At the age of fifty years they shall cease to render service, and shall serve no more; [26]they may minister with their kinsmen in the tent of meeting, to fulfil that duty, but shall perform no service. Thus shalt thou deal with the Levites concerning their duties.

§ 158. Consecration, Nu. 8[5-22]

Supplemental Priestly Codes

Rite of cleansing

Nu. 8 [5]Jehovah spoke thus to Moses, [6]Take the Levites from among the Israelites, and cleanse them. [7]Thus shalt thou deal with them, in cleansing them; sprinkle them with the water of expiation,[a] and let them shave all their flesh with a razor, and let them wash their clothes, and cleanse themselves.

Public sacrifice in their behalf

[8]Then let them take a young bullock, with its cereal-offering, fine meal mixed with oil;[b] and another young bullock shalt thou take as a sin-offering. [9]Then thou shalt present the Levites before the tent of meeting; and thou shalt assemble the whole congregation of the Israelites; [10]and thou shalt present the Levites before Jehovah. And the Israelites shall lay their hands upon the Levites.[c] [12]The Levites also shall lay their hands upon the heads of the bullocks; then thou shalt offer the one as a sin-offering, and the other as a burnt-offering, to Jehovah, to make atonement for the Levites. [13]Thou shalt also set the Levites before Aaron, and before his sons, and offer them as a sacred offering[d] to Jehovah.

---

§ 157 Nu. 4[3] fixes the minimum age of service at thirty years; cf. § 34; 8[24] at twenty-five and the Chronicler at twenty, I Chr. 23[24, 27], II 31[17], Ezra 3[8]. Apparently these different sources represent the usage in the succeeding periods to which they each belong. The increased duties of the Levites may well explain why in the Gk. period they were pressed into service at an earlier age.

§ 158 The law prescribing a detailed ceremony for the consecration of the Levites evidently belongs to the latest stratum of the Pentateuch. It is really an expansion of the simple law of Nu. 3[5-10]. In the process of repeated expansion several repetitions have crept in, cf. *e. g.*, vss. [6, 15] and [11, 13, 15]. Vss. [15b-22] contain an expanded version of the preceding regulations. Aaron is also assigned the central place in the narrative instead of Moses. The aim of the law is to provide a formal consecration for the Levites, as well as for the priests, Lev. 8.

a Nu. 8[7] Heb., *water of sin, i. e.*, for the removal of sin.

b Nu. 8[8] The phrase, *as a burnt-offering*, is perhaps to be added, though found in none of the versions, cf. [12].

c Nu. 8[10] Vs. [11] reads, *Then Aaron shall offer* (Heb., *wave*) *the Levites before Jehovah as a sacred offering* (Heb., *wave-offering*) *in behalf of the Israelites, that it may be theirs to perform the service of Jehovah;* it is clearly an explanatory interpolation. Aaron, not Moses, as in [13], is commanded to present the Levites to Jehovah.

d Nu. 8[13] Heb., *wave them as a wave-offering*. The original significance of the words apparently is lost here. So vss. [15-21].

Supplementary Priestly Codes

¹⁴Thus shalt thou separate the Levites from among the Israelites, that the Levites may be mine. ¹⁵Afterwards shall the Levites go in to perform the service of the tent of meeting; thus shalt thou cleanse them and offer them as a sacred offering; ¹⁶for they are wholly given to me from among the Israelites; instead of all that openeth the womb, even the first-born of all the Israelites, have I taken them for myself. ¹⁷For all the first-born among the Israelites are mine, both of man and of beast; on the first day when I smote all the first-born in the land of Egypt I sanctified them for myself. ¹⁸And I have taken the Levites instead of all the first-born among the Israelites. ¹⁹And I have given the Levites as a gift to Aaron and to his sons from among the Israelites, to perform the service of the Israelites in the tent of meeting and thus make atonement for the Israelites; that there may be no plague among the Israelites, when the Israelites come near the sanctuary.

²⁰So Moses and all the congregation of the Israelites dealt thus with the Levites; according to all that Jehovah commanded Moses* concerning the Levites, thus the Israelites dealt with them. ²¹So the Levites cleansed themselves from sin, and they washed their clothes; and Aaron offered them as a sacred offering before Jehovah; and Aaron made atonement for them to cleanse them. ²²Afterward the Levites went to perform their service in the tent of meeting before Aaron, and before his sons; as Jehovah had commanded Moses concerning the Levites, so they dealt with them. ᶠ

Presented to Jehovah in place of the first-born of the people

Traditional precedent

§ 159. **Duties,** Nu. 3⁵⁻⁹, 18¹⁻⁶ [8¹⁵, ²⁴⁻²⁶], 1⁴⁷⁻⁵³, 3²⁵, ²⁶, ²⁹⁻³², ³⁵⁻³⁷, 4⁴, ⁵, ¹⁵, ²⁴⁻³³, I Chr. 23¹⁻⁵ [⁶⁻²⁶] ²⁷⁻³², 25¹⁻⁸

Priestly Codes

Nu. 3 ⁵Jehovah spoke thus to Moses, ⁶Bring the tribe of Levi near, and set them before Aaron the priest, that they may minister to him. ⁷They shall obey his orders, and have charge of the whole congregation before the tent of meeting, to perform the service of the dwelling. ⁸They shall also care for all the furniture of the tent of meeting, and have charge of the Israelites, to perform the service of the dwelling. ⁹Thou shalt give the Levites to Aaron and his sons; they shall be wholly given to him in behalf of the Israelites.

To take charge of the sanctuary

18 ¹And Jehovah said to Aaron, Thou and thy sons and thy fathers' house with thee shall bear the consequences of the iniquity committed in the sanctuary;ᵍ and thou and thy sons with thee shall bear the consequences of the iniquity committed in the exercise of your priestly office. ²And thy kinsmen also, the tribe of Levi, the tribe of thy father, bring near with thee, that they may be associated with thee, and minister to thee, while thou and thy sons with thee are before the tent of the testimony. ³And they shall

To assist the priests

ᵉ Nu. 8²⁰ Heb. adds, *and Aaron*, a later gloss.
ᶠ Nu. 8²¹, ²² These vss. are very late additions to the law.
§ 159 The late priestly laws limit the duties of the Levites to the care of the sanctuary and its furnishings. They are simply the servants of the priests and perform the menial services which fell to the temple slaves in the pre-exilic temple, cf. § 152. The Chronicler, however, states that certain Levitical families or guilds were organized as temple singers. In I Chr. 6¹⁸ three such Levitical guilds are mentioned, which bear the names, Heman, Asaph and Ethan, cf. II Chr. 20¹⁹ Ezra 2⁴¹ and its parallel Neh. 7⁴⁴ speaks only of the sons or guild of Asaph. The superscriptions of the Pss. also bear testimony to the existence of these guilds of singers. In connection with Herod's temple the Levitical singers play an important rôle. Their prominent development appears, however, to have followed the reformation under Ezra and Neh. cf. Vol. V, Introd. *in loco.*
ᵍ Nu. 18¹ Heb., *bear the iniquity of the sanctuary.* The expression is apparently a technical priestly idiom and must be expanded to be intelligible. Cf. *e. g.* 1⁵⁰.

Priestly Codes

obey thy orders, and have the care of all the tent; only they shall not come near to the vessels of the sanctuary and the altar, that they die not, neither they, nor ye. ⁴And they shall be associated with thee, and have charge of the tent of meeting, to perform all the service of the tent, for no layman shall come near you. ⁵But ye shall have charge of the sanctuary and the altar, that wrath may never again come upon the Israelites there. ⁶And I, behold, I have taken your kinsmen the Levites from among the Israelites; they are a gift to you, given to Jehovah, to perform the service of the tent of meeting.

Supplemental Priestly Codes

To act as porters and guards

Nu. 1 ⁴⁷The Levites according to the tribe of their fathers were not numbered among the Israelites; ⁴⁸for Jehovah said to Moses, ⁴⁹Only the tribe of Levi shalt thou not number, neither shalt thou take a census of them among the Israelites, ⁵⁰but appoint the Levites over the dwelling of the testimony, and over all its furniture, and over all that belongeth to it; they shall carry the dwelling, and all its furniture; and they shall minister to it, and shall encamp round about the dwelling. ⁵¹And when the dwelling setteth forward, the Levites shall take it down, and when the dwelling halteth the Levites shall set it up; the layman who cometh near shall be put to death. ⁵²The Israelites shall encamp according to their hosts, each man by his own camp, and each man by his own standard. ⁵³But the Levites shall encamp about the dwelling of the testimony, that no wrath come upon the congregation of the Israelites; thus the Levites shall take charge of the dwelling of the testimony.

Special duties of the sons of Gershon

3 ²⁵And the charge of the sons of Gershon in the tent of meeting shall be the dwelling, the tent, its covering, the screen for the door of the tent of meeting, ²⁶the hangings of the court, and the screen for the door of the court which is by the dwelling, and by the altar round about, and the cords for all its service.

Of Kohath

²⁹The families of the sons of Kohath shall encamp on the side of the dwelling on the south. ³⁰And the prince of the fathers' house of the families of the Kohathites shall be Elizaphan the son of Uzziel. ³¹And their charge shall be the ark, the table, the candlestick, the altars, the vessels of the sanctuary with which they minister, the screen, and all its service. ³²And Eleazar the son of Aaron the priest shall be the prince of the princes of the Levites, having the oversight of those who have charge of the sanctuary.

Of Merari

³⁵And the prince of the fathers' house of the families of Merari was Zuriel the son of Abihail : they shall encamp on the north side of the dwelling. ³⁶And the appointed charge of the sons of Merari shall be the boards of the dwelling, and its bars, its pillars, its sockets, and all its instruments, and all its service, ³⁷and the pillars of the court round about, with their sockets, their pins, and their cords.

4 ⁴This is the service of the sons of Kohath in the tent of meeting, the care of the most holy things : ⁵when the camp sets forth, Aaron shall go in,

Supplemental Priestly Code

and his sons, and they shall take down the veil of the screen, and cover the Of the
sons of
Kohath
ark of the testimony with it.   ¹⁵And when Aaron and his sons have finished
covering the sanctuary, and all the furniture of the sanctuary, as the camp on the
march
is about to set forth, after that the sons of Kohath shall come to carry them,
without, however, touching the holy things lest they die.   To carry these things
is the duty of the sons of Kohath in connection with the tent of meeting.

²⁴This is the service of the families of the Gershonites in connection with Of the
Ger-
shon-
ites
serving and carrying: ²⁵they shall carry the curtains of the dwelling, and
the tent of meeting, its protecting covering, and the covering of Egyptian
leather which is over it, and the screen of the door of the tent of meeting,
²⁶and the hangings of the court, and the screen for the door of the gate of the
court, which surrounds the dwelling and the altar, and their cords, and all
the accessories of their service; whatever is to be done in connection with
them the Gershonites shall perform.   ²⁷At the bidding of Aaron and his
sons the Gershonites shall perform all their service in connection with all
that they have to carry, and all that is in their care.   Ye shall assign to them
by name all the things committed to them to carry.^h   ²⁸This is the service of
the families of the Gershonites in the tent of meeting; the performance of
their duties shall be under the supervision of Ithamar the son of Aaron the
priest.

²⁹As for the sons of Merari, thou shalt number them by their families, by Of the
sons of
Merari
their fathers' houses; ³⁰from thirty years old and upward even to fifty years
old thou shalt number them, every one who entereth upon the service,ⁱ to
do the work of the tent of meeting.   ³¹This is their responsibility in connection with carrying and all their service in the tent of meeting: the boards of
the dwelling, and its bars, and its pillars, and its sockets, ³²and the pillars of
the court round about, and their sockets, and their pins, and their cords,
with all their accessories, and with all the work which they require.^j   ³³This
is the service of the families of the sons of Merari in connection with all their
serving in the tent of meeting, under the supervision of Ithamar the son of
Aaron the priest.

Chronicler's Ecclesiastical History

I Chr. 23 ¹Now David was old and advanced in years when he made Varied
duties
of the
Levites
accord-
ing to
the
Chron-
icler
Solomon his son king over Israel.   ²And he gathered together all the princes
of Israel, with the priests and the Levites.   ³And the Levites thirty years
old and upward were numbered; and their number by their census, man by
man, was thirty-eight thousand.   ⁴Of these, twenty-four thousand were to
oversee the work of the temple of Jehovah; and six thousand were officers
and judges; ⁵and four thousand were door-keepers; and four thousand praised
Jehovah with the instruments which he^k made for giving praise.   ²⁷For in

---

^h Nu. 4²⁷ This last clause is perhaps a scribal addition.
ⁱ Nu. 4³⁰ Lit., *warfare.*
^j Nu. 4³² *Ye shall appoint to them* (cf. Gk. and ²⁷) *by name all* (so Gk. and Sam.) *the things
committed to their charge to carry,* is clearly a later gloss.
^k I Chr. 23⁵ So Gk.   Heb., *I made.*

Chronicler's Ecclesiastical History

accordance with the last words of David the sons of Levi twenty years old and upward were numbered. ²⁸For their official duty was to wait on the sons of Aaron in connection with the service of the temple of Jehovah, in the courts, and in the chambers, and in the purifying of all the holy things, even the work of the service of the house of God ²⁹in connection with the show-bread[1] and the fine meal for a cereal-offering, whether of unleavened wafers or of that which is baked in the pan or of that which is soaked, and in connection with all measurements of capacity or length;[m] ³⁰and to stand every morning to give thanks and praise to Jehovah, and likewise also in the evening; ³¹and to offer regularly all burnt-offerings to Jehovah, on the sabbaths, on the new moons, and on the appointed feasts, in their order according to the regulation concerning them. ³²They also had charge of the tent of meeting and of the holy place, and of the sons of Aaron their kinsmen in connection with the service of the house of Jehovah.

As temple singers 25 ¹Moreover David and the commanders of the army set aside for the service certain of the sons of Asaph and Heman and Jeduthun, who prophesied with harps, with lyres, and with cymbals. And the number of those who did the work according to their service was ²of the sons of Asaph: Zaccur, and Joseph, and Nethaniah, and Asharelah,[n] the sons of Asaph, under the charge[o] of Asaph, who prophesied at the direction of the king. ³Of Jeduthun;[p] the sons of Jeduthun: Gedaliah, Jizri,[q] Jeshaiah, Hashabiah, and Mattithiah, six,[r] under the direction of their father Jeduthun with the harp, who prophesied by giving thanks and praising Jehovah. ⁴Of Heman; the sons of Heman: Bukkiah, Mattaniah, Uzziel, Shebuel, and Jerimoth, Hananiah, Hanani, Eliathah, Giddalti, and Romamti-ezer, Joshbekashah, Mallothi, Hothir, Mahazioth.[s] ⁵All these were the sons of Heman the king's seer in accord with God's promise to exalt his horn.[t] And God gave to Heman fourteen sons and three daughters. ⁶All these were under the direction of their father for song in the temple of Jehovah, with cymbals, lyres, and harps in connection with the service of the house of God, Asaph, Jeduthun, and Heman being under the direction of the king. ⁷And their number, together with their kinsmen who were instructed in singing praise to Jehovah, even all who were skilful, was two hundred and eighty-eight. ⁸And they all cast lots for their offices, both the small and the great, the teacher and the one taught.

---

[1] I Chr. 23²⁸ *I. e.*, the baking of the bread.
[m] I Chr. 23²⁸ *I. e.*, to measure all gifts and offerings brought to the temple.
[n] I Chr. 25² In vs. ¹⁴ *Jesarel*, Luc., *Aseivela*.
[o] I Chr. 25² Heb., *under the hands of.*
[p] I Chr. 25³ Elsewhere, *Ethan.*
[q] I Chr. 25³ So ¹¹; Heb., *Zeri.*
[r] I Chr. 25³ But five are mentioned, unless the father be included.
[s] I Chr. 25⁴ A slight change in the vocalization of these proper names gives the fragment of a psalm which was probably in the Chr.'s mind:
Be gracious to me, O Jehovah, be gracious! Thou art my God!
Thou hast given great and signal aid to those in affliction;
Thou hast given many and full visions.
[t] I Chr. 25⁵ *I. e.*, to bless with many offspring.

§ 160. Property and Means of Support, Nu. 18²¹· ²³· ²⁴, 31²⁸· ³⁰· ⁴⁷, 35¹⁻⁸, Lev. 25²⁹⁻³⁴

Priestly Codes

Nu. 18 ²¹To the sons of Levi, behold, I give every tithe in Israel as an The inheritance, in return for their service which they perform, even the service tithes of the tent of meeting. ²³The Levites shall perform the service of the tent of meeting, and they shall bear the consequences of their iniquity; this shall be a statute forever throughout your generations:ᵘ among the Israelites they shall have no inheritance. ²⁴For the tithe of the Israelites, which they offer as a portion reserved for Jehovah, I have given to the Levites as an inheritance; therefore I have said concerning them, Among the Israelites they shall have no inheritance.

Supplemental Priestly Codes

Nu. 31 ²⁸Levy a contribution for Jehovah upon the warriors who went Share out to battle; one in five hundred, of the persons, and of the oxen, and of the of the asses, and of the flocks. ²⁹Take it from their half, and give it to Eleazar of war the priest, as a special contribution to Jehovah. ³⁰And from the Israelites' half, thou shalt take one drawn out of every fifty, of the persons, of the oxen, of the asses, and of the flocks, even of all the cattle, and give them to the Levites, who have the charge of the dwelling of Jehovah. ⁴⁷Of the Israelites' half, Moses took one drawn out of every fifty, both of man and of beast, and gave them to the Levites, who had charge of the dwelling of Jehovah, as Jehovah commanded Moses.

35 ¹Jehovah spoke thus to Moses in the plains of Moab by the Jordan Forty-at Jericho, ²Command the Israelites that they give to the Levites out of eight their hereditary possession cities to dwell in; and pasture land for the cities with round about them shall ye give to the Levites. ³The cities shall they have sub-to dwell in; and their pasture land shall be used for their cattle,ᵛ and for their urbs herds, and for all their beasts. ⁴The pasture land of the cities, which ye shall give to the Levites, shall extend outside the wall of the city a thousand cubits in every direction. ⁵Ye shall measure without the city on the east side two thousand cubits, and on the south side two thousand cubits, and on the west side two thousand cubits, and on the north side two thousand cubits, the city being in the midst.ʷ This shall serve them as pasture land belonging

---

§ 160 Cf. for the income of the pre-exilic Levitical priests, §§ 150, 157. The priestly law of Nu. 18²³ reiterates the older regulation of Dt. 18¹, *the Levites shall have no inheritance.* The priestly law, however, provides that they shall no longer be dependent upon the generosity of the individual offerers, but shall receive as their own nine-tenths of the annual tithes, the remaining tenth to be paid by them to the priests. This regulation establishes as a law the principle underlying Nehemiah's reform measures, Neh. 13¹⁰⁻¹³. The supplemental priestly codes added to the income of the Levites a portion of the spoils of war and reversed the earlier law to the effect that they should have no inheritance, and in a tradition connected with Moses, assigned to them certain cities, with the surrounding pasture lands. There is no evidence, however, that this provision was ever carried out. Like the regulation regarding the year of jubilee, it remained only a priestly ideal. Until the Levites became exceedingly numerous the tithe must have bountifully met their needs.

ᵘ Nu. 18²³ This is possibly all a gloss with the exception of the last clause.
ᵛ Nu. 35³ Lit., *property.*
ʷ Nu. 35⁵ Vss. ⁴· ⁵ cannot be harmonized as they stand, for the area is a circle in ⁴ and a square in ⁵. Either ⁵ is a gloss, or the author had not carefully considered his plan.

Supplemental Priestly Codes

to the cities. ⁶As for the cities which ye shall give to the Levites, ye shall set apart the six cities of refuge, whither the manslayer may flee;ˣ and besides these ye shall set apart forty-two cities. ⁷The whole number of the cities which ye shall give to the Levites shall be forty-eight cities; them shall ye give together with their suburbs. ⁸And concerning the cities which ye shall set apart from the possession of the Israelites, from the great tribe ye shall take many, and from the small tribe ye shall take few; each tribe according to its inheritance which it is to receive shall set apart some of its cities for the Levites.

Perpetual right in their hereditary possessions

Lev. 25 ²⁹If a man sell a dwelling-house in a walled city, he shall have the right of redeeming it for a whole year after it has been sold; for a year shall he retain the right of redemption. ³⁰Then if it is not redeemed within a year, the house that is in the walled city shall be assured in perpetuity to him who bought it, to him and his descendants; it shall not be released in the year of jubilee. ³¹But the houses of the villages which have no walls around them shall be reckoned as belonging to the fields of the country; the right of redemption shall be retained for them, and they shall be released in the year of jubilee. ³²But in the case of the houses in the cities of the Levites, the cities which belong to the Levites, the Levites shall have the perpetual right of redemption. ³³If, however, one of the Levites do notʸ redeem it, then the house that was soldᶻ the city that belongeth to him, shall be released at the year of jubilee; for the houses in the cities of the Levites are their possession among the Israelites. ³⁴But the pasture land belonging to their cities may not be sold, for it is their perpetual possession.

III

THE PRIESTS

§ 161. Qualifications, Lev. 21¹⁶⁻²⁴

Holiness Code

Freedom from every physical defect

Lev. 21 ¹⁶Jehovah gave this command to Moses, ¹⁷Say to Aaron, 'No one of thy descendants throughout their generations who hath a blemish, shall approach to offer the food of his God. ¹⁸For no one who hath a blemish may approach; no one who is blind, or lame, or he who is mutilated in the face,ᵃ

ˣ Nu. 35⁶ Slightly correcting the Heb., which is very awkward.
ʸ Lev. 25³³ The Heb. omits the negative.
ᶻ Lev. 25³³ Slightly correcting the text. The Heb. has, *and*, for, *in*.
§ 161 The term, *son of Aaron*, as the regular designation of a priest, does not appear to have been found either in Ezek. or the Holiness Code, cf. note § 156. In the later process of priestly redaction, *Aaron* and the *sons of Aaron* have been introduced at many points into the older Holiness Code. In most cases, however, the hand of the editor is readily detected. The belief that a priest should be physically perfect is very ancient, and is in harmony with the characteristic teachings of the Holiness Code. Corresponding perfection and ceremonial purity were demanded in the case of both the offering and the individual offerer. It was in this graphic way that the prophetic ideal of moral perfection was impressed upon the popular mind by the later priestly teachers.
ᵃ Lev. 21¹⁸ Gk. and Syr., *who hath a flat nose.*

Holiness Code

or who hath a limb too long, ¹⁹or a broken leg, or a broken arm, ²⁰or who is humpbacked or withered, or hath defective eyesight,ᵇ or scurvy, or is scabbed, or whose testicles are destroyed; ²¹no one of the descendants of Aaron the priest, may thus come near to offer the offerings made by fire to Jehovah; he hath a blemish; he shall not come near to offer the food of his God. ²²He may eat the food of his God, both of the most holy and of the holy; ²³only he shall not go in to the veil, nor come near to the altar, because he hath a blemish; lest he profane my sanctuaries; for I am Jehovah who sanctifieth them.' ²⁴Thus Moses spoke to Aaron, and to his sons, and to all the Israelites.

§ 162. **Consecration**, Ex. 29¹⁻⁴, ⁸⁻²⁵, ³⁵, ³⁶ᵃ [Lev. 8¹⁻⁶, ¹³⁻³⁶, Ex. 30²², 40¹², ¹⁴⁻¹⁶]

Priestly Codes

Ex. 29 ¹And this shall be thy method of procedure in consecrating Aaron and his sons to minister to me as priests : take one young bullock and two rams without blemish, ²and unleavened bread, and unleavened cakes mixed with oil, and unleavened wafers smeared with oil : of fine wheaten flour shalt thou make them; ³and thou shalt put them in a basket, and bring in the basket, with the bullock and the two rams. *Preparations*

⁴Then thou shalt bring Aaron and his sons to the entrance of the tent of meeting, and wash them with water. *Washing*

⁸And thou shalt bring his sons and clothe them with tunics, ⁹and shalt gird them with sashes,ᶜ and fasten turbans on them; and they shall have the priesthood by a statute forever. Thus thou shalt installᵈ Aaron and his sons. *Attiring in garb of office*

¹⁰Then thou shalt bring the bullock before the tent of meeting; and Aaron and his sons shall lay their hands upon the head of the bullock, ¹¹and thou shalt kill the bullock before Jehovah at the entrance of the tent of meeting. ¹²Thou shalt take some of the blood of the bullock, and put it on the horns of the altar with thy finger, and pour out all the rest of the blood at the base of the altar. ¹³And thou shalt take all the fat that covereth the entrails, and the fatty mass next to the liver, and the two kidneys, and the fat that is on them, and burn them upon the altar. ¹⁴But the flesh of the bullock, and its hide, and the contents of its entrails, thou shalt burn with fire outside the camp; it is a sin-offering. ¹⁵Thou shalt also take one of the rams; Aaron and his sons shall lay their hands on the head of the ram, ¹⁶and thou shalt slay the ram, and take some of its blood, and dash it round about against the altar. ¹⁷Then thou shalt cut the ram in pieces, and wash its entrails, and its legs, and put them with the rest of its pieces, and with its head, ¹⁸and thou shalt burn the whole ram upon the altar; it is a burnt-offering to Jehovah; it is a pleasant odor, an offering made by fire to Jehovah. *Sacrificial offerings*

ᵇ Lev. 21²⁰ Or, *white specks in the eye*, as Syr., or, *a running in the eye*, as Targ.

§ 162 These elaborate laws belong to the latest stratum of the Pentateuch and represent the extreme development in the O.T. of that ceremonialism which ultimately overshot its true mark—the moral purity of the state and individual. In slightly different terms the parallels in Lev. 8¹⁻⁶, ¹³⁻³⁶, Ex. 30²², 40¹², ¹⁴⁻¹⁶ reflect the detailed directions of Ex. 29.

ᶜ Ex. 29⁹ A scribe has added the awkward gloss, *Aaron and his sons*.

ᵈ Ex. 29⁹ Lit., *fill the hands of*.

Priestly Codes

Rite of initiation

¹⁹Then thou shalt take the other ram; and Aaron and his sons shall lay their hands on the head of the ram, ²⁰and thou shalt kill the ram and take some of its blood, and put it on the tip of the right ear of Aaron, and on the tip of the right ear of each of his sons, and upon the thumb of the right hand of each, and upon the great toe of the right foot, and dash the rest of the blood against the altar round about. ²¹Thou shalt take some of the blood that is on the altar, and some of the anointing oil, and sprinkle it upon Aaron, and upon his garments, and upon his sons, and upon the garments of his sons as well; thus he shall be consecrated, and his garments, and his sons, and his sons' garments as well.ᵉ ²²Thou shalt take also of the fat of the ram, and the fat tail, and the fat that covereth the entrails, and the fatty mass next to the liver, and the two kidneys, and the fat that is on them, and the right thigh—for it is a ram of consecration—²³and one loaf of bread, and one cake of oiled bread, and one wafer, out of the basket of unleavened bread that is before Jehovah; ²⁴thou shalt put them all on the hands of Aaron, and on the hands of his sons; and thou shalt wave themᶠ as a wave-offering before Jehovah. ²⁵Then thou shalt take them from their hands, and burn them on the altar upon the burnt-offering, as a pleasant odor before Jehovah; it is an offering made by fire to Jehovah.

Seven days' ceremony

³⁵So shalt thou deal with Aaron and his sons exactly as I have commanded thee; seven days shalt thou take in installing them. ³⁶ᵃEach day shalt thou offer the bullock of sin-offering for atonement.ᵍ

§ 163. Clothing, Ex. 28⁴⁰⁻⁴³ [29⁸, ⁹, Lev. 8¹³]

Priestly Codes

Costume while officiating

Ex. 28 ⁴⁰For Aaron's sons thou shalt make tunics, and thou shalt make for them sashes, and turbans shalt thou make for them, as splendid ornaments. ⁴¹Thou shalt put them on Aaron thy brother, and on his sons with him; and shalt anoint them, and install them, and consecrate them, that they may minister to me as priests. ⁴²Thou shalt make them linen drawers to cover their bare flesh; from the loins to the thighs they shall reach; ⁴³and his sons shall wear them when they go in to the tent of meeting, or when they come near the altar to minister in the holy place, lest they incur guilt, and so die; it shall be a statute forever for him and his descendants after him.ʰ

ᵉ Ex. 29²¹ This vs. is perhaps a later addition. In the Gk. it precedes the last clause of ²⁰.
ᶠ Ex. 29²⁴ *I. e.*, swing them towards and from the altar, to symbolize their presentation to Jehovah, and his return of them to the giver. The expression is often used in a more general sense, where the original ceremony has disappeared, but not its significance.
ᵍ Ex. 29³⁶ᵃ Possibly this vs. is later than the preceding law.
§ 163 Vs. ⁴¹ anticipates the directions in 29⁸ and interrupts the directions regarding the clothing in ⁴⁰, ⁴², ⁴³. The anointing of the priests also appears to be an addition peculiar to the supplemental codes. In the groundwork of the priestly codes the high priest alone is anointed, cf. § 168.
ʰ Ex. 28⁴², ⁴³ Prob. later than ⁴⁰

§ 164. **Ceremonial Cleanliness,** Lev. 21¹⁻⁹, 22¹⁻⁹, 10⁸, ⁹, ⁶, ⁷, Ex. 30¹⁷⁻²¹

Holiness Code

Lev. 21 ¹Jehovah gave this command to Moses, Speak to the priests, the sons of Aaron and say to them, 'No priest shall defile himself for any one who is dead among his people,ⁱ ²except for his nearest kin, for his mother and his father and his son and his daughter and his brother; ³for his sister a virgin, who is near to him and hath had no husband, he may defile himself. ⁴But he shall not defile himself for a sister betrothed to a husband,ʲ so as to profane himself. | *No contact with dead except nearest of kin*

⁵They shall not make bald spots on their heads, nor shave off the corners of their beards, nor make any cuttings in their flesh. ⁶They shall be holy to their God, and not profane the name of their God; for the offerings made by fire to Jehovah, the food of their God, they do offer; therefore they must be holy. | *No bodily mutilation*

⁷A priest shall not marry a woman who is a harlot or dishonored, nor shall heᵏ marry a woman who has been divorced from her husband, for a priest is consecrated to his God. ⁸Thou shalt regard him as sacred, therefore, for he offereth the food of thy God; thou shalt regard him as holy; for I, Jehovah, who sanctify them,ˡ am holy. ⁹If the daughter of a priest profane herself by playing the harlot, she profaneth her father; she shall be burnt with fire.' | *No social immorality*

22 ¹Jehovah gave this command to Moses, ²Speak to Aaron and his sons, that they keep themselves separate from the holy things of the Israelites, which they consecrate to me, and that they profane not my holy name: I am Jehovah. ³Say to them, 'Any one among all your descendants throughout your generations, who approacheth the holy things, which the Israelites consecrate to Jehovah, while he is unclean, that person shall be cut off from before me: I am Jehovah. ⁴No one of the descendants of Aaron who is a leper, or hath a discharge may eat of the holy things, until he become clean. | *Nor to defile holy things*

Anyone, moreover, who toucheth a thingᵐ that hath been made unclean by a dead body, or a man who hath an emission of semen, ⁵or anyone who toucheth any swarming creature which may occasion uncleanness, or a man from whom any sort of uncleanness may be contracted; ⁶the person who toucheth any such shall be unclean until evening and shall not eat of the holy things until he bathe his body in water. ⁷When the sun is set he shall become clean; and afterward he may eat of the holy things, because they | *Cleansing for ceremonial defilement*

---

§ 164 The ceremonial cleanliness of the priests was rigorously insisted upon by most ancient religions. The Egyptian priests wore linen and were required to bathe twice each day. The Persian priests observed strict rules of ceremonial cleanliness, and even wore a cloth over their mouth while sacrificing, lest their breath might contaminate the sacrificial offering. Thus by the example of the powerful nations with which they came into contact, as well as by the dominant forces at work in their midst, post-exilic Judaism was led to place the emphasis more and more on external forms. The passages from the Holiness Code, as usual, bring the ethical *motifs* to the front.

ⁱ Lev. 21¹ *I. e.*, by participating in the funeral rites.
ʲ Lev. 21⁴ Heb., *being a chief man* (or *husband*) *among his people.* The text is evidently corrupt and the versions differ. The reading adopted, though by no means certain, seems the most probable restoration.
ᵏ Lev. 21⁷ The Heb. has a pl. verb in this and the following clause.
ˡ Lev. 21⁸ So Gk. and Syr. Heb., *you.*
ᵐ Lev. 22⁴ Or, *a person.*

195

Holiness Code

are his food. [8]That which dieth a natural death, or is torn by beasts, he may not eat so as to be made unclean by it : I am Jehovah. [9]So shall they observe my injunction. If they incur sin on account of some holy thing, and die in consequence of profaning it : I am Jehovah who sanctifieth them.'

Priestly Codes

To take no intoxicants

Lev. 10 [8]Jehovah gave this command to Aaron, [9]Drink no wine or strong drink, either thou or thy sons, when ye go into the tent of meeting, lest ye die; this shall be a statute forever throughout your generations.

Supplemental Priestly Codes

To refrain from mourning

Lev. 10 [6]Moses said to Aaron, and to Eleazar and to Ithamar, his sons, Do not unbind your heads[n] or rend your clothes, lest ye die, and he be angry with all the congregation; but your fellow countrymen, the whole house of Israel, may bewail the burning which Jehovah hath kindled.[o] [7]Ye shall not go out from the entrance of the tent of meeting, lest ye die, for the anointing oil of Jehovah is on you. Then they did according to the command of Moses.

To wash before officiating

Ex. 30 [17]Jehovah also gave this command to Moses, [18]Thou shalt make a laver of brass, with its base of brass, to be used for washing. Thou shalt put it between the tent of meeting and the altar, and thou shalt put water in it, [19]so that Aaron and his sons may wash their hands and their feet in it; [20]whenever they enter the tent of meeting, they shall wash with water, that they die not; or whenever they come near the altar to minister, to burn an offering made by fire to Jehovah. [21]So they shall wash their hands and their feet, that they die not. This shall be a statute forever for them, even for him and his descendants throughout their generations.

§ 165. Authority over Levites, Nu. 3[5, 6, 9], 18[1, 2a], 4[27]

Priestly Codes

Levites their servants

Nu. 3 [5]Jehovah spoke thus to Moses, [6]Bring the tribe of Levi near, and set them before Aaron the priest, that they may minister to him. [9]And the Israelites shall give the Levites to Aaron and to his sons; they shall be wholly given to him in behalf of the Israelites.

Nu. 18 [1]Jehovah said to Aaron, Thou and thy sons and thy fathers' house with thee shall bear the guilt of the sanctuary;[p] and thou and thy sons with thee shall bear the guilt of your priesthood. [2a]Thy kinsmen also, the tribe of Levi, the tribe of thy father, bring thou near with thee, that they may join themselves to thee and minister to thee.

---

[n] Lev. 10[6] *I. e.*, by removing the turbans.
[o] Lev. 10[6] The reference is to the punishment of Aaron's sons, Nadab and Abihu, by fire from heaven because they had offered strange fire, [1-5].
[p] Nu. 18[1] *Guilt of the sanctuary, i. e.*, the consequences of guilt incurred in connection with the sanctuary; cf. similarly, *guilt of your priesthood.*

Supplemental Priestly Codes

4 ²⁷At the bidding of Aaron and his sons the Gershonites shall perform all their service in connection with all that they have to carry, and all that is in their care; ye shall assign to them by name^q all the things committed to their charge to carry.

§ 166. **Duties,** Lev. 10⁸ᵃ, ¹⁰, ¹¹, Nu. 18⁵, ⁷ᵃ, Lev. 2¹, ² [⁹, ¹⁴⁻¹⁶], 6⁶ᵇ⁻⁷ [¹³, ¹⁴], Nu. 4¹¹ ¹⁵ᵃ, ¹⁶

Priestly Codes

Lev. 10 ⁸ᵃJehovah said to Aaron, ¹⁰Thou and thy sons shall distinguish between the holy and the common, and between the unclean and the clean;^r ¹¹and ye shall teach the Israelites all the statutes which Jehovah hath revealed to them through Moses. To instruct the people

Nu. 18 ⁵And ye shall have charge of the sanctuary^s and the altar that wrath may never again come upon the Israelites. ⁷ᵃBut thou and thy sons with thee shall limit the duties of your priestly office to everything about the altar and to that which is within the veil. To officiate at the altar

Lev. 2 ¹When anyone offereth a cereal-offering as a gift to Jehovah, his gift shall be of fine meal; and he shall pour oil on it, and put frankincense on it. ²Then he shall bring it to Aaron's sons the priests; and the priest shall take from it a handful of the fine meal and oil, with all the frankincense. Then as a memorial of the offering, the priest shall burn them on the altar, an offering made by fire, of an odor pleasing to Jehovah. To present Jehovah's part of cereal-offering

Supplemental Priestly Codes

Lev. 6 ⁶ᵇIf a man bring a guilt-offering to Jehovah, ⁷the priest shall make atonement for him before Jehovah; and he shall be forgiven for anything which he may have done to incur guilt.^t Also guilt-offerings

Nu. 4 ¹¹Also over the golden altar the sons of Kohath shall spread a violet cloth, and cover it with a covering of Egyptian leather, and shall put in its staves.^u ¹²Then they shall take all the utensils of ministry which they use in ministering in the sanctuary, and put them in a violet cloth, and cover them with a covering of Egyptian leather, and put them on the frame. ¹³They shall also take away the ashes from the altar, and spread a purple cloth over it; ¹⁴and they shall put on it all the utensils of the altar which they use in ministering about it, the fire-pans, the fleshhooks, and the shovels, and the To take charge of the altar and its utensils

---

q Nu. 4²⁷ So Gk. and cf. ³⁰. Heb. omits, *by name.*
§ 166 For the duties of the pre-exilic priests, cf. § 149, and of Ezek.'s priesthood, § 153. Their earlier functions as guardians of the oracle and as judges in civil as well as ceremonial cases have disappeared in the priestly codes, and instead their activity is limited to the care of the sanctuary and its sacrificial ritual, to the instruction of the people concerning their ceremonial duties, and to distinguishing between real and apparent cases of leprosy, cf. § 179.
r Lev. 10¹⁰ In its present form in the Heb. this law is only a broken fragment, loosely connected with its context. It probably was originally a priestly direction.
s Nu. 18⁵ Possibly the reference is to the oracle or holy of holies as elsewhere, but here it seems to include the sanctuary as a whole. Cf. for the context Vol. I, § 93.
t Lev. 6⁷ Lev. 14 also provides that the priests officiate in the sacrificial ceremony for the cleansing of lepers, cf. § 179.
u Nu. 4¹¹ Vss. ¹¹, ¹², ¹⁶ are possibly later than the rest.

Supplemental Priestly Codes

basins, all the utensils of the altar; then they shall spread over it a covering of Egyptian leather, and put in its staves. ¹⁵ᵃWhen Aaron and his sons have finished covering the holy things,ᵛ and all the holy utensils,ʷ as the camp is about to set forth, after that the sons of Kohath shall come to carry them, without, however, touching the holy things lest they die. ¹⁶Eleazar the son of Aaron the priest shall have charge of the oil for the light, and the fragrant incense, and the dailyˣ cereal-offering, and the anointing oil; he shall have oversight over all the dwelling, and all that is in it, the holy thingsʸ and the utensils which go with them.ᶻ

Summary of ceremonial duties

§ 167. **Means of Support,** Lev. 23¹⁵⁻²⁰, Nu. 18²⁰, Lev. 7¹¹⁻¹⁴, ²⁸⁻³⁶ [37], 10¹⁴, ¹⁵, Ex. 29²⁷, ²⁸, Nu. 18⁹, ¹⁰ [Lev. 6²⁴⁻²⁶, 7¹⁻⁷, 5¹¹⁻¹³], 6¹⁴⁻¹⁸, 10¹², ¹³ [2¹⁻³], 7⁹, ¹⁰, Nu. 6¹⁹, ²⁰, 18²⁵⁻³², 5⁹, ¹⁰, 18¹¹, ¹⁴, ¹⁹, 15²⁰, ²¹ [Lev. 27¹⁻²⁹], Nu. 18¹², ¹³, ¹⁵⁻¹⁸ [34⁶⁻⁵¹], Lev. 24⁵⁻⁹ᵃ, Nu. 5⁵⁻⁸, Lev. 7⁸, Nu. 31²⁵⁻²⁹

Holiness Code

Offerings at the feast of weeks

Lev. 23 ¹⁵Ye shall count from the day following the sabbath, from the day that ye bring the sheaf of the wave-offering seven full weeks; ¹⁶until the day following the seventh sabbath shall ye count fifty days; then ye shall present a new cereal-offering to Jehovah. ¹⁷Ye shall bring out of your dwellings two wave-loaves of two-tenths of an ephah; they shall be of fine meal, and they shall be baked with leaven, as firstfruits for Jehovah. ¹⁸Ye shall present with the bread seven yearling lambs without blemish, and one young bullock, and two rams; they shall be a burnt-offering to Jehovah, with the accompanying cereal-offering and libations, an offering made by fire, of an odor pleasing to Jehovah. ¹⁹Ye shall also offer one male goat as a sin-offering, andᵃ two male lambs a year old as a sacrifice of peace-offerings. ²⁰Then the priest shall wave them with the bread of the firstfruits as a wave-offering before Jehovah, with the two lambs;ᵇ they shall be a holy gift for Jehovah and shall belong to the priest.

ᵛ Nu. 4¹⁵ᵃ Or, *sanctuary.*
ʷ Nu. 4¹⁵ᵃ Or, *utensils of the sanctuary.*
ˣ Nu. 4¹⁶ Heb., continual, cf. Lev. 6¹³⁻¹⁵.
ʸ Nu. 4¹⁶ Or, *sanctuary and its utensils.*
ᶻ Nu. 4¹⁶ This vs. was probably the latest addition to the chapter.
§ 167 The priestly codes provide a definite and greatly increased income for the priests. Instead of being subjects of individual charity, as under the Deuteronomic codes, the priests were now able to demand certain specific dues. Definite portions of every sacrifice that was offered went to them. The tithe of the tithe also added to their income. As already enacted by Ezek., all the special contributions and objects consecrated to Jehovah, § 153, fell to them. In addition the priestly laws provide that the money paid for the redemption of every first-born in a family, the best portions of the olive oil and wine and the first ripe fruits as well as the first of the dough of every baking, should go to the priests. In this way they shared in the fruits of practically every form of labor in which the later Jews engaged. The supplemental laws further roll up their income by enacting that the hides of the animals sacrificed as burnt-offerings and a portion of all the spoils of war should belong to the priests.
ᵃ Lev. 23¹⁸, ¹⁹ᵃ The original animal sacrifice appears to have consisted simply of two lambs, ¹⁹. This section was probably added by a scribe who had in mind Nu. 28²⁷⁻³⁰, but who confused the numbers of rams and bullocks.
ᵇ Lev. 23²⁰ A very late interpolation.

Priestly Codes

Nu. 18 ²⁰Jehovah said to Aaron, Thou shalt have no inheritance in No inheritance their land, nor shalt thou have any portion among them; I am thy portion and thy inheritance among the Israelites.

Lev. 7 ¹¹This is the law concerning the sacrifice of peace-offerings, Parts of the peace-offerings which one may offer to Jehovah : ¹²if he offer it as a thank-offering, then he shall offer with the sacrifice of thanksgiving unleavened cakes mixed with oil, and unleavened wafers smeared with oil, and cakes mixed with oil, of fine meal well mixed.   ¹³With cakes of unleavened bread in addition to the sacrifice of his peace-offerings, which are given as a thank-offering, shall he present his gift.   ¹⁴And out of his offering he shall present one cake of each kind as a contribution to Jehovah; it shall belong to the priest who dasheth the blood of the peace-offerings.ᶜ

²⁸Jehovah gave this command to Moses: ²⁹Say to the Israelites, 'He who sacrificeth his peace-offerings to Jehovah shall bring his gift to Jehovah out of the peace-offerings which he sacrificeth.ᵈ ³⁰With his own hands he shall bring the offerings to be made by fire to Jehovah; the fat with the breast shall he bring, that the breast may be waved as a wave-offering before Jehovah. ³¹The priest shall burn the fat on the altar; but the breast shall belong to Aaron and his sons.   ³²And the right thigh shall ye give to the priest as a contribution out of the peace-offerings which ye sacrifice.ᵉ ³³He among the sons of Aaron who offereth the blood of the peace-offerings and the fat shall have the right thigh as his due.   ³⁴For the wave-breast and the thigh that is set aside have I taken from the Israelites out of the peace offerings which they sacrifice and have given them to Aaron the priest and his sons as their due forever from the Israelites.ᶠ

³⁵This is the shareᵍ of Aaron, and the share of his sons, out of the offerings for Jehovah made by fire, in the day when Moses presented them to minister as priests to Jehovah, ³⁶which Jehovah commanded to be given by the Israelites on the day he anointed them.   It is a statute forever throughout their generations.'

10 ¹⁴Thou and thy sons and thy daughters with thee shall eat in a clean Of the private contributions place the wave-breast and the thigh of the contribution, for they are given as thy due, and thy sons' due, out of the peace-offerings which the Israelites sacrifice. ¹⁵The thigh of the contribution and the wave-breast shall they bring with the offerings of the fat made by fire to wave them as a wave-offering before Jehovah; they shall belong to thee and to thy sons as your due forever, as Jehovah hath commanded.ʰ

Ex. 29 ²⁷Thou shalt consecrate the breast of the wave-offering, and the thigh of the contribution, which is waved, and that which is contributed, of the ram of consecration, for Aaron and his sons; ²⁸and they shall belong to

---

c Lev. 7¹¹⁻¹⁴ The form and contents of this passage indicate that it is from the priestly directions.

d Lev. 7²⁸⁻³³ These vss. are evidently a supplement to the preceding priestly directions. They probably come, however, from the author of the priestly groundwork, cf. Introd., pp. 44, 45.

e Lev. 7³² Possibly a gloss.

f Lev. 7³⁴ This vs. has the characteristics of the latest priestly editors.

g Lev. 7³⁵ This word has been confused with one etymologically similar which means *anointing portion*, and this confusion has led to a gloss in ³⁶, *on the day that he anointed them.* Vss. ³⁵, ³⁶ may also be later additions to ¹¹⁻¹⁴.

h Lev. 10¹⁵ Probably a still later gloss.

Priestly Code

Aaron and his sons as their due forever from the Israelites; for it is a contribution; and it shall be a contribution from the Israelites out of the peace-offerings which they sacrifice, even their contribution to Jehovah.

Nu. 18 ⁹This shall be thy share of the most holy things, reserved from the fire: all their gifts, even all their cereal-offerings, all their sin-offerings, and all their guilt-offerings, with which they make restitution to me, shall be held most sacred by thee and thy sons. ¹⁰In a most holy place shalt thou eat it; every male shall eat it; it shall be held sacred by thee.

Of the cereal-offer-ings

Lev. 6 ¹⁴This is the law concerning the cereal-offering: the sons of Aaron[i] shall offer it before Jehovah, in front of the altar. ¹⁵And he shall take up a handful of the fine meal of the cereal-offering, and of the oil, and of the frankincense which is upon the cereal-offering, and shall burn it on the altar as an offering made by fire[j] of pleasing odor, as a memorial[k] to Jehovah. ¹⁶The rest of it Aaron and his sons shall eat; it shall be eaten unleavened in a holy place; in the court of the tent of meeting they shall eat it. ¹⁷It shall not be baked with leaven. I have given it as their portion of my offerings made by fire; like the sin-offering, and the guilt-offering, it is most holy. ¹⁸Any male among the sons of Aaron may eat of it, as his everlasting due throughout your generations, from the offerings made by fire to Jehovah; but any layman who toucheth these offerings shall become holy.[l]

Supplemental Priestly Codes

Lev. 10 ¹²Then Moses gave command to Aaron, and to Eleazar and Ithamar, his sons who were left to him, Take the cereal-offering that is left over from the offerings made by fire to Jehovah and eat it unleavened beside the altar; for it is most holy.[m] ¹³And ye shall eat it in a holy place, for it is thy due and thy sons' due of the offerings of Jehovah made by fire; for thus I am commanded.

7 ⁹Every cereal-offering that is baked in the oven, and whatever is prepared in the stew-pan or on the griddle shall belong to the priest who offereth it.[n] ¹⁰But every cereal-offering, whether mixed with oil or dry, shall belong to the sons of Aaron, to all alike.

Priestly Codes

Of the Nazi-rite of-fering

Nu. 6 ¹⁹The priest shall take the boiled shoulder of the ram, and one unleavened cake from the basket, and one unleavened wafer, and shall lay them on the hands of the Nazirite, after he hath shaved off the evidence of his separation.[o] ²⁰Then the priest shall wave them as a wave-offering

---

[i] Lev. 6¹⁴ The subsequent context indicates that this is a later insertion. The passage is from the priestly directions.

[j] Lev. 6¹⁵ So Gk. and Sam. Heb., *as a pleasing odor*, cf. 1⁹ and 2².

[k] Lev. 6¹⁵ *As a memorial*, possibly secondary, interrupting the usual form of expression.

[l] Lev. 6¹⁸ Lit., *whoever toucheth them shall be holy, i. e.*, infected with holiness, tabooed from any common occupation.

[m] Lev. 10¹² This vs. incorporates earlier data in a very late setting.

[n] Lev. 7⁹ Possibly this vs. is also one of the later additions to the priestly codes.

[o] Nu. 6¹⁹ Lit., *his separation, i. e.*, shaved off his hair which hitherto had symbolized his Naziriteship.

Priestly Code

before Jehovah; this is a holy gift for the priest, together with the wave-breast and thigh of the contribution; after this the Nazirite may drink wine.

18 ^{25}Jehovah gave this command to Moses, ^{26}Thou shalt speak to the Levites and say to them, 'When ye take from the Israelites the tithe which I have granted you from them as your inheritance, ye shall make a contribution from it to Jehovah, a tithe of the tithe. ^{27}Your contribution shall be accredited to you as though it were the grain of the threshing-floor and as the full produce of the winepress. ^{28}Thus ye also shall make a contribution to Jehovah of all your tithes which ye receive from the Israelites; and out of them ye shall give Jehovah's full contribution to Aaron the priest. ^{29}Out of all your gifts ye shall make the full contribution due to Jehovah, even the consecrated parts of these gifts, selecting it from the best of them.' ^{30}Therefore say to them, 'When ye have contributed from your gifts the best part[p] of them, the rest shall be reckoned to the Levites as the produce of the threshing-floor and of the winepress. ^{31}Ye may eat it anywhere, ye and your families, for it is your reward in return for your service in the tent of meeting. ^{32}When ye have made a contribution from the best of your tithes, ye shall incur no guilt on account of it; ye shall not profane the holy things of the Israelites, lest ye die.' A tithe of all the tithes

5 ^{9}Every contribution, even all the holy things of the Israelites, which they present to the priest, shall be his; ^{10}and as for every man's consecrated things, they shall belong to the priest;[q] whatever any man giveth to the priest, his shall it be.

18 ^{11}This is thine: the contribution from their gift, including all the wave-offerings of the Israelites; I have given them to thee, and to thy sons, and to thy daughters with thee, as an everlasting due; every one who is clean in thy family may eat of it. ^{14}Everything devoted in Israel shall be thine. ^{19}All the contributions, which the Israelites make to Jehovah from the holy things have I given thee and thy sons and thy daughters with thee, as an everlasting due; it is an inviolable covenant[r] forever before Jehovah for thee and for thy descendants with thee.[s] All special contributions

15 ^{20}Of the first of your dough ye shall offer a cake as a contribution; as ye offer the contribution from the threshing-floor, so shall ye contribute it. ^{21}Of the first of your dough ye shall give to Jehovah a contribution throughout your generations.

18 ^{12}All the best[t] of the oil, and all the best[t] of the new wine, and of the grain, the firstfruits of them which they give to Jehovah, to thee have I given them, ^{13}the first-ripe fruits of all that is in their land, which they bring to Jehovah, shall be thine; every one who is clean in thy family may eat of it. First-fruits of the ground

^{15}Everything that openeth the womb of all flesh which they offer to Je-

---

p Nu. 18^{30} Lit., *fat.*
q Nu. 5^{9} Heb., *be his.*
r Nu. 18^{19} Lit., *covenant of salt.* The root idea is that those who share the same food, are bound not only to refrain from injuring each other, but to help each other whenever occasion may demand.
s Nu. 18$^{14, 19}$ This law is developed in Lev. 27$^{1-29}$ where the different gifts vowed or dedicated to Jehovah are specified. Cf. § 193.
t Nu. 18^{12} Lit., *fat.*

Priestly Codes

First-born of family, herd, and flock — hovah, both of man and beast shall be thine; only for the first-born of man thou shalt receive a ransom, and for the firstling of an unclean animal thou shalt receive a ransom.ᵘ ¹⁶At a month old thou shalt receive itsᵛ ransom price according to thy valuation, the sum of five shekels, after the shekel of the sanctuary, which contains twenty gerahs. ¹⁷But for the first-born of a cow, or the first-born of a sheep, or the first-born of a goat, thou shalt not receive a ransom; they are holy; thou shalt dash their blood against the altar, and burn their fat as an offering made by fire, of an odor pleasing to Jehovah. ¹⁸Their flesh shall be thine; like the wave-breast and the right thigh, it shall be thine.

Show-bread — **Lev. 24** ⁵Thou shalt take fine meal and bake twelve cakes of it, with two-tenths of an ephah in each cake. ⁶Thou shalt set them in two rows, six in a row, upon the table of pure goldʷ before Jehovah. ⁷Thou shalt put pure frankincense upon each row, to serve as a memorial of the bread, an offering made by fire to Jehovah. ⁸Every sabbath day the priest shall set it in order before Jehovah regularly; it is offered in behalf of the Israelites, in token of an everlasting covenant. ⁹ᵃIt shall belong to Aaron and his sons; they shall eat it in a holy place, for it is most holy.

Supplemental Priestly Codes

Guilt-offerings — **Nu. 5** ⁵Jehovah gave this command to Moses : ⁶Say to the Israelites, 'When a man or woman shall commit any sin such as men commit,ˣ in breaking faithᵃ with Jehovah, and that person shall so incur guilt, ⁷he shall confess the sin which he hath committed,ᵇ and shall restore in full that which he holds wrongfully,ᶜ and shall add a fifth to it, and give it to him by wronging whom he hath incurred guilt. ⁸But if the man have no kinsman to whom the property wrongfully held may be restored, the property wrongfully held must be restored to Jehovah; the priest shall have it; besides the ram of the atonement, with which atonement is made for him.'

Hide of the burnt-offerings — **Lev. 7** ⁸As for the priest, who offereth any man's burnt-offering, he shall have as his own the hide of the burnt-offering which he hath offered.

Part of the spoils of war — **Nu. 31** ²⁵Jehovah gave this command to Moses : ²⁶Make an estimate of the booty that was taken, both man and beast, thou, and Eleazar the priest, and the heads of the fathers' houses of the congregation; ²⁷and divide the booty into two parts, between the men skilled in war, who went out to battle, and all the rest of the congregation. ²⁸Then levy a contribution for Jehovah upon the warriors who went out to battle : one in every five hundred, of the persons, and of the oxen, and of the asses, and of the flocks; ²⁹take it from their half and give it to Eleazar the priest as a special contribution to Jehovah.

ᵘ Nu. 18¹⁵ Lit., *thou shalt ransom.* The Heb. word is probably wrongly pointed.
ᵛ Nu. 18¹⁶ *Its* clearly refers to the first-born of man alone.
ʷ Lev. 24⁶ Lit., *pure table.*
ˣ Nu. 5⁶ Or, *against men.*
ᵃ Nu. 5⁶ Or, *and so break faith.*
ᵇ Nu. 5⁷ Heb., *they shall confess their sin which they have committed.*
ᶜ Nu. 5⁷ Or, *make restitution for his guilt.* Lit., *restore his guilt.* The word here used ordinarily means *guilt-offering;* and only here and in ⁸ has it the meaning indicated in the translation.

IV

THE HIGH PRIEST

§ 168. Installation, Ex. 29⁵⁻⁷, 40^{12, 13} [Lev. 8⁷⁻¹²]

Priestly Codes

Ex. 29 ⁵Thou shalt take the garments, and clothe Aaron with the tunic, *Investiture and anointing* and the robe of the ephod, and the ephod, and the breastplate, and gird him with the skillfully wrought band of the ephod; ⁶and thou shalt set the turban on his head, and put the holy crown upon the turban. ⁷Then thou shalt take the anointing oil, and pour it on his head, and anoint him.

Supplemental Priestly Codes

Ex. 40 ¹²Thou shalt bring Aaron and his sons to the entrance of the tent of meeting, and shalt wash them with water. ¹³Then thou shalt clothe Aaron with the holy garments; and thou shalt anoint him, and consecrate him, that he may minister to me in the priest's office.

§ 169. Clothing, Ex. 28¹⁻³⁹, 29^{29, 30} [39¹⁻³⁹]

Priestly Codes

Ex. 28 ¹Bring thou near to thee Aaron thy brother, and his sons with *Preparation* him, from among the Israelites, that he may minister to me in the priest's office, even Aaron, Nadab and Abihu, Eleazar and Ithamar, Aaron's sons. ²Thou shalt make holy garments for Aaron thy brother, as splendid adornments; ³and thou shalt give command to all who are gifted, whom I have filled with the spirit of wisdom,^a that they make Aaron's garments to consecrate him, that he may minister to me in the priest's office. ⁴And these are the garments which they shall make : a breastplate, and an ephod, and a robe,^b and a tunic of checker work, a turban and a sash; thus they shall make holy garments for Aaron thy brother, and his sons, that he may minister to me in the priest's office. ⁵They shall use thread of gold, and violet, and purple, and red cloth, and fine linen.

The High Priest.—From the days of Solomon a chief priest was ever to be found, except during the Bab. exile, at the head of the Jerusalem priesthood. The names of some of the pre-exilic officials are known: Zadok, Jehoida and Hilkiah. Their title appears in the later pre-exilic literature to have always been *chief priest*. The same designation is used in the Holiness Code. The title *high priest* is peculiar to the post-exilic priestly literature, and is suggestive of the exalted civil and religious authority exercised by the high priests who reigned over the sacred temple and the Jewish community that gathered about it. The exile brought the religious leaders of the Jewish race into close contact with the Babylonians and Egyptians among whom the high priests enjoyed similar commanding authority. It is probable, therefore, that many of the elements in the later Jewish regulations regarding the high priest were suggested by the example of these powerful nations.

§ 169 The high priest was in later Judaism the representative of the Heb. kings, as well as the head and crown of the hierarchy. His costume when officiating as the high priest of the nation was correspondingly regal. Each article of his clothing and adornment suggested its sacred symbolic meaning. The exact meaning of many of the Heb. words employed in the description is doubtful.

^a Ex. 28³ Lit., *wise of mind.*
^b Ex. 28⁴ Or, *mantle.*

Priestly Codes

Shoul-
der-
cape

⁶They shall also make the ephod of gold, of violet, and purple, and red cloth, and fine twisted linen, with skillful workmanship.ᶜ ⁷It shall have two shoulder-pieces fastened together, that it may be held together at the two ends.ᵈ ⁸The skillfully wrought band, which is upon it, with which to gird it on, shall be of like workmanship and of the same piece with it, of gold, and violet, and purple, and red cloth, and fine twisted linen. ⁹Thou shalt also take two onyx stonesᵉ and engrave on them the names of the sons of Israel : ¹⁰six of their names on the one stone, and the names of the remaining six on the other stone, in the order of their birth. ¹¹With the workmanship of an engraver in stone shalt thou engrave the two stones, with the names of the sons of Israel; thou shalt make them enclosed in settings of woven gold thread. ¹²Thou shalt fasten the two stones on the shoulder-pieces of the ephod, as stones of memorial for the Israelites; thus Aaron shall bear their names before Jehovah on his two shoulders as a memorial. ¹³Thou shalt also make settings of braided gold thread, ¹⁴and two chains of pure gold; like cords shalt thou make them, well twisted; and thou shalt attach the corded chains to the settings.

Jew-
elled
breast-
plate

¹⁵Thou shalt make a breastplate of judgment,ᶠ skillfully wrought; of like workmanship with the ephod thou shalt make it; of gold, of blue, and purple, and violet, and fine twisted linen, shalt thou make it. ¹⁶It shall be square and folded double, a span long, and a span wide. ¹⁷Thou shalt insert in it a setting of stones, four rows of stones; a row of carnelian, topaz, and emerald shall be the first row; ¹⁸and the second row shall contain a ruby,ᵍ a sapphire, and a jasper; ¹⁹and the third row a jacinth,ʰ an agate, and an amethyst; ²⁰and the fourth row a chrysalite,ⁱ and a beryl, and an onyx; they shall be interwoven with gold thread in their settings. ²¹The stones shall correspond to the names of the sons of Israel, twelve according to their names; as a seal is engraved with one's name, they shall stand for the twelve tribes. ²²Thou shalt make upon the breastplate cordlike chains, well twisted, of pure gold.ʲ ²³Thou shalt make upon the breastplate two rings of gold, and shalt attach the two rings at the two ends of the breastplate. ²⁴Then thou shalt put the two corded chains of gold in the two rings at the ends of the breastplate. ²⁵And the other two ends of the corded chains thou shalt attach to the two settings, thus sewing them to the shoulder-pieces of the ephod at the front of it. ²⁶Thou shalt also make two rings of gold, and attach them at the two ends of the breastplate, at the inner edge of it, which is toward the side facing the ephod.ᵏ ²⁷Thou shalt also make two rings of

---

ᶜ Ex. 28⁶ Lit., *the work of a skillful workman.*
ᵈ Ex. 28⁷ The text is not clear.
ᵉ Ex. 28⁹ Or, *beryl*, or *malachite.* Some gem, but just what kind is uncertain.
ᶠ Ex. 28¹⁵ Or, *pouch to hold the oracle.*
ᵍ Ex. 28¹⁸ Or, *carbuncle . . . onyx.*
ʰ Ex. 28¹⁹ Or, *amber*, or *carbuncle.*
ⁱ Ex. 28²⁰ Or, *yellow jasper, . . . onyx . . . jasper.*
ʲ Ex. 28²² Possibly a gloss; it is unnecessary after ¹⁴.
ᵏ Ex. 28²²⁻³⁰ The Gk. has a shorter and variant text for ²²⁻³⁰, omitting ²³, ²⁶⁻²⁸, and ²⁵ᵃ, placing ²⁹ before ²⁴, and omitting all mention of rings. The Gk. also represents the breastplate as suspended by two corded chains. Neither the Heb. or Gk. are satisfactory. Behind both lies apparently a description of the breastplate hung by golden chains fastened to it, with

Priestly Codes

gold, and attach them to the two shoulder-pieces of the ephod underneath, at the front of it, close to the place of joining, above the skillfully wrought band of the ephod. ²⁸The breastplate shall be secured by its rings to the rings of the ephod with a violet cord, so that it will be over the skillfully woven band of the ephod, and that the breastplate may not hang loose from the ephod. ²⁹Aaron shall bear the names of the Israelites in the breastplate of judgment upon his heart, when he goeth in to the holy place, as a memorial before Jehovah continually. ³⁰Thou shalt put inside the breastplate of judgment the Urim and the Thummim;[1] that they may be upon Aaron's heart, when he goeth in before Jehovah; thus Aaron shall bear the judicial decisions of the Israelites upon his heart before Jehovah continually.

³¹Thou shalt make the robe of the ephod all of violet. ³²There shall be Robe an opening at the top,[m] in the middle of it, with woven work about the opening, as in the case of a coat of mail,[n] that it be not torn. ³³On the lower edge of it thou shalt make pomegranates of violet, and purple, and red, round about the border of it; and bells[o] of gold between them round about, ³⁴a golden bell and a pomegranate, on the border of the robe round about. ³⁵And Aaron shall wear it while ministering; and the sound of it shall be heard when he goeth in to the holy place before Jehovah, and when he cometh out, that he die not.

³⁶Thou shalt make a diadem of pure gold and engrave on it, HOLY TO Dia-
dem or JEHOVAH. ³⁷Thou shalt attach to it a violet cord to secure it to the tur- mitre ban; at the front of the turban shall it be. ³⁸It shall be upon Aaron's forehead, and Aaron shall be responsible for the holy things, which the Israelites consecrate, for all their holy gifts; it shall be always upon his forehead, that they may be accepted before Jehovah. ³⁹Thou shalt weave the tunic of fine linen in checker work; and thou shalt make a turban of fine linen, and thou shalt make a sash of embroidered work.

29 ²⁹And the holy garments of Aaron shall be for his sons after him, in Rules
for use which to be anointed and installed. ³⁰Seven days shall the son who becometh high priest in his place put them on, when he cometh into the tent of meeting to minister in the holy place.

---

their other ends made fast to the settings on the shoulder-pieces. The Heb. of ²⁵ makes the settings separate from the shoulder-pieces, thus differing from the earlier description. This may be accounted for by supposing that the reference to the onyx stones, with their inscriptions corresponding to the twelve stones in the breastplate, is a later addition. Otherwise the Heb. is fairly consistent and intelligible.

[1] Ex. 28³⁰ Lit., *the lights and the perfections.* For the earlier oracular use of these, cf. I Sam. 14⁴¹, ⁴² (Gk.), Vol. II, § 7. Originally they appear to have been two stones used in casting the sacred lot to determine the divine will. Possibly they were still employed by the high priest in the same way; or they may have been simply worn by him when rendering sacred decisions, as symbols of his divine authority.

[m] Ex. 28³² Or, *there shall be an opening for the head.*

[n] Ex. 28³² Lit., *like the opening of a coat of mail.*

[o] Ex. 28³³ These bells are probably a survival from a more primitive period when they were deemed necessary to keep away the evil spirits.

§ 170. Ceremonial Cleanliness, Lev. 21^10-15, 10^8, 9

Holiness Code

Limitations **Lev. 21** ^10The priest who is chief among his brethren, on whose head the anointing oil has been poured, and who has been installed, so as to put on the garments,^p shall not unbind his head^q or rend his clothes, ^11nor shall he go in to any dead body, or defile himself for his father or for his mother; ^12neither shall he go out of the sanctuary nor profane the sanctuary of his God; for the consecration imparted by the anointing oil of his God is upon him: I am Jehovah.

Marriage ^13He shall take a virgin as his wife. ^14A widow, a divorced woman, or a dishonored woman, or a harlot, such he shall not take; but a virgin of his own father's kin shall he take as his wife, ^15that he may not make his descendants dishonored among his father's kin: I am Jehovah who sanctifieth him.

Priestly Codes

No intoxicants **Lev. 10** ^8Jehovah gave this command to Aaron, ^9Drink no wine or strong drink, either thou or thy sons, when ye go into the tent of meeting, lest ye die; this shall be a statute forever throughout your generations.

§171. Duties, Lev. 16^32-34a [1-31], Ex. 28^29, 30, 30^10, Lev. 6^19-22, Ex. 30^7, 8

Priestly Codes

On the day of atonement **Lev. 16** ^32The high priest, who shall be anointed and installed as priest in his father's place, shall make the atonement, and shall put on the holy

---

§ 170 Because of his superlatively sacred office and functions, especial sanctity was required of the high priest: he must always marry only a virgin and was absolutely debarred from coming into contact with a corpse, even though it be of his nearest kinsmen. This regulation appears to have applied also to the pre-exilic chief priests, as its presence in the Holiness Code suggests.

p Lev. 21^10 This is perhaps a later gloss.

q Lev. 21^10 I. e., remove his turban.

§ 171 The duties of the high priest as prescribed by the O.T. law, consisted simply in making the annual offering within the temple on the great day of atonement; for the details of this law cf. § 221. He was also under obligation to care for the lamps in the temple, to provide for the daily morning and evening sacrifice, cf. § 208, and to furnish the special daily offering for himself and the priests. Josephus states that the high priest officiated in person only on the feasts and sabbaths, Ant. III, 2^57. From Nu. 27^21 it may also be inferred that, as in the pre-exilic times, he had charge of the sacred oracle. As a matter of fact the high priest was responsible for the organization and direction of the entire ritual and temple corps.

Ben Sira has preserved a vivid and highly colored picture of a certain high priest, Simon of the Greek period, 50^5, 6, 11-21. The occasion was probably the service on the day of atonement.

> ^5How glorious was he when he looked forth from the temple,
> At his coming forth out of the sanctuary!
> ^6As the morning star in the midst of a cloud,
> As the full moon on the day of the passover feast!
> ^11When he put on the robe of glory,
> And clothed himself with the splendid garments
> And ascended to the holy altar,
> He made glorious the precincts of the sanctuary.
> ^12And when he received the portions from the priests' hands,
> Himself also standing by the altar-hearth,
> His brethren as a garland round about him,
> He was as a young cedar on Mount Lebanon,

linen garments; ³³and he shall make atonement for the holy sanctuary; and
he shall make atonement for the tent of meeting, and for the altar; and he
shall make atonement for the priests, and for all the people of the assembly.
³⁴ᵃAnd this shall be an everlasting statute for you, that atonement be made
for the Israelites because of all their sins once every year.

Ex. 28 ²⁹Aaron shall bear the names of the Israelites in the breastplate
of judgment upon his heart, when he goeth in to the holy place, as a memorial before Jehovah continually. ³⁰Thou shalt put inside the breastplate
of judgment the Urim and the Thummim; that they may be upon Aaron's
heart, when he goeth in before Jehovah; thus Aaron shall bear the judicial
decisions of the Israelites upon his heart before Jehovah continually.

Supplemental Priestly Codes

Ex. 30 ¹⁰Aaron shall make atonement on the horns of the altar of incense once a year; with the blood of the sin-offering for atonement; once a
year shall he make atonement upon it throughout your generations; it is
most holy to Jehovah.

Lev. 6 ¹⁹Jehovah spoke thus to Moses,ʳ ²⁰This is the offering of Aaron Daily
and of his sons, which they shall offer to Jehovah on the day when he is offer-
anointed:ˢ a tenth of an ephah of fine meal as a cereal-offering regularly, ings
half of it in the morning, and half of it in the evening. ²¹On a flat plate it
shall be prepared with oil; when it is soaked, he shallᵗ bring it in. He
shall break in piecesᵘ the cereal-offering and shall offer it as an odor
pleasing to Jehovah. ²²The anointed priest from among Aaron's descend-

And as stems of palm trees they encompassed him about,
¹³*All the sons of Aaron in their glory,*
With Jehovah's burnt-offering in their hands,
In the presence of all the congregation of Israel,
¹⁴*Until he had finished the service at the altar,*
And the offering to the Most High, the Almighty.
¹⁵*He stretched out his hand to the cup,*
And poured out the blood of the grape;
He poured it out at the foot of the altar,
A sweet-smelling savor to the Most High, the King of all.
¹⁶*Then shouted the sons of Aaron,*
They blew on the trumpets of beaten work,
They blew and sent forth a mighty blast,
As a remembrance before the Most High.
¹⁷*Then all the people together hasted,*
They fell down with their faces to the ground,
To worship their Lord, the Almighty, God Most High.
¹⁸*The singers also praised him with their voices;*
In the whole house was there made sweet melody.
¹⁹*And the people besought the Lord Most High,*
In prayer before him who is merciful,
Until the service at the altar was ended;
And his due had been rendered to him.
²⁰*Then the high priest went down and lifted up his hands,*
Over the whole congregation of the Israelites
To give blessing to the Lord with his lips,
And to glory in his name.
²¹*And he bowed himself down the second time,*
To pronounce the blessing from the Most High.

ʳ Lev. 6¹⁹ Heb. 6¹².
ˢ Lev. 6²⁰ This clause is inconsistent with the last half of the vs. and is evidently a gloss.
ᵗ Lev. 6²¹ Heb., *thou shalt,* a scribal error due to the misreading of the previous verb.
ᵘ Lev. 6²¹ Syr., *thou shalt break it in pieces.* The Heb. is corrupt, and the rendering
given is not certain

Supplemental Priestly Codes

ants, who shall minister in his place, shall offer it; all of it shall be burnt as an everlasting due to Jehovah.

Incense and lamps **Ex. 30** ⁷On the altar of incense Aaron shall burn incense of sweet spices; each morning, when he taketh care of the lamps, he shall burn it. ⁸When Aaron setteth the lamps in place towards evening, he shall burn it as a perpetual incense before Jehovah throughout your generations.

E

REGULATIONS REGARDING CEREMONIAL CLEANLINESS

I

FOOD

§ 172. Clean and Unclean Animals, Birds and Insects, Dt. 14³⁻²⁰,
Lev. 20²⁵, ²⁶, 11¹⁻²³, ²⁶, ²⁷, ²⁹, ³⁰, ⁴¹⁻⁴⁴ᵃ, ⁴⁴ᵇ⁻⁴⁷

Deuteronomic Codes

Animals mals suitable for food **Dt. 14** ³Thou shalt not eat any abominable thing. ⁴These are the beasts which ye may eat: the ox, the sheep, the goat, ⁵the hart, the gazelle, the roebuck, the wild goat, the addax,ᵃ the antelope, and the mountain sheep. ⁶And every beast that parteth the hoof and cleaveth the cleft of the two hoofs and cheweth the cudᵇ among the beasts, that ye may eat. ⁷Never-

---

Regulations Regarding Ceremonial Cleanliness.—An exalted conception of the holiness and perfection of the Deity underlies all the ceremonial laws. A holy and perfect God must be worshipped by a holy and perfect people. A prophet like Isaiah defined holiness and perfection in moral terms, cf. Is. 6; but Israel's priests, in common with those of Babylonia, where much the same ceremonial laws obtained, sought to give objective and concrete expression to the principle of purity and perfection. As has been already noted, the Bab, exile gave a great impetus to this tendency, which, however, is traceable to the very beginnings of human history. The same general distinctions between clean and unclean food, the same general conceptions of defilement through contact with things ceremonially unclean, and the same emphasis upon the special purity of the priesthood were shared in common by the early Semitic peoples. Natural aversion at once explains why many things, as for example men afflicted with loathsome leprosy, were classified as unclean. All that suggested death or corruption had no place in the presence of the Holy One. Possibly an intuitive sense also led the Israelites to place certain diseases and unsanitary practices under the ban. In some cases primitive totemistic ideas doubtless underlie even the later laws.

§ 172 The belief in the sanctity of the blood, which was regarded as the life of the animal, evidently explains why many of these animals were classified as unclean. Since blood was sacred to the Deity, no Israelite was allowed to eat it. Hence all animals mangled or dying a natural death, and therefore retaining their blood in their veins were unfit for food. The same was true of all beasts and birds of prey. Scavengers were classified as unclean for the same reason and because of their loathsome habits. These were excluded by the law concerning non-ruminating animals. The basis of the prohibition against ruminating animals which do not part the cleft hoof is not so clear. The camel may have been thus excluded either because of its great value, or more probably, because it was regarded as sacred among the early Arabs. The hare and the rock-badger may have been prohibited because their flesh or habits were repulsive to the Hebrews. The principle of natural aversion is evidently operative in the case of fish and insects, explaining why the eel and all swarming things are placed under the ban. The exception in the case of locusts is clearly a concession to prevailing usage. Evidently both the list in Dt. 14 and its close parallel in Lev. 11 are based on still earlier usage and may well be derived from an earlier written source. Possibly the passage in Lev. 11 originally belonged to the Holiness Code. It has been supplemented in the latter part of the chapter ²⁶⁻⁴⁴ᵃ, for these vss. are in part duplicates of ¹⁻²³.

ᵃ Dt. 14⁵ Gk., pygarg, followed by the English versions.
ᵇ Dt. 14⁶ Lit., *bringeth up the cud*.

Deuteronomic Codes

theless these ye shall not eat of those that chew the cud or of those that part the cleft hoof : the camel, the hare, and the rock-badger, because they chew the cud but do not part the hoof; they are unclean to you.   ⁸And the swine, because he parteth the hoof but cheweth not the cud, he is unclean to you. Of their flesh ye shall not eat, and their carcasses ye shall not touch.

⁹These ye may eat of all that are in the waters : whatever hath fins and scales may ye eat; ¹⁰and whatever hath not fins and scales ye shall not eat; it is unclean to you.   Fish

¹¹Of all clean birds ye may eat.   ¹²But these are they of which ye shall not eat : the griffon-vulture,ᶜ the bearded-eagle, the ospray, ¹³the falcon,ᵈ and the kite after its kind, ¹⁴and every raven after its kind, ¹⁵and the ostrich, the night-hawk, the sea-mew, and the hawk after its kind, ¹⁶the little owl, the great owl, the horned owl,ᵉ ¹⁷the pelican, the carrion-vulture, the cormorant, ¹⁸the stork, and the heron after its kind, and the hoopoe and the bat.   Birds

¹⁹And all winged swarming creatures are unclean to you; they shall not be eaten.   ²⁰Of all clean winged creatures ye may eat.   Insects

Holiness Code

Lev. 20 ²⁵Ye shall make a distinction between the clean beast and the unclean, and between the unclean fowl and the clean; and ye shall not make yourselves abominable with beast, or by bird, or by anything with which the ground teemeth, which I have distinguished for you as unclean.   ²⁶But ye shall be holy to me; for I, Jehovah, am holy, and have distinguished you from the peoples, that ye should be mine.   General rules

Priestly Codes

Lev. 11 ¹Jehovah gave this command to Moses and Aaron: ²Say to the Israelites, ' These are the living things which ye may eat among all the beasts that are on the earth: ³whatever parteth the hoof, and cleaveth the cleft of the hoofs, that cheweth the cud among the beasts, that ye may eat.   ⁴Nevertheless these shall ye not eat of those that chew the cud, or of those that part the hoof : the camel, because he cheweth the cud but parteth not the hoof, he is unclean to you; ⁵and the rock-badger, because he cheweth the cud but parteth not the hoof, he is unclean to you; ⁶and the hare, because she cheweth the cud but parteth not the hoof, she is unclean to you; ⁷and the swine, because he parteth the hoof, and cleaveth the cleft of the hoof, but cheweth not the cud, he is unclean to you.   ⁸Of their flesh ye shall not eat, and their carcasses ye shall not touch; they are unclean to you.   Animals

⁹These ye may eat of all that are in the waters : whatever in the waters, in the seas, and in the rivers, hath fins and scales, ye may eat.   ¹⁰But all   Fish

---

ᶜ Dt. 14¹² The Heb. word poetically translated, *eagle*, clearly refers to the griffon-vulture (cf. Mi. 1¹⁶, Job 39³⁰, Mt. 24²⁸), which is exceedingly common in Palestine.
ᵈ Dt. 14¹³ So Gk. and Sam., supported by the close parallel in Lev. 11.   A scribal corruption has crept into the Heb.
ᵉ Dt. 14¹⁶ Gk., *water hen*, or *ibis.*

Priestly Codes

that have not fins and scales, in the seas, and in the rivers, of all that move in the waters, and of all the living creatures that are in the waters, they are detestable to you, ¹¹and they shall be detestableᶠ to you; ye shall not eat of their flesh, and their carcasses ye shall detest. ¹²Whatever in the waters hath no fins nor scales is detestable to you.

Birds

¹³And these ye shall detest among the birds; they shall not be eaten, they are : the griffon-vulture, and the bearded-vulture, the ospray, ¹⁴the kite, and the falcon after its kind, ¹⁵every raven after its kind, ¹⁶and the ostrich, the night-hawk, the sea-mew, and the hawk after its kind, ¹⁷and the little owl, the cormorant, the great owl, ¹⁸the horned owl, the pelican, the carrion vulture, ¹⁹the stork, the heron after its kind, the hoopoe and the bat.

Small animals and insects

²⁰All winged swarming things that go upon all fours are detestable to you. ²¹Yet these may ye eat of all winged swarming things that go upon all fours, which have legs above their feet, with which to leap upon the earth; ²²even these of them ye may eat : the locust after its kind, and the bald locust after its kind, and the cricket after its kind, and the grasshopper after its kind. ²³But all winged swarming things, which have four feet, are an abomination to you.

⁴⁴ᵇNeither shall ye defile yourselves with any kind of swarming thing that moveth upon the earth. ⁴⁵For I am Jehovah that brought you out of the land of Egypt, to be your God : ye shall therefore be holy, for I am holy.

Résumé

⁴⁶This is the law of the beast, and of the bird, and of every living creature that moveth in the waters, and of every creature that swarmeth upon the earth, ⁴⁷to make a distinction between the unclean and the clean, and between the living thing that may be eaten and the living thing that may not be eaten.'

Supplemental Priestly Codes

Animals

Lev. 11 ²⁶'Every beast which parteth the hoof, but cleaveth not the cleft of the foot, nor cheweth the cud, is unclean to you; every one who toucheth them shall be unclean. ²⁷And whatever goeth upon its paws, of all beasts that go on all fours, is unclean to you; whoever toucheth their carcass shall be unclean until evening; they are unclean to you.

Small animals and insects

²⁹And these are they which are unclean to you among the swarming creatures that swarm upon the earth : the weasel, the mouse, the great lizard after its kind, ³⁰and the gecko, the land-crocodile, and the chameleon. ⁴¹And every swarming creature that swarmeth upon the earth is detestable; it shall not·be eaten. ⁴²Whatever goeth on the belly, and whatever goeth on all fours, or whatever hath many feet, even all swarming creatures that swarm upon the earth, ye shall not eat, for they are detestable. ⁴³Ye shall not make yourselves detestable with any swarming creatures that swarmeth, neither shall ye make yourselves unclean with them, that ye should be defiled thereby. ⁴⁴ᵃFor I am Jehovah your God : sanctify yourselves therefore, and be ye holy; for I am holy.'

ᶠ Lev. 11¹¹ Lit., *a detestation.*

§ 173. **Blood and Fat**, Dt. 12²³⁻²⁵ [¹⁶, 15²³], Lev. 19²⁶ᵃ, 17¹⁰⁻¹⁴, 3¹⁷, 7²³ᵇ⁻²⁵ [²⁶], Gen. 9⁴

Deuteronomic Code

Dt. 12 ²³Firmly resist the temptationᵍ to eat the blood; for the blood is Reason for not eating blood the life, and thou shalt not eat the life with the flesh. ²⁴Thou shalt not eat it; thou shalt pour it out on the earth as water.ʰ ²⁵Thou shalt not eat it, that it may go well with thee and with thy children after thee, in case thou doest that which is right in the sight of Jehovah.

Holiness Code

Lev. 19 ²⁶ᵃYe shall not eat anything with the blood.

17 ¹⁰If any man of the house of Israel or of the aliens residing among Prohibition universal them, eateth of any blood, I will set my face against him and will cut him off from among his people. ¹¹For the life of the flesh is in the blood; and I have given it to you upon the altar to make atonement for your souls; for it is the blood that maketh atonement by means of the lifeⁱ *in it*. ¹²Therefore I have said to the Israelites, None of you shall eat blood, neither shall any alien residing among you eat blood.

¹³And if any one of the Israelites, or of the aliens residing among them, Blood to be poured out taketh in hunting any beast or bird that may be eaten; he shall pour out its blood and cover it with dust. ¹⁴For the life of all flesh is contained in the blood; therefore I have said to the Israelites, Ye shall not eat of the blood of flesh; for the life of all flesh is its blood; whoever eateth of it shall be cut off.

Priestly Codes

Lev. 3 ¹⁷It shall be a perpetual statute throughout your generations in No fat nor blood to be eaten all your dwellings, that ye shall eat neither fat nor blood.

7 ²³ᵇYe shall eat no fat, neither of ox, or sheep, or goat. ²⁴And the fat

---

§ 173 The belief that the blood represented the individual sentient life of man or animal or bird was widely held in antiquity, cf. Frazer, *Golden Bough*, I, 178, 179. It originated with the observation that when the blood of a living being was poured out life ceased and only the cold clay remained. It was this belief that led many primitive people to drink the blood of the slain animal that they might thereby themselves receive the life and strength of the victim.

The Hebrews, however, believed that the life, of which the blood was the symbol, came from Jehovah and therefore was sacred to him. The fat, because of its resemblance to the blood, was likewise regarded as sacred. Hence the blood was poured out upon the ground or upon the altar which in ancient times was believed to contain the spirit of the Deity, that the life which it contained might return to the God who gave it. The fat was also usually consumed with fire on the altar.

The Heb. belief in the sanctity of the blood was evidently very old, as the passage in I Sam. 14³²⁻³⁵ indicates: the sin of the hungry warriors in eating the slain animals together with the blood is corrected by rearing an altar on which the blood could be first presented to Jehovah. Until the Deuteronomic code was promulgated, apparently every animal killed for food was slaughtered at some local sanctuary, that the blood might be poured out to Jehovah beside an altar. In centralizing all worship in Jerusalem, the Deuteronomic lawgivers were obliged to provide for the slaughter of animals simply for food. In this case the sacrificial element disappears. Cf. further *Sacrificial Offerings* under § 195. These laws throw much light upon the psychological ideas of the early Hebrews.

ᵍ Dt. 12²³ Lit., *be firm not to eat.*

ʰ Dt. 12²⁴ Dt. 12¹⁶ is practically a repetition of this vs.

ⁱ Lev. 17¹¹ Lit., *soul, i. e.,* the individual sentient life of each man and animal.

Priestly Codes

of that which dieth a natural death, and the fat of that which is torn by beasts may be put to any other use, but ye shall in no case eat of it.

²⁵For whoever eateth the fat of any animal, of which men offer an offering made by fire to Jehovah, shall be cut off from his people.

Gen. 9 ⁴Flesh in which is the life, that is, its blood, shall ye not eat.

§ 174. Flesh of Animals Torn by Beasts or Dying a Natural Death, Ex. 22³¹, Dt. 14²¹ᵃ, Lev. 22⁸, 7²⁴, 17¹⁵, ¹⁶

Primitive Codes

No meat torn

Ex. 22 ³¹Holy men shall ye be to me; therefore ye shall not eat any flesh that is torn by beasts in the field; ye shall cast it to the dogs.

Deuteronomic Codes

Or of animals dying a natural death

Dt. 14 ²¹ᵃYe shall not eat of anything that dieth a natural death.

Holiness Code

Lev. 22 ⁸That which dieth a natural death, or is torn by beasts, a priest shall not eat so as to be made unclean by it : I am Jehovah.

Priestly Codes

Nor the fat

Lev. 7 ²⁴The fat of that which dieth of itself, and the fat of that which is torn of beasts, may be put to any other use, but ye shall in no case eat of it.

Method of purification

17 ¹⁵Every person who eateth that which dieth a natural death, or that which is torn by beasts, whether he be a native-born or a resident alien, shall wash his clothes and bathe himself in water and be unclean until evening. ¹⁶If he doth not wash his clothes and bathe his body, he shall bear the consequences of his iniquity.

§ 175. Meat Ceremonially Unclean, Lev. 7¹⁹ᵃ

Priestly Codes

Polluted meat

Lev. 7 ¹⁹ᵃFlesh that toucheth any unclean thing shall not be eaten; it shall be burnt with fire.

---

§ 174 Defilement by contact with unclean animals and the danger of eating the blood with the flesh appear to be the two ideas underlying these laws. Although the plural, *ye*, instead of the ordinary, *thou*, possibly indicates that the regulation in Ex. 22³¹ is from a later editor, the law itself seems to be one of the oldest ceremonial commands in the O.T.

§ 175 The belief that ceremonial uncleanness could be communicated by contact is accepted as a basal principle in the priestly laws, cf. also Hag. 2¹³.

§ 176. Leavened Bread, Ex. 34²⁵ᵃ [23¹⁸], 12¹⁸⁻²⁰

Primitive Codes

Ex. 34 ²⁵ᵃThou shalt not offer the blood of my passover sacrifice with leavened bread.

No leaven at the passover

Supplemental Priestly Codes

Ex. 12 ¹⁸On the fourteenth day of the first month in the evening, ye shall eat unleavened bread, until the evening of the twenty-first day of the month. ¹⁹Seven days shall no leaven be found in your houses; for whoever eateth that which is leavened shall be cut off from the congregation of Israel, whether he be a resident alien, or a native-born. ²⁰Ye shall eat nothing leavened; in all your dwellings ye shall eat unleavened bread.

§ 177. Fruit of Young Trees, Lev. 19²³⁻²⁵

Holiness Code

Lev. 19 ²³When ye shall come into the land, and shall have planted any kind of trees for food, ye shall treat its fruit as uncircumcised; three years it shall be held by you to be uncircumcised; it shall not be eaten. ²⁴But in the fourth year all its fruit shall be holy, a praise offering to Jehovah. ²⁵And in the fifth year ye may eat of its fruit, that it may yield to you its increase: I am Jehovah your God.

First-fruit sacred to Jehovah

§ 178. Rules Regarding the Eating of Meat, Ex. 34²⁶ᵇ, Dt. 12 [15], 20-27, Lev. 17³⁻⁹, 19⁵⁻⁸, 22¹⁰⁻¹⁶, 7¹⁵⁻¹⁸

Primitive Codes

Ex. 34 ²⁶ᵇThou shalt not seethe a kid in its mother's milk.

Boiling a kid

---

§ 176 The use of unleavened bread was limited to the passover feast or originally to the agricultural spring festival, cf. note § 212. Amos speaks of the use of leavened bread in connection with the thanksgiving sacrifices at Bethel, 4⁵. Three explanations have been offered to explain the use of unleavened bread: (1) that it is a survival of the nomadic usage when leaven was rarely employed; (2) because yeast represents fermentation and therefore is a symbol of decay; (3) because at the early spring festival the bread was made from the first-ripe grain without waiting for the yeast to act. The latter may well have given rise to the custom and the second explains its perpetuation and emphasis in later laws.

§ 177 The first and best products of fruit trees, as well as the first-born of the herd and flock and the firstfruits of the field, were consecrated to Jehovah. Since the fruit of the earliest years was not the best, the law provides that that of the fourth year shall be brought as Jehovah's part. That the first to be used might go to the Divine King, all earlier fruits are declared ceremonially unfit for food.

§ 178 From earliest times the slaying of an animal among the Hebrews was regarded as a sacrificial act. The blood and fat at least were given to the Deity. It was easy to enforce this law when there were many local sanctuaries and when animals were rarely killed for food except at the religious festivals. When the Deuteronomic lawgivers centralized the worship in Jerusalem, they were obliged, as has been noted, to modify the ancient usage. The Holiness Code and later priestly codes, however, retain the early sacrificial idea, but provide that all animals must be slain at the temple and under the direction of the priests. These variant regulations illustrate clearly the revolutionizing character of the Deuteronomic legislation and the tenacity of custom and the tendency of the later priestly lawgivers to bow to popular usage. The law of Lev. 17³⁻⁷ also reveals the harmonizing work of the later priestly editor, who aimed to bring the original regulation into harmony with the wilderness point of view, cf. Introd., p. 46.

Deuteronomic Codes

Permission to kill animals at home

Dt. 12 [20]When Jehovah thy God shall enlarge thy territory, as he hath promised thee, and thou shalt say, I will eat flesh, because thy soul desireth to eat it; thou mayest eat as thou mayest desire. [21]If the place in which Jehovah thy God shall choose to put his name be too far from thee, thou shalt kill of thy herd and of thy flock, which Jehovah hath given thee, as I have commanded thee; and thou mayest eat in thine own home, as thou mayest desire. [22]Even as the gazelle and as the hart is eaten, so thou shalt eat of it: the unclean and the clean may both eat of it.

Disposal of the blood

[23]Only be sure that thou eat not the blood, for the blood is the life, and thou shalt not eat the life with the flesh. [24]Thou shalt not eat it; thou shalt pour it out upon the earth as water. [25]Thou shalt not eat it; that it may go well with thee, and with thy children after thee, when thou shalt do that which is right in the sight of Jehovah.

Sacrificial animals

[26]Only thou shalt take thy holy things which thou hast, and thy vows, and go to the place which Jehovah shall choose; [27]and thou shalt offer thy burnt-offerings, the flesh and the blood, upon the altar of Jehovah thy God; and the blood of thy sacrifices shall be poured out upon the altar of Jehovah thy God; and thou shalt eat the flesh.

Holiness Code

Later limitations: all animals to be killed at temple

Lev. 17 [3]If there be any man of the house of Israel who killeth an ox, or lamb, or goat, either within or without the camp [4]and doth not bring it to the entrance of the tent of meeting, to present it as an offering to Jehovah before the dwelling of Jehovah; blood-guilt shall be imputed to that man; he hath shed blood, and that man shall be cut off from among his people, [5]in order that the Israelites may bring their sacrifices, which they are wont to sacrifice in the open field,[j] to Jehovah, at the entrance of the tent of meeting, to the priest, and sacrifice them as sacrifices of peace-offerings to Jehovah. [6]And the priest shall dash the blood against the altar of Jehovah at the entrance of the tent of meeting, and burn the fat as an odor pleasing to Jehovah.

[7]And they shall no more offer their sacrifices to the satyrs,[k] which they faithlessly worship. This shall be an everlasting statute for them throughout their generations. [8]If there be any man of the house of Israel, or of the aliens who reside among them, who offereth a burnt-offering or sacrifice, [9]and doth not bring it to the door of the tent of meeting, to sacrifice it to Jehovah, that man shall be cut off from his people.

Eating the sacrificial food

19 [5]When ye offer a sacrifice of peace-offerings to Jehovah, ye shall offer it so that ye may be accepted. [6]It shall be eaten the same day ye offer it or on the following day; and if any of it remain until the third day, it shall be burnt with fire. [7]And if it be eaten at all on the third day, it is refuse; it shall not be accepted; [8]but every one who eateth it shall be held guilty, because he hath profaned Jehovah's holy thing, and that person shall be cut off from his people.

---

j Lev. 17⁵ The Heb. repeats, *that they may bring.*
k Lev. 17⁷ Cf. Is. 13²¹. 34¹⁴, II Chr. 11¹⁵ where they figure as demons living in lonely places.

Holiness Code

22 [10]No laymen[1] shall eat of the holy thing;[m] a settler residing with the Holy
priest or a hired servant shall not eat of that which is holy. [11]But a slave, parts belong-
whom a priest buyeth for money, shall eat of it, and such as are born in his ing to the
house, may eat of his bread. [12]And if a priest's daughter be married to a lay- priests
man, she shall not eat of the special gifts of the holy things. [13]But if a priest's
daughter be a widow, or divorced, and have no child, and hath returned to
her father's house, as in her youth, she may eat of her father's bread; but no
layman may eat of it. [14]And if a man eat of the holy thing inadvertently,
he shall add a fifth part to it, and shall give the holy thing to the priest.
[15]The priests also shall not profane the holy things of the Israelites, which
they offer to Jehovah, [16]so as to cause them to bear the iniquity that bringeth
guilt, when they eat their holy things : I am Jehovah who sanctifieth them.

Priestly Codes

Lev. 7 [15]The flesh of any man's peace-offerings, which are presented as Eating
a thanksgiving, shall be eaten on the day he offereth it; he shall leave none the sac-
of it until morning. [16]But if the sacrifice which he offereth be a votive food
offering or a voluntary-offering, it shall be eaten on the day that he offereth
his sacrifice; and on the following day that which remaineth of it may be
eaten; [17]but that which yet remaineth of the flesh of the sacrifice on the
third day must be burnt with fire. [18]If any of the flesh of the sacrifice of his
peace-offerings be eaten on the third day,[n] it shall not be accepted, neither
shall it be credited to him who offereth it; it shall be refuse and the person
who eateth of it shall be held guilty.

II

CAUSES AND PURIFICATION OF CEREMONIAL UNCLEANNESS

§ 179. **Loathsome Diseases,** Dt. 24[8], Lev. 22[4a], 13, 14[33-53, 1-32, 54-57], 15[2b, 3, 13-15]
[[16-18, 25-33], Nu. 5[1-3]]

Deuteronomic Codes

Dt. 24 [8]Take heed in the plague of leprosy, that thou carefully observe Priest-
and do just as the priests the Levites shall instruct you; as I commanded ly regu-
them, so shall ye take heed to do. lation of lep-
rosy

---

[1] Lev. 22[10] Lit., *one not belonging to the priest's family.*
[m] Lev. 22[10] *I. e.,* the part of the sacrificial offering which had first been presented to Jehovah and then went to the priest.
[n] Lev. 7[18] In a tropical country meat was in danger of becoming putrid on the third day.
In keeping with their usual method, the later priests guarded against this possibility, not by
leaving the decision to the individual offerer, but by fixing a definite date.
    Causes and Purification of Ceremonial Uncleanness.—The tendency to increase the
list of things which would produce ceremonial defilement is already marked in the priestly
codes, although it reached its culmination in the laws of later Judaism. The roots of this tendency are traceable in earliest Semitic thought. Many of the strange provisions for ceremonial
cleansing are also clearly inherited from Israel's Semitic ancestors.
    § 179 Lepers are classed as unclean because the disease is so repulsive and incurable. It
was also popularly regarded as a mark of divine judgment, cf. Job, and, hence contact with
the one thus smitten was doubly defiling.
    Two kinds of real leprosy are still found in Palestine, (1) the *anœsthetic elephantiasis*

Holiness Code

Priest disqualified

Lev. 22 ⁴ᵃNo one of the descendants of Aaron who is a leper, or hath a discharge may eat of the holy things until he become clean.

Priestly Codes

Investigation of leprosy by the priest

Lev. 13 ¹Jehovah gave this command to Moses and Aaron, ²When a man shall have in his skin a rising, or an eruption or a bright spot, and it become in his skin the markᵃ of leprosy, then he shall be brought to Aaron the priest, or to one of his sons the priests, ³and the priest shall look at the plague in his skin; and if the hair in the plague be turned white, and the plague be seen to be deeper than his skin, it is the plague of leprosy; and the priest shall look at him, and pronounce him unclean. ⁴But if the bright spot in his skin be white and be seen to be no deeper than the skin, and the hair be not turned white, then the priest shall confine *him who hath* the plague seven days; ⁵and the priest shall look at him the seventh day, and if in his eyes the plague be stayed and hath not spread in the skin, then the priest shall confine him seven days more; ⁶and the priest shall look at him again the seventh day; and if the plague be dim, and hath not spread in the skin, the priest shall pronounce him clean, it is an eruption; and he shall wash his clothes, and be clean. ⁷But if the eruption spread in the skin, after he hath showed himself to the priest for his cleansing, he shall show himself to the priest again, ⁸and the priest shall look; and if the eruption hath spread in the skin, the priest shall pronounce him unclean, it is leprosy.

Real and white leprosy

⁹When the plague of leprosy is in a man, then he shall be brought to the priest; ¹⁰and the priest shall look; and, if there be a white rising in the skin, and it have turned the hair white, and there be a raw, open sore in the rising, ¹¹it is an old leprosy in his skin and the priest shall pronounce him unclean; he shall not confine him, for he is unclean. ¹²And if the leprosy break out in the skin, and the leprosy cover all the skin of *him who hath* the plague, from his head even to his feet, as far as the priest can see; ¹³then the priest shall look; and if the leprosy have covered all his flesh, he shall pronounce *him* clean *who hath* the plague; it is all turned white;ᵇ he is clean. ¹⁴But whenever raw flesh appeareth on him, he shall be unclean. ¹⁵And the priest shall look on the raw flesh, and pronounce him unclean; the raw flesh is unclean; it is

---

which first attacks the extremities with the result that the fingers and toes fall off at the joints. The limbs also gradually lose all sense of feeling as the disease gradually advances. Under proper care the malady may be kept partially in control and its victims have been known to live to an advanced age. More repulsive and malignant and common is the second type of leprosy, the *tubercular elephantiasis*, which first takes the form of red patches that later develop tubercles which in time ulcerate and eat far down into the flesh. The face and limbs swell, the eyes and tongue become affected and, at the end of about ten years, vital organs are attacked by the disease and death ensues. This is the form of leprosy referred to in Job 2⁷, ⁸, 7⁵, ¹⁵, 16¹⁶ and is one of the most horrible and incurable of maladies. With these types of true leprosy the Hebrews associated certain skin diseases, as for example, white leprosy, which took the form of white scales that often extended over most of the body and then gradually peeled off and disappeared, when the disease had run its course. Certain kinds of mould or fungus growth in garments and houses were also, because of the points of similarity, classified with human leprosy.
ᵃ Lev. 13² Lit., the mark left by a stroke. RV., *plague*. It is the mark left by some malign disease like leprosy.
ᵇ Lev. 13¹³ Evidently the disease is the white leprosy, which in time left the patient well and sound.

Priestly Codes

leprosy. ¹⁶Or if the raw flesh change again, and turn white, then he shall come to the priest, ¹⁷and the priest shall look on him; and if the plague be turned white, then the priest shall pronounce *him* clean *who hath* the plague; he is clean.

¹⁸And when there is a boil in the skin of the body and it is healed, ¹⁹and in the place of the boil there is a white rising, or a bright, reddish-white spot, then it shall be shown to the priest, ²⁰and the priest shall look; and if the spot be seen to be lower than the skin, and the hair be turned white, then the priest shall pronounce him unclean; it is the plague of leprosy, it hath broken out in the boil. ²¹But if the priest look at it, and there be no white hairs in it and it be no lower than the skin, but be dim, then the priest shall confine him seven days; ²²and if it be then spread in the skin, the priest shall pronounce him unclean; it is a plague. ²³But if the bright spot stay in its place, and be not spread, it is the scar of the boil; and the priest shall pronounce him clean. *(Real leprosy or a boil)*

²⁴Or when the flesh hath in the skin a burn caused by fire, and the sore of the burn become a bright spot, reddish-white or white, ²⁵then the priest shall look at it; and if the hair in the bright spot be turned white, and it appear to be deeper than the skin, it is leprosy that hath broken out in the burn, and the priest shall pronounce him unclean; it is the mark of leprosy. ²⁶But if the priest look at it, and there be no white hair in the bright spot, and it be no lower than the skin, but be dim, then the priest shall confine him seven days, ²⁷and the priest shall look at him the seventh day; if it be then spread in the skin, the priest shall pronounce him unclean; it is the mark of leprosy. ²⁸But if the bright spot stay in its place, and be not spread in the skin, but be dim, it is the rising of the burn, and the priest shall pronounce him clean, for it is the scar of the burn. *(White spots)*

²⁹And when a man or woman hath a mark on the head or on the beard, ³⁰the priest shall look at the mark; and if it appear to be deeper than the skin, and there be in it thin yellow hair, the priest shall pronounce him unclean; it is a scall,ᶜ it is leprosy of the head or beard. ³¹And if the priest look on the mark of the scall, and it appear to be no deeper than the skin, and there be no black hair in it, the priest shall confine *him who hath* the mark of the scall seven days; ³²and on the seventh day the priest shall look at the mark, and if the scall be not spread, and there be no yellow hair in it, and the scall appear to be no deeper than the skin, ³³he shall shave himself, but the scall shall he not shave; and the priest shall confine *him who hath* the scall seven days more; ³⁴and on the seventh day the priest shall look at the scall, and if the scall be not spread in the skin, and appear to be no deeper than the skin, the priest shall pronounce him clean; and he shall wash his clothes, and be clean. ³⁵But if the scall spread in the skin after his cleansing, ³⁶the priest shall look at him, and if the scall be spread in the skin, the priest need not look for the yellow hair; he is unclean. ³⁷But if in his eyes the *(Spots on the head or face)*

ᶜ Lev. 13³⁰ Probably a dry scale.

Priestly Codes

scall be stayed, and black hair be grown up in it, the scall is healed; he is clean, and the priest shall pronounce him clean.

A tetter

³⁸And when a man or a woman hath in the skin bright spots, bright white spots, ³⁹the priest shall look; and if the bright spots in the skin be of a dull white, it is a tetter, it hath broken out in the skin; he is clean.

Mark on a bald spot

⁴⁰And if a man lose his hair from his head, he is bald; *yet* he is clean. ⁴¹And if his hair be fallen off from the front part of his head, he is forehead-bald; *yet* he is clean. ⁴²But if there be on the bald head, or the bald fore-head, a reddish-white mark, it is leprosy breaking out on his bald head, or his bald forehead. ⁴³Then the priest shall look upon him, and if the rising caused by the mark be reddish-white on his bald head, or on his bald fore-head, like the appearance of leprosy in the skin, ⁴⁴he is a leprous man, he is unclean; the priest shall pronounce him unclean; his plague is on his head.

Obliga-tions of lepers

⁴⁵And when a leper hath the mark of leprosy upon him, his clothes shall be rent, and the hair of his head shall go loose, and he shall cover his upper lip, and cry, Unclean! unclean!ᵈ   ⁴⁶All the days during which the mark is upon him he shall be unclean; *and since* he is unclean, he shall dwell alone; his dwelling shall be outside the camp.

Lep-rosy spread-ing in a gar-ment

⁴⁷When the mark of leprosy is in a garment, whether it be a woolen garment, or a linen garment; ⁴⁸whether it be in the warp, or in the woof, of linen or of wool, either in a skin, or in anything made of skin; ⁴⁹if the mark be greenish or reddish in the garment, or in the skin, or in the warp, or in the woof, or in anything of skin, it is the mark of leprosy, and shall be shown to the priest. ⁵⁰And the priest shall look upon the mark and shut up *that which hath* the mark seven days : ⁵¹and he shall look on the mark on the seventh day; if the mark be spread in the garment, either in the warp, or in the woof, or in the skin, whatever be the purpose for which skin is used, the mark is that of malignant leprosy; it is unclean. ⁵²And he shall burn the garment, or the warp or the woof, whether it be of wool or of linen, or anything of skin, in which the mark is; for it is a malignant leprosy; it shall be burnt in the fire.

Per-manent marks

⁵³And if the priest shall look, and the mark be not spread in the garment, either in the warp, or in the woof, or in anything of skin, ⁵⁴the priest shall command that they wash the thing in which the plague is, and he shall shut it up seven days more : ⁵⁵and the priest shall look, after the mark is washed; and if the mark have not changed its color, and the mark be not spread, it is unclean; thou shalt burn it in the fire; it is malignant, whether the bareness be within or without.

Disap-pearing marks

⁵⁶But if the priest look, and the mark be dim after it hath been washed, he shall tear it out of the garment, or out of the skin, or out of the warp, or out of the woof; ⁵⁷and if it still appear in the garment, either in the warp, or in the woof, or in anything of skin, it is breaking out; thou shalt burn with fire that in which the mark is. ⁵⁸But if the mark disappear from the gar-ment, either from the warp or the woof, or whatever thing of skin it be,

---

ᵈ Lev. 13⁴⁵ *I. e.*, he shall assume the garb and rôle of a mourner.

Priestly Codes

when thou hast washed it, it shall be washed a second time, and shall be clean.

⁵⁹This is the law of the mark of leprosy in a garment of wool or linen, either in the warp, or the woof, or anything of skin, to *determine when* to pronounce it clean, or to pronounce it unclean.

³³Jehovah said to Moses and Aaron,ᵉ ³⁴When ye have come into the land of Canaan, which I give to you as a possession, and I put the mark of leprosy on a house in the land of your possession; ³⁵then he who owneth the house shall come and say to the priest: 'There seemeth to me to be a kind of mark in my house.' ³⁶And the priest shall command the house to be emptied before he goeth in to examine the mark, so that all that is in the house be not made unclean; and afterward the priest shall go in to examine the house; ³⁷and he shall look at the mark; and if the mark on the walls of the house be in greenish or reddish patches which appear to be deeper than *the surface* of the wall, ³⁸the priest shall go out to the door of the house, and shut up the house seven days. ³⁹And the priest shall come again on the seventh day and shall look; and if the mark be spread in the walls of the house, ⁴⁰the priest shall command that they take out the stones in which the mark is, and cast them into an unclean place outside the city. ⁴¹Then he shall cause the house to be scraped throughout inside, and they shall pour out the mortar, that they scrape off, outside the city into an unclean place; ⁴²and they shall take other stones, and put them in the place of those stones; and he shall take other mortar, and shall plaster the house.

Leprosy in a house

⁴³And if the mark break out again in the house, after he hath taken out the stones, and after he hath scraped the house, and after it is plastered, ⁴⁴the priest shall come in and look; and if the mark be spread in the house, it is a malignant leprosy in the house; it is unclean. ⁴⁵And he shall break down the house, its stones, and its timber, and all the mortar of the house; and he shall carry them out of the city to an unclean place. ⁴⁶Moreover he who goeth into the house during the time that it is shut up shall be unclean until evening. ⁴⁷And he who sleepeth in the house shall wash his clothes; and he who eateth in the house shall wash his clothes.

A malignant type

⁴⁸But if the priest come in, and look, and find that the mark hath not spread in the house, after the house was plastered; he shall pronounce the house clean, because the mark hath disappeared. ⁴⁹And he shall take to cleanse the house two birds, with cedar wood and scarlet, and hyssop: ⁵⁰and he shall kill one of the birds in an earthen vessel over running water: ⁵¹and he shall take the cedar wood, and the hyssop, and the scarlet, and the living bird, and dip them in the blood of the slain bird, and in the running water, and sprinkle the house seven times; ⁵²and he shall cleanse the house with the blood of the bird, and with the running water, and with the living bird, and with the cedar wood, and with the hyssop, and with the scarlet; ⁵³but he shall let the living bird go out of the city into the open field; so he shall make atonement for the house, and it shall be clean.

Ceremonial cleansing of a leprous house

14 ¹Jehovah gave this command to Moses: ²This shall be the law of the leper in the day when he is cleansed; he shall be brought to the priest; ³and the priest shall go out of the camp; and the priest shall look; and if the mark of leprosy be healed in the leper, ⁴the priest shall command to take for him who is to be cleansed two living clean birds, cedar wood, scarlet, and hyssop; ⁵and the priest shall command to kill one of the birds in an earthen vessel over running water. ⁶He shall then take the living bird, the cedar wood, the scarlet, and the hyssop, and shall dip them and the living bird in the blood of the bird that was killed over the running water; ⁷and the blood he shall sprinkle seven times upon him who is to be cleansed from the leprosy, and shall pronounce him clean, and shall set free the living bird in the open field. ⁸And he who is to be cleansed shall wash his clothes, and shave off all

Ritual for the cleansing of a leper

ᵉ Lev. 14³³⁻⁵³ The contents, as well as the colophon in ⁵⁴⁻⁵⁷, indicate that this section belongs at the close of 13⁷. While it doubtless records a very ancient ritual, its literary style and allusions to the rite of atonement, ⁵³, indicate that it is a late addition.

Priestly Codes

his hair, and bathe himself in water; and he shall be clean; and after that he shall come into the camp, but shall dwell outside his tent seven days. ⁹And on the seventh day he shall shave off all the hair of his head and his beard and his eyebrows, even all his hair he shall shave off, and he shall wash his clothes, and shall bathe his flesh in water; then he shall be clean.

Completion of the rite of cleansing

¹⁰And on the eighth day he shall take two male lambs without blemish, and one ewe-lamb a year old without blemish, and as a cereal-offering three-tenths *of an ephah* of fine meal mixed with oil, and one log^f of oil.   ¹¹And the priest who cleanseth him shall set the man who is to be cleansed and these things before Jehovah, at the entrance of the tent of meeting.   ¹²And the priest shall take one of the male lambs, and offer it with the log of oil as a guilt-offering, and wave them as a wave-offering before Jehovah; ¹³then he shall kill the male lamb in the place where they kill the sin-offering and the burnt-offering in the place of the sanctuary; for the guilt-offering like the sin-offering belongeth to the priest; it is most holy.   ¹⁴And the priest shall take some of the blood of the guilt-offering, and shall put it on the tip of the right ear of him who is to be cleansed, and on the thumb of his right hand, and on the great toe of his right foot.   ¹⁵And the priest shall take some of the log of oil, and pour it into the palm of his own left hand; ¹⁶and the priest shall dip his right finger in the oil that is in his left hand, and shall sprinkle some of the oil with his finger seven times before Jehovah.   ¹⁷And of the rest of the oil that is in his hand the priest shall put some on the tip of the right ear of him who is to be cleansed, and on the thumb of his right hand, and on the great toe of his right foot, and upon the blood of the guilt-offering; ¹⁸and the rest of the oil that is in the priest's hand he shall put on the head of him who is to be cleansed.   Thus the priest shall make atonement for him before Jehovah.   ¹⁹And the priest shall offer the sin-offering, and make atonement for him who is to be cleansed because of his uncleanness; and afterward he shall kill the burnt-offering; ²⁰and the priest shall offer the burnt-offering and the cereal-offering upon the altar.   Thus the priest shall make atonement for him, and he shall be clean.

Offering and rite in the case of a poor man

²¹And if he be poor, and his means are not sufficient for this, he shall take one male lamb as a guilt-offering to be waved, to make atonement for him, and one-tenth *of an ephah* of fine meal mixed with oil as a cereal-offering, and a log of oil, ²²and two turtle-doves, or two young pigeons, such as his means permit; and the one shall be a sin-offering, and the other a burnt-offering. ²³And on the eighth day he shall bring them for his cleansing to the priest, at the entrance of the tent of meeting, before Jehovah; ²⁴and the priest shall take the lamb of the guilt-offering, and the log of oil, and the priest shall wave them as a wave-offering before Jehovah.   ²⁵And he shall kill the lamb of the guilt-offering; and the priest shall take some of the blood of the guilt-offering, and put it on the tip of the right ear of him who is to be cleansed, and on the thumb of his right hand, and on the great toe of his right foot. ²⁶And the priest shall pour some of the oil into the palm of his own left hand;

---

f Lev. 14¹⁰ According to the Rabbis the log was one-twelfth of a hin, *i. e.*, about five-sixths of a pint.

Priestly Codes

27and the priest shall sprinkle with his right finger some of the oil that is in his left hand seven times before Jehovah; 28and the priest shall put some of the oil that is in his hand on the tip of the right ear of him who is to be cleansed, and on the thumb of his right hand, and on the great toe of his right foot, and on the place of the blood of the guilt-offering; 29and the rest of the oil that is in the priest's hand he shall put on the head of him who is to be cleansed, to make atonement for him before Jehovah. 30And he shall offer one of the turtle-doves, or of the young pigeons, as his means permit,[g] 31the one as a sin-offering, and the other as a burnt-offering, with the cereal-offering; and the priest shall make atonement for him who is to be cleansed before Jehovah. 32This is the law of him on whom is the mark of leprosy, whose means do not permit him *to bring the regular sacrifices* for his cleansing.

54This is the law for every kind of mark of leprosy, and for a scall, 55and for the leprosy of a garment and of a house, 56and for a rising, and for a scab, and for a bright spot, 57to show when each is unclean, and when it is clean; this is the law of leprosy. Colophon

15 2bWhen any man hath a discharge from his body,[h] his discharge is unclean; 3and his uncleanness shall continue as long as he hath the discharge; whether the discharge continue or be stopped so that no discharge appeareth, he is in a state of uncleanness. Chronic discharges

13And when he who hath a discharge is cleansed of his discharge, he shall count seven days for his cleansing, and wash his clothes; and he shall bathe his body in running water, and become clean. 14And on the eighth day he shall take two turtle-doves, or two young pigeons, and come before Jehovah at the entrance of the tent of meeting, and give them to the priest; 15and the priest shall offer them, the one as a sin-offering, and the other as a burnt-offering; and the priest shall make atonement for him before Jehovah for his discharge.[i] Rite of cleansing

§ 180. **Childbirth, Lev. 12**^1-8

Priestly Codes

Lev. 12 1Jehovah gave this command to Moses: 2Speak thus to the Israelites, 'If a woman become pregnant, and bear a male child, she shall be unclean seven days; as the days of the uncleanness of her monthly infirmity she shall be unclean. 3And on the eighth day the flesh of his foreskin shall be circumcised. 4And she shall continue in the blood of her purification thirty-three days; she shall touch no holy thing, nor come into the sanctuary, until the days of her purification are fulfilled. 5But if she bear a female child she Period of ceremonial uncleanness

g Lev. 14^30 Through a scribal error the last clause of ^30 has been repeated in ^31.
h Lev. 15^2b Lit., *flesh, i. e.*, euphemism for *urethra.*
i Lev. 15^13-15 The same directions are repeated in ^25-30, for a woman afflicted with an irregular or prolonged monthly sickness.
§ 180 This law appears to be one of the later additions to the ceremonial system. Possibly it came in through the influence of Persia, where childbirth was regarded as especially defiling. The primitive idea at the root of the law is the supreme mystery of childbirth, which profoundly impressed the minds of the ancients. The ceremonial precautions were in all probability originally intended to guard against the influence of the spirits which were supposed to be present especially at childbirth, cf. Frazer, *Golden Bough*, II, 238-42.

Priestly Codes

shall be unclean two weeks,[j] as in her monthly uncleanness; and she shall continue in the blood of her purification sixty-six days.

Rite of cleansing ⁶And when the days of her purification are fulfilled, for a son or for a daughter, she shall bring a yearling lamb as a burnt-offering, and a young pigeon or a turtle-dove, as a sin-offering, to the entrance of the tent of meeting, to the priest, ⁷and he shall offer it before Jehovah, and make atonement for her; thus she shall be cleansed from her flow of blood. This is the law for her who beareth either a male or a female. ⁸And if her means be not sufficient for a lamb, she shall take two turtle-doves or two young pigeons; the one as a burnt-offering, and the other as a sin-offering; and the priest shall make atonement for her, and she shall be cleansed.[k]

§ 181. Contact with the Dead, Dt. 21²², ²³, ¹⁻⁵, Lev. 22⁴ᵇ, ⁶ᵃ, Nu. 19¹⁴⁻²¹, ¹¹⁻¹³, 31¹⁹

Deuteronomic Codes

Disposal of body of capital offender **Dt. 21** ²²If a man have committed a sin deserving of death, and he be put to death, and thou hang him on a tree,[l] ²³his body shall not remain all night upon the tree, but thou shalt surely bury him the same day, for he that is hanged is accursed of God, that thou defile not thy land which Jehovah thy God is about to give thee as an inheritance.

Rite in case of undetected murder ¹If one be found slain in the land which Jehovah thy God is about to give thee as a possession, lying in the open field, and it be not known who hath smitten him, ²then thy elders and thy judges shall come out, and they shall measure the distance to the cities round about the one who is slain: ³and the elders of the city which is nearest to the slain man shall take from the herd a heifer which hath done no work[m] nor drawn in the yoke; ⁴and the elders of that city shall bring down the heifer to a valley with running water, which hath been neither plowed nor sown, and shall break the heifer's neck there in the valley. ⁵And the priests the sons of Levi shall come near; for them Jehovah thy God hath chosen to minister to him and to bless in the name of Jehovah, and every controversy and every blow shall be according to their sentence.

Holiness Code

Period of defilement **Lev. 22** ⁴ᵇIf any man touch a thing that hath been made unclean by a dead body, ⁶ᵃthe person who toucheth any such thing shall be unclean until evening.

---

[j] Lev. 12⁵ This was because it was widely held in antiquity that the abnormal puerperal conditions lasted longest after the birth of a girl.

[k] Lev. 12⁸ This vs. appears to be a later addition, since it follows the colophon in ⁷. The evidence, however, is not decisive.

§ 181 The belief that a murdered man's blood defiled a land or people, until proper atonement was made, is an inheritance from earliest times. The rite in Dt. 21¹⁻⁵ is doubtless very ancient. The priests do not appear to have participated in the ceremony, but are simply present to lend their religious sanction. In the priestly codes any contact with a corpse or with anything that has touched it means ceremonial defilement.

[l] Dt. 21²² *I. e.*, as a solemn warning to all evil-minded members of the community.

[m] Dt. 21³ Lit., *which hath not been wrought with.*

Priestly Codes

Nu. 19 ¹⁴This is the law when any man dieth in a tent: Every one who cometh into the tent and every one who is in the tent shall be unclean seven days. ¹⁵And every open vessel which hath no covering tied over it is unclean. ¹⁶And whoever in the open field toucheth any one who has been slain with a sword, or a dead body, or a bone of a man, or a grave, shall be unclean seven days. ¹⁷And for the one who is unclean they shall take of the ashes of the burning of the sin-offering; and running[a] water shall be added to it in a vessel; ¹⁸and a man ceremonially clean shall take hyssop, and dip it in the water, and sprinkle it over the tent and over all the vessels, and over the persons who were there, and over him who touched the bone, or the slain, or the dead, or the grave; ¹⁹and the one who is ceremonially clean shall sprinkle it over the one who is unclean both on the third day and on the seventh day; and on the seventh day he shall purify him; and he shall wash his clothes, and bathe himself in water, and shall be clean in the evening.

²⁰But the man who is unclean and doth not purify himself shall be cut off from the midst of the assembly, because he hath defiled the sanctuary of Jehovah; the water of impurity hath not been sprinkled over him; he is unclean. ²¹And it shall be a perpetual statute to them; and he who sprinkleth the water of impurity shall wash his clothes; and he who toucheth the water of impurity shall be unclean until evening.

Supplemental Priestly Codes

Nu. 19 ¹¹He who toucheth the dead, even any human corpse shall be unclean seven days; ¹²he must purify himself therewith on the third day and on the seventh day, and so become clean;[o] but if he do not purify himself on the third day, he shall not become clean. ¹³Whoever toucheth a dead person, the corpse of any man that may have died, and doth not purify himself, defileth the dwelling of Jehovah; and that one shall be cut off from Israel, because the water of impurity was not sprinkled over him; he shall be unclean; his uncleanness is yet upon him.

31 ¹⁹Encamp outside the camp seven days; whoever hath killed any person, and whoever hath touched any slain, purify yourselves on the third day, and on the seventh day you and your captives.

§ 182. **The Carcasses of Animals,** Lev. 5², 11⁸, ²⁴⁻²⁸, ²⁹ᵇ⁻⁴⁰

Priestly Codes

Lev. 5 ²If any one touch any unclean thing, either the carcass of an unclean beast, or the carcass of an unclean domestic animal, or the carcass of an unclean swarming creature, and the fact be hidden from him, and he be unclean, he shall be guilty.

11 ⁸Of the flesh of swine ye shall not eat, and their carcasses ye shall not touch; they are unclean to you.

Side notes: Period and rite of purification after contact with the dead — Penalty for neglecting this law — Later versions of the law — Contact with unclean animals — Swine's flesh

---

[a] Nu. 19¹⁶ *I. e.*, spring water, cf. Gen. 26¹⁹, Zech. 14⁸, Lev. 14⁵, ⁶, ⁵⁰⁻⁵².
[o] Nu. 19¹² So the Gk. and Syr.

Supplemental Priestly Codes

Means and period of pollution

Lev. 11 ²⁴By all kinds of unclean beasts and birds and swarming creatures ye shall become unclean; whoever toucheth their carcasses shall be unclean until evening; ²⁵and whoever carrieth the carcass of any of them shall wash his clothes and be unclean until evening. ²⁶Every beast which parteth the hoof, but cleaveth not the cleft of the foot nor cheweth the cud, is unclean to you; every one who toucheth them shall be unclean. ²⁷And whatever goeth upon its paws, of all beasts that go on all fours, is unclean to you; whoever toucheth the carcass of any of them shall be unclean until evening. ²⁸And he who carrieth the carcass of any of them shall wash his clothes and be unclean until evening; they are unclean to you. ²⁹ᵇThe weasel, the mouse, the great lizard after its kind, ³⁰the gecko, the land-crocodile, and the chameleon, ³¹these are they which are unclean to you among all swarming creatures; whoever toucheth them, when they are dead shall be unclean until evening.

Cleansing of objects polluted by swarming creatures

³²And everything upon which any of them, when it is dead, doth fall, shall be unclean; whether it be a wooden vessel, or clothing, or a skin, or a sack; whatever vessel it be, with which any work is done, it must be put into water, and it shall be unclean until the evening; then it shall be clean. ³³And if any of them fall into an earthen vessel, whatever is in it shall be unclean, and the vessel itself ye shall break. ³⁴All food in it which may be eaten, which is prepared with water, shall be unclean; and any liquid which may be drunk out of any such vessel shall be unclean. ³⁵And everything on which the carcass of any of these creatures falleth shall be unclean; whether oven or chaffing pot, it shall be broken in pieces; they are unclean and shall be unclean to you. ³⁶Nevertheless a fountain or a cistern in which water is collected shall be clean, but that which toucheth their carcass shall be unclean. ³⁷And if the carcass of any of these fall upon any seed grain which is to be sown, it is clean. ³⁸But if water be put upon the seed, and the carcass of any of these fall upon it, it is unclean to you.

Carcasses of clean animals

³⁹And if any animal, the flesh of which ye may eat, die, he who toucheth its carcass shall be unclean until evening. ⁴⁰And he who eateth of the carcass must wash his clothes, and be unclean until evening; he also who carrieth the carcass shall wash his clothes and shall be unclean until evening.ᴾ

§ 183. With Persons or Things Ceremonially Unclean,
Nu. 19²², Lev. 5³ [15¹⁻²⁴]

Priestly Codes

Contagion of uncleanness

Nu. 19 ²²Whatever a person ceremonially unclean toucheth shall be unclean; and the one who toucheth it shall be unclean until evening.

ᴾ Lev. 11³⁹, ⁴⁰ These vss. probably contain the earlier law which has been expanded in the preceding vss.

§ 183 A natural aversion, which was felt toward that which was revolting to the senses, is undoubtedly the basis of these as well as many other ceremonial laws. Lev. 15 develops this principle in detail. Persons of either sex afflicted with normal, abnormal or chronic discharges were regarded as unclean and capable of imparting ceremonial pollution to everything or everyone with which they came into direct contact. All imparted ceremonial impurity which required thorough washing and bathing, and meant uncleanness, at least until sunset.

Priestly Codes

Lev. 5 ³If one touch the uncleanness of man, whatever it be, and the fact be hid from him, when he knoweth of it, he shall be guilty.

§ 184. With Spoils of War, Nu. 31²⁰⁻²⁴

Supplemental Priestly Codes

Nu. 31 ²⁰*Of the spoils of war* every garment and all that is made of skin, and all work of goats' hair, and all things made of wood, ye shall purify. To be purified

²¹And Eleazar the priest said to all the warriors who went to the battle, This is the statute of the law which Jehovah hath commanded Moses, ²²'Only the gold, the silver, the brass, the iron, the tin, and the lead—²³everything that may be put into the fire—ye shall put through the fire, that it may be clean; it shall surely be purified by means of the water of impurity; and all that cannot be put into the fire ye shall put through the water. ²⁴And ye shall wash your clothes on the seventh day and shall be clean, and afterwards ye shall come into the camp.' By fire and water

§ 185. Special Laws Governing the Nazirites, Nu. 6¹⁻¹²

Priestly Codes

Nu. 6 ¹Jehovah gave this command to Moses, ²Speak to the Israelites and say to them, 'When any man or a woman shall make a special vow, the vow of a Nazirite, to separate himself to Jehovah, ³he shall separate himself from wine and strong drink; he shall drink no vinegar of wine, or vinegar of strong drink, neither shall he drink any drink of grapes, nor eat fresh or dried grapes. ⁴All the days of his separation he shall eat nothing that is borne by the grapevine, not even the unripe grapes or tendrils.[q] To reject all products of the vine

---

§ 184 In this very late traditional precedent, associated with the war with the Midianites, the later Jewish belief that everything that had been touched by heathen hands was unclean assumes binding legal form.

§ 185 The word *Nazirite* means, *one separated* or *one who separates himself, i. e.*, from certain ordinary practices. The Nazirite was also *separated to Jehovah*, that is, his separation was intended to symbolize especial devotion to Jehovah. The custom of abstaining from certain acts or kinds of food in connection with a vow to the Deity appears to have been in vogue among the nomadic ancestors of the Hebrews. Throughout a millennium of Israel's history, Nazirites figure more or less prominently. Two kinds of Nazirites may be distinguished, (1) those who like Samson were bound for life by certain obligations assumed by themselves or their parents; or (2) those who for a limited period assumed the Nazirite vow. The second appear to have been by far the most common. The law of Nu. 6 contemplates only the latter type. In later Jewish history the Nazirite vow is very common, but is taken only for a specified time, cf. the Jewish tractat, *Nazir*, I Mac. 3⁴⁹, ⁵⁰, Jos. Ant. xix, 6¹. From the Samson stories and the earliest references it would seem that the abstinence from cutting the hair was the oldest and most characteristic element in the Nazirite vow, cf. for the widespread reverence for the hair, Frazer, *Golden Bough*,² I, 362–89. The other elements may have been added later. The refraining from wine and grapes and all the products of the vine may well be due to the aversion, long felt by the more zealous worshippers of Jehovah, the God of their nomadic ancestors, for the agricultural civilization of the Canaanites. The Nabateans were not allowed to sow or to set out fruit-bearing plants or to build houses or to use wine, cf. Diod. Sic. xix, 94³. Similar restrictions were laid upon the Recabites, who appear to have cherished the older nomadic ideals, Jer. 35⁶, ⁷. Amos classifies the Nazirites with the prophets, as sent by Jehovah to teach his people, Am. 2¹¹, ¹². Self-denial and devotion to Jehovah are the two central ideas inherent in the ancient institution. For the somewhat similar regulations concerning the priests, cf. §§ 164, 170. The basis of the law regarding the Nazirite is evidently an early priestly direction which has many points of kinship with the Holiness Code.

[q] Nu. 6⁴ RV, *from the kernels even to the husk*. The Heb. words occur nowhere else in the O.T. and the exact meaning is uncertain.

Priestly Codes

To leave hair un-cut

⁵All the days of his vow of separation no razor shall pass over his head;ʳ until the completion of the days which he separated himself to Jehovah, he shall be holy; he shall let the locks of the hair on his head grow long.

Not to touch the dead

⁶All the days that he separateth himself to Jehovah he shall not come near a dead body. ⁷He shall not make himself unclean for his father or his mother, for his brother or his sister, when they die, because his separation to God is upon his head. ⁸All the days of his separation he is holy to Jehovah.

Procedure if accidentally defiled

⁹And if any man die very suddenly beside him, and he defile the head thus separated, the Nazirite shall shave his head on the day of his cleansing, on the seventh day shall he shave it.ˢ ¹⁰And on the eighth day he shall bring two turtle-doves or two young pigeons, to the priest, at the entrance of the tent of meeting: ¹¹and the priest shall offer one as a sin-offering, and the other as a burnt-offering, and make atonement for him, for he hath sinned by coming into contact with the dead; thus he shall hallow his head that same day. ¹²And he shall separate to Jehovah the days of his separation,ᵗ and shall bring a male lamb a year old as a trespass-offering; but the preceding days shall not count, because his separation was defiled.'

F

THE LAW OF CIRCUMCISION

§ 186. Origin and Requirements, Gen. 17⁹⁻¹⁴, 21⁴, Lev. 12³, Ex. 12⁴⁸

Priestly Codes

Divine command to the race

Gen. 17 ⁹God said to Abraham, As for thee, thou shalt keep my covenant, thou, and thy descendants after thee throughout their generations.

ʳ Nu. 6⁵ *I. e.*, shall not even be trimmed, cf. Judg. 13⁵, 16¹⁷, I Sam. 1¹¹.
ˢ Nu. 6⁹ According to the Mishna, *Temurah*, vii, 4, the hair thus cut off was to be buried, because unclean.
ᵗ Nu. 6¹² *I. e.*, he shall observe his vow the full time originally agreed upon.
§ 186 The rite of circumcision was generally in force among western Semites. Herodotus asserts that they adopted it from the Egyptians, II, 36, 204. An intuitional appreciation of its hygienic importance, especially in hot tropical countries, may lie at the root of the institution, but more probably it is a survival from the phallic worship that was widely extended in antiquity and still survives in portions of the far East to-day. It is certainly safe to say that circumcision was originally regarded as a religious rite.
The peculiar story in Ex. 4²⁴⁻²⁶ connects the institution with Moses. It is his Kenite wife, however, who circumcised their son to deliver Moses from the wrath of Jehovah. The implication is that the custom was already in vogue among the Kenites. The priestly traditions represent it as revealed to Abraham and imposed upon all his descendants as a symbol of cleansing and consecration to Jehovah, and of the sacred covenant between God and his people. Closely connected with its religious origin was its early significance as a tribal and national mark. This meaning of the rite was strongly emphasized as distinctive by later Judaism, although the term *uncircumcised Philistines* implies the recognition by the biblical writers of the fact that, with this exception, the other peoples of Palestine, as well as the Hebrews, practiced circumcision.
The expression *bridegroom of blood* in Ex. 4²⁵ and the tradition in Josh. 5². ³, ⁸, ⁹ suggest that with the Israelites in the earlier periods, as among the ancient Arabs, circumcision did not take place until adolescence or young manhood was reached. It was then the symbol of the admission of a youth to full marital, tribal, and religious rights. Only in later periods was it transferred to infancy, perhaps that the child from its earliest years might thus be placed

Priestly Codes

[10]This is my covenant, which ye shall keep, between me and you and thy descendants after thee : every male among you shall be circumcised. [11]Whenever ye are circumcised, the flesh of your foreskin shall be a sign of a covenant between me and you. [12]And every male when he is eight days old, shall be circumcised throughout your generations, he who is born in the house, or bought with money of any foreigner who is not of thine offspring. [13]He who is born in thy house and he who is bought with thy money must surely be circumcised. Thus my covenant shall be in your flesh for an everlasting covenant. [14]As for the uncircumcised male, who is not circumcised in the flesh of his foreskin, that one shall be cut off from among his people; he hath broken my covenant.

21 [4]So Abraham circumcised his son Isaac, when he was seven days old, as God had commanded him. Traditional precedent

Lev. 12 [3]On the eighth day the flesh of the foreskin shall be circumcised. Age

Ex. 12 [48]When an alien shall reside with thee, and wish to keep the passover to Jehovah, let all the male members of his family be circumcised, and then let him come near and keep it; and he shall be as a native born; but no uncircumcised person shall eat of it. Resident aliens

G

THE SACRED DUES

§ 187. **First-born Sons,** Ex. 34[19a, 20c], 22[19b], Ex. 13[1, 2], Nu. 3[11-13, 44-51] [8[16-18]]

Primitive Codes

Ex. 34 [19a]All that openeth the womb is mine.
[20c]All the first-born of thy sons shalt thou redeem.
22 [19b]The first-born of thy sons shalt thou give to me. Jehovah's due

under the protection of the Deity, or possibly because the later priests desired to break with the ideas and practices associated with the earlier usage. Cf. the varying usages in the rite of baptism. Thus transformed and interpreted, circumcision became finally the distinctive religious and racial mark of the Jew.

The Sacred Dues.—The fundamental idea of the theocracy can be traced to the beginnings of Israel's history. It developed as Heb. political institutions unfolded. Gifts to the divine head of the tribe and nation were presented from earliest times, as they were to the primitive tribal chieftain and later to the king. In the case of the human and Divine King the gifts were practically the same both in character and purpose. They were the evidences of loyalty and the surest means of securing and retaining royal favor. Only the best of everything would be accepted. In most cases this meant also the first. Certain dues must be regularly rendered by each man. Additional gifts might be brought as the desires or feelings or vows of the individual offerers dictated. Custom, as well as the influence of the priests, constantly tended to increase the volume of these sacred dues. In the earliest times they included little more than the offerings brought to the local sanctuaries at the three great festivals. The disappearance of the monarchy, with the destruction of Jerusalem in 586 B.C., left the people free to bring all their gifts to Jehovah. The strong desire of the exiles to win again the favor of Jehovah also tended to multiply the number of sacred dues, with the result that under the priestly laws a very large proportion of the income of every Israelite found its way in one form or other to the sanctuary.

§ 187 The first-born of family and herd and flock was universally believed to be the best. It was appropriate, therefore, that it should be given to Jehovah. Another illustration of the belief in the pre-eminence of the first-born is the law of primogeniture, cf. § 30.

Priestly Codes

Ex. 13 ¹Jehovah gave this command to Moses: ²Sanctify to me all the first-born, whatever openeth the womb among the Israelites, both of man and of beast; it is mine.

Levites a substitute

Nu. 3 ¹¹Jehovah spoke thus to Moses, ¹²I have taken the Levites from among the Israelites in the place of all the first-born that openeth the womb among the Israelites; ¹³for all the first-born are mine; on the day that I smote all the first-born in the land of Egypt I consecrated to myself all the first-born in Israel, both man and beast; mine they shall be: I am Jehovah.

⁴⁴Jehovah also gave this command to Moses: ⁴⁵Take the Levites in the place of all the first-born among the Israelites, and the cattle of the Levites in the place of their cattle; and the Levites shall be mine: I am Jehovah.

Supplemental Priestly Codes

Money-equivalent

Nu. 3 ⁴⁶And for the redemption of the two hundred and seventy-three of the first-born of the Israelites, who are over and above the number of the Levites, ⁴⁷thou shalt take five shekels[a] apiece according to the census; by the standard of the shekel of the sanctuary shalt thou take them (the shekel is twenty gerahs). ⁴⁸And thou shalt give the money, with which the odd number of them is redeemed, to Aaron and to his sons. ⁴⁹And Moses took the redemption-money from them who were over and above those who were redeemed by the Levites. ⁵⁰From the first-born of the Israelites he took the money, one thousand three hundred and sixty-five shekels, by the standard of the shekel of the sanctuary; ⁵¹and Moses gave the redemption-money to Aaron and to his sons, according to the word of Jehovah, as Jehovah commanded Moses.

§ 188. **First-born of Flock and Herd**, Ex. 34¹⁹ᵇ, ²⁰, 13¹¹⁻¹³ᵃ, 22³⁰,
Dt. 14²³⁻²⁷, 15¹⁹⁻²², Nu. 18¹⁵⁻¹⁸ [Lev. 27²⁶, ²⁷]

Primitive Code

Jehovah's due

Ex. 34 ¹⁹ᵇAll thy male cattle, the first-born of cow and sheep are mine. ²⁰And the firstling of an ass thou shalt redeem with a lamb; and if thou dost not wish to redeem it, then thou shalt break its neck.

13 ¹¹When Jehovah shall bring thee into the land of the Canaanites, as he promised by oath to thee and to thy fathers, and shall give it thee, ¹²thou shalt set apart[b] to Jehovah all that openeth the womb; of all the first offsprings of beasts, which thou shalt have, the males shall belong to Jehovah. ¹³ᵃAnd every first-born of an ass thou shalt redeem with a sheep; but if thou dost not wish to redeem it, then thou shalt break its neck.

22 ³⁰Thou shalt give[c] to me the first-born of thine oxen, and thy sheep; seven days shall it be with its dam; on the eighth day thou shalt give it me.

---

[a] Nu. 3⁴⁷ About three dollars or twelve shillings.
§ 188 This institution is firmly established in the earliest codes and dates from the nomadic period of Israel's history. The primitive Arabs also appear to have had it.
[b] Ex. 13¹² Lit., *cause to pass over.*
[c] Ex. 22³⁰ Heb., *Likewise shalt thou do.*

Deuteronomic Codes

Dt. 14 ²³Before Jehovah thy God, in the place in which he shall choose to have his name dwell, thou shalt eat the tithe of thy grain, of thy new wine, and of thine oil, and the first-born of thy herd and of thy flock, that thou mayest learn to fear Jehovah thy God always. ²⁴And if the way be too long for thee, so that thou art not able to carry it, because the place, where Jehovah thy God shall choose to set his name, is too far from thee; when Jehovah thy God shall bless thee, ²⁵thou shalt exchange thy offering for money, and shalt bind up the money in thy hand, and shalt go to the place which Jehovah thy God shall choose; ²⁶and thou shalt spend the money for whatever thou desireth, for oxen, or for sheep, or for wine, or for strong drink, or for whatever thine appetite craveth; and thou shalt eat there before Jehovah thy God, and thou shalt rejoice, together with thy household. ²⁷Thou shalt not forsake the Levite who is within thy city, for he hath no portion nor inheritance with thee. *(margin: Presentation at the sanctuary)*

15 ¹⁹All the first-born males of thy herd and of thy flock thou shalt consecrate to Jehovah thy God; thou shalt do no work with the first-born of thy herd, nor shear the first-born of thy flock. ²⁰Thou, together with thy household, shalt eat it before Jehovah thy God year by year in the place which Jehovah shall choose. ²¹And if it have any blemish, such as lameness or blindness or any evil blemish whatever, thou shalt not sacrifice it to Jehovah thy God. ²²Thou shalt eat it within thy gates; the unclean and the clean shall eat it alike, as the gazelle, and as the hart. *(margin: Only perfect animals acceptable)*

Priestly Codes

Nu. 18 ¹⁵Everything that openeth the womb, of all flesh which they offer to Jehovah, both of man and beast shall be thine; only for the first-born of man thou shalt receive a ransom, and for the first-born of unclean beasts thou shalt receive a ransom. ¹⁶At a month old thou shalt receive its ransom price according to thy valuation, the sum of five shekels, after the shekel of the sanctuary, which contains twenty gerahs. ¹⁷But for the first-born of a cow, or the first-born of a sheep, or the first-born of a goat, thou shalt not receive a ransom; they are holy; thou shalt dash their blood upon the altar, and shalt burn their fat as an offering made by fire as an odor pleasing to Jehovah. ¹⁸Their flesh shall be thine; like the wave-breast and the right thigh, it shall be thine. *(margin: Only unclean animals to be redeemed)*

§ 189. **Firstfruits**, Ex. 34²⁶ᵃ [23¹⁹ᵃ], Dt. 18⁴, 26¹⁻¹¹, Lev. 19²⁴, 23¹⁰, ¹¹, Nu. 15¹⁷⁻²¹, Lev. 2¹⁴⁻¹⁶

Primitive Codes

Ex. 34 ²⁶ᵃThe first of the firstfruits of thy ground thou shalt bring to the house of Jehovah thy God. *(margin: Presentation)*

---

§ 189 It was natural that as the Hebrews passed over to the agricultural stage, they should also bring to Jehovah the first products of the field, as well as of the herd and flock. Among the Canaanites this institution was probably in force long before the Hebrews appeared in Palestine. With the Babylonians vegetable offerings were in the preponderance. The formula of Dt. 26, to be used when the firstfruits were presented, is in perfect keeping with the religious and didactic aims of the Deuteronomic lawgivers.

Deuteronomic Codes

Method and ritual of presentation

Dt. 18 ⁴The firstfruits of thy grain, of thy new wine, and of thine oil, and the first of the fleece of thy sheep, shalt thou give to Jehovah.

26 ¹When thou shalt come into the land which Jehovah thy God is about to give thee as an inheritance, and shalt possess it, and dwell therein, ²thou shalt take a part of the first of all the fruit of the ground, which thou shalt bring in from thy land that Jehovah thy God giveth thee; and thou shalt put it in a basket, and shalt go to the place in which Jehovah thy God shall choose to have his name dwell. ³And thou shalt come to the priest who shall be officiating in those days, and say to him, I declare this day to Jehovah thy God, that I have come to the land which Jehovah promised by oath to our fathers to give to us. ⁴Then the priest shall take the basket out of thy hand, and set it down before the altar of Jehovah thy God. ⁵And thou shalt speak out and say before Jehovah thy God, An Aramean[d] ready to perish was my father; and he went down into Egypt, and resided there as an alien, few in number; and he became there a nation, great, mighty, and populous. ⁶And the Egyptians dealt evilly with us, and afflicted us, and laid upon us hard bondage. ⁷Then we cried to Jehovah, the God of our fathers, and Jehovah heard our cry, and saw our affliction, and our toil, and our oppression; ⁸and Jehovah brought us forth from Egypt with a strong hand, and with an outstretched arm, and with great terrors, and with signs, and with wonders; ⁹and he hath brought us into this place, and hath given us this land, a land abounding in milk and honey. ¹⁰Now, therefore, I have brought the first of the fruit of the ground, which thou, O Jehovah, hast given me. And thou shalt set it down before Jehovah thy God; ¹¹and thou shalt rejoice in all the good which Jehovah thy God hath given to thee and to thy household, together with the Levite and the alien who resideth in thy midst.

Holiness Code

Fruit of trees

Lev. 19 ²⁴On the fourth year all the fruit of a young tree shall be holy, a praise-offering to Jehovah.

First sheaf

23 ¹⁰Speak to the Israelites and say to them, When ye come into the land which I am about to give to you, and reap its harvest, ye shall bring the sheaf of the firstfruits of your harvest to the priest, ¹¹and he shall wave the sheaf before Jehovah that ye may be accepted; on the day following the sabbath the priest shall wave it.

Priestly Codes

First of the dough

Nu. 15 ¹⁷Jehovah gave this command to Moses: ¹⁸Speak to the Israelites and say to them, ' When ye come into the land to which I am about to bring you, ¹⁹and when ye eat of the bread of the land, ye shall offer up a special offering to Jehovah. ²⁰Of the first of your dough ye shall offer up a cake as a special offering; like the special offering from the threshing-floor, shall ye offer it.

---

d Dt. 26⁵ *I. e., Jacob,* cf. Gen. 24¹⁰, ²⁴.

Priestly Codes

²¹Of the first of your dough ye shall give to Jehovah a special offering throughout your generations.'ᵉ

Supplementary Priestly Codes

Lev. 2 ¹⁴If thou offer a cereal-offering of firstfruits to Jehovah, thou shalt offer for the cereal-offering of thy firstfruits fresh grain in the ear, parched with fire and crushed. ¹⁵And thou shalt put oil on it, and lay frankincense on it; it is a cereal-offering. ¹⁶And as a memorial of it the priest shall burn part of the crushed grain and part of the oil, with all the frankincense; it is an offering made by fire to Jehovah.

Pres-
enta-
tion of
first of
grain

§ 190. Tithes, Dt. 14²²⁻²⁷, 26¹²⁻¹⁵, Nu. 18²⁵⁻³², Lev. 27³⁰⁻³³

Deuteronomic Codes

Dt. 14 ²²Of all the produce of thy seed thou shalt take a tenth of all that groweth in the field each year, ²³and before Jehovah thy God, in the place in which he shall choose, to have his name dwell, thou shalt eat the tithe of thy grain, of thy new wine, and of thine oil, and the first-born of thy herd and of thy flock, that thou mayest learn to fear Jehovah thy God always. ²⁴And if the way be too long for thee, so that thou art not able to carry it, because the place which Jehovah thy God shall choose to set his name, is too far from thee; when Jehovah thy God shall bless thee, ²⁵thou shalt exchange thy offering for money, and shalt bind up the money in thy hand, and shalt go to the place which Jehovah thy God shall choose; ²⁶and thou shalt spend the money for whatever thou desireth, for oxen, or for sheep, or for wine, or for strong drink, or for whatever thine appetite craveth; and thou shalt eat there before Jehovah thy God, and thou shalt rejoice together with thy household. ²⁷Also thou shalt not forget the Levite who dwelleth within thy town, for he hath no portion nor inheritance with thee.

Pres-
enta-
tion of
the reg-
ular
tithes

26 ¹²When thou hast made an end of tithing all the tithe of thy produce in the third year, which is the year of tithing, then thou shalt give it to the Levite, to the resident alien, to the fatherless, and to the widow, that they

Trien-
nial
tithe
for the
needy

ᵉ Nu. 15¹⁸ᵇ⁻²¹ This passage appears to have been taken from an earlier collection of priestly directions.

§ 190 The tithe, as a rate of taxation, was known among many early peoples, including the Babylonians (Jastrow, *Relig. of Babs. and Assyrs.*, 668), the Egyptians (Maspero, *Struggle of the Nats.*, 312), Sabeans (Plin. *NH.* 12⁶³), Carthagenians (Diod. Sic. 20¹⁴) and Syrians (I Mac. 10³¹, 11³⁵). From I Sam. 8¹⁵, ¹⁷ it appears that a tithe of the product of the fields and vineyards and flocks was also levied as a tax by Solomon or later Israelitish kings. There is no trace, however, of the sacred tithe in the oldest Heb. codes. It appears first in Northern Israel in the days of Amos, 4⁴; but the law of Dt. 14²²⁻²⁷ suggests that in the days of Josiah the institution had long been established.

In the Deuteronomic codes the tithe is only levied on the products of the field and olive and vineyard. Two out of every three years it or the equivalent was consumed by the individual offerer and his family and dependents at the central sanctuary; on the third year it was distributed among the needy in the community. Since this law is bound up with that of the sabbatical year, it would appear that only three out of every cycle of seven years was the special tithe thus set aside for the needy. From the first Jehovah's special part in the tithe doubtless went to the Levitical priests. As has already been noted, § 160, until the days of Nehemiah, however, their income was very uncertain, cf. Neh. 13¹⁰⁻¹³. In the priestly codes all the tithe goes to the Levites. The supplemental priestly passage, Lev. 27 also adds the tithe of the herd and flock, *i. e.*, of the increase of each year. As interpreted by the Rabbis this went to the priests, cf. Tobit 1, Jubilees, 32¹⁵.

Dt. 26^{12}]   THE SACRED DUES

Deuteronomic Codes

may eat within thy city, and be filled. ¹³And thou shalt say before Jehovah thy God, I have put away the consecrated things out of my house, and have also given them to the Levite, and to the resident alien, to the fatherless and to the widow, just as thou hast commanded me; I have not transgressed any of thy commands, neither have I forgotten them : ¹⁴I have not eaten it in my mourning,ᶠ neither have I put away any of it, while I was unclean, nor given of it for the dead;ᵍ I have hearkened to the voice of Jehovah my God; I have done just as thou hast commanded me. ¹⁵Look down from thy holy habitation, from heaven, and bless thy people Israel, and the ground which thou hast given us, as thou promised by oath to our fathers, a land abounding in milk and honey.

Priestly Codes

Tithe of the tithe for the priests

Nu. 18 ²⁵Jehovah gave this command to Moses, ²⁶Thou shalt speak to the Levites, and say to them, 'When ye take from the Israelites the tithe which I have granted you from them as your inheritance, ye shall make a contribution from it to Jehovah, a tithe of the tithe. ²⁷And your contribution shall be accredited to you, as though it were the grain of the threshing-floor, and as the full produce of the winepress. ²⁸Thus ye also shall make a contribution to Jehovah of all your tithes which ye receive of the Israelites; and out of themʰ ye shall give Jehovah's full contribution to Aaron the priest. ²⁹Out of all your gifts ye shall make the full contribution due to Jehovah, even the consecrated parts of these gifts, selecting it from the best of them.' ³⁰Therefore say to them, 'When ye have contributed from your gifts the best of them, the rest shall be reckoned to the Levites as the produce of the threshing-floor and of the winepress. ³¹And ye may eat it anywhere, ye and your families; for it is your reward in return for your service in the tent of meeting. ³²When ye have contributed the best of your tithes, ye shall incur no guilt on account of it; and ye shall not profane the holy things of the Israelites, lest ye die.'

Supplemental Priestly Codes

Tithe of the herd and flock

Lev. 27 ³⁰All the tithe of the land, whether the seed of the land, or of the fruit of the tree, belongeth to Jehovah; it is holy to Jehovah. ³¹And if a man wish to redeem any of his tithe, he shall add to it the fifth part of it. ³²And all the tithe of the herd or the flock, the tenth of whatever passeth under the rod,ⁱ shall be holy to Jehovah. ³³The owner shall not look to see whether it is good or bad, nor shall he change it; and if he change it, both it and that for which it is changed shall be holy; it may not be redeemed.

ᶠ Dt. 26¹⁴ *I. e.*, while ceremonially unclean.
ᵍ Dt. 26¹⁴ Probably referring to the custom of sending gifts of food to the relatives and friends of the dead, cf. II Sam. 3³⁵, Jer. 16⁷, Ezek. 24¹⁷. Possibly the allusion is to the practice of putting food on the grave, cf. Tobit 4¹⁸.
ʰ Nu. 18²⁸ *I. e.*, the tithes.
ⁱ Lev. 27³² *I. e.*, is counted.

§ 191. Poll Tax, Ex. 30$^{11-16}$

Supplemental Priestly Codes

Ex. 30 ^{11}Jehovah gave this command to Moses: ^{12}When thou takest the census of the Israelites according to their numbering, they shall give each a ransom for his life to Jehovah, when thou numberest them, that no plague come upon them. ^{13}This is the sum that each shall give who passeth over to those who are numbered, half a shekel according to the standard of the sanctuary^j (the shekel is twenty gerahs); half a shekel as an offering to Jehovah. ^{14}Every one who passeth over to those who are numbered, from twenty years old and upward,^{k} shall present the offering of Jehovah. ^{15}The rich shall not give more, and the poor shall not give less than the half shekel when they present the offering of Jehovah to make atonement for your lives. ^{16}And thou shalt take the atonement money from the Israelites and shall give it for the service of the tent of meeting that it may be a memorial before Jehovah in behalf of the Israelites, to make atonement for their^l lives.

To be paid by every adult male

§ 192. **Voluntary Offerings,** Ex. 34^{20c}, 22^{29a}, Dt. 16$^{10, 16, 17}$ [12$^{5-8}$], Lev. 22$^{17-20}$

Primitive Codes

Ex. 34 ^{20c}None shall appear before me empty-handed.
Ex. 22 ^{29a}Thou shalt not delay to offer of thy harvest, and of the outflow of thy presses.

Required of all

Deuteronomic Codes

Dt. 16 ^{10}Thou shalt keep the feast of weeks to Jehovah thy God according to the measure of the voluntary offering which thy hands shall present, in proportion as Jehovah thy God blesseth thee. ^{16}Three times in a year shall all thy males appear before Jehovah thy God in the place which he shall choose: at the feast of unleavened bread, and at the feast of weeks, and at the feast of tabernacles; and they shall not appear before Jehovah empty-handed; ^{17}every man shall give as he is able, according to the individual gift with which Jehovah thy God hath blessed thee.

To be presented at the annual feasts

Holiness Code

Lev. 22 ^{17}Jehovah gave this command to Moses: ^{18}Speak to Aaron, and to his sons, and to all the Israelites, and say to them, 'If any man of the house of

Only perfect animals acceptable

---

§ 191 According to Neh. 10^{33} the annual temple tax consisted of one-third of a shekel. The present law evidently comes from a period later than the great reformation of 400 B.C. This poll tax, about thirty-three cents, in the subsequent period was faithfully paid by all loyal Jews, and brought into the temple a very large income.
^{j} Ex. 30^{13} *I. e.*, full weight, not depreciated, as were most of the current coins of Palestine.
^{k} Ex. 30^{14} Cf. § 34.
^{l} Ex. 30^{16} Heb., *your.*
§ 192 Voluntary gifts, depending upon the prosperity and generosity of the individual giver, constituted the chief offerings presented at the pre-exilic sanctuaries. After the exile the required offerings were greatly increased, but the zeal of the worshippers also increased, so that many voluntary gifts were doubtless still brought to the sanctuary.

Holiness Code

Israel, or of the aliens residing in Israel, bring his offering, whether it be any of the vows, or any of the voluntary offerings, which are brought to Jehovah as a burnt-offering; ¹⁹in order that ye may be accepted, ye shall offer a male without blemish, of the bullocks, of the sheep, or of the goats. ²⁰But whatever hath a blemish ye shall not offer, for it will not be accepted for you.'

§ 193. Things Vowed or Devoted, Dt. 23²¹⁻²³, ¹⁸, 12²⁶, Nu. 30, 6¹³⁻²¹, Lev. 27¹⁻²⁹

Deuteronomic Codes

A vow made to be paid

Dt. 23 ²¹When thou vowest a vow to Jehovah thy God, thou shalt not delay to pay it; for Jehovah thy God will surely require it of thee and it will be sin on thy part. ²²But if thou refrain from making a vow, it shall be no sin on thy part. ²³That which thy lips have declared thou shalt faithfully do, according as thou hast vowed to Jehovah thy God, a voluntary offering, which thou hast promised by word of mouth. ¹⁸Thou shalt not bring the hire of a harlot, or the wages of such a dog, into the temple of Jehovah thy God for a vow; for both these are an abomination to Jehovah thy God.

Not with immoral gain

At the temple

12 ²⁶Thou shalt take the consecrated things which thou hast, and thy votive-offerings, and go to the place which Jehovah shall choose.

Supplemental Priestly Codes

A man's vow

Nu. 30 ¹Moses said to the heads of the tribes of the Israelites, This is the thing which Jehovah hath commanded : ²'When a man voweth a vow to Jehovah, or sweareth an oath to bind himself with a bond, he shall not break his word; he shall do just as he declared.

Vow made by an unmarried daughter

³Also when a woman maketh a vow to Jehovah and bindeth herself by a pledge, while she is still in her father's house, in her youth, ⁴and her father heareth her vow, and her pledge with which she hath bound herself, and her father say nothing to her; then all her vows shall be valid, and every pledge with which she hath bound herself shall be valid. ⁵But if her father express his disapproval of her on the day that he heareth, none of her vows, or of her pledges with which she hath bound herself, shall be valid; and Jehovah will forgive her, because her father expressed his disapproval of her.

By a wife

⁶And if she be married while her vows are upon her, or the rash utterance of her lips, with which she hath bound herself, ⁷and her husband hear it, and

§ 193 The widespread Semitic custom of making vows is assumed by these laws. The classic O.T. example of a vow are, (1) that of Jephthah, Judg. 11³⁰ᶠᶠ, according to which he promised if Jehovah would give him the victory over his foes, to sacrifice the first one who came to meet him on his return; and (2) Saul's similar vow, which would have cost the life of his valiant son Jonathan had not the people interfered, I Sam. 14²⁴⁻⁴⁵. The vow was of the nature of a contract between the individual and Jehovah and was all the more binding because the Deity was one of the parties to it. The present laws, however, no longer recognize human sacrifice, but provide an equivalent offering in case a man, for example, vows that he will give one of his children to Jehovah. The priest, as Jehovah's representative determines the valuation. Especially in the case of the poor, the danger of extortion was great as the law itself recognizes by making a special provision, Lev. 27⁸. The law regarding the redemption of persons and things vowed is very late, for it assumes the late regulation regarding the year of jubilee, but II Kgs. 12⁴ contains a reference to the custom which indicates that the institution was in vogue at an early date. The Marseilles Tablet also demonstrates that it was known to the Phœnicians and probably the ancient Canaanites, as well as to the Hebrews, cf. Appendix VIII.

Supplemental Priestly Codes

say nothing to her on the day that he heareth it; then her vows shall be valid, and her pledges with which she hath bound herself shall be valid. [8]But if her husband express his disapproval of her on the day that he heareth it, then he rendereth her vow invalid, and the rash utterance of her lips, with which she hath bound herself, and Jehovah will forgive her.

[9]But in the case of the vow of a widow, or of one who is divorced, everything with which she hath bound herself, shall be valid against her. [10]And if she vowed in her husband's house, or bound herself with a pledge by an oath, [11]and her husband heard it, and said nothing to her, and expressed no disapproval of her, then all her vows shall be valid, and every pledge with which she bound herself shall be valid. [12]But if her husband made them null and invalid, on the day that he heard them, then whatever she declared concerning her vows, or her pledge shall not be valid; her husband hath made them invalid, and Jehovah will forgive her. [13]Every vow, and every oath pledging some self-infliction, her husband may render valid or invalid. [14]But if her husband say nothing to her from day to day, then he rendereth all her vows, or all her pledges which rest upon her valid; he hath rendered them valid because he said nothing to her on the day that he heard them. [15]But if he render them null and invalid after he hath heard them, then he taketh her iniquity upon himself. [16]These are the statutes, which Jehovah commanded Moses, between a man and his wife, between a father and his daughter, while she is still a girl in her father's house.'

By a widow or divorced woman

Priestly Codes

Nu. 6 [13]This is the law of the Nazirite: When the days of his separation[m] are at an end he shall come[n] to the entrance of the tent of meeting. [14]And he shall offer as his gift to Jehovah, one yearling male lamb without blemish as a burnt-offering, and one ewe-lamb a year old without blemish as a sin-offering, and one ram without blemish as a peace-offering, [15]and a basket of unleavened bread, cakes of fine meal mixed with oil, and unleavened wafers anointed with oil, and their cereal-offering and libations.[o] [16]And the priest shall present them before Jehovah, and shall offer his sin-offering, and his burnt-offering; [17]and he shall sacrifice the ram as a peace-offering to Jehovah, together with the basket of unleavened bread; the priest shall also present its cereal-offering and its libation.

Nazirite's offering at end of his period

[18]Then the Nazirite shall shave his consecrated[p] head at the entrance of the tent of meeting, and shall take his consecrated[p] hair,[q] and put it on the fire which is under the sacrifice of peace-offering. [19]And the priest shall take the boiled shoulder of the ram, and one unleavened cake from the basket, and one unleavened wafer, and shall lay them on the hands of the Nazirite,

Ritual to be observed

---

[m] Nu. 6^{13} Or, *Naziriteship.*

[n] Nu. 6^{13} Through what must be a scribal error the Heb. reads, *he shall be brought.*

[o] Nu. 6^{15} According to Nu. 15^{4-6} these consisted of about three and one-half pints of fine meal and about seven pints of wine.

[p] Nu. 6^{18} Lit., *of his separation* or *Naziriteship.*

[q] Nu. 6^{18} The hair was regarded as sacred by many ancient peoples, and therefore suitable as a special offering.

Priestly Codes

after he hath shaved off the evidence of his separation.   ²⁰Then the priest shall wave them as a wave-offering before Jehovah; this is an holy gift for the priest, together with the wave-breast and the thigh of the contribution; after that the Nazirite may drink wine.

Résumé of his obligations   ²¹This is the law of the Nazirite who taketh a vow in regard to his gift to Jehovah in accordance with his separation, in addition to what he is able to offer; according to his vow which he voweth, so he must do in accordance with the law of his separation.

Supplemental Priestly Codes

Tariff for redemption of things vowed: individuals   **Lev. 27** ¹Jehovah gave this command to Moses: ²Speak to the Israelites, and say to them, 'When a man fulfilleth a vow to Jehovah which involveth thy valuation of persons, ³for a male between twenty and sixty years of age thy valuation shall be fifty shekels of silver, by the standard ʳ of the sanctuary.   ⁴And if it be a female, thy valuation shall be thirty shekels. ⁵And if it be between the age of five years and twenty years, thy valuation shall be for a male twenty shekels, and for a female ten shekels.   ⁶And if it be between the ages of one month and five years, thy valuation shall be for a male five shekels of silver, and for a female three shekels of silver.   ⁷And if it be for the age of sixty years and upward, thy valuation shall be for a male fifteen shekels, and for a female ten shekels.   ⁸But if the man be too poor to pay the valuation, the person vowed shall be placedˢ before the priest, and the priest shall value him; according to the means of him who made the vow shall the priest value him.

Animals   ⁹And if it be a beast, of a kind which may be offered to Jehovah, all that any man giveth of such to Jehovah shall be holy.   ¹⁰He shall not alter or exchange it, a good for a bad, or a bad for a good; and if he exchange beast for beast, then both it and that for which it is exchanged shall be holy.   ¹¹And if it be an unclean beast, of a kind which they do not offer to Jehovah, then he shall set the beast before the priest; ¹²and the priest shall value it, estimating how good or bad it is; as thou, the priest, valuest it, so shall it be. ¹³But if he wish to redeem it, he shall add the fifth part to thy valuation.

Houses   ¹⁴And when a man consecrateth his house to be holy to Jehovah, the priest shall value it, estimating how good or bad it is; as the priest valuest it, so shall it stand.   ¹⁵And if he who consecrated it wish to redeem his house, he shall add the fifth part of the money of thy valuation to it, and it shall be his.

Hereditary fields and growing crops   ¹⁶And if a man consecrate to Jehovah part of the field of his possession, thy valuation shall be in proportion to the seed sown upon it to the sowing thereof: if sown with a homer of barley it *shall be valued* at fifty shekels of silver.   ¹⁷If he consecrate his field from the year of jubilee, it shall stand according to thy valuation.   ¹⁸But if he consecrate his field after the jubilee, the priest shall reckon to him the money in proportion to the years that remain until the year of jubilee; and an abatement shall be made from thy

---

ʳ Lev. 27³ Lit., *shekel.*
ˢ Lev. 27⁸ Lit., *one shall set;* so also in ¹¹.

Supplemental Priestly Codes

valuation. ¹⁹And if he who consecrated the field wish to redeem it, then he shall add the fifth part of the money of thy valuation to it, and it shall be assured to him. ²⁰But if he will not redeem the field, or if he have sold the field to another man, it shall not be redeemed any more; ²¹but the field, when it is released in the jubilee, shall be holy to Jehovah, as a field devoted; it shall be the possession of the priest. ²²And if he consecrate to Jehovah a field which he hath bought, which is not one of the fields of his possession, ²³the priest shall reckon to him the amount of thy valuation until the year of jubilee; and he shall give thy valuation in that day, as a thing holy to Jehovah. ²⁴At the year of jubilee the field shall return to him of whom it was bought, even to him to whom the possession of the land belongeth. ²⁵And all thy valuations shall be according to the shekel of the sanctuary; twenty gerahs shall be the shekel.

²⁶Only the firstling of animals, which as such belongeth to Jehovah, no man shall consecrate whether it be ox or sheep, it is Jehovah's. ²⁷And if it be the firstling of an unclean beast, he shall ransom it according to thy valuation, and shall add to it the fifth part of it; or if it be not redeemed, then it shall be sold according to thy valuation. _{First-lings of clean and un-clean animals}

²⁸Nevertheless, no devoted thing, that a man may devote to Jehovah of all that he hath, whether of man or beast, or of the field of his possession, shall be sold or redeemed; every devoted thing is most holy to Jehovah. ²⁹None devoted, that shall be devoted from among men, shall be ransomed; he shall surely be put to death.' ᵗ _{Things devot-ed to Jeho-vah}

§ 194. Spoils of War, Nu. 31²⁵⁻³¹

Supplemental Priestly Codes

Nu. 31 ²⁵Jehovah commanded Moses, ²⁶Make an estimate of the booty that was taken, both of man and of beast, thou, and Eleazar the priest, and the heads of the fathers' houses of the congregation; ²⁷and divide the booty into two parts between the men skilled in war, who went out to battle, and all the congregation. ²⁸And levy a contribution for Jehovah upon the warriors who went out to battle: one in five hundred, of the persons, and of the oxen, and of the asses, and of the flocks; ²⁹take it from their half, and give it to Eleazar the priest, as a special contribution to Jehovah. ³⁰And from the Israelites' half thou shalt take one drawn out of every fifty, of the persons, of the oxen, of the asses, of the flocks, *even* of all the cattle, and give them to the Levites, who have charge of the dwelling of Jehovah. ³¹And Moses and Eleazar the priest did as Jehovah commanded Moses. _{Part due Je-hovah}

ᵗ Lev. 27²⁹ This law doubtless refers to heathen captives or idolaters placed under the ban, cf. §§ 58–60.
§ 194 This late traditional precedent represents one of the many ways in which later Judaism sought to secure for the temple and its officials a definite and generous income. From the earliest times a part of the spoils of war were doubtless dedicated to the Deity, cf. *e. g.*, Josh. 7. The Moslem law enacts that one-fifth of the spoil belongs to God, Kor. 8⁴².

H

SACRIFICIAL OFFERINGS

§ 195. Animals Suitable for Sacrifice, Dt. 15²¹, 17¹, Lev. 22¹⁸ᵇ⁻²⁷ [12ᵇ, ³]

Deuteronomic Codes

Only
perfect
animals

Dt. 15 ²¹If an animal have any blemish, such as lameness or blindness or any evil blemish whatever, thou shalt not sacrifice it to Jehovah thy God.

17 ¹Thou shalt not sacrifice to Jehovah thy God an ox, or a sheep, in which is a blemish or anything evil, for that is an abomination to Jehovah thy God.

Holiness Code

De-
tailed
specifi-
cations

Lev. 22 ¹⁸ᵇIf any man of the house of Israel or of the aliens residing in Israel bring his offering, whether it be any of the vows or voluntary offerings

Sacrificial Offerings.—The prophetic tradition in the story of Cain and Abel traces the institution of sacrifice back to the beginnings of human history. The earliest Bab. inscriptions contain frequent references to both animal and vegetable sacrifices. The Babylonians believed that the institution originated with the creation of the world. Thousands of years before the beginnings of Hebrew history the usages and laws of sacrifice had been developed, subject to local modifications. Most of the sacrificial terms employed in the O.T. had long been in use among the Babylonians. Like prayer and song, sacrifice in antiquity was almost universally regarded as a necessary element in all religious worship. Perhaps the original, and certainly in the O.T. the prevailing idea of sacrifice is that of a gift or tribute to the Deity. Thus the oldest common designation of a sacrificial offering, *minḥah*, was also employed to describe a gift proffered to a friend or a chieftain or an offended brother (as when Jacob returned to his brother Esau, Gen. 32¹³, ¹⁸). In the ritual the *minḥah* included animal as well as other sacrificial offerings. The corresponding late priestly term, *korban*, gift or present, has a similar broad content. The laws and literature of sacrifice reflect the idea of the primitive age when the prevailing conceptions of the gods were exceedingly anthromorphic. Since early man was, like the normal small boy, usually possessed of a strongly developed appetite, it was inevitable that he should regard food as the gift most suitable and acceptable to his god. In the Bab. literature this idea is clearly and frequently expressed. In the Bab. account of creation the gods are represented as feasting and drinking together, cf. Vol. I, p. 366. Elsewhere we are told that the *glorious gods smell the incense, the noble food of heaven, they enjoy the pure wine which no hand hath touched*, 4 R. 19⁵⁴, or again we find the parallel expressions, *eat the food, accept his sacrifice*, 4 R. 17⁵⁶.

As man's conceptions of the Deity became more spiritualized, he recognized that the god could not, as a human being, partake of the offerings brought to him; accordingly the parts set aside for the Deity were consumed by fire that he might *smell the pleasant odor*, even as when Noah sacrificed to Jehovah, Gen. 8²¹. At other times, Jehovah's portion was consumed by his representatives, the priests. In the case of animal sacrifices the most sacred part, the blood that represents the life, cf. note § 173, was poured out upon the ground or dashed against the altar that it might thus be presented to the Deity.

It was natural that out of the belief that the Deity was pleased with gifts of food should grow the kindred conception of sacrifice as a sacrificial meal. Even in the later priestly ritual an ordinary sacrifice had all the ordinary accessories of the usual Heb. meal: the meat, cakes of meal mixed with olive oil, and a measure of wine. Judg. 6¹⁹ contains one of the most striking of the many illustrations of this popular belief, for it states that when the Messenger of Jehovah came to him, *Gideon went in and prepared a kid, and unleavened cakes from an ephah of flour; he put the broth in a pot, and brought it out to the divine Messenger.* The tradition adds that after this meal had been laid out on the rock, and the broth had been poured out, the divine Messenger touched with his staff the food thus prepared, and a fire went up from the rock and consumed the food.

The early narrative in I Sam. 9 and the sacrificial laws in Dt. give vivid pictures of the pre-exilic sacrificial meals at the local shrines and later at the central sanctuary in Jerusalem. Amid great rejoicing they shared their sacrificial offerings with their Divine Host, their families, and the needy in the community. Each individual offerer slew and prepared his own sacrificial animal. As has already been noted, Introd., p. 43, the exile changed these feasts to fasts; the performance of the sacrificial offering also passed largely from the hands of the individual offerer to the priests, as the ritual became more elaborate and was more carefully guarded from all ceremonial defilement. The chief aim of sacrifice ceased to be praise and homage, and it came to represent more and more the effort of the individual and community to appease Jehovah's wrath and secure and retain his favor.

Holiness Code

which are brought to Jehovah as a burnt-offering, ^{19}in order that ye may be accepted, ye shall offer a male without blemish, of the bullocks, of the sheep, or of the goats. ^{20}But ye shall not offer anything that hath a blemish, for it will not be accepted for you. ^{21}Whoever bringeth a sacrifice of peace-offerings to Jehovah as a votive-offering[a] or as a voluntary offering from the herd or the flock, it must be perfect to be accepted; there must be no blemish in it. ^{22}Animals that are blind, or broken, or maimed, or that have running sores, or scurvy or are scabbed, ye shall not offer to Jehovah, nor make of them an offering by fire on the altar to Jehovah. ^{23}A bullock or a lamb, however, which hath any part too long or too short,[b] thou mayest offer as a voluntary offering, but it will not be accepted as a votive-offering. ^{24}Ye shall not offer to Jehovah that which hath the testicles bruised, or crushed, or torn off, or cut off; ye shall not sacrifice such animals in your land;[c] ^{25}nor shall ye offer any of these from the hand of a foreigner as food for your God; because they are corrupt, there is a blemish in them,[d] they will not be accepted for you.

^{26}Jehovah gave this command to Moses: ^{27}When a bullock, or a sheep, or a goat, is born, it shall be seven days with its mother; and from the eighth day and after it may be accepted as a gift, an offering made by fire to Jehovah. *Age of victim*

I

THE DIFFERENT FORMS OF OFFERINGS

§ 196. **Ordinary Animal Sacrifice** (*Zĕbhăch*), Ex. 10$^{24, 25}$, 18^{12}, Dt. 12^{11}, Lev. 3^{1-7a}

Primitive Codes

Ex. 10 ^{24}Pharaoh summoned Moses, and said, Go ye, worship Jehovah; only let your flocks and your herds remain behind; let your little ones also go with you. ^{25}But Moses said, Thou must also give into our hand sacrifices and burnt-offerings, that we may sacrifice to Jehovah our God. *Early precedents*

18 ^{12}Jethro, Moses' father-in-law, took a burnt-offering and sacrifices for God, and Aaron came with all the elders of Israel to eat with Moses' father-in-law before God.

---

[a] Lev. 22^{21} Lit., *to fulfil a special vow.*
[b] Lev. 22^{23} Or, *superfluous* or *lacking.*
[c] Lev. 22^{24} Lit., *and in your land ye shall not do, i. e.*, sacrifice. Jos. interprets, *nor shall ye do thus, i. e.*, practice any of these four methods of castrating animals. The former rendering does better justice to the text.
[d] Lev. 22^{25} Lit., *their corruption is in them.*
Different Forms of Offerings.—At least five distinct forms of sacrificial offerings can be distinguished in the earliest periods of Israel's history. The form chosen depended upon the occasion, the object of the offering, and to a great extent at first upon the feeling of the individual offerer. In the later ritual, however, the form of the sacrifice was definitely prescribed. Several of the earlier independent offerings were combined; thus the bloody sacrifices assumed the central place, and the cereal-offerings and the libations were required simply as accessories.
§ 196 By far the most common form of sacrifice both in the earlier and later periods was the ordinary private animal sacrifice in which the victim was killed by the offerer at the sanctuary. Probably before, as after the exile, the priest dashed its blood against the altar and burnt the fat upon the altar, as Jehovah's portion. A part went to the officiating priest in return for his services and the rest was consumed by the offerer, his family, friends, and dependents in the temple courts.

Deuteronomic Codes

To be
pre-
sented
at the
temple
Dt. 12 ¹¹At the place in which Jehovah your God shall choose to have his name dwell, thither shall ye bring all that I command you : your burnt-offerings, and your sacrifices, your tithes, and the individual contributions of your hand,ᵉ and your choice vows which ye vow to Jehovah.

Priestly Codes

Method
of pres-
enta-
tion
Lev. 3 ¹When a man's gift is a sacrifice of peace-offerings,ᶠ if he bring it from the herd, whether male or female, he shall offer one that is without blemish before Jehovah. ²He shall lay his hand on the head of his offering and kill it at the entrance of the tent of meeting; and Aaron's sons, the priests, shall dash the blood against the altar round about. ³Then he shall present from the sacrifice of peace-offerings an offering made by fire to Jehovah; the fat that covereth the entrails, and all the fat that is about the entrails, ⁴and the two kidneys, and the fat that is on them near the loins, and the fatty mass next to the liver, which mass he shall remove as far as the kidneys.ᵍ ⁵Aaron's sons, the priests,ʰ shall burnⁱ it on the altar over the burnt-offering, which is upon the wood that is on the fire; it is an offering made by fire of an odor pleasing to Jehovah.

⁶If his gift as a sacrifice of peace-offerings to Jehovah be from the flock, a male or a female, he shall offer it without blemish. ⁷ᵃIf he bring a lamb as his offering, he shall present it before Jehovah. ⁎

§ 197. **The Holocaust** (*Ôlâh*), Gen. 8²⁰, Ex. 20²⁴, Dt. 27⁶, 12¹¹, ²⁷ᵃ, Lev. 1³⁻¹⁷, 6⁸⁻¹³

Primitive Code

An
early
prece-
dent
Gen. 8 ²⁰Noah built an altar to Jehovah, and took of every clean beast and of every clean bird, and offered burnt-offerings on the altar.

On
many
altars
Ex. 20 ²⁴An altar of earth thou shalt make to me, and shalt sacrifice on it thy burnt-offerings, and thy peace-offerings, thy sheep, and thine oxen; in every place where I record my name I will come to thee and will bless thee.

Dt. 27 ⁶Thou shalt build the altar of Jehovah thy God of unhewn stones; and thou shalt offer burnt-offerings on it to Jehovah thy God.

Deuteronomic Codes

Only at
the
temple
Dt. 12 ¹¹At the place in which Jehovah your God shall choose to have his name dwell, thither shall ye bring all that I command you : your burnt-

---

ᵉ Dt. 12¹¹ Lit., *reserved portions of your hands.*
ᶠ Lev. 3¹ Or, *thank-offerings.* So vs. ⁶. The term denotes primarily a sacrifice in token of alliance or friendship. This law in 3¹⁻⁷ᵃ was probably found originally among the priestly directions.
ᵍ Lev. 3⁴ Or, *with the kidneys.*
ʰ Lev. 3⁵ So Gk. Heb. omits, *the priests.*
ⁱ Lev. 3⁵ Lit., *cause it to ascend in smoke.*
§ 197 The holocaust or whole burnt-offering goes back to the beginnings of Heb. history. The entire animal was consumed on the altar that it might thus be given entirely to Jehovah. In the priestly codes the victim itself appears to have been slain by the offerer; but in later practice it was left to the priests. The priestly laws also specify very definitely the ritual to be observed by them.

Deuteronomic Codes

offerings, your sacrifices, your tithes, your individual contributions, and all your choice vows which ye vow to Jehovah. 27[a]And thou shalt offer thy burnt-offerings, both the flesh and the blood, upon the altar of Jehovah thy God.

Priestly Codes

Ritual in offering animals from the herd

Lev. 1 3If his gift be a burnt-offering from the herd, he shall offer a male[j] without blemish; he shall present it at the entrance of the tent of meeting, that he may be accepted before Jehovah. 4He shall lay his hand on the head of the burnt-offering, and it shall be accepted in his behalf to make atonement for him. 5Then he[k] shall kill the bullock before Jehovah; and Aaron's sons, the priests, shall bring the blood, and dash the blood round about against the altar that is at the entrance of the tent of meeting. 6Then he shall flay the burnt-offering and cut it into pieces. 7And Aaron's sons, the priests,[l] shall put fire on the altar, and lay wood in order upon the fire; 8and Aaron's sons, the priests, shall lay the pieces, together with[m] the head and the suet, in order upon the wood that is on the fire which is upon the altar; 9but its entrails and its legs shall be washed[n] with water. Then the priest shall burn the whole on the altar; it is[o] a burnt-offering, an offering made by fire, of an odor pleasing to Jehovah.

From the flock

10If his gift be from the flock, a sheep or a goat[p] as a burnt-offering, he shall offer a male without blemish.[q] 11And he shall kill it on the north side of the altar before Jehovah; and Aaron's sons, the priests, shall dash its blood against the altar round about. 12Then he shall cut[r] it into pieces; and the priest[s] shall lay them together with the head and the suet in order on the wood that is on the fire which is upon the altar; 13but the entrails and the legs shall be washed with water. Then the priest shall offer the whole, and burn it upon the altar; it is a burnt-offering, an offering made by fire, of an odor pleasing to Jehovah.

Birds

14If his gift[t] to Jehovah be a bird[u] as a burnt-offering, he shall bring as his offering a turtle-dove or a young pigeon.[v] 15Then the priest shall bring it to the altar, and wring off its head, and burn it on the altar; its blood shall be drained out against the side of the altar; 16and he shall take away its crop with the feathers, and cast it into the ash-pit[w] on the east side of the altar. 17Then he shall cleave it at its wings, without wholly severing them; and the priest shall burn it on the altar

---

j Lev. 1[3] Heb., *offer it a male.* So in [10]. The law of Lev. 1 appears to come from the priestly directions and to have been adjusted to the groundwork.

k Lev. 1[5] Gk., *they shall kill;* so also in [11]. The Heb. may be rendered impersonally with the same meaning as the Gk., but the reading adopted accords with Arab. usage.

l Lev. 1[7] So Gk., Sam., and Syr. Heb., *priest.* It is possible that the priest alone figured in the original law and that *Aaron's sons* was added by a late editor.

m Lev. 1[8] So Gk., Sam., and Syr. Heb. omits, *together with.*

n Lev. 1[9] The Heb. has the transitive form. The Gk. and Sam. have the plural. The evidence for plural form is rather slight, and it seems unlikely that anyone but the priests should perform this service, so that the above rendering seems to be the original.

o Lev. 1[9] So Gk., Sam., and Syr. Heb. lacks, *it is.*

p Lev. 1[10] Lit., *of the sheep or of the goats.*

q Lev. 1[10] Gk. adds, *and he shall lay his hand on its head.*

r Lev. 1[12] Gk. and Syr. have the verb in plural.

s Lev. 1[12] Gk., *the priests.*

t Lev. 1[14-17] A later supplement, as the title in [2] implies.

u Lev. 1[14] Heb., *of birds.*

v Lev. 1[14] Heb., *of turtle-doves or of young pigeons.*

w Lev. 1[16] So Gk., Sam., and Vulg. The Heb. does not justify the translation, *filth,* as in RV. By a slight correction the above reading is restored.

Deuteronomic Codes

on the wood that is upon the fire; it is a burnt-offering, an offering made by fire, of an odor pleasing to Jehovah.

Rules regarding the daily burnt-offering

Lev. 6 ⁸Jehovah spoke thus to Moses, ⁹Command Aaron and his sons as follows: 'This is the law concerning the burnt-offering: The burnt-offering shall remain on the hearth upon the altar all night until the morning; and the fire of the altar shall be kept burning by means of it. ¹⁰The priest shall clothe himself in his linen garment,^x and put on his linen breeches; and he shall take up the ashes to which the fire hath consumed the burnt-offering on the altar, and he shall put them beside the altar. ¹¹Then he shall take off his garments, and put on other garments, and carry the ashes out of the camp to a clean place. ¹²The fire on the altar shall be kept burning by means of the burnt-offering, it shall not go out; the priest shall burn wood on it every morning; and he shall arrange the burnt-offering upon it, and shall burn on it the fat of the peace-offerings. ¹³Fire shall be kept burning on the altar continually; it shall not go out.'

§ 198. Cereal-offerings, Ex. 34^{25a} [23^{18a}], Nu. 15¹⁻¹⁶, Lev. 2^{1a, 2b-16} [6¹⁹⁻²³]

Primitive Codes

With animal sacrifices

Ex. 34 ^{25a}Thou shalt not offer the blood of my sacrifice with leavened bread.

Priestly Code

To accompany every animal-offering

Nu. 15 ¹Jehovah gave this command to Moses, ²Speak to the Israelites, and say to them, 'When ye come into the land of your dwellings, which I give you, ³and wish to make an offering made by fire to Jehovah, a burnt-offering, or a sacrifice, as a votive-offering^a or as a voluntary offering, or at your appointed seasons, to make an odor pleasing to Jehovah, from the herd or from the flock, ⁴then he who bringeth his offering shall present to Jehovah a cereal-offering of a tenth of an ephah of fine meal mixed with the fourth of a hin of oil; ⁵and as wine for the libation, the fourth of a hin shalt thou prepare with the burnt-offering or the sacrifice, for each lamb.^b ⁶Or for a ram, thou shalt prepare as a cereal-offering two-tenths of an ephah of fine meal mixed with a third of a hin of oil;^c ⁷for the libation thou shalt bring a third of a hin of wine, an odor pleasing to Jehovah. ⁸When thou preparest a bullock as a burnt-offering or as a sacrifice in fulfillment of a vow, or offered as any other form of peace-offerings^d to Jehovah, ⁹thou shalt^e offer with the bullock a

---

^x Lev. 6¹⁰ Syr., *garments.*

§ 198 Among the Babylonians the most common offerings were grain, fruit, and other products of the soil. In the earlier days these forms of offerings were also very common among the Hebs.; but in the priestly codes the cereal-offerings are only the necessary accompaniments of the animal sacrifices. Possibly they are assigned to this secondary place in the sacrificial system because grain was regarded as a product of the Canaanitish agricultural civilization, while animal sacrifices came from the flock and herd, and, therefore, were the gifts originally presented to Jehovah by the nomadic ancestors of the Hebs.

^a Nu. 15³ Lit., *to fulfil a special vow.*
^b Nu. 15⁵ The Gk. adds, *thou shalt do this as an offering of pleasant odor to Jehovah*
^c Nu. 15⁶ Gk. adds, *when ye offer it for a burnt-offering or for a sacrifice.*
^d Nu. 15⁸ Lit., *for peace-offerings.*
^e Nu. 15⁹ Heb., *he shall.*

Priestly Code

cereal-offering of three-tenths of an ephah of fine meal mixed with half a hin
of oil; ¹⁰thou shalt offer as the libation half a hin of wine, as an offering made
by fire, of an odor pleasing to Jehovah.[f]

¹¹So shall it be done for each bullock, or for each ram, or for each of the
male lambs, or of the kids. ¹²According to the number that ye shall prepare,
so shall ye do in the case of every one according to their number. ¹³All
who are native born shall do these things in this way, in offering an offering
made by fire, of an odor pleasing to Jehovah. ¹⁴If an alien reside among
you, or if any one else be among you throughout your generations, and wish
to present an offering made by fire, of an odor pleasing to Jehovah; as ye do,
so shall he do. ¹⁵ᵃThere shall be but one statute for the assembly,[g] both
for you and for the alien who resideth among you, a statute forever throughout your generations; ye and the resident alien shall both be alike before
Jehovah. ¹⁶There shall be one law and one regulation for you, and for the
alien who resideth among you.'

Binding upon Israelites and resident alien alike

Lev. 2 ¹ᵃIf anyone presenteth a cereal-offering as a gift to Jehovah, the
priest[h] shall take from it a handful of the fine meal and oil, with all the frankincense. ²ᵇThen as a memorial of it the priest shall burn it on the altar, an
offering made by fire of an odor pleasing to Jehovah. ³The remainder of
the cereal-offering shall belong to Aaron and his sons; it is a thing most holy,
being a part of the offerings made by fire to Jehovah.

Method of presentation

Supplemental Priestly Codes

Lev. 2 ⁴When thou bringest as a gift a cereal-offering baked in the oven,
it shall be in the form of unleavened cakes of fine meal mixed with oil, or
unleavened wafers smeared with oil. ⁵If thy gift be a cereal-offering baked
on a flat plate, it shall consist of fine meal unleavened, mixed with oil. ⁶Thou
shalt break it in pieces and pour oil on it; it is a cereal-offering. ⁷If thy gift
be a cereal-offering prepared in a sauce-pan, it shall be made of fine meal
with oil. ⁸Thou shalt bring the cereal-offering that is made in any of these
ways[i] to Jehovah; it shall be presented to the priest, and he shall bring it to
the altar. ⁹Then the priest shall take up part of the cereal-offering as a
memorial, and shall burn it on the altar, an offering made by fire, of an odor
pleasing to Jehovah. ¹⁰The remainder of the cereal-offering shall belong to
Aaron and his sons, as a thing most holy, being a part of the offerings made
by fire to Jehovah.

Additional directions

¹¹No cereal-offering, which ye shall offer to Jehovah, shall be made with
leaven; for ye shall offer[j] neither leaven nor honey as an offering made by
fire to Jehovah. ¹²As an offering of firstfruits ye shall bring them to Jehovah; but they shall not be burnt on the altar, to give forth a pleasant odor.[k]

Accessories cereal-offerings

---

[f] Nu. 15¹⁰ Most of this vs. is lacking in Gk.
[g] Nu. 15¹⁵ Cf. § 22, note ᵉ.
[h] Lev. 2² Heb., *he.* Cf. ⁹. The rest of the vs. as far as *frankincense* is perhaps a gloss.
[i] Lev. 2⁸ Or, *of these materials.*
[j] Lev. 2¹¹ So Gk., Sam., Syr., and Targ. Heb., *cause to ascend in smoke.*
[k] Lev. 2¹² Heb., *come up as a pleasant odor on the altar.*

Priestly Codes

hovah.ᵏ ³¹The priest shall burn the fat on the altar, but the breast shall belong to Aaron and his sons. ³²And the right thigh shall ye give to the priest as a contribution out of the peace-offerings which ye sacrifice.

§ 203. **Guilt-offerings,** Lev. 19²⁰⁻²², 5¹⁴⁻¹⁹, 6¹⁻⁷ [Nu. 5⁵⁻⁸], Lev. 7¹⁻⁷

Holiness Code

A moral offence

Lev. 19 ²⁰If any man lieth carnally with a woman, who is a slave, betrothed to another man, but who hath in nowise been redeemed nor given her freedom, there shall be a judicial inquiry, but they shall not be put to death, because she was not free.

Priestly Codes

Its expiation

Lev. 19 ²¹The man shall bring his guilt-offering to Jehovah, to the entrance of the tent of meeting, a ram as a guilt-offering; ²²and the priest shall make atonement for him with the ram of the guilt-offering before Jehovah for his sin which he hath committed; and the sin which he hath committed shall be forgiven him.

Of failure to meet the demands of the ritual

5 ¹⁴Jehovah spoke thus to Moses : ¹⁵If any one commit a treacherous act, and sin inadvertently with respect to the holy things of Jehovah,ˡ he shall bring from the flock as his guilt-offering to Jehovah, a ram without blemish, according to thy valuation, by the shekel of the sanctuary, as a guilt-offering; ¹⁶he shall also make restitution for his sin in connection with the holy thing, and shall add a fifth to the amount, and give it to the priest. Then the priest shall make atonement for him with the ram of the guilt-offering, and he shall be forgiven.

Expiation of any offence

¹⁷If any one sin,ᵐ by doing any of the things which Jehovah hath forbidden,ⁿ even without being aware of it, yet is he guilty and shall bear the consequences of his iniquity. ¹⁸He shall bring to the priest a ram without blemish out of the flock, according to thy valuation,ᵒ as a guilt-offering. Then the priest shall make atonement for him on account of the error which he hath inadvertently committed without being aware of it, and he shall be forgiven. ¹⁹It is a guilt-offering for he is guilty before Jehovah.

ᵏ Lev. 7³⁰ *I. e.,* swung toward the altar and back to symbolize the presentation of this portion of the offering to Jehovah, and his return of it to the priest. Later the term lost the original significance which seems to be found here.

§ 203 The guilt-offering appears to be a very ancient institution. According to I Sam. 6 the Philistines sent back a guilt-offering with the ark to avert the wrath of Jehovah, because they had desecrated his sacred palladium.   The guilt-offerings in II Kgs. 12¹⁶ are paid in money to the temple treasury.   In the latter passage, as frequently, the guilt- and sin-offerings are closely associated.   The laws do not make the distinction between the two entirely clear. The original object of the guilt-offering appears to have been to make restitution to anyone, whether man or God, for the infringement of his rights or for theft or injury to his property. The wrong might be done intentionally or unintentionally.   In either case the offender must make reparation.   If the offence was against the property or rights of another man, restitution was due not only to the man wronged but also to Jehovah, whose laws had been disobeyed.

ˡ Lev. 5¹⁵ *I. e.,* by keeping back gifts due to sanctuary and portions due to priests.

ᵐ Lev. 5¹⁷⁻¹⁹ These vss. were taken from the priestly directions.

ⁿ Lev. 5¹⁷ Lit., *commanded not to be done.*

ᵒ Lev. 5¹⁸ *I. e.,* to be accepted, subject to Moses' estimation of its value, as sufficient.

Supplemental Priestly Codes

round about with his finger, and so purified the altar from sin, and poured out the rest of the blood at the base of the altar and so consecrated it, making atonement for it.

Priestly Codes

Lev. 6 ²⁴Jehovah said to Moses: Speak to Aaron and to his sons, and say to them, ' This is the law of the sin-offering: In the place where the burnt-offering is killed shall the sin-offering be killed before Jehovah; it is most holy. ²⁶The priest who offers it for sin shall eat it; in a holy place shall it be eaten, in the court of the tent of meeting. ²⁷Whoever toucheth the flesh of it shall become holy; and if any of the blood of it shall be sprinkled on a garment, thou shalt wash the garment thus sprinkled in a holy place. ²⁸And every earthen vessel in which the flesh hath been boiled shall be broken; and if it be boiled in a bronze vessel, this shall be scoured, and rinsed with water. ²⁹Any male among the priests may eat of it; it is most holy.ᵐ ³⁰And no sin-offering, of which any of the blood is brought into the tent of meeting to make atonement in the holy place, shall be eaten; it shall be burnt with fire.'ⁿ

Disposal of the sin-offering

§ 205. **The Yearly Sin-offering,** Nu. 16²⁹⁻³⁴ᵃ [1-28]

Priestly Codes

Nu. 16 ²⁹It shall be an everlasting statute for you: On the tenth day of the seventh month, ye shall afflict yourselves, and shall do no work at all, whether it be the native born or the alien who resideth among you; ³⁰for on this day shall atonement be made for you, to cleanse you; ye shall be cleansed from all your sins before Jehovah. ³¹It is a sabbath of complete rest for you, and ye shall afflict yourselves; it is a statute forever. ³²And the high priest who shall be anointed and installed as priest in his father's place shall make the atonement, and shall put on the holy linen garments; ³³and he shall make atonement for the holy sanctuary; and he shall make atonement for the tent of meeting, and for the altar; and he shall make atonement for the priests, and for all the people of the assembly. ³⁴ᵃAnd this shall be an everlasting statute for you, that atonement be made for the Israelites because of all their sins once every year.

Ritual of cleansing for people and sanctuary

§ 206. **The Red Cow,** Nu. 19¹⁻¹³ [14-22, 31²¹⁻²⁴]

Supplemental Priestly Codes

Nu. 19 ¹Jehovah spoke thus to Moses and Aaron: ²This is the statute of the law which Jehovah hath commanded, 'Speakᵒ to the Israelites, that

Preparation of the water of cleansing

ᵐ Lev. 6²⁴⁻²⁹ The basis of this law is the earlier priestly directions.
ⁿ Lev. 6³⁰ This vs. is an awkward addition to the preceding law.
§ 205 For the detailed ceremony to be observed on the great day of of atonement, cf. § 221.
§ 206 This rite, like the kindred one in Dt. 21¹⁻⁵, § 181, is evidently very old. In both cases the rôle of the priest is unimportant. He has evidently been introduced by the later lawgivers to give a deeper religious significance to the institution. Originally private individuals probably attended to all the details. The belief that a corpse brought ceremonial defilement to all with which it came in contact was widely held by primitive peoples, cf. § 181. Hos. 9⁴, as well as the law of Dt. 21¹⁻⁵, indicates that the early Hebrews shared it. In the

ᵒ Nu. 19² Heb., *speak thou;* Moses alone is addressed and Aaron is disregarded. The plural subject is resumed in ³, but the Gk. has the singular.

Supplemental Priestly Codes

they bring thee a red cow,[p] faultless in which there is no blemish, and upon which a yoke hath never come. [3]And ye shall give her to Eleazar[q] the priest, and she shall be taken outside the camp and be slain before him; [4]and Eleazar the priest shall take some of her blood with his finger, and sprinkle it toward the front of the tent of meeting seven times. [5]Then the cow shall be burnt in his sight; her hide and her flesh, and her blood,[r] with her dung, shall he burn. [6]And the priest shall take cedar wood, hyssop,[s] and scarlet thread, and cast them into the midst of the burning carcass of the cow. [7]Then the priest shall wash his clothes and bathe his flesh in water, and afterwards he shall come into the camp, and the priest shall be unclean until evening. [8]And he that burneth her shall wash his clothes and bathe his flesh in water, and shall be unclean until evening. [9]And a man ceremonially clean shall collect the ashes of the cow and lay them up without the camp in a clean place; and it shall be kept for the congregation of the Israelites as a water for the removal of impurity; it is a means of removing sin. [10]And he who collecteth the ashes of the cow shall wash his clothes, and be unclean until the evening; and it shall be for the Israelites and the alien who resideth among them, a statute forever.

Its use

[11]He that toucheth the dead, even any human corpse, shall be unclean seven days; [12]that one must purify himself therewith on the third day and on the seventh day, and so become clean; but if he do not purify himself the third day and on the seventh, he will not become clean. [13]Every one who toucheth a dead person, the corpse of any man who may have died, and doth not purify himself, defileth the dwelling of Jehovah. That person shall be cut off from Israel; because the water for impurity was not thrown over[t] him, he shall be unclean; his uncleanness is yet upon him.

---

older and yet in many respects parallel regulation of Dt. 21, moral as well as ceremonial guilt is assumed; but in both cases a young cow (in Dt., *heifer*), which has done no work nor borne the yoke, is sacrificed. While the institution is evidently very old and may well come from an age when it was thought necessary to sacrifice to the spirit of the dead lest he take vengeance upon the living (cf. Bewer in *JBL* XXIV., 1 pp. 41-44), the law in Nu. 19[1-13] reveals the marks of late priestly adaptation. Its object is purely ceremonial cleansing. The sacrifice takes the form of a whole burnt-offering. Cedar wood, hyssop and scarlet thread, used in the cleansing of lepers, Lev. 14, are added to the mixture. These may be simply symbolic, or may represent primitive survivals or later importations.

The closest parallel to the rite as a whole is the Roman custom of using the ashes of calves in lustration, Ovid, *Fast.* IV. 639, 725, 733. Cows' urine was also frequently employed in India for ceremonial purification, cf. Gray, *Numbers*, 246, 247. Red oxen were required for certain sacrifices by the Egyptians. It seems clear that in this law several primitive *motifs* have been combined and adapted by the priestly lawgivers to the higher religious ends. The exact meaning of all the symbolism is not certain. The final product, *the water for the removal of impurity*, contained and therefore represented sacrificial blood and flesh and the whole burnt-offering, as well as medicating herbs, and therefore symbolized the methods of ceremonial purification in vogue in later priestly codes. Aside from the subsequent detailed directions, [14-22], regarding the use of the water of purification in the case of contact with a corpse, cf. § 181, and in the late law regarding the purification of the spoils of war, Nu. 31[23], § 184, there is no reference to this rite in the O.T. Hence if ancient, it was only at a later period inserted in the Pentateuch.

[p] Nu. 19[2] Not necessarily a heifer, as the current translations assume without any support in the Heb.

[q] Nu. 19[3] Eleazar, not Aaron, is appointed to this task, for it involves ceremonial pollution.

[r] Nu. 19[5] This is the only case in the O.T. law when the blood was burnt; the reason is because the ashes were later used for purification, or else it is a survival from a primitive age when the blood as well as the flesh was consumed in the burnt-offering.

[s] Nu. 19[6] *Hyssop* is but a late conjecture of the Talmudists. From I Kgs. 4[33] it may be inferred that it was a climbing plant.

[t] Nu. 19[13] The verb means to throw in copious quantities.

§ 207. Leprosy Offering, Lev. 14²⁻⁷, ¹⁰ [11-20], 21-23 [24-32, 48-52]

Priestly Codes

Lev. 14 ²This shall be the law of the leper in the day when he is cleansed : Ritual
he shall be brought to the priest; ³and the priest shall go out of the camp; of
and the priest shall look, and if the mark of leprosy be healed in the leper, ing
⁴the priest shall command to take for him who is to be cleansed two living
clean birds, cedar wood, scarlet, and hyssop; ⁵and the priest shall command
to kill one of the birds in an earthen vessel over running water. ⁶He shall
then take the living bird, the cedar wood, the scarlet and the hyssop, and
shall dip them and the living bird in the blood of the bird that was killed over
the running water; ⁷and he shall sprinkle the blood seven times upon him
who is to be cleansed from the leprosy, and shall pronounce him clean; then
he shall set free the living bird in the open field. ¹⁰And on the eighth day
the cleansed leper shall take two male lambs without blemish, and one female
lamb a year old without blemish, and as a cereal-offering, three-tenths of
an ephah of fine meal mixed with oil, and one log of oil.

²¹And if the cleansed leper be poor, and his means are not sufficient for Poor
this, he shall take one male lamb as a guilt-offering to be waved, to make man's
atonement for him, and one-tenth of an ephah of fine meal mixed with oil offering
as a cereal-offering, and a logᵘ of oil, ²²and two turtle-doves or two young
pigeons, as his means permit; and the one shall be a sin-offering and the
other a burnt-offering. ²³And on the eighth day he shall bring them for his
cleansing to the priest, at the entrance of the tent of meeting, before Jehovah.ᵛ

§ 208. Jealousy Offering, Nu. 5¹²ᵇ, ¹³ᵃ, ᶜ, ¹⁵, ¹⁸, ²¹, ²³, ²⁴, ²⁶ᵃ, ²⁷ᵇ, ³¹

Priestly Codes

Nu. 5 ¹²ᵇIf a man's wife turn aside and is unfaithful to him, ¹³ᵃ,ᶜand Form
a man enter into illicit relations with her and it be hid from her husband, and of the
there be no witness against her and she be not caught in the act, ¹⁵then the offering
man shall take his wife to the priest, and shall bring an offering for her, the
tenth of an ephah of barley meal; he shall pour no oil upon it nor put frankincense on it for it is a cereal-offering of jealousy, a memorial cereal-offering,
bringing iniquity to remembrance.

¹⁸Then the priest shall place the woman before Jehovah, and loosen the Admin-
hair of her head, and put in her hands the memorial cereal-offering, which istra-
is the cereal-offering of jealousy, and the priest shall hold in his hand the of the
water of bitterness which causeth the curse. ²¹Then the priest shall make oath
the woman swear with the oath of execration, and the priest shall say to the
woman, Jehovah make you an execration and an oath among thy people,
when Jehovah causeth your thigh to fall away, and your body to swell.

---

§ 204 For the full details regarding the presentation of the different leprosy offerings, cf.
§ 179.
ᵘ Lev. 14²¹ According to the Rabbis a little less than a pint.
ᵛ Lev. 14²¹⁻²³ Possibly this provision for the poor man's offering is a later addition.
§ 208 For the origin and analysis of the law cf. note § 70.

Priestly Codes

Water of bitterness

²³Then the priest shall write these execrations in a book, and he shall wipe them off into the water of bitterness, ²⁴and he shall make the woman drink the water of bitterness that causeth the curse, so that the water that causeth the curse may enter into her and become bitter.   ²⁶ᵃThe priest shall also take a handful of the cereal-offering, as its memorial-offering, and burn it upon the altar.   ²⁷ᵇThus the woman shall become an execration among her people.   ³¹The man shall be free from guilt, but the woman must bear her own guilt.

§ 209. **The Daily Sacrifice,** Ex. 29³⁸⁻⁴² [Nu. 28¹⁻⁸], Ex. 30⁷, ⁸

Supplemental Priestly Codes

Morning offering

Ex. 29 ³⁸Now this is what thou shalt offer upon the altar: two yearling lambs regularly each day.   ³⁹One lamb thou shalt offer in the morning, and the other lamb thou shalt offer towards evening; ⁴⁰and with the one lamb a tenth of an ephah of fine meal mixed with the fourth of a hin of beaten oil, and the fourth of a hin of wine as a libation.

Evening offering

⁴¹The other lamb thou shalt offer towards evening, and shalt deal with it as with the cereal-offering of the morning and its libation, as a pleasant odor, an offering made by fire to Jehovah.   ⁴²It shall be a regular burnt-offering throughout your generations at the entrance of the tent of meeting before Jehovah, where I will meet with thee,ʷ to speak there to thee.ˣ

Incense and lamps

Ex. 30 ⁷On the altar of incense Aaron shall burn incense of sweet spices; each morning, when he taketh care of the lamps, he shall burn it.   ⁸When Aaron lighteth the lamps towards evening, he shall burn it as a perpetual incense before Jehovah throughout your generations.

---

§ 209 Neh. 10²³ seems to imply that in the days of Ezra and Nehemiah but one animal was offered daily.   Before the exile the daily offering consisted of a burnt-offering in the morning and a cereal-offering in the evening, II Kgs. 16¹⁵.   Ezek. assigns both of these offerings to the morning.   The Chronicler, however, speaks of two burnt-offerings, I Chr. 16⁴⁰, II Chr. 13¹¹, 31³.   It would appear that the double offering was introduced some time after 400 B.C. and that these laws, therefore, belong to the latest supplements to the priestly codes.
ʷ Ex. 29⁴² So Gk., Syr., and Sam.   Heb., *you.*
ˣ Ex. 29⁴² Gk., *reveal myself to you.*

I

THE PRE-EXILIC SACRED CALENDAR

§ 210. **The Sabbath,** Ex. 34²¹, 23¹² [20⁸⁻¹¹], Dt. 5¹²⁻¹⁵

Primitive Codes

Ex. 34 ²¹Six days shalt thou work, but on the seventh day thou shalt Seventh rest; in plowing time and in harvest thou shalt rest. day of rest

---

The Pre-Exilic Sacred Calendar.—The external religious life of most peoples of antiquity centred about certain great festivals. This fact is especially true of the Semitic nations. In the earliest days the festivals were supremely significant, since they represented the united worship of the family or tribe or nation. Through them the bond between the different members of the community was strengthened by social intercourse and common feasting, merrymaking and worship. The joyous element was also very prominent. *To rejoice before Jehovah,* is the ordinary idiom used in Dt. to describe a feast. Songs, music, dancing, drinking and processions probably all entered into the great sacrificial meals, cf. Am. 2⁸, 5²¹, Judg. 21¹⁹, Is. 28⁷· ⁸, I Sam. 1¹⁴. At these times, also, the covenant between Jehovah and his people was renewed, as the men and women brought up their gifts as tribute to their Divine King.

In the early period there were three great annual festivals. The oft-reiterated command, *Three times in the year shall all thy males appear before the Lord Jehovah, the God of Israel,* belongs to the oldest decalogues. It voices one of the fundamental requirements of Israel's primitive faith. In addition to the early festivals, the new moon and the sabbath apparently also date from Israel's earliest historical period. The moon, called by the Hebrews *the wanderer,* not only fixed by its different phases the calendar, but also seems to have occupied a central place in the religion of the primitive ancestors of the Israelites. At Ur and Haran, whence the Heb. traditions trace the origin of their ancestors, Sin, the moon god, was the chief deity. Even the sacred Mount Sinai bears the name of the moon god. Job 31²⁶ refers to the worship of the moon; cf. also Ezek. 8¹⁴ and Is. 3¹⁸. The new moon festival is frequently mentioned in the earliest O.T. books, and was clearly one of the oldest of Israel's institutions; it was, in fact, shared with all primitive Semitic peoples. According to I Sam. 20⁴⁻⁶· ²⁷· ³⁴ it was celebrated by the clan with sacrificial offerings. II Kgs. 4²³ indicates that it was also made the occasion for visits to the prophets. Am. 8⁵, Is. 1¹⁴ and Hos. 2¹¹ classify it with the sabbath and suggest that it was an occasion of merrymaking and cessation from labor. Its omission in the pre-exilic laws is probably because the lawgivers were unwilling to countenance its rites and associations. Throughout all the pre-exilic laws the divinely inspired prophetic endeavor to eliminate the older heathen customs and ideas associated with the ancient festivals and to introduce nobler usages and to give them a more ethical and spiritual content is prominently in evidence.

§ 210 It is very probable that originally the sabbath was connected with the four phases of the moon and that, like the feast of the new moon, its background is the primitive moon worship, suggested by many of Israel's earliest institutions. Whether the derivation of the Heb. word sabbath be traced to the Assyrian, *shabatu,* to *cease, be completed,* or the Arabic root meaning to *cut off, interrupt,* it suggests the changing phases of the moon. The division of the month into weeks in accordance with the four quarters of the moon was known in many parts of the ancient world. Thus the Hindus had such a division, with special sacrifices at the new and full moon, cf. Ps. 81³. In this connection it is interesting to note that when the dates of the Israelitish feasts were definitely fixed the days selected were the full moons. The moon itself also establishes the unit seven, for seven days after the first appearance of the new moon it is half full, and on the fourteenth it is full. The arbitrary fixing of the sabbath at the end of every six days, irrespective of the lunar month, appears to have resulted from the strong tendency already observed in the pre-exilic lawgivers to break away from all traditions connected with primitive moon worship.

The week among the Egyptians contained ten days, and there are no clear indications of the division of the month into weeks among the Babylonians. The forbidding of certain acts as unlucky on the 7th, 14th, 19th, 21st and 28th of the intercalary month Elul perhaps suggests, but certainly does not prove the existence of an institution in Babylonia similar to the Heb. sabbath. Furthermore at the time when the Jews came into closest contact with the Babylonians, the priestly lawgivers emphasized sabbath observance most strongly as a distinctively Israelitish institution. More probably it was inherited from the agricultural Canaanites. Ultimately the origin of the sabbath is to be traced back to those nomadic ancestors of the Hebrews and the Canaanites, who paid chief homage to the moon, whose benign light guided them in their night journeys over the plains of Northern Arabia. Originally, like the new moon, it was doubtless observed as a festival. As a natural sequel came that remission of labor which accompanied every ancient feast, cf. Strabo, 3⁹. In the hands of Israel's prophetic lawgivers the element of rest was given the first place, and that of worship was made secondary, probably because of its heathen associations. Cf. for its later history, note § 217.

257

Supplemental Priestly Codes

fourteenth day of the second month, towards evening, they shall keep it; they shall eat it with unleavened bread and bitter herbs; ¹²they shall leave none of it until the morning nor break a bone of it; according to all the statute of the passover shall they keep it.   ¹³But the man who is ceremonially clean and is not on a journey and neglecteth to keep the passover, that one shall be cut off from his people; because he offered not the gift to Jehovah in its appointed season, that man shall bear his guilt.   ¹⁴And if a foreigner reside among you and wish to keep the passover to Jehovah according to the statute of the passover and the ordinance regarding it, so shall he do; ye shall have one statute, both for the resident alien and the native born.'

§ 219. Feast of Weeks or Firstfruits, Lev. 23¹⁵⁻²¹, Nu. 28²⁶⁻³¹

Holiness Code

Date and ritual

Lev. 23 ¹⁵Ye shall count from the day following the sabbath, from the day that ye bring the sheaf of the wave-offering [at the beginning of the feast of unleavened bread], seven full weeks; ¹⁶until the day following the seventh sabbath shall ye count fifty days; and ye shall present a new cereal-offering to Jehovah.   ¹⁷Ye shall bring out of your dwellings two wave-loaves of two-tenths of an ephah; they shall be of fine meal, and they shall be baked with leaven, as firstfruits for Jehovah.   ¹⁸Ye shall present with the bread seven yearling lambs without blemish, and one young bullock, and two rams; they shall be a burnt-offering to Jehovah, with the cereal-offerings and libations, an offering made by fire, of an odor pleasing to Jehovah.   ¹⁹Ye shall also offer one male goat as a sin-offering, and two male lambs a year old as a sacrifice of peace-offerings. ²⁰And the priest shall wave them with the bread of the firstfruits as a wave-offering before Jehovah, with the two lambs; they shall be a holy gift for Jehovah and shall belong to the priest.   ²¹And he shall make proclamation on that same day,ᵐ and there shall be a religious assembly for you in the sanctuary; ye shall do no toilsome work; it is a statute forever in all your dwellings throughout your generations.

Supplemental Priestly Codes

Additional directions and offerings

Nu. 28 ²⁶On the day of the firstfruits, when ye offer a new cereal-offering to Jehovah in your feast of weeks, ye shall hold a religious assembly at the sanctuary; ye shall do no toilsome work, ²⁷but ye shall offer a burnt-offering as an odor pleasing to Jehovah : two young bullocks, one ram, seven male lambs a year old, ²⁸and their cereal-offering, fine meal mingled with oil, three-tenths of an ephah for each bullock, two-tenths for the one ram, ²⁹a tenth for each of the seven lambs, ³⁰one male goat to make atonement for you. ³¹Besides the regular burnt-offering, and its cereal-offering, ye shall offer them—they shall be without blemish,—and their libations.

---

§ 219 The Holiness Code, like that of Dt. leaves the exact date of the feast indeterminate, simply fixing it on the fiftieth day (hence the N.T. designation, *Pentecost*) after the beginning of the feast of unleavened bread.   The details of the sacrificial offering in ¹⁸ᵇ, ¹⁹ᵃ appear to have been added by a late priestly editor, cf. § 167 note ᵃ.
    ᵐ Lev. 23²¹ The characteristic formulas of the priestly lawgivers reappear in this vs.

§ 220. Feast of Trumpets, Lev. 23²³⁻²⁵, Nu. 29¹⁻⁶

Priestly Codes

Lev. 23 ²³Jehovah gave this command to Moses: ²⁴Speak thus to the Israelites, 'On the first day of the seventh month ye shall have a complete rest, a memorial day celebrated by the blowing of trumpets, a religious assembly at the sanctuary. ²⁵Ye shall do no toilsome work, and ye shall present an offering made by fire to Jehovah.' *(marginal: Date and method of observance)*

Supplemental Priestly Codes

Nu. 29 ¹On the first day of the seventh month ye shall hold a religious assembly at the sanctuary; ye shall do no toilsome work; it shall be to you a day for blowing trumpets. ²And ye shall offer a burnt-offering as an odor pleasing to Jehovah: one young bullock, one ram, seven male lambs a year old without blemish, ³and their cereal-offering, fine meal mingled with oil, three-tenths of an ephah for the bullock, two-tenths for the ram, ⁴and one-tenth for each of the seven lambs, ⁵and one male goat as a sin-offering, to make atonement for you, ⁶in addition to the burnt-offering of the new moon, and its cereal-offering, and the regular burnt-offering, and its cereal-offering, and their libations in accordance with their ordinance, as a pleasant odor, an offering made by fire to Jehovah. *(marginal: Specific offerings)*

§ 221. Day of Atonement, Lev. 16, 23²⁶⁻³², Nu. 29⁷⁻¹¹ [Ex. 30¹⁰]

Priestly Codes

Lev. 16 ¹Jehovah spoke to Moses, after the death of the two sons of Aaron, when they drew near before Jehovah and died, ²and Jehovah said *(marginal: High priest's preparations)*

---

§ 220 There are no traces of this feast in the pre-exilic literature. It falls, however, on the first day of the early Heb. year which began in Sept., cf. Ex. 23¹⁶, Lev. 25⁹, Ezek. 40¹, rather than in the spring. Most Semitic peoples celebrate the beginning of a new year with some religious festivities, so that the present laws may simply represent the revival of a very old institution. From the time of Alexander the Jews have celebrated this feast as the New Year's Day. The priestly lawgivers doubtless desired to emphasize the first day of the seventh Bab. month, doubling as they did at that time the regular offerings of the new moon, because of the important feasts which fell in that month.

§ 221 The day of atonement represents the culmination of the ritualistic tendencies of the late priestly schools. It is nowhere mentioned in the pre-exilic or Holiness codes. Ezek. did not know of it in its present form, but provides rather for two days of atonement, one on the first day of the first month, and on the first of the seventh month, 45¹⁸⁻²⁰. In the account of the great priestly reformation in Neh. 8, the tenth of the seventh month is passed over without any reference to it, but on the twenty-fourth a general feast and confession was held. The laws regarding the day of atonement, therefore, appear to be among the latest sections of the Pentateuch. Its background is the Bab. exile and its motive is its deep sense of guilt which that overwhelming national experience impressed on the minds of the Jews. But the Holy One must be served by a holy people. In the doctrines of the priestly schools holiness meant ceremonial purity. Therefore the ritual of the day of atonement was developed to remove from the nation and sanctuary all possible forms of defilement overlooked or not provided for by the other detailed ceremonial laws. It was natural that in the minds of later Jews it should become the most important day in the calendar. It was equivalent to a great national confession. In the deeply spiritual prayers of the later ritual and of Judaism to-day it is essentially a common confession of individual as well as national guilt.

Whether or not the institution is derived from the Bab. day of appeasement (*shabattum*, cf. Lev. 23²⁴) cannot be definitely determined. The aim, to win the favor of the Deity by special offerings, is the same in both. Doubtless the Jewish priests in Babylonia were influenced, indirectly at least, by prominence of this kindred idea and institution among their neighbors and masters.

The goat, sent forth to Azazel, like the bird released in connection with the leprosy offering, § 207, reflects the very ancient and widespread belief that human ills or guilt could thus be

Supplemental Priestly Codes

own family, and to the possession of his fathers shall he return.   ⁴²For they are my servants whom I brought from the land of Egypt; they shall· not be sold as slaves.

Hebrews sold subject to this law

⁴⁷ᵇIf thy fellow countryman become poor beside him and sell himself to a foreigner or alien residing with thee, or to a descendant of the foreigner's family, ⁴⁸he may be redeemed after he has sold himself; one of his kinsmen may redeem him, ⁴⁹or his uncle, or his uncle's son, may redeem him, or one of his near kinsmen may redeem him; or, if he become rich, he may redeem himself.   ⁵⁰He shall reckon with his purchaser from the year that he sold himself to him to the next year of jubilee; and the price of his release shall be according to the number of years of service; on the terms of a hired servant shall he be with him.   ⁵¹If there are yet many years, in proportion to them he shall give back the price of his redemption out of the money for which he was bought.   ⁵²And if there remain but few years until the year of jubilee, then he shall reckon with his master; according to the years of service still remaining shall he pay back the price of his redemption.   ⁵⁴And if he be not redeemed in any of these ways, then he shall go free in the year of jubilee, together with his children.

APPENDIX

APPENDIX

I

SELECTED BIBLIOGRAPHY AND DETAILED REFERENCES

GENERAL INTRODUCTIONS TO THE OLD TESTAMENT
LEGAL BOOKS

Addis, *The Documents of the Hexateuch*, I, II, 1893–1898.
Baudissin, *Einleitung in die Bücher des A.T.*, 1901.
Briggs, *The Higher Criticism of the Hexateuch*,[2] 1897.
Carpenter, *The Composition of the Hexateuch*, 1902.
Carpenter and Harford-Battersby, *The Hexateuch*, I, II, 1900.
Cornill, *Einleitung in das A.T.*,[3] 1896.
Cullen, *The Book of the Covenant in Moab*, 1903.
Driver, *An Introduction to the Literature of the O.T.*,[8] 1901.
Fries, *Der Gesetzschrift des Königs Josia*, 1903.
Holzinger, *Einleitung in den Hexateuch*, 1893.
Kautzsch, *Literature of the O.T.*, 1899.
Kent, *The Messages of Israel's Lawgivers*, 1902.
Kent and Sanders, *The Origin and Growth of Israelitish Law*, in *Historical and Critical Contributions to Biblical Science*, 1901.
König, *Einleitung in das A.T.*, 1893.
Kuenen, *The Hexateuch*, 1886.
McFadyen, *An Introduction to the O.T.*, 1905.
Smith, *The Old Testament in the Jewish Church*,[2] 1892.
Steuernagel, *Allgemeine Einleitung in den Hexateuch*, 1900.
Wellhausen, *Composition des Hexateuchs und der historischen Bücher des A.T.*,[3] 1899.
" *Prolegomena to the History of Israel*, 1885.
Wildeboer, *Die Litteratur des A.T.*, 1895.

DICTIONARIES AND ENCYCLOPÆDIAS

Cheyne and Black, *Encyclopædia Biblica*, I–IV, 1899–1903.
Hastings, *A Dictionary of the Bible*, I–V, 1898–1904.
Herzog-Hauck, *Realencyclopädie für protestantische Theologie und Kirche*,[3] 1896.
Singer, *The Jewish Encyclopedia*, I–XII, 1901–1906.
Smith, *A Dictionary of the Bible*,[2] 1893.

SELECTED BIBLIOGRAPHY

ISRAELITISH AND CONTEMPORARY SEMITIC HISTORY

See Kent, *Student's O.T.*, Vol. II, pp. 485–487.

THE CODE OF HAMMURABI AND THE OLD TESTAMENT CODES

Cohn, *Die Gesetze Hammurabi's*, 1903.

Cook, *The Laws of Moses and the Code of Hammurabi*, 1903.

Edwards, *The Hammurabi Code and the Sinaitic Legislation*, 1904.

Grimme, *Das Gesetz Chammurabis und Moses*, 1903.

Harper, *The Code of Hammurabi*, 1904.

Jeremias, *Moses und Hammurabi*, 1903.

Johns, *Babylonian and Assyrian Laws, Contracts, and Letters*, 1904.

" Article, *The Code of Hammurabi*, Hastings's D.B. (Extra Volume, 1904).

Kent, "*The Recently Discovered Civil Code of Hammurabi*," Biblical World, Vol. XXI, pp. 175–190, 1903.

Kohler und Peiser, *Hammurabi's Gesetz*, I: *Uebersetzung, juristiche Wiedergabe, Erläuterung*, 1903.

Lyon, *The Structure of the Hammurabi Code*, Journal of the American Oriental Society, Vol. XXV, pp. 248–265, 1904.

Müller, *Die Gesetze Hammurabis und ihr Verhältnis zur Mosaischen Gesetzgebung so wie zu den XII Tafeln*, 1903.

Oettli, *Das Gesetz Hammurabis und die Thora Israels*, 1903.

Rosenbacher, *Moses und Hammurabi*, 1904.

Sayce, *The Legal Code of Babylonia*, American Journal of Theology, pp. 256–266, 1904.

Scheil, *Memoires de la delegation en Perse*, Tome IV, 1902.

" *La loi de Hammurabi*, 1904.

Winckler, *Die Gesetze Hammurabis*, 1903.

" *Die Gesetze Hammurabis in Umschrift und Uebersetzung herausgegeben*, 1904.

OTHER ANCIENT CODES

Amos, *The History and Principles of the Civil Law of Rome*, 1883.

Burnell, *The Ordinances of Manu*, 1884.

Ball, *Light from the East*, 1886.

Bühler, *Sacred Books of the East*, Vol. XXV, *The Laws of Manu*, 1886.

Herrick, *The Attic Law of Status, Family Relations, and Succession in the Fourth Century B.C.*, 1890.

Lee, *Historical Jurisprudence*, 1900.

Leist, *Altarisches Jus Gentium*, 1889.

von Lingenthal, *Geschichte des griech-römischen Rechts*,[2] 1877.

ANCIENT LEGAL CODES

Macdonald, *Muslim Theology, Jurisprudence and Constitutional Theory*, 1903.
Maine, *Ancient Law*, 1888.
Merriam, *The Gortyan Code*, Journal of the American Archæological Society, 1899.
Monro, *The Digest of Justinian*, translated 1904.
Moyle, *Imperatoris Justiniani Institutionum*, 1890.
Voigt, *Die XII Tafeln Geschichte und System des Civil und Criminal-Rechts, wie Process der XII Tafeln*, I, II, 1883.

SEMITIC AND ISRAELITISH INSTITUTIONS AND ARCHÆOLOGY

Baethgen, *Beiträge sur semitischen Religionsgeschichte*, 1888.
Barton, *A Sketch of Semitic Origins—Social and Religious*, 1902.
Baudissin, *Studien zur semitischen Religionsgeschichte*, 2 vols., 1876, 1878.
" *Die Geschichte des alttestamentlichen Priesterthums*, 1889.
Benzinger, *Hebräische Archäologie*, 1894.
Bertholet, *Die Stellung der Israeliten und Juden zu den Fremden*, 1896.
Bissell, *The Law of Asylum in Israel*, 1888.
Bohn, *Der Sabbat im A.T.*, 1903.
Curtiss, *Primitive Semitic Religion To-Day*, 1902.
" *The Levitical Priests*, 1877.
Duschak, *Das Mosaische Strafrecht*, 1869.
Förster, *Das Mosaische Strafrecht in seiner geschichtlichen Entwickellung*, 1900.
Frazer, *Golden Bough*, I, II, 1890.
Frenkel, *Der gerichtliche Beweis*, 1846.
Green, *The Hebrew Feasts in their Relation to Recent Critical Hypotheses Concerning the Pentateuch*, 1885.
Harper, *The Priestly Element in the O.T.*,[2] 1905.
Hogarth, *Authority and Archæology*, 1899.
van Hoonacker, *Le Sacerdoce levitique*, 1899.
Hummelauer, *Das vormosaische Priesterthum in Israel*, 1899.
Jastrow, *The Religion of Babylonia and Assyria*, German translation, 1905–1907.
King, *Babylonian Religion and Mythology*, 1899.
Klein, *Das Gesetz über das gerichtliche Beweisverfahren nach mosaisch-talmudisches Recht*, 1885.
Lagrange, *Études sur les religions Sémitiques*, 1903.
Leighton, *The Jewish Altar*, 1886.
Nowack, *Lehrbuch der hebräischen Archäologie*, I, II, 1894.
Priestel, *Baugeschichte der jüdischen Heiligtümer und die Tempel-Salomos*, 1904.
Rosenau, *Jewish Ceremonial Institutions and Customs*, 1903.
Sayce, *The Religions of Ancient Egypt and Babylonia*, 1902.

DETAILED REFERENCES

Origin and Growth of Israelitish Law: Hastings DB III, 64–67; Encyc. Bib. III, 2714–18; Kent and Sanders OGIL in Contribs. to Bib. Sci., 41–67; Wellhausen PHI 392–401.

The Primitive Hebrew Codes: Hastings DB III, 67, 68; Carpenter and Battersby H II, 112–17; Driver LOT⁸ 30–40; Encyc. Bib. II, 1444–48; III, 2733–35; *Baentsch EL*, 177–212.

The Deuteronomic Codes: McFadyen IOT 46–61; Hastings DB III, 68, 69; I, 597–603; Encyc. Bib. I, 1079–88; Carpenter and Battersby H I, 70–97; Driver D XXV–LXXVII; LOT⁸ 69–99; Smith OTJC 346–360; Wellhausen PHI 402–10; *Holzinger EH* 255–331.

Ezekiel and the Holiness Code: Hastings DB III, 68, 69; Encyc. Bib. III, 2737–39; Carpenter and Battersby H I, 145–51; Driver LOT⁸ 292–98; *Holzinger EH*, 406–18.

The Priestly Codes: Hastings DB III, 70–72; Encyc. Bib. III, 2739–43; Carpenter and Battersby H I, 121–44, 152–57; Driver LOT⁸ 128–59; *Holzinger EH* 332–405, 418–65.

PERSONAL AND FAMILY LAWS

Parents and Children: Article, *Family* in Hastings DB and Encyc. Bib.; Smith KMEA; *Post, Familienrecht; Benzinger HA* 133–38, 147–59; *Nowack HA* I, 152–55, 180–82.

Marriage Relation: Smith KMEA; article, *Marriage* in Hastings DB and Encyc. Bib. and Jewish Encyc.; *Benzinger HA* 138–47, 342–47; *Nowack HA* I, 155–64, 341–48.

Masters and Slaves: Article, *Servant* in Hastings DB; *Slavery* in Encyc. Bib. and Jewish Encyc.; McCurdy HPM II, 168–75; *Benzinger HA* 159–63; *Nowack HA* I, 173–80.

Aliens: Article, *Ger* in Hastings DB; *Stranger and Sojourner* in Encyc. Bib.; Smith KMEA; RS 75–81; McCurdy HPM II, 177–83; *Bertholet SIJF; Benzinger HA* 339–42; *Nowack HA* I, 336–41.

Rights of Property: Encyc. Bib. III, 2725–28; *Klein GGBMR; Benzinger HA* 347–54; *Nowack HA* I, 350–56.

Rights of Inheritance: Encyc. Bib. III, 2728–29; article *Inheritance* in Hastings DB and Jewish Encyc.; *Benzinger HA* 354–56; *Nowack HA* I, 348–50.

CONSTITUTIONAL LAWS

Political Organization: Article, *Government* in Hastings DB and Encyc. Bib.; McCurdy HPM I, ch. III; Smith RS 70–75; KMEA; *Benzinger HA* 292–319; *Nowack HA* I, 300–16.

Military Regulations: Articles, *War, Camp* and *Fenced Cities* in Hastings DB; *War* in Encyc. Bib.; *Benzinger HA* 356–63; *Nowack HA* I, 357–75; *Schwally SK* I.

The Judiciary: Article, *Judges* in Hastings DB; *Law and Justice* in Encyc. Bib.; Bissel LAI; *Benzinger HA* 320–30; *Nowack HA* I, 317–26; *Frenkel GB; Klein GGBMR.*

REGARDING THE CONSTITUTIONAL LAWS

Public Instruction: Article, *Education* in Hastings DB and Encyc. Bib.; Schürer HJPTJ, Div. II, Vol. I, § 25; Laurie, Hist. Survey of Pre-Christian Educ., 69–105; *Simon, L'Éducation des Enfants chez les anciens Juifs; Strassburger, Gesch. der Erziehung bei den Israeliten; Dushak, Schulgesetzgebung und Methodik der alten Israeliten.*

CRIMINAL LAWS

Crimes and Penalties: Article, *Crimes and Punishments* in Hastings DB; Schürer HJPTJ, Div. II, Vol. II, 90 ff.; Smith OTJC[2], 340–45, 368–70; *Post, Familienrecht,* 358; *Benzinger HA* 331–39; *Nowack HA* I, 327–53; *Förster MSGE.*

HUMANE LAWS

Humane and Philanthropic Provisions: Hastings DB I, 579, 580; Extra Vol. 357–59; IV, 323–26; Encyc. Bib. III, 3791–93; *Benzinger HA* 168–77; *Nowack HA* I, 353–56.

CEREMONIAL LAWS

The Tent of Meeting or Tabernacle: Article, *Tabernacle* in Hastings DB, Encyc. Bib., and Jewish Encyc.; Brown, The Tabernacle; Ottley, Aspects of the O.T., 261–65; *Benzinger HA* 370, 395–99; *Nowack HA* III, 53–70.

The Ark: Article, *Ark of the Covenant* in Hastings DB, Encyc. Bib., and Jewish Encyc.; *Kraetzschmar, Die Bundesvorstellung,* 208–20; *Bähr, Symbolik* I, 482; *Benzinger HA,* 367–70.

Solomon's Temple: Cf. Vol. II, p. 490, for detailed bibliography.

Ezekiel's Temple Plan: Hastings DB IV, 703–10; Encyc. Bib. IV, 4941–43; Sulley, The Temple of Ezekiel's Prophecy; Toy E, 177–92; *Benzinger HA* 393, 394; *Nowack HA* II, 50–53.

The Pre-exilic Priests: Hastings DB IV, 67–77; Encyc. Bib. III, 3837–43; Jewish Encyc. VIII, 49, 50; *Benzinger HA* 405–18; *Nowack HA* II, 87–104; *Hummelauer VPI; Baudissin GAP.*

Sacred Officials in Ezekiel's Hierarchy: Hastings DB IV, 77–79; Encyc. Bib.; Toy E 192–205; *Benzinger HA* 419; *Nowack HA* II, 104–6.

The Post-exilic Hierarchy: Levites: Hastings DB IV, 80, 92–96; Encyc. Bib. III, 3843–46; Gray N 21–26; *Benzinger HA* 420–1; *Baudissin GAP; Nowack HA* II, 106–29.

Priests: Hastings DB IV, 85–92; Encyc. Bib. III, 3843–46; Jewish Encyc. X, 192–97; *Benzinger HA* 421–29; *Baudissin GAP; Nowack HA* II, 106–29.

High Priest: Hastings DB IV, 79, 84; Jewish Encyc. VI, 389–93; *Benzinger HA* 422, 423; *Nowack HA* II, 115–20.

DETAILED REFERENCES

Food Ceremonially Clean and Unclean: Articles, *Food* and *Unclean* in Hastings DB; *Food* and *Clean and Unclean* in Encyc. Bib.; *Stade GVI* I, 481–87; *Benzinger HA* 483, 490.

Ceremonial Uncleanness: Hastings DB IV, 825–29; Encyc. Bib. I, 836–41, 845–48; Smith RS 152–64; article, *Taboo* in Encyc. Brit.; Gray N 241–48; *Benzinger HA* 478–83; *Nowack HA* II, 275–99.

Nazirites: Article, *Nazirite* in Hastings DB, Encyc. Bib., and Jewish Encyc.; Smith RS 323–33, 481–85; Gray N 56–60, 65, 69; *Smend LAR* 93–96; *Benzinger HA* 429, 430; *Nowack HA* II, 133–37; *Gruneisen, Der Ahnencultus*, 46, 71, 92, 112–50.

Circumcision: Article, *Circumcision* in Hastings DB, Encyc. Bib., and Jewish Encyc.; Asher, The Jewish Rite of Circumcision; *Ploss, Das Kind*, 360–66; *Wellhausen AH* 154; *Glassberg, Die Beschneidung; Smend ATRG* 37–40; *Marti GIR* 43, 163, 164.

Sacred Dues: Articles, *First-born, Firstfruits, Tithes, Tax, Vows* in Bible Dicts.; Gray N 225–29, 236–41; Smith RS 244–53, 458–65; *Benzinger HA* 457–61; *Nowack HA* II, 254–59.

Vows: Article, *Vow* in Hastings DB; *Vows* in Encyc. Bib., and Jewish Encyc.; *Nowack HA* II, 262–68.

Sacrifice: Article, *Sacrifice* in Encyc. Bib., Hastings DB, and Jewish Encyc.; Smith RS 213–43, 253–440; *Benzinger HA* 431–56; *Nowack HA* II, 203–54.

Sabbath: Article, *Sabbath* in Hastings DB, Encyc. Bib., and Jewish Encyc.; *Bohn, Der Sabbat im A.T; Benzinger HA* 465, 473; *Nowack HA* II, 140–44, 159–62.

New Moon: Article, *New Moon* in Hastings DB, Encyc. Bib., and Jewish Encyc.; *Benzinger HA* 464, 473; *Nowack HA* II, 138–40, 158, 159.

Passover and Feast of Unleavened Bread: Articles, *Passover* and *Feasts* in Hastings DB, Encyc. Bib., and Jewish Encyc.; Trumbull, The Blood Covenant; Edersheim, The Temple; Gray N, 404–7; *Benzinger HA* 466–71, 475; *Nowack HA* II, 145–49, 153–57, 172–78.

Feast of Weeks: Article, *Pentecost* in Hastings DB, Encyc. Bib., and Jewish Encyc.; Edersheim, The Temple, ch. XIII; *Benzinger HA* 476; *Nowack HA* II, 149–50, 178–80.

Feast of Tabernacles: Article, *Feast of Tabernacles* in Hastings DB, Encyc. Bib., and Jewish Encyc.; *Benzinger HA* 476; *Nowack HA* II, 150–70, 180–82.

Day of Atonement: Article, *Day of Atonement* in Hastings DB, Encyc. Bib., and Jewish Encyc.; Edersheim, The Temple, 263–88; Schultz OTT I, 367, 368, 402–6; *Nowack HA* II, 183–94; *Stade GVI* II, 182, 258–60; *Benzinger HA* 477.

Sabbatical Year: Article, *Sabbatical Year* in Hastings DB, Encyc. Bib., and Jewish Encyc.; *Benzinger HA* 474; *Nowack HA* II, 163–65.

Year of Jubilee: Article, *Jubilee* in Encyc. Bib.; *Sabbatical Year* in Hastings DB; *Sabbatical Year and Jubilee* in Jewish Encyc.; Wellhausen PHI 116, 117; *Benzinger HA* 474; *Nowack HA* II, 165–72.

II

THE CIVIL AND CRIMINAL DECALOGUES OF EXODUS 21 AND 22

The following decalogues, together with that in Exodus 34, represent the oldest Hebrew laws which have been preserved. The few supplemental laws are reproduced in the footnotes; the evidence that these were not found in the original versions of these decalogues has already been presented in the Introduction, p. 25.

Superscription

Ex. 21 [1]Now these are the ordinances which thou shalt set before them:

First Decalogue: The Rights of Slaves

First Pentad: Males

I. Ex. 21 [2]If a man buy a Hebrew slave, the slave shall serve six years; but in the seventh he shall go free without having to pay any ransom.

II. [3]If he come in single, he shall go free unmarried.

III. If he be married, then his wife shall go out with him.

IV. [4]If his master give him a wife and she bear him sons or daughters, the wife and her children shall be her master's, but the man shall go out by himself.

V. [5]If, however, the slave shall definitely say, I love my master, my wife, and my children; I will not go free, [6]then his master shall bring him before God, and shall lead him to the door, or the door-post, and his master shall bore through his ear with an awl; and the man shall be his slave as long as he liveth.

Second Pentad: Females

VI. [7]If a man sell his daughter to be a slave, she shall not go free as do the male slaves.

VII. [8]If she do not please her master, who hath espoused her to himself, then he may let her be redeemed; only he shall have no power to sell her to a foreign people seeing he hath dealt deceitfully with her.

VIII. [9]If he espouse her to his son, he shall deal with her as with a daughter.

IX. [10]If he marry another wife, her food, her raiment, and her duty of marriage shall he not diminish.

X. [11]If he do not these three things to her, then she may go out without having to pay any money.

Second Decalogue: Assaults

First Pentad: Capital Offences

I. Ex. 21 [12]If a man strike another so that he die the manslayer shall be put to death.

II. [13]If a man lie not in wait, but God deliver him into his hand, then I will appoint thee a place to which he may flee.

III. [14]If a man attack another maliciously to slay him by treachery, thou shalt take him from mine altar, that he may be put to death.

IV. [15]He who striketh his father or his mother shall be put to death.

V. [16]He who stealeth a man, and selleth him, or if he still be found in his hand, shall surely be put to death.[a]

Second Pentad: Minor Offences

VI. [18]If men contend and one strike the other with a stone or a club, and he die not, but is confined to his bed, [19]then if he rise again, and can walk out supported on his staff, the one who struck him shall be acquitted; only he must pay for the loss of the other man's time until he is thoroughly healed.

VII. [20]If a man strike his male or female slave with a stick so that he die at once, the master must be punished.

VIII. [21]If, however, the slave survive a day or two, the master shall not be punished for it is his own loss.[b]

IX. [26]If a man smite the eye of his male or female slave, so that it is destroyed, he shall let him go free for his eye's sake.

X. [27]If he knock out a tooth of his male or female slave, he shall let him go free for his tooth's sake.

Third Decalogue: Laws Regarding Domestic Animals

First Pentad: Injuries by Animals

I. Ex. 21 [28]If an ox fatally gore a man or a woman, the ox shall be stoned, and its flesh shall not be eaten, but the owner of the ox shall be acquitted.

II. [29]But if the ox was already in the habit of goring, and it hath been reported to its owner, and he hath not kept it in, with the result that it hath killed a man or a woman, the ox shall be stoned, and its owner shall also be put to death.

---

[a] 21[16] Although it cuts athwart the context, the following ancient law was inserted here because it likewise imposed capital punishment:
[17]*Whoever curseth his father or his mother shall be put to death.*

[b] 21[21] Clearly [26] is the original sequel of [21]. The following early laws have later been inserted:
[22]*If men strive together and hurt a pregnant woman so that she hath a miscarriage and yet no harm to her result, he shall be fined as the woman's husband shall determine; and he shall pay for the miscarriage.* [23]*But if any harm follow, then thou shalt give life for life,* [24]*eye for eye, tooth for tooth, hand for hand, foot for foot,* [25]*branding for branding, wound for wound, stripe for stripe.*

IX. **22** [1]If a man steal an ox, or a sheep, and kill it, or sell it, he shall restore five oxen for one ox, and four sheep for a sheep.[c] [3b]If he have nothing, then he shall be sold to pay for what he hath stolen.

X. [4]If the theft be found in his hand alive, whether it be ox, or ass, or shee... he must pay twice its value.

Fourth Decalogue : Responsibility for Property

First Pentad: *Property in General*

I. **Ex. 22** [5]If a man burn over a field or vineyard and let the fire s... so that it devoureth a neighbor's field, out of the best of his own field, the best of his own vineyard shall he make restitution.

II. [6]If fire break out, and catch in thorns, so that the shocks of grain, ... the standing grain, or the field are consumed, he that kindled the fire mus... make restitution.

III. [7]If a man deliver to his neighbor money or personal property to keep, and if it be stolen out of the man's house, if the thief be found, the man shall make double restitution.

IV. [8]If the thief be not found, then the master of the house shall come before God to prove whether or not he hath taken his neighbor's goods.

V. [9]In every case of breach of trust whether it concern an ox, or ass, or sheep, or clothing, or any kind of lost thing of which one saith, This is it, the case of both parties shall come before God; he whom God shall condemn shall make double restitution to his neighbor.

---

[c] 22[1] The sequel of [1] is [3b]. Vss.[2], [3a] deal with a related but distinct theme:
[2]*If the thief be found breaking in and be struck down so that he dieth, the one who striketh him is not guilty of murder.* [3]*If the sun hath risen, the one who striketh him, is guilty of murder; he must make restitution.*

I. Dt. 22 [13]If, after a man hath married a wife and entered into marital relations with her, he turn against her, [14]and frame against her shameful charges, . . . [15]then the father of the young woman and her mother shall ʈake and bring evidences of the young woman's virginity to the elders of the ʈy at the gate; . . . [18]And the elders of that city shall take the man and ʈish him; [19]and they shall fine him a hundred shekels of silver, and give ʈn to the young woman's father because the man hath given an evil name ʈ virgin of Israel; and she shall be his wife; he may not divorce her as long ʈ liveth. [d]

ʈ. [20]But if it prove to be true that the evidences that the young woman ʈ a virgin were not found, [21a]then they shall bring out the young woman ʈ the door of her father's house, and the men of her city shall stone her to ʈeath because she hath committed a shameful act in Israel, in that she hath ʈeen a harlot in her father's house.

III. [22a]If a man be found lying with a married woman, they shall both of them die, the man who lay with the woman and the woman.

IV. [23a]If a man find in the city a young woman who is a virgin betrothed to a husband, and lie with her, [24]then ye shall bring them both out to the gate of that city and stone them to death, the damsel because she did not cry out, although she was in the city, and the man because he hath seduced his neighbor's wife.

V. [25]If the man find a young woman, who is betrothed in the field, and force her and lie with her, then simply the man who lay with her shall die; [26a]but thou shalt do nothing to the young woman; she hath committed no sin worthy of death.

---

[d] Dt. 13[13-19] The original decalogue versions of this and the four succeeding laws were undoubtedly at first far briefer, but, in common with most of the early laws in Dt., they have been freely worked over and expanded. Cf. Ex. 22[16-20].

FIFTH DECALOGUE: SOCIAL PURITY

Second Pentad: Fornication and Apostasy

VI. Ex. 22 [16]If a man entice a young girl who is not betrothed, and lie with her, he must make her his wife by paying a dowry for her.

VII. [17]If her father utterly refuse to give her to him, he shall pay money equivalent to the dowry of young girls.

VIII. [18]A sorceress shall not be allowed to live.

IX. [19]Whoever lieth with a beast shall surely be put to death.

X. [20]He who sacrificeth to other gods, except to Jehovah, shall be placed under the ban.

III

RIGHTS AND DUTIES OF WIVES IN HAMMURABI'S CODE

The following are the more important laws in the Code of Hammurabi regarding the rights of wives and the subject of divorce; the translation is from Johns' *Bab. and Assyr. Laws, Contracts and Letters:*

§ 133. If a man has been taken captive, and there was maintenance in his house, but his wife has left her house and entered into another man's house; because that woman has not preserved her body, and has entered into the house of another, that woman shall be prosecuted and shall be drowned.

§ 134. If a man has been taken captive, but there was not maintenance in his house, and his wife has entered into the house of another, that woman has no blame.

§ 135. If a man has been taken captive, but there was no maintenance in his house for his wife, and she has entered into the house of another, and has borne him children, if in the future her [first] husband shall return and regain his city, that woman shall return to her first husband, but the children shall follow their own father.

§ 136. If a man has left his city and fled, and, after he has gone, his wife has entered into the house of another; if the man return and seize his wife, the wife of the fugitive shall not return to her husband, because he hated his city and fled.

§ 137. If a man has determined to divorce a concubine who has borne him children, or a votary who has granted him children, he shall return to that woman her marriage-portion, and shall give her the usufruct of field, garden, and goods, to bring up her children. After her children have grown up, out of whatever is given to her children, they shall give her one son's share, and the husband of her choice shall marry her.

§ 138. If a man has divorced his wife, who has not borne him children, he shall pay over to her as much money as was given for her bride-price and the marriage-portion which she brought from her father's house, and so shall divorce her.

§ 139. If there was no bride-price, he shall give her one mina of silver, as a price of divorce.

§ 140. If he be a plebeian, he shall give her one-third of a mina of silver.

§ 141. If a man's wife, living in her husband's house, has persisted in going out, has acted the fool, has wasted her house, has belittled her husband, he shall prosecute her. If her husband has said, "I divorce her," she shall go her way; he shall give her nothing as her price of divorce. If her husband has said, "I will not divorce her," he may take another woman to wife; the wife shall live as a slave in her husband's house.

§ 142. If a woman has hated her husband and has said, "You shall not possess me," her past shall be inquired into, as to what she lacks. If she has been discreet, and has no vice, and her husband has gone out, and has greatly belittled her, that woman has no blame, she shall take her marriage-portion and go off to her father's house.

§ 143. If she has not been discreet, has gone out, ruined her house, belittled her husband, she shall be drowned.

IV

REPARATION FOR DAMAGE TO PROPERTY

Hammurabi's laws regarding reparation for damage or loss of property reveal the stern paternal ruler (cf. for the corresponding Hebrew laws § 25):

§ 229. If a builder has built a house for a man, and has not made his work sound, and the house he built has fallen, and caused the death of its owner, that builder shall be put to death.

§ 230. If it is the owner's son that is killed, the builder's son shall be put to death.

§ 231. If it is the slave of the owner that is killed, the builder shall give slave for slave to the owner of the house.

§ 232. If he has caused the loss of goods, he shall render back whatever he has destroyed. Moreover, because he did not make sound the house he built, and it fell, at his own cost he shall rebuild the house that fell.

§ 233. If a builder has built a house for a man, and has not jointed his work, and the wall has fallen, that builder shall make that wall firm at his own expense.

§ 235. If a boatman has built a boat for a man, and has not made his work sound, and in that same year that boat is sent on a voyage and suffers damage, the boatman shall rebuild that boat, and, at his own expense, shall make it strong, or shall give a strong boat to the owner.

§ 236. If a man has let his boat to a boatman, and the boatman has been careless and the boat has been sunk or lost, the boatman shall restore a boat to the owner.

§ 237. If a man has hired a boat and boatman, and loaded it with corn, wool, oil, or dates, or whatever it be, and the boatman has been careless, and sunk the boat, or lost what is in it, the boatman shall restore the boat which he sank, and whatever he lost that was in it.

V

HAMMURABI'S LAWS OF INHERITANCE

The Babylonian laws regarding inheritance concede many rights to women, although they carefully preserve within each family the title to its hereditary possessions. The laws of Hammurabi present suggestive parallels to and variations from the Old Testament usages:

§ 150. If a man has presented field, garden, house, or goods to his wife, has granted her a deed of gift, her children, after her husband's death, shall not dispute her right; the mother shall leave it after her death to that one of her children whom she loves best. She shall not leave it to her kindred.

§ 162. If a man has married a wife, and she has borne him children, and that woman has gone to her fate, her father shall lay no claim to her marriage-portion. Her marriage-portion is her children's only.

§ 163. If a man has married a wife, and she has not borne him children, and that woman has gone to her fate; if his father-in-law has returned to him the bride-price, which that man brought into the house of his father-in-law, her husband shall have no claim on the marriage-portion of that woman. Her marriage-portion indeed belongs to her father's house.

§ 164. If the father-in-law has not returned the bride-price, the husband shall deduct the amount of her bride-price from her marriage-portion, and shall return her marriage-portion to her father's house.

§ 165. If a man has presented field, garden, or house to his son, the first in his eyes, and has written him a deed of gift; after the father has gone to his fate, when the brothers share, he shall keep the present his father gave him, and over and above shall share equally in the goods of his father's estate.

§ 167. If a man has taken a wife, and she has borne him children and that woman has gone to her fate, and he has taken a second wife, and she also has borne children; after the father has gone to his fate, the sons shall not share according to mothers, but each family shall take the marriage-portion of its mother, and all shall share the goods of their father's estate equally.

§ 168. If a man has determined to disinherit his son and has declared before the judge, "I cut off my son," the judge shall inquire into the son's past, and, if the son has not committed a grave misdemeanor such as should cut him off from sonship, the father shall disinherit his son.

§ 170. If a man has had children borne to him by his wife, and also by a maid, if the father in his lifetime has said, " My sons," to the children whom his maid bore him, and has reckoned them with the sons of his wife; then after the father has gone to his fate, the children of the wife and of the maid shall share equally. The children of the wife shall apportion the shares and make their own selection.

§ 171. And if the father, in his lifetime, has not said, " My sons," to the children whom the maid bore him, after the father has gone to his fate, the children of the maid shall not share with the children of the wife in the goods of their father's house. The maid and her children, however, shall obtain their freedom. The children of the wife have no claim for service on the children of the maid.

The wife shall take her marriage-portion, and any gift that her husband has given her and for which he has written a deed of gift and she shall dwell in her husband's house; as long as she lives, she shall enjoy it, she shall not sell it. After her death it is indeed her children's.

§ 172. If her husband has not given her a gift, her marriage-portion shall be given her in full, and, from the goods of her husband's estate, she shall take a share equal to that of one son.

If her children have persecuted her in order to have her leave the house, and the judge has inquired into her past, and laid the blame on the children, that woman shall not leave her husband's house. If that woman has determined to leave, she shall relinquish to her children the gift her husband gave her, she shall take the marriage-portion of her father's estate, and the husband of her choice may marry her.

§ 173. If that woman, where she has gone, has borne children to her later husband, after that woman has died, the children of both marriages shall share her marriage-portion.

§ 174. If she has not borne children to her later husband, the children of her first husband shall take her marriage-portion.

§ 175. If either a slave of a patrician, or of a plebeian, has married the daughter of a free man, and she has borne children, the owner of the slave shall have no claim for service on the children of a free woman. And if a slave, either of a patrician or of a plebeian, has married a free woman and when he married her she entered the slave's house with a marriage-portion from her father's estate, be he slave of a patrician or of a plebeian, and from the time that they started to keep house, they have acquired property; after the slave, whether of a patrician or of a plebeian, has gone to his fate, the free woman shall take her marriage-portion, and whatever her husband and she acquired, since they started house-keeping. She shall divide it into two portions. The master of the slave shall take one half, the other half the free woman shall take for her children.

§ 176. If the free woman had no marriage-portion, whatever her husband and she acquired since they started house-keeping, she shall divide into two portions. The owner of the slave shall take one half, the other half the free woman shall take for her children.

§ 177. If a widow, whose children are young, has determined to marry again, she shall not marry without consent of the judge. When she is allowed to remarry, the judge shall inquire as to what remains of the property of her former husband, and shall intrust the property of her former husband to that woman and her second husband. He shall give them an inventory. They shall watch over the property, and bring up the children. Not a utensil shall they sell. A buyer of any utensil belonging to the widow's children shall lose his money and shall return the article to its owners.

§ 178. If a female votary, or vowed woman, has had given her by her father a portion, as for marriage, and he has written her a deed, and in the deed which he has written her he has not written that she may leave it as she pleases, and has not granted her all her desire, after her father has gone to his fate, her brothers shall take her field, or garden, and, according to the value of her share, shall give her corn, oil, and wool, and shall content her heart. If they do not give her corn, oil, and wool, according to the value of her share, and do not satisfy her, she shall let her field and garden to a farmer, whom she chooses, and the farmer shall support her. The field, garden, or whatever her father gave her, she shall enjoy, as long as she lives. She shall not sell it, nor mortgage it. The reversion of her inheritance indeed belongs to her brothers.

§ 179. If a female votary, or vowed woman, has had a portion given her by her father, and he has written her a deed, and in the deed that he has written her has [declared] that she may give it as she pleases, and has granted her all her desire; after her father has gone to his fate, she shall leave it as she pleases; her brothers shall make no claim against her.

§ 180. If the father has not given a portion to his daughter, who is a female votary, or vowed woman; after her father has gone to his fate, she shall share in the property of her father's house, like any other child. As long as she lives, she shall enjoy her share; after her, it indeed belongs to her brothers.

§ 181. If a father has vowed his daughter to a god, as a temple maid, or a virgin, and has given her no portion; after the father has gone to his fate, she shall share in the property of her father's estate, taking one-third of a child's share. She shall enjoy her share, as long as she lives. After her, it belongs to her brothers.

§ 182. If a father has not given a portion, as for marriage, to his daughter, a votary of Marduk of Babylon, and has not written her a deed; after her father has gone to his fate, she shall share with her brothers from the goods of her father's estate, taking one-third of a child's share. She shall not be subject to duty. The votary of Marduk shall leave it after her to whom she pleases.

§ 183. If a father has given a portion, as for marriage, to his daughter by a concubine, and has given her to a husband, and has written her a deed; after her father has gone to his fate, she shall not share in the goods of her father's house.

§ 184. If a man has not given a portion, as for marriage, to his daughter by a concubine, and has not given her to a husband; after her father has gone to his fate, her brothers shall present her with a marriage-portion, according to the wealth of her father's estate, and shall give her to a husband.

VI

HAMMURABI'S LAWS REGARDING ASSAULT

§ 196. If a man has knocked out the eye of a patrician, his eye shall be knocked out.

§ 197. If he has broken the limb of a patrician, his limb shall be broken.

§ 198. If he has knocked out the eye of a plebeian or has broken the limb of a plebeian, he shall pay one mina of silver.

§ 199. If he has knocked out the eye of a patrician's servant, or broken the limb of a patrician's servant, he shall pay half his price.

§ 200. If a patrician has knocked out the tooth of a man that is his equal, his tooth shall be knocked out.

§ 201. If he has knocked out the tooth of a plebeian, he shall pay one-third of a mina of silver.

§ 202. If a man has smitten the privates of a man, higher in rank than he, he shall be scourged with sixty blows of an ox-hide scourge, in the assembly.

§ 203. If a man has smitten the privates of a patrician, of his own rank, he shall pay one mina of silver.

§ 204. If a plebeian has smitten the privates of a plebeian, he shall pay ten shekels of silver.

§ 205. If the slave of anyone has smitten the privates of a free-born man, his ear shall be cut off.

§ 206. If a man has struck another in a quarrel, and caused him a permanent injury, that man shall swear, "I struck him without malice," and shall pay the doctor.

§ 207. If he has died of his blows, [the man] shall swear [similarly], and pay one-half a mina of silver; or,

§ 208. If [the deceased] was a plebeian, he shall pay one-third of a mina of silver.

§ 209. If a man has struck a free woman with child, and has caused her to miscarry, he shall pay ten shekels for her miscarriage.

§ 210. If that woman die, his daughter shall be killed.

§ 211. If it be the daughter of a plebeian, that has miscarried through his blows, he shall pay five shekels of silver.

§ 212. If that woman die, he shall pay half a mina of silver.

§ 213. If he has struck a man's maid and caused her to miscarry, he shall pay two shekels of silver.

§ 214. If that woman die, he shall pay one-third of a mina of silver.

VII

HAMMURABI'S PENALTIES FOR THEFT

The following are the more important laws in the Code of Hammurabi concerning robbery:

§ 6. If a man has stolen goods from a temple, or house, he shall be put to death; and he that has received the stolen property from him shall be put to death.

§ 7. If a man has bought or received on deposit from a minor or a slave, either silver, gold, male or female slave, ox, ass, or sheep, or anything else, except by consent of elders, or power of attorney, he shall be put to death for theft.

§ 8. If a patrician has stolen ox, sheep, ass, pig, or ship, whether from a temple, or a house, he shall pay thirtyfold. If he be a plebeian, he shall return tenfold. If the thief cannot pay, he shall be put to death.

§ 9. If a man has lost property and some of it be detected in the possession of another, and the holder has said, "A man sold it to me, I bought it in the presence of witnesses"; and if the claimant has said, " I can bring witnesses who know it to be property lost by me "; then the alleged buyer on his part shall produce the man who sold it to him and the witnesses before whom he bought it; the claimant shall on his part produce the witnesses who know it to be his lost property. The judge shall examine their pleas. The witnesses to the sale and the witnesses who identify the lost property shall state on oath what they know. Such a seller is the thief and shall be put to death. The owner of the lost property shall recover his lost property. The buyer shall recoup himself from the seller's estate.

§ 10. If the alleged buyer on his part has not produced the seller or the witnesses before whom the sale took place, but the owner of the lost property on his part has produced the witnesses who identify it as his, then the [pretended] buyer is the thief; he shall be put to death. The owner of the lost property shall take his lost property.

§ 11. If, on the other hand, the claimant of the lost property has not brought the witnesses that know his lost property, he has been guilty of slander, he has stirred up strife, he shall be put to death.

§ 12. If the seller has in the meantime died, the buyer shall take from his estate fivefold the value sued for.

§ 21. If a man has broken into a house he shall be killed before the breach and buried there.

§ 22. If a man has committed highway robbery and has been caught, that man shall be put to death.

§ 23. If the highwayman has not been caught, the man that has been robbed shall state on oath what he has lost and the city or district governor in whose territory or district the robbery took place shall restore to him what he has lost.

§ 24. If a life [has been lost], the city or district governor shall pay one mina of silver to the deceased's relatives.

§ 25. If a fire has broken out in a man's house and one who has come to put it out has coveted the property of the householder and appropriated any of it, that man shall be cast into the self-same fire.

VIII

THE MARSEILLES SACRIFICIAL TABLET

Near the ruins of ancient Carthage a Phœnician inscription has been found which throws much light upon the old Canaanitish sacrificial customs. Although it cannot be dated earlier than the fourth or fifth century before the Christian era, it doubtless faithfully reflects much earlier institutions. In general the same sacrificial terms are used and the same laws prevail as among the Hebrews during the same period. Unfortunately the tablet, which is now at Marseilles, has been broken in many places and the meaning of several of the terms used is still doubtful. By the aid of parallels and the implications of the context the text may, however, be tentatively restored as follows :

[1]Temple of Baal[   ]. Tariff of dues, set up by the superintendents of the dues in the time of [   ]baal the governor[a], son of Bodtanit, son of Bodeshmun, and of Halazbaal, the governor, son of Bodeshmun, son of Halazbaal and their colleagues.

[3]For an ox, whether it be a whole-offering, or a prayer-offering, or a whole thank-offering, the priests shall have ten shekels of silver for each; and if it be a whole-offering, they shall have, besides this payment, three hundred shekels of flesh; and if it be a prayer-offering, the . . . and the . . . ; but the skin, and the . . . , and the feet, and the rest of the flesh, shall belong to the person offering the sacrifice.

[5]For a calf whose horns are imperfect . . . , or for a hart, whether it be a whole-offering, or a prayer-offering, or a whole thank-offering, the priests shall have five shekels of silver for each; and if it be a whole-offering, they shall have, besides this payment, one hundred and fifty shekels of flesh; and if it be a prayer-offering, the . . . and the . . . ; but the skin, and the . . . , and the feet, and the rest of the flesh, shall belong to the person offering the sacrifice.

[7]For a ram, or for a goat, whether it be a whole-offering, or a prayer-offering, or a whole thank-offering, the priests shall have one shekel, and two zars, of silver for each; and if it be a prayer-offering, they shall have, besides this payment, the . . . , and the . . . ; but the skin, and the . . . , and the feet, and the rest of the flesh, shall belong to the person offering the sacrifice.

[9]For a lamb, or for a kid, or for the young of a hart, whether it be a whole-offering, or a prayer-offering, or a whole thank-offering, the priests shall have three-fourths of a shekel, and two zars of silver for each; and if it be a prayer-offering, they shall have, besides this payment, the . . . , and the . . . ; but the skin, and the . . . , and the feet, and the rest of the flesh, shall belong to the person offering the sacrifice.

[11]For a bird, whether domestic or wild, whether it be a whole thank-offering, or a . . . , or a . . . , the priests shall have three-fourths of a shekel, and two zars of silver for each; but the flesh shall belong to the person offering the sacrifice.

[12]For a bird, or sacred firstfruits, or a sacrifice of game, or a sacrifice of oil, the priests shall have ten gerahs for each.

[13]In every prayer-offering, which is presented before the gods, the priests shall have the . . . , and the . . . in the prayer-offering.

[14]For a cake, and for milk, and for fat, and for every sacrifice which a man may offer as a cereal-offering, the priests shall have . . .

[15]For every sacrifice which a poor man may offer in cattle or birds, the priests shall have nothing.

[16]Every . . . , and every . . . , and every . . . , and all men who may

---

[a]Lit., *suffete*, or, *judge, i. e.*, the chief ruler of Carthage.

sacrifice, [17]these men shall give as payment for each sacrifice, according as is prescribed in the regulations . . .

[18]Every due which is not prescribed in this table shall be made according to the regulations which were drawn up by the superintendents of the dues in the time of [   ]baal son of Bodtanit, [19]and Halazbaal son of Bodeshmun, and their colleagues.

[20]Every priest who may accept a due other than that which is prescribed in this table, shall be fined . . .

IX

TABLES OF WEIGHTS AND MEASURES

These tables will give the approximate equivalents of the weights and measures employed in this volume. The following weights are computed according to the Troy standard:

	BABYLONIAN		PHŒNICIAN	
	HEAVY	LIGHT	HEAVY	LIGHT
Shekel..............	.7 oz.	.35 oz.	.47 oz.	.23 oz.
Mina...............	3.5 lbs.	1.75 lbs.	2.33 lbs.	1.17 lbs.
Talent.............210.4 "		105.19 "	140.25 "	70.12 "

DRY AND LIQUID MEASURES

	LITRES	GALLONS
Log..	.50	.11
Cab..	2.02	.44
Omer...	3.63	.80
Sacred Hin...	4.54	1.00
Hin..	6.06	1.33
Great Hin..	9.09	2.00
Seah...	12.12	2.67
Bath...	36.37	8.00
Homer...	363.70	80.05

LINEAR MEASURES

	LONGER SYSTEM		SHORTER SYSTEM	
	METRES	INCHES	METRES	INCHES
Finger's breadth.............	.022	.86	.019	.74
Palm.......................	.087	3.44	.075	2.95
Span	.262	10.33	.225	8.86
Cubit......................	.525	20.67	.450	17.72

X

THE POST–EXILIC SACRED CALENDAR

The following table will indicate in outline the dates and history of the more important feasts and fasts of later Judaism:

SABBATICAL FEASTS AND SACRED YEARS

References Outside the Legal Books

Sabbath	I Sam. $20^{5,\,6}$, II Kgs. 4^{23}, 11^{5-7}, Neh. 8^{9-13}, 10^{31}, 13^{15-22}, Is. 56^{2-6}, 58^{12}, Jer. 17^{20-27}, Ezek. 20^{12-16}, Hos. 2^{13}, Am. 8^5, Mt. 12^{9-13}, Mk. 3^{1-5}, Lu. 6^{6-10}, 13^{10-17}, Jn. 5^{1-16}, 9^{14-16}
New Moon	I Sam. 20^5, Ps. $81^{3,\,4}$, Is. $1^{13,\,14}$, Am. 8^5, I Mac. 10^{34}
Sabbatical Year	Jer. 34, II Chr. 36^{21}, Neh. 10^{31}, I Mac. 6^{53}
Year of Jubilee	Is. $61^{1,\,2}$, 63^4, Lk. 4^{18-21}

THE ANNUAL FEASTS AND FASTS

	Pre-exilic Date	Post-exilic Date	Important References Outside the Legal Books
Feast of Passover	In first month (March-April)	Fourteenth day of first month (March-April)	Josh. 5^{10}, II Chr. 30, 35, Ezra 6^{19}, Mt.26^2, Acts 12^4
Feast of Wood Offering	. . . .	Fifteenth of first month	Jos. BJ II, 17^6
Feast of Unleavened Bread	Seven days in first month	Fifteenth to twenty-second of first month	Josh. 5^{11}, II Chr. 35^{17}, Ezra 6^{22}
Feast of Weeks or Pentecost	Seven weeks after the beginning of grain harvest	Fifty days after passover; about the eighth of third month (early in June)	II Mac. 12^{32}, Acts 2^1, 20^{16}, I Cor. 16^8
New Year's Day or Feast of Trumpets	. . . .	First day of seventh month (Sept.-Oct.)	Neh. $8^{9,\,10}$
Day of Atonement	. . . .	Seventh day of seventh month	Ben S. 50^{5-21}, Acts 27^9, Heb. 2^{18}, 4^{14-16}, 5^{1-10}
Feast of Tabernacles	Seven days at the end of the year, when all the fruits had been harvested	Fifteenth to twenty-second of seventh month (Sept.-Oct.)	I Kgs. 8^2, 12^{32}, II Chr. 5^3, 7^8, Ezra 3^4, 8^{14-17}, Zech. 14^{16-19}, Jn. $7^{1-}$$10^{21}$

THE ANNUAL FEASTS AND FASTS

	Pre-exilic Date	Post-exilic Date	Important References Outside the Legal Books
Feast of Dedication or Lights	....	Eight days, beginning the twenty-fifth day of ninth month (Nov.-Dec.)	I Mac. 4$^{56-59}$, II Mac. 10$^{6-8}$, Jos. Ant. XII, 7^7
Nicanor's Day (later Fast of Esther)	....	Thirteenth of twelfth month (Feb.-March)	I Mac. 7^{49}, II Mac. 15^{36}
Feast of Purim	....	Fourteenth and fifteenth of twelfth month	II Mac. 15^{36}

as in a harmony, that they may be studied comparatively and as independent literary units.

(3) A lucid, exact translation. The third essential is a clear, vivid, dignified translation, which will represent not merely the words but also the ideas, the spirit, and the beauty of the original, and which will put the reader, unacquainted with Hebrew, in possession of the latest contributions of philology, exegesis, and theology.

(4) Clear literary analysis. The fourth is a clear literary analysis, which will make it possible readily to trace the logical thought of a story, law, sermon, or poem, and to note the relation of the different parts to each other and to the whole.

(5) Illuminating introductions and foot-notes. Finally concise, lucid notes are demanded, which will at once present the historical background and the critical, geographical, and archæological data required to illuminate the obscurities of the text, without distracting attention from its beauty and thought.

Aims and plan of the Student's Old Testament. These five absolute essentials the *Students' Old Testament* aims to supply in the fullest measure and in the most direct and usable form. The general plan is unique in its simplicity and economy of space. By combining a lucid, scholarly translation, a logical and chronological classification, and a critical and a literary analysis of the text with brief introductions and notes at the foot of the page, the reader is at once placed in command of the practical results of modern biblical research, many of which are otherwise found only in cumbersome technical works, intelligible only to the specialist.

Its origin. The sane, careful scholarship and the reverent constructive spirit of the author are already known to a wide circle of Bible students through his *History of the Hebrew People* and his volumes in the *Messages of the Bible*. The present extensive work is the result of years of preparation, in which he has also been able to profit by the generous suggestions and criticisms of a large number of biblical scholars and practical teachers. The whole has been prepared to meet not theoretical but practical needs and has been tested at each point in university and Bible classes.

The work embodies the positive conclusions of **Its point of view and method.** the many hundreds of earnest critical scholars, who have during the past two centuries been grappling with the intricate problems of the Old Testament. For the first time in its history the various versions of its more important stories and historical records are printed throughout in parallel columns so that they can be readily studied in approximately their original form. In the introductions and foot-notes the biblical data upon which these results are based are cogently presented so that the ordinary Bible reader can readily understand and estimate their significance. Where the positions are established the fact is indicated, and where there is still uncertainty this is also frankly stated. When at times the author's conclusions differ from those of the majority of scholars the reasons for the departure are fully outlined.

To the ordinary conservative biblical student, **Its practical value.** who rejects or views with alarm the critical positions of modern Old Testament teachers, an opportunity is offered, for the first time, of ascertaining just what those positions are and the chief reasons therefor. To many it will be a genuine relief to find that the foundations of Christian faith, instead of being destroyed, are simply being laid on a deeper and broader historical basis, and that the newer methods of interpretation are supremely helpful in gaining a true knowledge of the eternal messages of the Bible. To the rapidly increasing body of progressive Bible readers, who accept the principles and in general appreciate the practical value of critical biblical research, this clear, definite presentation of its more important fruits cannot fail to be most welcome. It furnishes to the historian the data for the easy reconstruction of biblical history, to the literary student the basis for a new understanding and appreciation of the wonderful literature of the Old Testament, and to the pastor, the Sunday-school teacher, the parent, and the individual reader positive religious facts and teachings, the want of which is being strongly felt in this age, when destructive conclusions are much in evidence. Above all the *Student's Old Testament* presents those foundations—laid bare through the untiring labors of generations of Christian scholars and by the faithful application of scientific method—upon which Old Testament interpretation and doctrine promise in the future to rest.

No effort or expense has been spared to make this work a complete manual for class-room study, for reading, and for reference. Each volume is complete in itself, embodying all the cognate Old Testament and apocryphal literature in its given field. A detailed table of contents, index, page-headings, and cross-references facilitate its use by primary as well as advanced readers.

Each volume is also fully equipped with thoroughly modern topographical and historical maps, which are introduced in connection with the literature of each period. Comparative chronological charts make it possible to trace readily the growth and approximate dates of the Old Testament and apocryphal writings in connection with the events and movements which determined their form and which in turn they record. Tables of weights and measures and carefully selected and detailed bibliographies, introduced in connection with each epoch, supply both elementary and advanced students with a complete equipment for intelligent reading and fruitful study.

Terms of Subscription

SINGLE VOLUMES. The publishers will supply any single volume of the series for $2.75 net (postage, 15 cents).

ADVANCE SUBSCRIPTIONS. As an inducement to advance subscribers, the publishers will accept subscriptions for the complete set of six volumes for $13.50, payable in instalments on the publication of each volume.

DELIVERY. Each volume will be sent to subscribers as soon as published. Books will be sent by mail or express as requested.

CHARLES SCRIBNER'S SONS
153-157 Fifth Avenue   **NEW YORK**